Now is the Time

Also by Angus Buchan and published by Monarch Books:

Faith Like Potatoes

A Farmer's Year

Come of Age

A Mustard Seed

The Secret Place

A Rushing Mighty Wind

NOW IS THE TIME
A DAILY DEVOTIONAL

ANGUS BUCHAN

MONARCH
BOOKS
Oxford, UK & Grand Rapids, Michigan, USA

Published by Monarch Books
an imprint of
Lion Hudson plc
Wilkinson House, Jordan Hill Road,
Oxford OX2 8DR, England
Email: monarch@lionhudson.com
www.lionhudson.com/monarch

ISBN 978 0 85721 580 2
e-ISBN 978 0 85721 581 9

First edition 2014

Acknowledgments
Unless otherwise stated scripture taken from the New King James Version. Copyright © 1982 by Thomas Nelson, Inc. Used by permission. All right reserved.
Extracts from The Authorized (King James) Version. Rights in the Authorized Version are vested in the Crown. Reproduced by permission of the Crown's patentee, Cambridge University Press.
Scripture taken from the New American Standard Bible®, Copyright © 1960, 1962, 1963, 1968, 1971, 1972, 1973, 1975, 1977, 1995 by The Lockman Foundation. Used by permission.
Scripture quotations taken from the Holy Bible, New International Version, copyright © 1973, 1978, 1984 International Bible Society. Used by permission of Hodder & Stoughton, a member of the Hodder Headline Group. All rights reserved. 'NIV' is a trademark of International Bible Society. UK trademark number 1448790.
Scripture taken from The Message. Copyright © by Eugene H. Peterson 1993, 1994, 1995, 1996, 2000, 2001, 2002. Used by permission of NavPress Publishing Group.

A catalogue record for this book is available from the British Library

Printed and bound in Malta, July 2014, LH28

This book is dedicated to those believers who really mean business with God. There is an old saying:
"To be forewarned is to be forearmed."
I pray that this devotional will help you as a believer: To go out each day and be an ambassador for Jesus Christ, ready for whatever comes your way.

NOW IS THE TIME ...

of God's favour, now is the day of salvation.

Behold, now is the accepted time; behold, now is the day of salvation.

2 Corinthians 6:2b

JANUARY

Now is the time … to live as God's ambassador

An ambassador of the highest rank

An ambassador with a special mission

An ambassador preaches an authentic gospel

An ambassador shares the love of God

An ambassador has the authority to witness

An ambassador is faithful to his calling

An ambassador fearlessly seizes the moment

An ambassador is not ashamed of the gospel

An ambassador stands up and is counted

An ambassador wisely manages his home

An ambassador walks the talk

An ambassador is well informed

An ambassador knows that God honours His Word

An ambassador accurately portrays his master

An ambassador is a servant of the Lord

An ambassador of Jesus knows that he is forgiven

An ambassador of Jesus forgives others

An ambassador of Jesus forgives no matter what

An ambassador has a love relationship with Jesus

An ambassador of Jesus loves others

An ambassador obeys God's commands

An ambassador is a blessing to everyone

An ambassador is a man of courage

An ambassador lives a life of gratitude

An ambassador is humble before his God

An ambassador of Jesus Christ honours his marriage

An ambassador abides in the truth

An ambassador lives a life of praise

An ambassador of Jesus Christ does not grow weary

An ambassador never stops growing in God

An ambassador is a man of promise

An ambassador of the highest rank

Read 2 Corinthians 5:17–21

Now then, we are ambassadors for Christ, as though God were pleading through us: we implore you on Christ's behalf, be reconciled to God. For He made Him who knew no sin to be sin for us, that we might become the righteousness of God in Him. (2 Corinthians 5:20–21)

As we begin our journey together at the start of this new year I want to take a look at what it means to be an ambassador of Jesus Christ. If ever the world needed to hear about Eternal Life, about Jesus Christ, about forgiveness of sins, about vision and about purpose – it is now. I want to challenge you today: How are people going to know if we don't tell them? Saying it is the minister's job is a fallacy. It is not the minister's job, my friend. It is the believer's job. It is your job and it is my job.

Our Scripture reading tells us:

Therefore, if anyone is in Christ, he is a new creation; old things have passed away; behold, all things have become new. Now all things are of God, who has reconciled us to Himself through Jesus Christ, and has given us the ministry of reconciliation, that is, that God was in Christ reconciling the world to Himself, not imputing their trespasses to them, and has committed to us the word of reconciliation. (2 Corinthians 5:17–19)

God has called us; He has given us a job to do, my friend. We are called to reconcile our fellow man to God; and God to man. We are His ambassadors. It is a very special thing to be an ambassador. The dictionary says that an ambassador is a diplomat of the highest rank. Isn't that a beautiful description of what we are meant to be? We should live in such a way that the people we work with know that we are diplomats of the highest rank for Jesus Christ. Do your colleagues even know that you are a Christian? There is no such thing as a secret-agent Christian. So called secret-agent Christians say: "My beliefs are private. I live out my Christianity in my own way." No, sir, this is not an option for you. God saved you so that you can be a blessing to other people and to the world. He saved you to be an ambassador of the highest rank.

Prayer

Dear Father, at the start of this new year I come before You with praise and thanksgiving. Thank You for my salvation; thank You that You have saved me to be a blessing to others. Help me to live as Your ambassador every day. Amen.

An ambassador is a diplomat of the highest rank.

An ambassador with a special mission

Read 2 Corinthians 5:14–21

For the love of Christ compels us, because we judge thus: that if One died for all, then all died; and He died for all, that those who live should live no longer for themselves, but for Him who died for them and rose again. (2 Corinthians 5:14–15)

People will not know about Jesus Christ if you do not tell them. You are a diplomat of the highest rank who has been tasked with a special mission. You have to choose whether you will step up and accept the mission God has for you. You might well be thinking to yourself, I am not an evangelist. I don't have that gift. My dear friend, listen to me. Evangelism is very simple. This is what evangelism is: One hungry beggar showing another hungry beggar where to find bread.

If you have been watching my television broadcasts or reading my devotionals over the past few years then you will know that I constantly refer to the great men and women of God who went before us. The reason that I never tire of sharing their stories is because there is so much that we can learn from their individual walks of faith with God. These men and women knew what hardship was; many of them knew great sorrow in their lives; they certainly sacrificed much for the privilege of being an ambassador of Jesus Christ. Above all, my friends, they knew great victory and great joy as they faithfully fulfilled the purpose to which God had called them. As a result of their faithfulness we can look at their lives and be encouraged in our walk with the Lord.

Gypsy Smith was such a man; he was a true ambassador of his master and a great evangelist. One day a part-time preacher who was burnt out asked Gypsy Smith what he should do. "Keep telling them what Jesus means to you," was Gypsy Smith's advice. This is what being an ambassador is. An ambassador is a representative of Jesus Christ.

A South African ambassador, who is sent overseas to represent South Africa, promotes the country; and tells people about all the good things that are to be found there. You need to tell people about Jesus Christ and what He means to you. You are an ambassador of the highest rank on a special mission.

Prayer

Father God, I come before You worshipping You as the God of this universe. I am so awed that You have called me to represent You in this world. I commit my life anew to You – use me I pray. Make me a witness to everyone that I meet today. Amen.

You need to tell people about Jesus Christ and what He means to you.

An ambassador preaches an authentic gospel

Read Mark 16:9–20

And He said to them, "Go into all the world and preach the gospel to every creature."
(Mark 16:15)

As God's ambassador your orders are to *go into all the world and preach the gospel to every creature* (Mark 16:15). You have been given treaty-signing powers; this means you can pray the sinner's prayer with people, facilitating them receiving a passport to heaven. You can do this because you are His ambassador. However, the responsibility rests with you to be an authentic representative of your King. You cannot say one thing and live another. Your life must speak for you.

Augustine, a mighty man of God, said: "What I live by, I impart." Another man of God, Francis of Assisi, said: "Preach the gospel at all costs, and if you really have to, use words." Profound, don't you think? You don't have to keep telling people how to live; all you have to do is live the life, and they will see that you are an ambassador of Jesus Christ. An ambassador is an authorised representative, or a messenger.

If you are a farmer your farm workers will know that you are a Christian by the way that you treat them. You will pay them a fair day's wages for a fair day's work. I am not suggesting you pay a man for being lazy. I don't care who he is; if he doesn't work, he doesn't get paid. However, if he does the job, you pay him. Do the people with whom you work know that you are a Christian, my friend? They should know this not because you shoot your mouth off, but because of your lifestyle. Does your boss consider you a good ambassador of Jesus Christ? A good ambassador is honest and doesn't steal the boss's time; he would not use the telephone, the company vehicles, or company equipment for his private use. People will soon see who you are or aren't by the way you live. You know that old saying: "You might be able to fool some of the people some of the time, but you cannot fool all of the people all of the time."

Prayer

Father God, You have saved me and brought me into Your kingdom of light. You have called me to be an ambassador for You. Help me to live a life of honesty and integrity. I want my life to be an authentic witness for You, so that my walk and my talk line up. Amen.

You don't have to keep telling people how to live; all you have to do is live the life.

An ambassador shares the love of God

Read John 15:9–17

Greater love has no one than this, than to lay down one's life for his friends. (John 15:13)

Mahatma Gandhi led India to independence. He had a quarter of the world's population eating out of the palm of his hand. He said that he would have no problem following after the man Jesus Christ; but he felt he could not reconcile himself to Jesus' followers. This is a sad indictment against Christians as ambassadors of Jesus.

Mahatma Gandhi came out from England to South Africa as a lawyer. One day he was travelling on a train. Even though he had a first-class ticket he was thrown off the train in Pietermaritzburg because he was the wrong colour. That night he sat in the waiting room and he made a decision that he would stand up for righteousness and truth. Later he was escorted out of a church in Johannesburg, a guard on each arm, again because he was the wrong colour. My dear friend, an ambassador of Jesus Christ is not a racist. We don't even know what colour Jesus is. I would say He is probably more Mahatma Gandhi's colour than my colour.

You see, if we are ambassadors then our lives have to correlate with what we are saying. Are you an ambassador? One man put it like this: "We are not Christ's lawyers; we are His witnesses." We don't have to argue with people about Jesus: we don't have to try and persuade people to become Christians. The greatest asset that we have – the greatest credential that the church of Jesus Christ has – is love. There are other religions that frighten people into believing what they want them to believe. As Christians we are to love people into the kingdom of God. *Greater love has no one than this, than to lay down one's life for his friends* (John 15:13). You need to know in Whom you believe and you need to know what you believe. In order to be good at his job an ambassador must both believe in his country as well as know about his country.

Prayer

Father God, today I come before You acknowledging that there are times that I allow prejudice to overrule my desire to share Your love with others. Forgive me, I pray. Wash me clean and give me a heart filled with love. My witness is worth nothing if it is not infused with love for others. Amen.

The greatest asset that we have – the greatest credential that the church of Jesus Christ has – is love.

An ambassador has the authority to witness

Read Matthew 28

And Jesus came and spoke to them, saying, "All authority has been given to Me in heaven and on earth. Go therefore and make disciples of all the nations, baptizing them in the name of the Father and of the Son and of the Holy Spirit, teaching them to observe all things that I have commanded you; and lo, I am with you always, even to the end of the age." Amen. (Matthew 28:18–20)

Many years ago, I had the privilege of visiting King Goodwill Zwelithini, the king of the Zulus. He is directly descended from Shaka Zulu and he has around 10 million subjects. We arrived at the village of Nongoma, where his palaces are situated. Our group of ambassadors consisted of: My InDuna – Simeon Bengo; Mark Berret, my pastor; Oom Johannes Nel (who has gone to be with the Lord); and me. As we entered the palace the guards stood to attention with their AK-47 rifles. Their job was to protect their king. Outside the stockade hundreds of people stood shouting to the king: "We salute you; you are the elephant!"

My knees were knocking together, I was so nervous. I had never before had the privilege of meeting a king and I didn't know the correct protocol when it came to greeting him. I will never forget it. The moment I walked through the door the Holy Spirit came upon me and told me: "Angus, this man is a king: treat him with respect. He represents the Zulu nation; but don't forget you represent the King of kings and the Lord of lords. Remember, I am his King as well."

With those words in my heart I had the confidence, with the humility, to go in and greet the king. He was very courteous towards us. I then had the opportunity to preach the gospel to him. He insisted that I preach in Zulu. Having only recently come to South Africa from Zambia, my Zulu was limited. However, I believe that at that moment the promise of Luke 12:12 – that the Holy Spirit will give you the words you need to speak – was true for me. It wasn't me speaking; it was the Holy Spirit. As an ambassador of Jesus Christ I was able to minister to the King of the Zulus. My friend, you can speak to anyone, because you have the authority of Jesus Christ.

Prayer

Father, You are God of this whole universe. Kings and queens bow before Your throne. There is none greater than You. The wonder of this is that I am Your child; a child of the King of kings. Help me to live up to my royal birthright. Help me to witness with authority. Amen.

You can speak to anyone, because you have the authority of Jesus Christ.

An ambassador is faithful to his calling

Read 2 Timothy 1:1–14

Therefore do not be ashamed of the testimony of our Lord … who has saved us and called us with a holy calling. (2 Timothy 1:8a, 9a)

In 1979 I played polocrosse (a combination of lacrosse and polo). I was an unbeliever and one of the boys. Then on the 18th of February, 1979, I signed up for God's Army and I became an ambassador of Jesus Christ. Shortly after this I was refereeing a game with Jannie Bernhard. We stood talking and he commented that there was something different about me. He said I was no longer angry and aggressive. He noticed a joy and peace in my life. I told him that I had given my life to Jesus. His eyes grew big and he told me that he wanted what I had. We agreed that he would come to the farm the following day.

When he arrived I didn't know what to say or do. Remember Gypsy Smith's advice: "Keep telling them what Jesus means to you." As we walked together in my mielie fields I asked him whether he was ready. He assured me that he was. We were both half crying. I started to tell him about my friend, Jesus Christ. I told him that He is known by many names. He is known as the Lion of Judah; the Lily of the Valley; the great Plough Man; the Shepherd of the sheep, but He is also known as the Friend of sinners like us. Jannie wanted to know what he had to do. I explained that he had to repent; that he had to say sorry. I told him that he had to ask Jesus to come into his life and take it over, and then Jesus would change his life.

I don't know what kind of prayer we prayed, but the Holy Spirit knew what it was. Jannie Bernhard gave his life to Jesus Christ. He was the first person I had ever led to Jesus Christ. I was an ambassador of Jesus Christ. I was new at it, but He gave me the words to say. All I had to do was to be obedient and share with my friend. The Holy Spirit did the rest.

Prayer

Father God, You have called me with a holy calling. I am Your workman, Your ambassador. Help me to live up to my calling every day of my life. I want to bring honour and glory to Your precious name, my Father. Amen.

All I had to do was to be obedient. The Holy Spirit did the rest.

An ambassador fearlessly seizes the moment

Read 2 Timothy 1:1–14

Therefore I remind you to stir up the gift of God which is in you through the laying on of my hands. For God has not given us a spirit of fear, but of power and of love and of a sound mind. (2 Timothy 1:6–7)

n world affairs there are moments when ambassadors play a critical role. Events occur where key decisions have to be made, conveyed and executed. It often falls to the ambassador to be fearless in acting on the instructions of his government. It is his job to share the message that his government wishes to convey to another country. There have been times in history when it has been a matter of life and death. It is no different for us as ambassadors of Jesus Christ: we are involved in life and death matters. The salvation of mankind is a life and death matter.

It is our mandate as ambassadors of the kingdom of God to lead people to Jesus Christ. Now we are not going to get all technical about it, and argue that nobody can lead a person to Christ; that it is only the Holy Spirit who can lead someone to Christ. We know this. However, you cannot get away from the fact that God uses people like you and me to share the the gospel with other people. So I ask you, have you ever led anybody to Jesus Christ? If you are an ambassador of Jesus Christ you have to be His representative.

Returning to my story about my friend Jannie Bernhard; a couple of years after sharing the gospel with him, he was involved in a motor car accident and he died. I know he is in heaven. Good people don't go to heaven, my friend; believers go to heaven. Jannie is waiting for me in heaven, and I cannot wait to see him, together with so many others who have gone before. I want to assure you that God will give us the power, the strength and the ability to be His ambassadors. We are busy with life and death matters; nobody deserves to hear the gospel twice, until everyone in the world has heard it once. The question is: How are they going to hear it if you and I don't tell them? Be an ambassador who fearlessly seizes the moment.

Prayer

Father, I praise You and thank You that You would choose to use me to carry Your precious gospel message to people. Help me to be a worthy ambassador; help me to seize every opportunity You bring my way to share the good news of Jesus Christ with others. Amen.

Nobody deserves to hear the gospel twice, until everyone in the world has heard it once.

An ambassador is not ashamed of the gospel

Read Romans 1:1–17

For I am not ashamed of the gospel of Christ, for it is the power of God to salvation for everyone who believes, for the Jew first and also for the Greek. (Romans 1:16)

During the period of 1881 to 1994 there was a famous fighting regiment in Scotland called the Gordon Highlanders. They were formidable men, skilled in combat and killing: professional soldiers feared by everyone. A young new recruit joined the regiment. He arrived at the barracks, settled in, and before climbing into bed knelt by the side of his bed to pray. The other men mocked him. Those tough, battle-scarred soldiers had no place for religion in their lives.

The staff sergeant came back drunk from the pub. He was an older man with the scars of battle etched upon his face. He saw the young soldier on his knees praying. He sat down and took off his heavy, hobnailed boots. Then he stood up, and he threw his boot at the young boy, hitting him on the side of the head. There was a gash on his head and the blood started running down his neck. Not satisfied, he threw the other boot as well. He called him a sissy, and told him that he wasn't a soldier. He shouted at him that they were men in the Gordon Highlanders; and with that he fell onto his bed and passed out.

At four o'clock the following morning he woke up, and before he got out of bed he remembered his boots. He recalled what had happened the night before. He swung his legs out of bed intending to go and retrieve his boots. As he sat on the side of his bed, there right in front of him were his boots. They were shined, spit and polished; nicely lined up, ready for him to put on. The young soldier had got up in the middle of the night, and polished the staff sergeant's boots. That big, tough soldier stood up calling to the boy. He asked him to tell him about his Jesus. The staff sergeant accepted Christ as his saviour. That young soldier was not ashamed of the gospel of Christ. As His ambassadors we must not be ashamed of the gospel; we must stand up for the gospel of Jesus Christ.

Prayer

Father, I hang my head in shame as I think of the many times I have either avoided standing up for the gospel or I have silently prayed that the situation would go away so that it would not be necessary to take a stand. Father, I pray, fill me with Your Spirit; give me boldness to declare Your name for all to hear. Amen.

As His ambassadors we must not be ashamed of the gospel; we must stand up for the gospel of Jesus Christ.

An ambassador stands up and is counted

Read Mark 8:38

Therefore do not be ashamed of the testimony of our Lord, nor of me His prisoner, but share with me in the sufferings for the gospel according to the power of God. (2 Timothy 1:8)

We must never be ashamed to tell people what Jesus means to us. In Romans 8:19, the Bible says: *For the earnest expectation of the creation eagerly waits for the revealing of the sons of God.* (That is you and me.) If we're not going to speak up about Jesus, who is? The Lord chose to use you and me. He could use the angels but He doesn't. He uses us. Every time you are quiet you're depriving somebody of the good news. The worst that can happen to you, my dear friend, is that they mock you or scorn you. I would like to encourage you, as you begin this new year, to become more outspoken about what you believe.

On our farm we gather together every morning to sing hymns, pray and read the Scriptures in Zulu. I want to tell you that since the day we began worshipping together things on our farm have changed completely. Why? Because Jesus became our focal point. There's no one else like Jesus, and the time of worship changes the whole atmosphere on the farm. You may say to me that you do not have any Christians on your farm. Have you ever asked the people who work with you? You may well be surprised. Maybe you work in a factory; don't assume that there are no Christians. There are probably a whole group of Christians waiting for you to have the courage to invite them to a lunchtime prayer meeting.

Difficult work environments can be changed by bringing Jesus into the midst of the situation. If you are facing challenges with the people who work with you, invite Jesus to come in and be a part of your daily routine. The gospel is the power of God at work amongst us. Do not be ashamed to stand up for the gospel, even if it means that you must bear the insults of people who do not believe. Paul encouraged Timothy to stand up for what he believed in no matter what he would have to endure. People will never know if you do not tell them.

Prayer

Father, like the Apostle Paul, help me to stand up tall and proud for what I believe in. Thank You that I do not believe in a list of rules and regulations, but I believe in Jesus Christ, the Risen Lord, Your One and Only Son, the saviour of my soul. Amen.

People will never know if you do not tell them.

An ambassador walks the talk

Read Ephesians 4:17–32

You should no longer walk as the rest of the Gentiles walk … put off, concerning your former conduct, the old man which grows corrupt according to the deceitful lusts, and be renewed in the spirit of your mind, and that you put on the new man which was created according to God, in true righteousness and holiness. (Ephesians 4:17b, 22–24)

Are you an effective ambassador of Jesus Christ? Do people recognize that you are a witness for God? If not you need to pray: "Lord, please, whatever it takes, make me Your ambassador so that people will see Jesus in me. Help them to recognize Him by the way I live as well as by the things I say." Many years ago a family of missionaries felt God leading them to go to one of the South Sea Islands and preach the gospel. Missionaries had stopped going to these islands because the inhabitants, who were cannibals, killed and ate every missionary who set foot on their shores.

When the missionary and his family arrived ashore, the islanders gathered around them on the beach. The family knelt down, opened the Bible and the missionary began preaching about the Lord Jesus Christ. As he preached the people nodded their heads, as if they knew the story. The preacher asked them if they had heard the gospel before. They replied that they hadn't. He was confused and told them that by their nodding he assumed that they had heard it. They told him that the man he was talking about used to live amongst them.

They offered to take the missionary to the man's grave and they told him the story. Many years ago, a man came on a sailing ship. All the other people with him had been killed. The islanders realized that this man could be useful to them, so they allowed him to live. There was one condition though; they told him that the first time he opened his mouth and spoke they would kill him. He could stay with them but he was never to utter a single word. That man was a missionary who never verbally preached the gospel once; but through his life and by his example he lived the gospel every day. The islanders became Christians. They said he lived the life of Jesus; in fact they mistook him for Jesus. Do people see Jesus in you – do they mistake you for Jesus? Do you walk your talk, my friend?

Prayer

Father God, what a wonderful testimony this is. I pray today as I rededicate myself to You, that You will place Your fire within me. Fill me with Your Spirit, I pray. Help me to walk the talk. Help me to be a worthy and honourable ambassador for You. I want people to mistake me for Jesus. Amen.

Do people see Jesus in you? Do they mistake you for Jesus?

An ambassador wisely manages his home

Read Ephesians 5:15–33

Therefore do not be unwise, but understand what the will of the Lord is. (Ephesians 5:17)

I am talking to you, sir: it is your job to head up your home in a godly way. Ephesians 5:15–16 admonishes men to: *See then that you walk circumspectly, not as fools but as wise, redeeming the time, because the days are evil.* It is your God-given privilege to be the head of your family. It is not your wife's job, my friend. Too many men are abdicating their responsibility. It wasn't Sarah who headed up the ministry in their household: it was Abraham. It wasn't Zipporah who led the household: it was Moses.

Men, you need to stand up and be counted. You are the high priest of your house. If you are a child of God then 1 Peter 2:9 says: *But you* are *a chosen generation, a royal priesthood, a holy nation, His own special people, that you may proclaim the praises of Him who called you out of darkness into His marvelous light.* This means that God has given you everything you need to fulfil His purposes in your life. He has given you all that you need to be able to walk in obedience to His commands.

God has called you to walk in His light and to lead your family into that light. If your children are not following Jesus it's not your wife's fault: it's your fault, sir. Don't look around for someone else to blame. You need to go before the Lord and ask Him to help you. Take up your position as His ambassador in your family. Claim your family for Jesus. You need to hear my heart, and understand that I am saying these things to you in love. I love you with the love of the Lord, my dear friend. I am being forthright today because the Lord says that we are not to be ashamed of the gospel. This means that we must stand tall and be counted. As an ambassador of Jesus you must love your wife as He loves the church; you must draw your children to Jesus and not push them away from Him.

Prayer

My Father God, I praise You and worship You. Thank You that You have called me out of darkness into Your marvellous light. Thank You that You have made me a priest. Today, with Your help I take up my privileged position as Your ambassador in my family. Help me to love and serve my loved ones with the love of the Lord. Amen.

Take up your position as His ambassador in your family.

An ambassador is well informed

Read 1 Peter 3:8–15

But sanctify the Lord God in your hearts, and always be ready to give a defence to everyone who asks you a reason for the hope that is in you, with meekness and fear. (1 Peter 3:15)

I n order to become an ambassador of a country a person needs to be knowledgeable about their country. They have to be able to expertly discuss and promote their country. They must be able to defend and explain the policies of their country. Often they will be the one who has to help people understand a certain course of action that their government has taken. They have to be equipped to give an effective answer to people's questions.

Being an ambassador means that often the person is in the line of fire, so to speak – they are out there on display. People are watching them, looking at what they do and listening carefully to what they have to say. It is no different as an ambassador of Jesus Christ. You represent the kingdom of God. You need to know the Word of God, my friend. It saddens me to hear of so many Christians who don't know the Word of God. You need to memorise it; you need to absorb it into your spirit-man. You can't walk around with a Bible in your hand all day – it will likely frighten people away – so you need to have the Word of God in your heart.

An ambassador has to present his credentials to the President (or the Monarch) of the host country he is going to be serving in. These credentials prove that he or she has been authorized by their government to represent their country. *For God so loved the world that he gave his only begotten Son, that whoever believes in Him should not perish but have everlasting life* (John 3:16). These are the credentials you present when you want to tell somebody about your saviour. What a beautiful introduction this is. Being an effective ambassador of Jesus means that you will be able to give an adequate explanation to those who question you. Our Scripture verse says it so well: … *always be ready to give a defence to everyone who asks you a reason for the hope that is in you, with meekness and fear.*

Prayer

Father, I thank You for the privilege of representing You here on earth. Help me to equip myself. I want to hide Your Word in my heart so that I will always be ready to give an answer for the hope that is within me. Amen.

As an ambassador of Jesus Christ you need to know the Word of God.

An ambassador knows that God honours His Word

Read Psalm 40:9

For I am not ashamed of the gospel of Christ, for it is the power of God to salvation for everyone who believes, for the Jew first and also for the Greek. For in it the righteousness of God is revealed from faith to faith; as it is written, "The just shall live by faith." (Romans 1:16–17)

If you're not ashamed of the gospel the Lord will honour His Word with power, signs and wonders following the preaching of His Word. You know we have regular healing meetings here at Shalom. In fact wherever I go I always pray for the sick. However, I want to tell you today that if I cut corners when it comes to preaching the gospel in truth, I can feel it when I start praying for the sick. It is almost as if there is no power.

Paul understood about the power of the gospel. He proclaimed the gospel fearlessly throughout the then-known world. When Paul came to salvation in Jesus Christ he became totally sold out to the gospel of Jesus Christ. We are called to preach the gospel in the same way. When we are outspoken and we proclaim: "There has never been another God, there will never be another God, that there is only one God, and He is the Father of Abraham, Isaac and Jacob. He is the Almighty God and His name is Jesus Christ!" When I preach like this folks, I want to tell you that before we even lay hands upon the sick they are healed. Why? It is because of His Word: there is power in the Word; in the spoken Word of God.

Paul exhorted the people of God wherever he went to stand up and proudly proclaim the gospel; no matter what the personal consequences were for them. Wherever Paul went his preaching was followed by signs and wonders. This same power is available to you and me, my friend. There was nothing different about Paul; he didn't receive anything that you and I haven't received. Everyone who is a child of God receives the power of God. However, it is like a switch – if you don't switch on the light, the electricity cannot light up the room. You need to yield to the Holy Spirit and allow Him to work through you; then you will see the power of God flowing through you as you obediently proclaim His gospel.

Prayer

Father God, I lift my hands to You; I lift up my heart to You; I give my life to You. Father, You have called me; You have empowered me. Help me to proclaim Your gospel fearlessly. It is the power to salvation. As I proclaim Your Word You will honour it with signs, wonders and miracles. The honour and the glory belong to You. Amen.

Everyone who is a child of God receives the power of God.

An ambassador accurately portrays his master

Read Matthew 28

And Jesus came and spoke to them, saying, "All authority has been given to Me in heaven and on earth. Go therefore and make disciples of all the nations, baptizing them in the name of the Father and of the Son and of the Holy Spirit, teaching them to observe all things that I have commanded you; and lo, I am with you always, even to the end of the age." Amen. (Matthew 28:18–20)

A good ambassador is someone who portrays the master. When Jesus walked on this earth He was the perfect representation of His heavenly Father's kingdom. He came to earth to reveal God to man. Jesus gathered twelve disciples around Him. He walked with them. He lived intimately with them. He taught them the principles of God's kingdom. Then He commissioned them: *"Go therefore and make disciples of all the nations, baptizing them in the name of the Father and of the Son and of the Holy Spirit, teaching them to observe all things that I have commanded you"* (Matthew 28:19–20a).

This does not mean that we lecture people on how to be Christians. It means that we show them by example. We teach them by the way we live our lives. We have to back our words up with actions. The talk is an important part of the process, but without the walk it is of no lasting value. Too many people have been turned off Christianity by the bad witness of a so-called ambassador of Christ. We have a huge responsibility resting on our shoulders to walk our talk.

What does an ambassador of Jesus Christ look like? He is slow to anger and quick to forgive. He doesn't easily get angry and when he does he is quick to ask forgiveness. He is somebody who goes the extra mile, who gives his coat to somebody in need. I don't know how you feel when you see the little street kids. I have to admit that I am often irritated by them; especially when they stand at the door of my car, knocking on the window and asking for money. Like me you may think that they just use the money to buy alcohol or glue. However, Jesus says we must bless those who have nothing and be what He wants us to be. We are to follow His example. Did He ever turn away a beggar? No, never. He kept company with the beggars.

Prayer

My Father in heaven, I bow before Your throne. I acknowledge You as my Lord and master. You have commissioned me to go into the entire world and walk my talk. Help me to live today in a way that will bring only glory and honour to Your holy name. Amen.

We have a huge responsibility resting on our shoulders to walk our talk.

An ambassador is a servant of the Lord

Read 1 Corinthians 12:1–14

There are diversities of gifts, but the same Spirit. There are differences of ministries, but the same Lord. And there are diversities of activities, but it is the same God who works all in all. But the manifestation of the Spirit is given to each one for the profit of all.
(1 Corinthians 12:4–7)

God has gifted each one of us. As an ambassador of Jesus Christ, you represent the kingdom of God here on earth. You have a purpose for being on this earth, and part of that purpose is for you to exercise the gifts that God has given you. You need to know your gifts and operate within your gifting. If you are working within the gifting that God has given you then you should never grow tired. Your gift has been given to you not for your enjoyment only; but in order that you can serve the Lord, and the body of Christ: the church.

My late dad was a blacksmith. He had a limited education but he was a wise man. He told my brother and me that if we didn't feel like getting up in the morning and going to work then we were in the wrong job. What did he mean by this? Most of your life is spent in the workplace, and if you hate what you do it will kill you quicker than any disease. The same goes for your Christian service. If you don't know what your spiritual gifting is then you need to find out. Otherwise you will become frustrated. God has gifted you so that you can serve Him and bless your fellow brothers and sisters.

The job God gave His disciples was to preach the gospel, and lay hands upon the sick so that they could be healed. They were ambassadors of Jesus Christ. The Lord healed the sick through their faith and through the anointing He had placed upon them. I am not an apostle, a prophet, a teacher or a pastor. In fact, I wonder sometimes if I am even an evangelist. What I am though is a servant of the Lord. That's it! Your gifting is given to you *for the profit of all*. If you only want to exercise your gifts as and when it suits you then you have missed the point: you do not understand what it means to be an ambassador of the kingdom of God.

Prayer

Father, I praise You today. You are a great God. I am so grateful that You have chosen me to be Your servant. I want to serve You first, and then my fellow brothers and sisters. Help me to faithfully exercise the gifting that You have given me to the honour and glory of Your name. Amen.

As an ambassador of Jesus Christ, you represent the kingdom of God on earth.

An ambassador of Jesus knows that he is forgiven

Read Luke 7:36–50

Therefore I say to you, her sins, which are many, are forgiven, for she loved much. But to whom little is forgiven, the same loves little. Then He said to the woman, "Your faith has saved you. Go in peace." (Luke 7:47, 50)

What an amazing story this is. Jesus said that if you have been forgiven much you will love much; if you have been forgiven little you will love little. My friend, there isn't a person walking on this earth who doesn't need the forgiveness of God. Romans 3:23 says, *for all have sinned and fall short of the glory of God.* So if you are sitting reading this and you think there is no sin in your life, my dear friend, then you are deluding yourself. The biggest sin of all is when you cannot acknowledge that Jesus died on the Cross of Calvary for your sin.

I know for a fact that if it were not for Jesus Christ I would not be preaching or serving the Lord in any capacity whatsoever. He took my ragged life; He restored it, He renewed it and He made me a brand new person. He forgave me all the sins I had committed in the past. Some people say: "Angus, you are over the top." I don't accept this for a moment. I am an ordinary, normal Christian; but I serve a mighty God! As a sinner saved by grace I know that I am forgiven. I walk daily in God's forgiveness. You cannot be an effective ambassador for Jesus Christ if you do not know that your sins are forgiven. If you do not have the assurance of your salvation, how are you going to help others to find salvation and forgiveness?

Romans 8:1–2 tells us: *There is therefore now no condemnation to those who are in Christ Jesus, who do not walk according to the flesh, but according to the Spirit. For the law of the Spirit of life in Christ Jesus has made me free from the law of sin and death.* This verse assures us that if we have confessed our sins, and repented of them, then we are forgiven. You can walk tall in your forgiveness. You can have the confidence to be an ambassador of Jesus because your sins are forgiven.

Prayer

Father God, I humbly thank You for Your grace and mercy that You have poured out upon my life. I would be nothing without You. You have forgiven me for so much; I will never stop praising You and thanking You for the blessing of forgiveness. Thank You that I can walk tall as Your ambassador because I walk in the power of Your Spirit. Amen.

You can have the confidence to be an ambassador of Jesus because your sins are forgiven.

An ambassador of Jesus forgives others

Read Matthew 6:9–15

"For if you forgive men their trespasses, your heavenly Father will also forgive you. But if you do not forgive men their trespasses, neither will your Father forgive your trespasses." (Matthew 6:14–15)

Today I want us to look at a subject that I think affects all of us, especially me. It is the subject of forgiving others. Isn't it interesting that it is the one aspect that Jesus lifts out and highlights from the Lord's Prayer? Verse 12 says: *And forgive us our debts, as we forgive our debtors.* My dear friends, Jesus doesn't stop there. Just in case we didn't get the point, He underlines what He has been telling His disciples: "*For if you forgive men their trespasses, your heavenly Father will also forgive you. But if you do not forgive men their trespasses, neither will your Father forgive your trespasses*" (Matthew 6:14–15).

This is not a request; it is not an optional extra – it is a command. If you want Jesus to forgive you all of your sins, then you have to be prepared to forgive others all of their sins. I know that it is not always easy. In fact there are times when, without the help of the Lord, there is no way we would be able to forgive. God understands this. Forgiveness is not meant to be cheap. Grace isn't cheap, my friend. It cost God everything to extend His grace and forgiveness to us – it cost Him His one and only Son, Jesus Christ. God knows all about the cost of forgiveness.

Even so, He tells you to forgive. Some of you are saying: "Angus, my wife betrayed me. I am heartbroken." It could be you had a business partner whom you trusted because he said he was a Christian, and he stabbed you in the back. I know exactly how that feels. If you look at my bare back you will see the scars between my shoulder blades. The only people who can get that close to me are the people I trust. Maybe you have a child who has let you down. Remember that you are an ambassador of Jesus Christ, representing the kingdom of God; this means that you forgive others. Whatever your situation God commands you to forgive.

Prayer

Father God, again as I contemplate Your forgiveness of my sins I realize that I have no right to withhold forgiveness from anyone else. Help me to obey Your Word and Your command to me to forgive. Thank You that I don't have to do this in my own strength. You give me the power to forgive. Fill me with Your love for those who have wronged me. Amen.

Whatever your situation God commands you to forgive.

An ambassador of Jesus forgives no matter what

Read Ephesians 4:25–5:2

Let all bitterness, wrath, anger, clamor, and evil speaking be put away from you, with all malice. And be kind to one another, tenderhearted, forgiving one another, even as God in Christ forgave you. Therefore be imitators of God as dear children. And walk in love, as Christ also has loved us and given Himself for us, an offering and a sacrifice to God for a sweet-smelling aroma. (Ephesians 4:31–5:2)

A few years ago I preached in a big church in Johannesburg. I had two services back to back, with ten minutes between the services. At the end of the first service the ushers were escorting me to a room where I could have a cup of tea before the next service. I had been speaking on forgiveness. Before we could leave the auditorium a lady in her mid-forties, dressed in black, hurried up to me – crying bitterly. She asked to speak to me.

The ushers wanted to move her along, but I stopped and turned around. I asked them to leave us for a moment. I enquired what the problem was. Weeping, she told me: "I hate him, I hate him." I asked her whom she hated. She replied, "I hate the man who killed my daughter." I didn't ask her for the details of who had killed her daughter or how she had died. All I told her was that she had to forgive him. She told me that she couldn't. I replied, "Yes, you can. You just don't want to. If you cannot forgive him, then God cannot forgive you." The tears ran down her face. She was in an absolute state. "Will you do it?" I asked her. "Because I have to go." We were standing in the aisle and the ushers wanted to clear the auditorium. She said that she would forgive him. So I invited her to pray after me. "Dear Lord Jesus, I forgive (I told her to say his name)."

She gritted her teeth and said she couldn't say it. "You can and you have to," I said. "I forgive John," she said and she passed out. She went down under the power of the Holy Spirit. As she lay there a smile came over her face; she was tranquil and peaceful. We picked her up; she dusted herself off and walked away totally transformed. As an ambassador of Jesus Christ you are called *to be imitators of God as dear children. And walk in love, as Christ also has loved us.*

Prayer

Father, there are times when it is very hard to forgive; when I have been so badly hurt that I feel like my heart will break. Help me, I pray, in those times to turn to You. You are my strength. You are my Strong Tower. It is only as I imitate You and walk in love as Christ loves me that I can forgive. Amen.

Walk in love, as Christ also has loved you.

An ambassador has a love relationship with Jesus

Read John 15:1–17

"If you keep My commandments, you will abide in My love, just as I have kept My Father's commandments and abide in His love." (John 15:10)

S ome time back I shared this lovely quote with my wife, Jill: *Without romance there can be no holiness.* Isn't that fantastic? She asked me what I meant by it. This is how I understand it: If you don't have a love relationship with Jesus Christ, you will never be holy. You see, holiness is the end product of obedience. When you become obedient and you love your enemy, you don't steal, you don't fornicate and you don't swear – that is holiness. You can only live consistently in this way if you have a relationship with God. You won't have success by trying to obey the Ten Commandments.

God intended that we should obey the Ten Commandments; but He saw that we were failing miserably. He loved us so He had to come up with another solution. *For God so loved the world that He gave His only begotten Son, that whoever believes in Him should not perish but have everlasting life. For God did not send His Son into the world to condemn the world, but that the world through Him might be saved* (John 3:16–17). This is why we remain faithful to Him, not because we have to but because we love Him.

There is no fear in love; but perfect love casts out fear (1 John 4:18a). It covers a multitude of sins. If you are in a love relationship with Jesus Christ then you have nothing to fear. You can trust Him completely. He will give you everything that you need to live a holy life through the infilling and empowering of His Holy Spirit. Jesus said that: *"If you keep My commandments, you will abide in My love."* He went on to say: *"These things I have spoken to you, that My joy may remain in you, and that your joy may be full"* (John 15:10a, 11). He promises you abundant joy. You will never be able to live a holy life if you do not love God. Only love can motivate us to obey Him. Love is the key to living an abundant, joy-filled life.

Prayer

Father, my heart is filled with love and gratitude to You. You are my great and wonderful God. I come before You today to tell You that I love You. I want to be in a love relationship with You. I want Your love to fill me to overflowing. I want to live out of the abundance of Your love. I want to walk in obedience to You and abide in Your commands. Amen.

Love is the key to living an abundant, joy-filled life.

An ambassador of Jesus loves others

Read John 15:11–27

"This is My commandment, that you love one another as I have loved you." (John 15:12)

My friends, you can never outlove God. *For God so loved the world that He gave His only begotten Son, that whoever believes in Him should not perish but have everlasting life. For God did not send His Son into the world to condemn the world, but that the world through Him might be saved* (John 3:16–17).

This is the ultimate love. Nothing can top God's love for us; it cost Him everything. *In this the love of God was manifested toward us, that God has sent His only begotten Son into the world, that we might live through Him. In this is love, not that we loved God, but that He loved us and sent His Son to be the propitiation for our sins. Beloved, if God so loved us, we also ought to love one another* (1 John 4:9–11). It is because of His love for you that you can love other people, even the unlovely.

Jesus commanded us: "*A new commandment I give to you, that you love one another; as I have loved you, that you also love one another. By this all will know that you are My disciples, if you have love for one another*" (John 13:34–35). It is this love that inspired people such as Mother Teresa to leave the comforts of home and go to Calcutta to work among the poorest of the poor. If you don't have love in your heart, then you cannot call yourself a Christian. You might say: "Angus, you are getting a little heavy now." When did you last look at 1 John 4:7–8? *Beloved, let us love one another, for love is of God; and everyone who loves is born of God and knows God. He who does not love does not know God, for God is love.* Sir, if you don't have love in your heart then Jesus has departed. You cannot be an ambassador of Jesus Christ and not have love for your fellow man in your heart. Ask Him to fill your heart with His love, so that you can love with His love.

Prayer

My Father God, this is a hard message to absorb. You have spoken clearly to me through Your Word. There is no way around it – I have to love others if I am to have the right to call myself Your child. Help me, I pray. Fill me afresh with Your love. Love is a choice and I choose to love. Amen.

Ask Him to fill your heart with His love, so that you can love with His love.

An ambassador obeys God's commands

Read 1 Samuel 15:16–31

"Has the Lord as great delight in burnt offerings and sacrifices, as in obeying the voice of the Lord? Behold, to obey is better than sacrifice, and to heed than the fat of rams." (1 Samuel 15:22)

Today we are going to look at God's command to be obedient to Him and the consequences of not obeying Him. Take another look at 1 Samuel 15:22: *So Samuel said: "Has the Lord as great delight in burnt offerings and sacrifices, as in obeying the voice of the Lord? Behold, to obey is better than sacrifice, and to heed than the fat of rams."* In the portion of Scripture we read this morning God is pronouncing His judgment upon King Saul. This is the Word of the Lord to King Saul, but it could just as easily be us that God is speaking to today. An ambassador of Jesus Christ will delight in obeying God's commands.

What God is actually saying to us through His Word is that it is better to obey Him than to keep saying sorry to Him. It is better to do what God is telling you to do than to continually offer sacrifices. This is what the Israelites did. They would sin and then they would come before God and offer the fat of rams to Him (the fat is the choicest part of a ram). They offered the fat of rams to Him as atonement for their sin; then they went away, and they continued sinning. There was no change in their behaviour. Repentance means changing your behaviour.

My friend, there is no short cut to heaven. As an ambassador of Jesus Christ obedience is what God requires of you. The Bible says the greatest commandment is to love the Lord your God. You do not purposefully disobey someone you love. If you love someone you do not want to cause them hurt or heartache. For instance, if you love your wife you will not be unfaithful to her. Why? Because you love her. This is what God is asking of us. You cannot love Him and consistently disobey Him. Jesus warns us in Matthew 7:21: *"Not everyone who says to Me, 'Lord, Lord,' shall enter the kingdom of heaven, but he who does the will of My Father in heaven."*

Prayer

My Father God, I come humbly before You. Forgive me, I pray, for so often taking Your grace for granted. I repent before You today and I turn from my sin. I choose to walk in obedience to You and Your commands. Amen.

As an ambassador of Jesus Christ obedience is what God requires of you.

An ambassador is a blessing to everyone

Read 1 Peter 3:8–17

Finally, all of you be of one mind, having compassion for one another; love as brothers, be tenderhearted, be courteous; not returning evil for evil or reviling for reviling, but on the contrary blessing, knowing that you were called to this, that you may inherit a blessing. (1 Peter 3:8–9)

Y ou are called to be a blessing to others. Do you intentionally look for opportunities to bless other people as you go through your day? It starts with your family; then it branches out to encompass your friends and work colleagues. Read the verses above again. Before you can receive a blessing, you have to first be a blessing. So often we only want to stand with our hands outstretched to receive. Jesus said that we must be a blessing so that He can bless us. You know, Christianity is a very simple way of life. There is nothing complicated about it. That is why little children came to Jesus to be blessed and to hear from Him. I personally believe that too many theologians complicate Christianity. It is a walk of love and being a blessing to others.

1 Peter 3:10 continues: For "He who would love life and see good days, let him refrain his tongue from evil, and his lips from speaking deceit." Refrain means; to restrain or to muzzle. In other words in the same way you would muzzle a dog, so you need to muzzle your jaw to refrain your tongue from evil. Some of us have foul mouths. I was one of the worst. It was the first miracle that I experienced when I gave my life to Jesus. From that day to this I have never again sworn. Watch that tongue, my friend. Something said in the heat of the moment can never be taken back. Even if you say sorry the damage is done. The Bible tells us that: A soft answer turneth away wrath: but grievous words stir up anger (Proverbs 15:1 KJV).

We are promised that if we behave in this way we will know good days. As an ambassador of Jesus Christ you have the power to defuse a difficult situation. Choose to restrain your tongue and the situation will calm down. It takes two people to argue, my friend. If your heart's desire is to be a blessing then the outcome will be that God is glorified and others are blessed.

Prayer

Father, thank You that You bless me in so many ways every day of my life. You have called me to be a blessing to other people. I cannot choose the people whom I will bless. I know that I must bless even the difficult people. Help me to extend Your love and grace to everyone in my life. Amen.

Before you can receive a blessing, you have to first be a blessing.

An ambassador is a man of courage

Read Deuteronomy 31:1–8

"Be strong and of good courage, for you must go with this people to the land which the Lord has sworn to their fathers to give them, and you shall cause them to inherit it. And the Lord, He is the One who goes before you. He will be with you, He will not leave you nor forsake you; do not fear nor be dismayed." (Deuteronomy 31:7–8)

People commonly report that they are driven by adrenalin when they have to take a big step of courage. For example, when on the spur of the moment someone saves a person trapped in a burning car. They just do it. It is a spontaneous and impulsive reaction. Make no mistake: it still takes great courage, but it is not premeditated. There are times when courage is required for the big issues in life and we need the courage to walk on water. We have to step out into the unknown and trust God with our very lives.

However, the type of courage I want us to look at today is the kind we need for the day-to-day issues of life. I am referring to the courage you need to stand up and be counted. The kind of courage we are talking about is the courage that allows you to take a stand against popular opinion, and declare something to be wrong. It is often very hard for us to exhibit this sort of courage, because it can bring with it criticism and ridicule. This is not the kind of courage that the world admires or aspires to. You need the kind of courage that helps you go to work every day, to consistently work hard, in order to put food on the table to feed your family.

The kind of courage I am talking about is the courage to choose to live a holy life. It is about making the choice to obey God's commands and what He is telling you to do through His Word. God tells us in His Word that He expects us to live lives of integrity. This can take great courage. God instructed Joshua through Moses to be strong and courageous; God promised that if he obeyed Him then He would never leave him, nor forsake him. God's promise is the same to you today. He says that you do not need to fear or be dismayed. God will give you the courage to do the right thing – trust Him today.

Prayer

Father, I thank You for Your promise to me that if I am strong and courageous You will always be with me. Fill me with Your Spirit, I pray. Empower me and give me the courage that I need to walk in holiness before You so that my life will glorify You. Amen.

God will give you the courage to do the right thing – trust Him today.

An ambassador lives a life of gratitude

Read Philippians 4:4–13

Be anxious for nothing, but in everything by prayer and supplication, with thanksgiving, let your requests be made known to God; and the peace of God, which surpasses all understanding, will guard your hearts and minds through Christ Jesus. (Philippians 4:6–7)

Timothy 6:6 says: *Now godliness with contentment is great gain.* Contentment is not to be found in money. Some of the most contented people I have ever met are not rich: in fact, they are poor. (I am not knocking rich people. God has blessed my family with three farms.) It is a fact, though, that money will not make you happy. Often you will find that it is the poor person who is the most grateful for the little that they have; whereas rich people can sometimes be very discontented. There is little that is more uplifting than being around a person who has an attitude of gratitude. You cannot control your circumstances, but you can control the way that you react to them. Paul walked the talk when it came to gratitude.

When Paul wrote the Letter to the Philippians he was in jail. In those days jails were dark, damp, smelly and ugly places. Rats ran rampant. Paul was thrown in with murderers and all types of criminals. That was the environment he found himself in when he wrote to the Philippians. Reading Philippians chapter four helps us understand what the Lord means when He talks about being grateful and content. Paul's life is a great example for us to follow. Paul said: *for I have learned in whatever state I am, to be content: I know how to be abased, and I know how to abound. Everywhere and in all things I have learned both to be full and to be hungry, both to abound and to suffer need* (Philippians 4:11b–12).

Paul gives us the secret as to why he could be content no matter what his circumstances; because *I can do all things through Christ who strengthens me* (Philippians 4:13). This is the reason that we too can be content no matter what our circumstances. Isn't it a wonderful thing to know that you are not at the mercy of what happens to you or around you? As an ambassador of Jesus Christ you can live a life of gratitude no matter what your circumstances.

Prayer

Father, forgive me that so often I am discontented with my life and my circumstances. I am so encouraged by Paul and his example. I choose today to live a life of gratitude and contentment no matter what is happening to me or around me. Thank You for Your love, grace and mercy that is new to me every morning. Amen.

As an ambassador of Jesus Christ you can live a life of gratitude no matter what your circumstances.

An ambassador is humble before his God

Read James 4:1–10

Humble yourselves in the sight of the Lord, and He will lift you up. (James 4:10)

*H*umble *yourself in the sight of the Lord, and He will lift you up.* So in other words, contrary to what popular culture would have us believe, we don't have to climb over other people to get to the top. Have you heard this adage: "Each man for himself and God for us all"? This does not apply to us. This is not what the Bible teaches us. It is not the way Jesus lived when He walked on earth. It is not the way He taught His disciples to behave. No, the Jesus way is to humble yourself before God and He will raise you up. He will give you the place that you need in order to fulfil His purpose for your life.

A. W. Tozer was a mighty man of God, who went to be with the Lord in 1963. He has spoken into my life a great deal recently. If you haven't read any of his books I encourage you to do so. Tozer told a story found in *The Best of A. W. Tozer* (1978) about a minor prophet: On the day of his ordination there was a solemn service. The elders and ministers together with other dignitaries laid hands upon him and prayed. After the pomp and ceremony he withdrew to meet his saviour in a secret place. There he made his personal, private covenant with God and he was ordained by the Holy Spirit. As he did this he was taken into a deeper place than any man could ever have led him.

If you want to be used by Jesus Christ, you need to humble yourself before God. You must submit yourself to His Holy Spirit and allow Him to fill you. He is the One who will ultimately ordain you with power to do the will of Him who called you. At the end of the day it is between you and God. When the minor prophet that Tozer speaks of went before God to make his commitment this is the prayer that he prayed. I invite you as a humble ambassador of Jesus Christ to pray it with me...

Prayer

Oh Lord, I have heard Your voice and I was afraid. You have called me to an awesome task in a grave and perilous hour. You are about to shake the nations and also heaven, that the things that cannot be shaken may remain. Lord, my Lord, You stooped down to honour me, Your servant. I humbly bow before You today. It is an honour to serve You. Amen.

The Jesus way is to humble yourself before God and He will raise you up.

An ambassador of Jesus Christ honours his marriage

Read Malachi 2:10–16

But did He not make them one, having a remnant of the Spirit? And why one? He seeks godly offspring. Therefore take heed to your spirit, and let none deal treacherously with the wife of his youth. (Malachi 2:15)

Marriage is a two-way covenant; first between you and God, and secondly between you and your wife. When you make this covenant you promise to be faithful to your wife until one or the other of you dies. This is a serious promise to make. You promise to be faithful through health, sickness, riches and poverty. You make yourself accountable before God. It is this covenant that you have made that will see the marriage through. There is no such thing as a marriage without problems. There is no such thing as the perfect marriage. We live in an impure and imperfect world. Every single marriage has to be worked at. Only when we get to heaven will things be perfect, but not until then.

When a couple is not married and they live together there is no obligation. It is easy come, easy go. There is no commitment and you stand the chance of ending up old and alone, because a rolling stone gathers no moss, as they say. There is nowhere in the Bible that the Lord condones sleeping with another person to whom you are not married to. No, you must be the husband of one wife. Why? Because this is what the Bible says. A man of honour obeys God's Word. If you are an ambassador of Jesus Christ He has called you to live honourably; this means that you will be faithful to your wife.

Young man, you may be in love with the most beautiful girl; but if she is not convicted regarding the sin of sleeping around, could you be satisfied, knowing that she is sleeping with other boys? Surely it would make you jealous and unhappy. The same goes for you: it is not possible for you to serve God and sleep around. God is a jealous God. He doesn't want us serving any other gods. He says in Exodus 34:14b: *the Lord, whose name is Jealous, is a jealous God.* Living according to God's laws is the only road to honour and happiness.

Prayer

Father, I thank You that You have given me clear guidelines on how I am to live my life in Your Word. I recognize that Your laws are there for my benefit and not to inhibit me. Help me, like the Psalmist, to be able to say from the bottom of my heart that I love Your laws. Amen.

Living according to God's laws is the only road to honour and happiness.

An ambassador abides in the truth

Read 1 John 2:24–27

Therefore let that abide in you which you heard from the beginning. If what you heard from the beginning abides in you, you also will abide in the Son and in the Father. (1 John 2:24)

We need to abide in the truth. In the last days the Lord has told us there will be many wolves in sheep's clothing. What does this mean? It means that many people coming in the name of the Lord will be imposters. They will be deceivers. The Word tells us they will deceive even the very elect. They will lead people astray from the truth of God's Word. We need to know not only the Word of God but also the Author of the Word of God. 1 John 2:24a says: *Therefore let that abide in you which you heard from the beginning.* Oh, my friend, don't lose your first love. Do you remember when you first met Jesus Christ and the love you felt for Him? Do you still love Him like this, or has it all become old hat to you?

Therefore let that abide in you which you heard from the beginning. If what you heard from the beginning abides in you, you also will abide in the Son and in the Father (1 John 2:24). Our television programme, *Grassroots*, is about getting back to basics. God's Word also reminds us to continue abiding in the basics. I don't care how many revelations you have received from God. The Bible says there is nothing new under the sun. I am not interested in any theology that is not found in the Bible. I don't care how important someone is; if what they say cannot be found in the Bible, don't listen to them. That is why God tells us to abide in the truth.

The truth will set you free. Truth is a person, my friend, not a philosophy. Truth is Jesus Christ. He is the only truth; He is the one you can trust. Jesus prayed this prayer for His disciples and He prays it for you and me today: *Sanctify them by Your truth. Your Word is truth* (John 17:17). An ambassador knows that his security is found in abiding in the truth – Jesus Christ. Don't allow yourself to be sidetracked – hold fast to the truth.

Prayer

Father God, I praise You and worship You. You are a great God. I love You and thank You for reminding me today of my first love for You. Help me to abide in Jesus Christ – who is my truth. Constantly remind me, I pray, of the things that I heard from the beginning. Amen.

An ambassador knows that his security is found in abiding in the truth – Jesus Christ.

An ambassador lives a life of praise

Read Numbers 21:14–18

"Call to Me, and I will answer you, and show you great and mighty things, which you do not know." (Jeremiah 33:3)

Praise and faith are closely interlinked with each other. In Numbers chapter twenty-one we read that the children of Israel were thirsty. If you are thirsty today the Lord invites you in Jeremiah 33:3: "*Call to Me, and I will answer you, and show you great and mighty things, which you do not know.*" If we reach out to God in faith He will answer us. The Israelites were in the desert: can you imagine the shimmering heat and how thirsty they would have been? Moses told them to praise God and sing about the water that was about to come out of the ground. *Then Israel sang this song: "Spring up, O well! All of you sing to it"* (Numbers 21:17).

The Israelites were walking around in the desert dying of thirst; and so Moses told them to start digging in the sand. They hadn't seen any water yet but they sang in faith, praising God for the water that would come. Are you praising God for your circumstances, despite the fact that things might look dark and gloomy right now? Moses told them God would provide water for them. They dug down and water came bubbling up. The lesson here, my friend, is that they were praising God before they saw the water. It's easy to praise God when everything is going well; but the bottom line is, are you praising God before He gives you your heart's desire?

Faith is a "doing" word, it involves action. This means that you have to start praising God for what He is going to do for you. I am not talking about a "name it and claim it" theology; I am not into that kind of thing. The Bible clearly tells us, though, that: *faith is the substance of things hoped for, the evidence of things not seen* (Hebrews 11:1). My friend, no matter what your circumstances today, you need to praise God. There is nothing too difficult for Him. Your very life is in His hands. An ambassador lives a lifestyle of praise no matter what his circumstances.

Prayer

Father, I praise You today. I glorify Your Holy name. You are a mighty God and there is none besides You. I praise You for Your faithfulness. I give You the praise and honour due to You. I bow in Your presence and humbly submit to You as You work out Your plans and purposes in my life. Amen.

An ambassador lives a lifestyle of praise no matter what his circumstances.

An ambassador of Jesus Christ does not grow weary

Read Romans 8:18–39

What then shall we say to these things? If God is for us, who can be against us?
(Romans 8:31)

The old saints were passionate about prayer. It is said that one of John Wesley's men, by the name of Fletcher, had indentations in the wooden floorboards of his room, where he knelt at night to pray. He used to wail, and cry out to God for lost souls. Is it any wonder that there were revivals through people like Wesley that changed the world? They did not grow weary. Their passion never wavered.

The church of today has lacked passion and perseverance; but I thank God that this is changing. Passion and perseverance are being reborn. This passion and perseverance will become evident as men take up their positions as ambassadors of Jesus Christ, and stand for what is right. The righteous will become more righteous, and the filthy more filthy. This is what the Bible tells us; and we need to understand it. The battle lines are drawn and we need to choose on whose side we stand.

You do not have to fear man and what man can do to you. Our Scripture verse encourages us: *If God is for us, who can be against us? Yet in all these things we are more than conquerors through Him who loved us* (Romans 8:31b, 37). What does it mean to be more than a conqueror? It means that the battle has been fought; that we can do things that we never dreamt of doing. How? Through the power of the Lord Jesus Christ. That is what God wants to do for us. This is something to get excited and passionate about. It is something worth persevering for. My friends, now is not the time to grow weary. As an ambassador of Jesus Christ you have everything you need to fight the battle before you. As you enter this New Year be known as a man who is a true ambassador of Jesus Christ. Be characterized by your passion and your perseverance. Be known as someone who does not grow weary because you are more than a conqueror through Christ who strengthens you.

Prayer

Father, I want to ask You to please forgive me for being so dry. Forgive me for being so matter of fact. Forgive me that there is so little passion evident in my life. Forgive me that I am so easily discouraged. Give me perseverance, I pray. Fill me with passion for You, Your Word and Your work. Thank You that I am more than a conqueror through Christ who strengthens me. Give me the grace, Lord, to keep running with passion, perseverance and desire. Amen.

Let your passion and perseverance for the things of God characterize your life this year.

An ambassador never stops growing in God

Read John 12:2–26

Most assuredly, I say to you, unless a grain of wheat falls into the ground and dies, it remains alone; but if it dies, it produces much grain. (John 12:24)

I want to ask you to turn off your brain for the next few minutes as you read this and open your heart to what the Spirit is saying to you today. Yes, switch off the intellect and open up your heart. The Lord says: *For the wisdom of this world is foolishness with God* (1 Corinthians 3:19a). Jesus also said: *"Assuredly, I say to you, unless you are converted and become as little children, you will by no means enter the kingdom of heaven"* (Matthew 18:3).

If you begin believing the Word of God as it is written you will enjoy a brand new way of life. If we want to grow in God one of the first things we have to do is to die to self. John 12:24 says: *... unless a grain of wheat falls into the ground and dies, it remains alone; but if it dies, it produces much grain.* Believe me when I tell you that my biggest enemy isn't Satan. His neck was broken when Jesus died on the Cross of Calvary, and He rose from the dead three days later. My biggest enemy is me, Angus Buchan. The "I" must come out of me. I have a word for you if you are married and you are having problems in your marriage. When you take the "I" out of your marriage and insert "we" instead, you will have a new marriage. It is not about "yours" or "mine" – it is about "ours".

If you want to grow in God then Jesus Christ must be in the driver's seat of your life. Imagine you are actually driving down the road in your car or Land Rover. Stop your vehicle. Put it into neutral and pull up the handbrake; then climb out, walk around to the other side and sit in the passenger's seat. Then allow Jesus to sit in the driver's seat and take the wheel. Now you are in the place where you will be able to begin growing in God. Try it – it is the only way to grow in God.

Prayer

Father, thank You for Your Word to me today. I realize that "I" is still so prevalent in my life. Today I am stopping the car and I am going to sit in the passenger seat so that You can take control of my life. Help me through Your Spirit to die daily to self so that I can become less, and You can become more in my life. Help me to grow in You. Amen.

Only once Jesus is in the driver's seat will you be able to begin growing in God.

An ambassador is a man of promise

Read Galatians 4:28–5:6

Now we, brethren, as Isaac was, are children of promise. (Galatians 4:28)

Like Isaac we are men of promise. What kind of a man is a man of promise? He is a man of faith. I want you to remember one thing even if you forget everything else: HOPE is for the future, and FAITH is for now. Are you walking by faith or by presumption; by faith or by sight; by faith or by how much money you have in the bank? Folks, hear me: this is why so many people are so desperate today. We receive calls from people all over the country who are suffering from depression, not knowing which way to turn. I want to tell you that Jesus Christ has not changed. *Jesus Christ is the same yesterday, today, and forever* (Hebrews 13:8). You had better believe this; because if you do then everything else in your life will change.

You can depend upon God's Word and what He says in His Word. *For assuredly, I say to you, till heaven and earth pass away, one jot or one tittle will by no means pass from the law till all is fulfilled* (Matthew 5:18). The truth of the matter is this: if you want to finish the race, complete the journey, have the victory, be on top and not underneath, then you need to be a person of faith. There is no other way, my friend. Nothing is impossible with God.

God is also able to accomplish the humanly impossible in your life. As you move into this new year take your place as a man of promise. Your birthright as a child of God is to walk in victory no matter what your circumstances. We have spent the past month looking at some of the aspects of being an ambassador of Jesus Christ. You are a citizen of the kingdom of God. Don't sell your birthright. You are a man of promise – an ambassador of Jesus. Now is the time for you to live by faith: to live in the fullness of all that Jesus accomplished for you on Calvary.

Prayer

My Father God, I bow before You. Thank You for the incredible privilege of being Your child. I am so grateful that I am a man of promise. I lift my hands and open my heart to You today. Fill me with Your Spirit, I pray. Give me the gift of faith, so that I can be known as a man of faith. Father, I love You. Amen.

You are a man of promise – an ambassador of Jesus. Now is the time for you to live by faith.

FEBRUARY

Now is the time ... to live in obedience

Obedience is ...loving the Lord my God with all my heart
Obedience is ...doing the will of my Father
Obedience is ...turning from my sins
Obedience is ...bearing good fruit
Obedience is ...loving my neighbour as myself
Obedience is ...being a law-abiding citizen
Obedience is ...rendering to Caesar what is Caesar's
Obedience is ...loving, not judging, my neighbour
Obedience is ...walking in the Spirit
Obedience is ...forgiving those indebted to me
Obedience is ...living so that Jesus will know me
Obedience is ...not being a fair-weather Christian
Obedience is ...living a life of contentment
Obedience is ...obeying God rather than man
Obedience is ...sharing the good news
Obedience is ...fearlessly proclaiming the gospel
Obedience is ...choosing to serve God and not man
Obedience is ...not compromising
Obedience is ...believing in the truth
Obedience is ...worshipping only the King of Kings
Obedience is ...trusting God in the midst of trials
Obedience is ...living a holy life
Obedience is ...being a living sacrifice
Obedience is ...binding myself to the altar
Obedience is ...walking in freedom
Obedience is ...trusting in God's forgiveness
Obedience is ...staying close to God
Obedience is ...my attitude determining my altitude
Obedience is ...being an overcomer

Loving the Lord my God with all my heart

Read Mark 12:28–34

"'And you shall love the LORD your God with all your heart, with all your soul, with all your mind, and with all your strength.' This is the first commandment. And the second, like it, is this: 'You shall love your neighbor as yourself.' There is no other commandment greater than these." (Mark 12:30–31)

One of the scribes asked Jesus: *"Which is the first commandment of all?"* Jesus' answer to him is found in the verses we have just read: *"'And you shall love the LORD your God with all your heart, with all your soul, with all your mind, and with all your strength.' This is the first commandment. And the second, like it, is this: 'You shall love your neighbor as yourself.' There is no other commandment greater than these"* (Mark 12:28b–31).

So the scribe said to Him, "Well said, Teacher. You have spoken the truth, for there is one God, and there is no other but He. And to love Him with all the heart, with all the understanding, with all the soul, and with all the strength, and to love one's neighbor as oneself, is more than all the whole burnt offerings and sacrifices" (Mark 12:32–33). This reminds me of 1 Samuel 15:22–23a: *So Samuel said: "Has the LORD as great delight in burnt offerings and sacrifices, as in obeying the voice of the LORD? Behold, to obey is better than sacrifice, and to heed than the fat of rams. For rebellion is as the sin of witchcraft, and stubbornness is as iniquity and idolatry."*

What is the Lord actually saying to us? He is saying that it is better to obey than to keep saying we are sorry. It is better to do what God has told you to do than to be continually offering sacrifices of remorse. This is what the Israelites did; they brought the fat of the rams. They offered the choicest part of a ram to God and then they went away and they continued to sin. The scribe understood that the evidence of loving God was not about burnt offerings and sacrifices. *Now when Jesus saw that he answered wisely, He said to him, "You are not far from the kingdom of God"* (Mark 12:34a). So the bottom line of what Jesus is saying to us today is that if we love God with all our heart we will live lives of obedience to Him.

Prayer

Father God, I come to You with a humble heart. Lord, help me to live a life that will demonstrate my love for You. I know that obedience is what You require of me. I want to walk in obedience to You so that You can say to me: *"You are not far from the kingdom of God."* Amen.

The result of my loving God with all my heart is that I will live a life of obedience to Him.

Doing the will of my Father

Read Matthew 7:13–23

"Not everyone who says to Me, 'Lord, Lord,' shall enter the kingdom of heaven, but he who does the will of My Father in heaven." (Matthew 7:21)

To obey is better than sacrifice. In the early days the church practised indulgences. A person would commit a sin: For instance, if a man had slept with his friend's wife, stolen from his employer or become involved in a drunken fight on a Saturday night, all he would do is confess his sins to the priest on the Sunday morning. The priest gave him a fine to pay, wrote him a receipt and proclaimed his sins forgiven. When Monday arrived he would do the same things all over again. My dear friend, you cannot behave in this way because it makes a mockery of God.

This still goes on today. The form it takes is different, but in essence it is the same principle. The InDuna on our farm once came to me very annoyed; he told me there were ministers telling people to pay them money and they would give them a ticket to heaven. It's laughable, but sad. There is no shortcut to heaven. God requires obedience of us. The Bible tells us that the greatest commandment is to *"love the Lord your God with all your heart, with all your soul, with all your mind, and with all your strength"* (Mark 12:30).

If you love somebody you are not purposefully going to disobey them, are you? You will not wilfully hurt them. If you love your wife you will be faithful to her. God challenges us with these words: *"Not everyone who says to Me, 'Lord, Lord,' shall enter the kingdom of heaven, but he who does the will of My Father in heaven."* God is not interested in your words; He is interested in what you do. Don't tell people that you love them; show them. Sir, don't keep telling your wife that you love her. She is sick and tired of hearing you say it, rather show her by your actions. The greatest commandment in the Bible is that you must love the Lord your God. We show our love for God by walking in obedience to Him. Words are cheap; it is actions that count.

Prayer

Father God, You have spoken to my heart today. Father, forgive me that so often I do not put You first in my life. Lord, I never want You to look at me and say that You do not know me. I want to spend my life doing Your will and walk in obedience to You. Help me to love the people close to me with integrity and passion. Amen.

I show my love for God by walking in obedience to Him.

Turning from my sins

Read Luke 6:46

"Many will say to Me in that day, 'Lord, Lord, have we not prophesied in Your name, cast out demons in Your name, and done many wonders in Your name?' And then I will declare to them, 'I never knew you; depart from Me, you who practice lawlessness!'"
(Matthew 7:22–23)

As you know, before I was saved I spent a lot of time in pubs. In the pubs they used to say that words are cheap, but that money buys the whiskey. What does this mean? The guy sitting next to you keeps telling you that he is going to buy you a beer, but he never does. His intentions are good but he never delivers. This is a very bad example because I don't want any of you sitting in the pub, okay? What I am trying to illustrate is that Christianity is about action, it is about making good on what we promise. Faith has to have feet. It is a "doing" word.

Often when someone is addicted to alcohol or drugs, they come to me and tell me that they cannot stop drinking or using drugs. The bottom line is that they actually can; they just don't want to. Sorry that I have to be harsh about this, but I am telling you the truth. If you have an alcohol or drug problem you can stop by the grace of God. You can say: "Today I am stopping this filthy habit and I am never going to do it again." The harsh truth is that if you don't stop, the drugs and the alcohol will kill you. If you are involved in pornography, or some other form of immorality, stop it today before you become exposed. How many of our Christian leaders across the world have fallen into adultery and immorality through disobedience?

Don't tell people that you love them; show them that you love them. Don't tell Jesus that you are committed to loving Him with all your heart, and all of your mind, and all your soul, and all your strength, and then disobey Him. Jesus tells us in Matthew 7:22–23 that He is not interested in the things that you do for Him. He is only interested in the way that you live. Rather start to live a life of obedience that brings glory to God. Then He will be able to honour you and bless you.

Prayer

Father, as I bow in Your presence I pray that You will shine Your light into the innermost parts of my heart. Reveal my sins to me so that I can repent before You. I thank You for Your grace and Your forgiveness. Help me to go forward in obedience, demonstrating my love for You by doing Your will. Amen.

When I live a life of obedience that brings glory to God, He will honour me and bless me.

Bearing good fruit

Read Romans 2:13

"A good tree cannot bear bad fruit, nor can a bad tree bear good fruit. Every tree that does not bear good fruit is cut down and thrown into the fire. Therefore by their fruits you will know them." (Matthew 7:18–20)

I am convinced that if a person has a regular quiet time with God they cannot blatantly sin against Him. I am telling you it is impossible. If you get up every morning and spend time in the presence of God – if you pray and read His Word – you will not be able to continue in a particular sin. Spending time in God's Word is one of the ways that you build a good strong life. Jesus likened our lives to trees. He said that a good tree bears good fruit and a bad tree bears bad fruit. It is impossible for a good tree to produce bad fruit. It is also impossible for a bad tree to produce good fruit. What you put in is what you are going to get out.

It starts by spending time in the Word of God. Psalm 119:105 tells us that *Your word is a lamp to my feet and a light to my path.* You cannot get lost or go astray when you are being guided by the Word of God. His Word will never lead you into sin. So many times we look everywhere else for wisdom and guidance, and God's Word is the last place we go.

God has told you that to obey is better than sacrifice. He says that He is more interested in the quality of your fruit than He is in what you do for Him. "*Enter by the narrow gate; for wide is the gate and broad is the way that leads to destruction, and there are many who go in by it. Because narrow is the gate and difficult is the way which leads to life, and there are few who find it*" (Matthew 7:13–14). A life of obedience is not to be found on the broad road that leads to destruction; it is to be found by entering through the narrow gate. Jesus' words "*and there are few who find it*" are chilling. My friend, what will you choose today: the road of obedience leading to eternal life or the road to destruction?

Prayer

Father God, thank You for Your Word. Help me to be faithful in guarding the time I spend with You in Your Word and in prayer. Help me to not allow anything to erode this time. I realize that it is my safety net. I want to live a life of obedience to You that bears good fruit to the glory of Your name. Amen.

The road of obedience leads to eternal life.

Loving my neighbour as myself

Read Mark 12:28–34

"'And you shall love the LORD your God with all your heart, with all your soul, with all your mind, and with all your strength.' This is the first commandment. And the second, like it, is this: 'You shall love your neighbor as yourself.' There is no other commandment greater than these." (Mark 12:30–31)

L ove the Lord your God is the first commandment in the Bible. The second is: *Love your neighbour as yourself.* My friends, now we are getting to the hard part. *Love your neighbour as yourself.* You might ask, "Who is my neighbour?" In Genesis chapter four we read the story of Cain and Abel. Cain asked God: *"Am I my brother's keeper?"* (Genesis 4:9c) The answer is yes: you are your brother's keeper. If you want to live in obedience to God you have to love your neighbour.

Maybe you are thinking that if I knew what that person had done to you, and how they had hurt you, I wouldn't be telling you to forgive them. Yes I would. *Then Peter came to Him and said, "Lord, how often shall my brother sin against me, and I forgive him? Up to seven times?" Jesus said to him, "I do not say to you, up to seven times, but up to seventy times seven"* (Matthew 18:21–22). There is nothing complicated about understanding what the Bible teaches; however, I want to tell you that implementing what the Bible teaches is another thing altogether. Being a Christian is not for the faint hearted. It takes courage to forgive someone who has deeply hurt you. It takes a real man to do it.

I often smile to myself when someone says that because he is not making it in the world he is going into the ministry to serve the Lord. I want to say to him, if you cannot make it in the world, you will never make it in the ministry. The ministry is much tougher because God requires so much more from you. The Bible says in James 3:1: *My brethren, let not many of you become teachers, knowing that we shall receive a stricter judgment.* I have certainly found this to be true in my own life. The bottom line about loving your neighbour is that if you want to please God then loving your neighbour is not an optional extra. Now is the time to walk in love and obedience.

Prayer

My Father God, You have called me into a love relationship with You. You have forgiven me all my sins. In the same way You call me to love my neighbour. If I love You then I have to love my neighbour. I have to forgive him when he wrongs me. Help me, I pray, to walk in obedience to You. Amen.

Now is the time to walk in love and obedience.

Being a law-abiding citizen

Read Titus 3:1–8

Remind them to be subject to rulers and authorities, to obey, to be ready for every good work. (Titus 3:1)

My dear friend, if you love God you have to obey Him. Obedience to God includes obeying the rules of our country. He has quite a lot to say in His Word about this. One aspect of obeying God is being a good citizen and abiding by the laws of the land. In Titus we are taught *to be subject to rulers and authorities, to obey, to be ready for every good work.* Verse eight reinforces this, saying that *those who have believed in God should be careful to maintain good works.*

Obeying rulers and authorities includes obeying the rules of the road. That is right. South Africans are very lawless when it comes to their behaviour on the road. Sadly Christians are often no better than the next person in this regard. If the speed limit says you must drive up to 120 kilometres an hour then you are not to travel any faster than that. How many Christians have you seen flying past you at 180 kilometres an hour, jumping red lights or not stopping at stop signs? There are people who ride around with bumper stickers proclaiming one or another Christian slogan, and they drive like absolute maniacs. What kind of a witness is that?

Ecclesiastes 8:2 has good advice for us: *"Keep the king's commandment for the sake of your oath to God."* This is why you obey the speed limit and the other rules of the road, my friend. You have made a commitment to Jesus Christ. It is because of this commitment that you do the right thing. People are looking at you and the way you behave. Your actions speak far louder than your words ever will. You cannot obey God and not obey the laws of the land. The two go together. So many people think it is smart to see how much they can get away with. This is not the way a servant of God behaves. Now is the time to obey God by doing the right thing. *Remind them to be subject to rulers and authorities, to obey … showing all humility to all men* (Titus 3:1, 2b).

Prayer

Father God, I come before You today in repentance. I am sorry that my actions do not always line up with my talk. This is often most apparent by the way I behave behind the wheel of my car. I realize that obeying the laws of the land are an indication of my commitment to You. Forgive me, I pray. Help me to obey for the sake of my oath to You. Amen.

My actions speak far louder than my words ever will.

Rendering to Caesar what is Caesar's

Read Matthew 22:15–22

And He said to them, "Render therefore to Caesar the things that are Caesar's, and to God the things that are God's." When they had heard these words, they marveled, and left Him and went their way. (Matthew 22:21–22)

A s was their practice, the Pharisees were looking for a way to catch Jesus out. *"Teacher, we know that You are true, and teach the way of God in truth; nor do You care about anyone, for You do not regard the person of men. Tell us, therefore, what do You think? Is it lawful to pay taxes to Caesar, or not?"* But Jesus perceived their wickedness, and said, *"Why do you test Me, you hypocrites? Show Me the tax money."* So they brought Him a denarius. And He said to them, *"Whose image and inscription is this?"* They said to Him, *"Caesar's."* And He said to them, *"Render therefore to Caesar the things that are Caesar's, and to God the things that are God's."* When they had heard these words, they marveled, and left Him and went their way (Matthew 22:16b–22).

Passages like this in the Bible sometimes make us uncomfortable. You may be thinking that I am becoming legalistic. No, my friend, I am not. We cannot choose what we will obey in God's Word and what we won't. The truth is we are talking about the greatest commandment in the Bible: *Love the Lord your God with all your heart, with all your soul, with all your mind, and with all your strength* (Mark 12:30). If you love someone you obey them. The two are intertwined.

You might ask me why you should pay your income taxes. Simple: Because God says so. In Romans Paul says: *Let every soul be subject to the governing authorities. For there is no authority except from God, and the authorities that exist are appointed by God. Therefore whoever resists the authority resists the ordinance of God, and those who resist will bring judgment on themselves. Therefore you must be subject, not only because of wrath but also for conscience' sake. For because of this you also pay taxes, for they are God's ministers attending continually to this very thing. Render therefore to all their due: taxes to whom taxes are due, customs to whom customs, fear to whom fear, honor to whom honor* (Romans 13:1–2, 5–7).

Prayer

Father, for all sorts of reasons I often don't want to give the government what I should be giving them. I realize that it is not about whether I want to or not. It is not about whether the government deserves it or not. I must do it because You have commanded me to do so in Your Word. If I love You I will obey You. Amen.

If I love someone I obey them. The two are intertwined.

Loving, not judging, my neighbour

Read Mark 12:28–34

"'And you shall love the LORD your God with all your heart, with all your soul, with all your mind, and with all your strength.' This is the first commandment. And the second, like it, is this: 'You shall love your neighbor as yourself.' There is no other commandment greater than these." (Mark 12:30–31)

As you may know, my dad only became a Christian towards the end of his life. I was so grateful that I had the privilege of leading him to the Lord before he died. However, even when he was still very much in the world he was the most honest man that I have ever met. He used to continually embarrass and humble me with his integrity; because he showed qualities that I never showed even as a Christian.

I will never forget the day in the 1970s when one of the world's top evangelists was exposed for his involvement with a prostitute. I walked into my dad's house as this news was being broadcasted on national television. There the man was on the screen for the whole world to see. The tears were running down his face as he repented of what he had done. I wanted to find a hole and crawl into it. I was waiting for my dad to make a comment about Christians not walking their talk again. Instead he said, "Angus, we are all human." I was so touched by his attitude. He didn't judge. Once again he was an example to me.

In Matthew 7:1–5 Jesus tells us: *"Judge not, that you be not judged. For with what judgment you judge, you will be judged; and with the measure you use, it will be measured back to you. And why do you look at the speck in your brother's eye, but do not consider the plank in your own eye? Or how can you say to your brother, 'Let me remove the speck from your eye'; and look, a plank is in your own eye? Hypocrite! First remove the plank from your own eye, and then you will see clearly to remove the speck from your brother's eye."* My friend, the message is clear: Don't be so quick to judge, especially when you are still dealing with issues in your own life. Make sure that you are obeying God in every area of your own life. Walk your talk. Love your neighbour – don't judge him.

Prayer

Father God, I humbly bow before You. I realize that I am so quick to judge others. Often this is so that I can deflect attention away from myself and my own sins. Forgive me, I pray. I repent before You. Fill me with love for You, my Lord, and love for my fellow man. Amen.

I must obey God in every area of my life and love my neighbour instead of judging him.

Walking in the Spirit

Read Romans 8:1–17

There is therefore now no condemnation to those who are in Christ Jesus, who do not walk according to the flesh, but according to the Spirit. For the law of the Spirit of life in Christ Jesus has made me free from the law of sin and death. (Romans 8:1–2)

The road to hell is paved with good intentions. We all fall prey to the sin of procrastination. I must go visit my neighbour, I must go and repay the money that I owe, or I must return something that I borrowed. Don't delay any longer; do it today. On a very practical level this is what Christianity is. Faith is practical, not pie-in-the-sky theory. You need to be obedient to what the Holy Spirit is telling you to do. Walk according to the Holy Spirit and His prompting in your life. Then you will see the difference in your life, you will experience liberty and freedom. Walk in obedience according to the Spirit and not your flesh; and you will definitely sleep better at night.

You might think that you cannot afford to pay back the money that you owe. So you are avoiding the person. This is the worst thing that you can do. If you owe somebody money phone them up, or better yet, climb in your car and go and see them. Tell them you are sorry that you don't have the money to pay them now. Assure them that you will pay as soon as you can and settle on an amount that you will pay. There are very few people who will not be prepared to accept an arrangement. The important thing is that you do what you say you are going to do. If you don't take the initiative and make an arrangement they will hand you over and then you will be in even more trouble. Be honest. Be obedient. Galatians 5:25 encourages us: *If we live in the Spirit, let us also walk in the Spirit.*

Paul also admonishes us in Romans 14:17, *for the kingdom of God is not eating and drinking, but righteousness and peace and joy in the Holy Spirit.* You will know righteousness, peace and joy when you obey the Holy Spirit. Paul also says to us: *I, therefore, the prisoner of the Lord, beseech you to walk worthy of the calling with which you were called* (Ephesians 4:1).

Prayer

Father God, You have spoken clearly to me again through Your Word. Help me, I pray, to be obedient even when it is difficult. Give me courage to walk my talk. Now is the time for me to be obedient to Your Holy Spirit and His prompting in my life. Amen.

I must walk worthy of my calling.

Forgiving those indebted to me

Read Matthew 18:21–35

"'Should you not also have had compassion on your fellow servant, just as I had pity on you?' And his master was angry, and delivered him to the torturers until he should pay all that was due to him. 'So My heavenly Father also will do to you if each of you, from his heart, does not forgive his brother his trespasses.'" (Matthew 18:33–35)

We need to take this parable to heart on two levels. First, there is the irrefutable fact that God has forgiven us so much that we have no right to withhold forgiveness from anyone else – no matter what they have done to us. Jesus doesn't say to us that He will forgive us one thing but not another. No, He says: *If we confess our sins, He is faithful and just to forgive us our sins and to cleanse us from **all** unrighteousness* (1 John 1:9). How many times have you had to go to God and ask forgiveness for the same sin; and has He ever turned you away?

Secondly, it is sad that we so often choose to withhold forgiveness from other people. It is one thing if we owe someone money. However, it is often quite another when someone owes us money. Take a moment and look at our Scripture reading again. Are you like the gracious king or the unforgiving servant? There is a harsh reality awaiting those who will not forgive. God takes forgiveness very seriously, my friend. Jesus says in Matthew 6:14: *"For if you forgive men their trespasses, your heavenly Father will also forgive you."*

If you do not forgive you will not be forgiven. The Bible is clear on this point. If there are people from whom you are withholding forgiveness you need to carefully examine your heart today. *"But if you do not forgive men their trespasses, neither will your Father forgive your trespasses"* (Matthew 6:15). *"And whenever you stand praying, if you have anything against anyone, forgive him, that your Father in heaven may also forgive you your trespasses"* (Mark 11:25). This takes us back to our earlier Scripture in 1 Samuel 15:22–23a: *So Samuel said: "Has the Lord as great delight in burnt offerings and sacrifices, as in obeying the voice of the Lord? Behold, to obey is better than sacrifice, and to heed than the fat of rams. For rebellion is as the sin of witchcraft, and stubbornness is as iniquity and idolatry."*

Prayer

Father, I hang my head in shame when I realize that so often I withhold forgiveness from people. So often I take revenge when the opportunity presents itself. Forgive me, I pray. You are so gracious to me, forgiving me over and over again. I choose today to be obedient to You and forgive those who have wronged me. Amen.

Am I like the gracious king or the unforgiving servant?

Living so that Jesus will know me

Read Matthew 7:21–29

"Many will say to Me in that day, 'Lord, Lord, have we not prophesied in Your name, cast out demons in Your name, and done many wonders in Your name?' And then I will declare to them, 'I never knew you; depart from Me, you who practice lawlessness!'"
(Matthew 7:22–23)

I advised my two farmer sons to invite the bank manager to visit their farms when their crops are looking fantastic, their cattle are fat and they don't owe any money. This way the bank manager will see how well they are doing. If they wait until they need money, all he will see is the crop taking strain and thin cattle. Then the bank manager is more likely to phone and tell them to come to his office, which usually means trouble. It is much too late then – it is better to take the initiative and go to him before he calls you.

We used to show animals at the local show. The sheep and cattle received the best of care and food. We had grooms working on the animals 24/7. However, we made no profit on those animals, even though we walked away with all the prizes and the big silver trophies. You can't eat them or trade them in for money though, can you? My boys queried why we went to all this trouble for very little return. I explained that it was about collateral and reputation. The bank, co-op and agricultural managers, as well as the managers of all the tractor, seed and fertilizer companies, attended the show and saw us win. At the back of their minds they had the perception "those guys are good farmers; they know how to produce good animals and good crops." As a result they were more likely to help us out.

In the lean times when you phone to ask them for an extension of your overdraft facility or your production line they have a positive memory of you. The same applies to the kingdom of God. Your lifestyle counts: love the Lord your God and walk in His ways. Then in times of leanness, in times of hardness, you will be able to withstand the onslaught of the evil one. Jesus will know you because you have done the will of His Father in heaven. You have walked in obedience and not practised lawlessness. Always remember that obedience is better than sacrifice.

Prayer

Father, thank You that You will never leave me nor forsake me if I continue to faithfully walk with You. Help me to live in obedience in the good times and the bad times. Help me to always seek to do Your will no matter what happens to me or around me. Amen.

Jesus will know me because I have done the will of His Father in heaven.

Not being a fair-weather Christian

Read Philippians 3:1–14

Not that I have already attained, or am already perfected; but I press on, that I may lay hold of that for which Christ Jesus has also laid hold of me. ...forgetting those things which are behind and reaching forward to those things which are ahead, I press toward the goal for the prize of the upward call of God in Christ Jesus. (Philippians 3:12, 13b–14)

Being a fair-weather Christian means that when things are going well we praise God. However when things go badly we are in the pub drowning our sorrows. That is not Christianity and it isn't how you demonstrate that you love the Lord your God with all your heart, with all your soul, with all your mind and with all your strength. Your love has to be unconditional.

I love the book of Job; you need to read it again sometime soon. There is nowhere in the Bible where it says that if you come to Jesus you are going to be a prosperous Christian. Nowhere! Come to Jesus and you will never ever have any problems in your home; you will never ever have sickness at your door; you will never ever have financial difficulties. Those are lies from the pit of hell. You have to love the Lord your God unconditionally no matter what comes your way. Job understood this. In Job 13:15a he says: *Though He slay me, yet will I trust Him*. Folks, this is love and commitment. This is obedience. The reason that Job endured was because he knew his God.

The apostle Paul understood that following Jesus was about obedience. He says in Philippians 3:10–11: *...that I may know Him and the power of His resurrection, and the fellowship of His sufferings, being conformed to His death, if, by any means, I may attain to the resurrection from the dead*. You see, sir, if you kick a dead dog it feels nothing because it is dead; so if someone kicks you and you react to them then you are not dead, are you? Paul continues in Galatians 2:20: *I have been crucified with Christ; it is no longer I who live, but Christ lives in me; and the life which I now live in the flesh I live by faith in the Son of God, who loved me and gave Himself for me*. How you react to hardship will determine whether you are a fair-weather Christian or an obedient servant of the Lord Jesus Christ.

Prayer

Father, thank You for the wonderful examples that I find in Your Word of people who were not fair-weather followers of You. People like Job and Paul were faithful servants no matter what happened in their lives. They loved You and were obedient to You unconditionally. Help me to follow their example. Amen.

How I react to hardship will determine what kind of a Christian I am.

Living a life of contentment

Read 1 Timothy 6:1–16

Now godliness with contentment is great gain. For we brought nothing into this world, and it is certain we can carry nothing out. (1 Timothy 6:6–7)

I f you are a Christian then it doesn't really matter what happens in your life. What matters is that you love the Lord your God with all your heart, with all your soul, with all your mind and with all your strength; and that you love your neighbour as yourself. This is what God asks of us. If you love Him you will do what He tells you to do. You will be obedient no matter what the outcome or the consequences. This is the only way for you to live an abundant life filled with joy and peace. We so often confuse joy and peace with everything going well in our lives. This is not so. Joy and peace are not about our circumstances. They are about having Jesus in our hearts. He is our Joy and He is our Peace.

As Christians we are meant to live lives of contentment. One of my wife Jill's favourite Scriptures is 1 Timothy 6:6. It says: *Now godliness with contentment is great gain.* How many truly contented Christians do you know? Sadly, not too many, I am sure. It seems that many Christians are just as frustrated and fearful as people who don't even know Jesus. Many Christians are as driven by the quest for material gain and ambition as the next man. Paul gives this warning in 1 Timothy 6:8–10: *And having food and clothing, with these we shall be content. But those who desire to be rich fall into temptation and a snare, and into many foolish and harmful lusts which drown men in destruction and perdition. For the love of money is a root of all kinds of evil, for which some have strayed from the faith in their greediness, and pierced themselves through with many sorrows.*

We have forgotten that godliness with contentment is great gain. We are called to live a life of obedience. God is saying to us that it is time to walk in obedience. Paul said in Philippians 1:21: *For to me, to live is Christ, and to die is gain.* This is true contentment.

Prayer

Father, You have given me so much to be grateful for. Forgive me that so often I am striving and straining for more. I realize that as I increasingly find my joy and peace in Jesus I will want for less and less. The more I walk in obedience to You the more content I will become. Fill me with Your Spirit, I pray. Amen.

Godliness with contentment is great gain.

Obeying God rather than man

Read Acts 5:17–32
But Peter and the other apostles answered and said: "We ought to obey God rather than men."
(Acts 5:29)

Peter and the other apostles had been thrown in the common prison by the high priest and a sect of the Sadducees. During the night an angel came and freed them from prison. This was done for the express purpose of them being able to continue preaching the gospel. During the night an angel of the Lord opened the prison doors and brought them out, and commanded them to: *"Go, stand in the temple and speak to the people all the words of this life"* (Acts 5:20). Now, don't you agree that after being thrown in prison – which couldn't have been very pleasant – and then being freed, one's first inclination would have been to run and hide?

The apostles knew that if they obeyed God's command they would be in trouble again. However, running and hiding was not an option for them. God told them to preach the gospel and they obeyed Him. The apostles went to the temple and they shared the words of life with the people. My friends, we have the same privilege of sharing *the words of this life* with other people. Jesus commanded us in Matthew 28:18–20: *"All authority has been given to Me in heaven and on earth. Go therefore and make disciples of all the nations, baptizing them in the name of the Father and of the Son and of the Holy Spirit, teaching them to observe all things that I have commanded you; and lo, I am with you always, even to the end of the age."*

The high priest was incensed and he went to the temple to confront them. Peter and the other apostle's answer to him is an example to us. *"We ought to obey God rather than men."* This is the bottom line – will you obey God or man, my friend? It is so easy to make excuses as to why we do not stand up and speak out the truth of God's Word. We come up with all kinds of reasons, but God's command to us is clear. Who will you obey, my friend: God or man?

Prayer

Father God, I am so inspired by the obedience of Peter and the apostles. I realize that the time has come to stand up and be counted. I also recognize that their obedience stemmed from their love for You. I want to love You like this. Fill me with Your Spirit, I pray. Amen.

I have to choose whether I will obey God or man.

Sharing the good news

Read Acts 3:1–16

"And His name, through faith in His name, has made this man strong, whom you see and know. Yes, the faith which comes through Him has given him this perfect soundness in the presence of you all." (Acts 3:16)

You have the words of life, my friend; why aren't you sharing them? In our reading today Peter and John went up to the temple as was their custom, as Jesus used to do. Outside the temple was a 40-year-old man who had been lame from birth, begging for money. *Then Peter said, "Silver and gold I do not have, but what I do have I give you: In the name of Jesus Christ of Nazareth, rise up and walk"* (Acts 3:6). The man expected Peter to give him money, but instead Peter gave him something so much more precious. *And he took him by the right hand and lifted him up, and immediately his feet and ankle bones received strength. So he, leaping up, stood and walked and entered the temple with them – walking, leaping, and praising God. And all the people saw him walking and praising God* (Acts 3:7–9).

When he ran into the temple praising God it caused a real stir, because everyone recognized him as the man who begged at the gate beautiful. What was the outcome of this miracle: *… and they were filled with wonder and amazement at what had happened to him* (Acts 3:10b). The people came running to Peter and John. They didn't take the glory for themselves. Peter immediately used it as an opportunity to point the people towards Jesus.

"Men of Israel, why do you marvel at this? Or why look so intently at us, as though by our own power or godliness we had made this man walk? … And His name, through faith in His name, has made this man strong, whom you see and know. Yes, the faith which comes through Him has given him this perfect soundness in the presence of you all" (Acts 3:12,16). Obedience to God was the hallmark of the apostles' lives. They took every opportunity presented to them to share the good news of Jesus Christ with people. The result of this obedience was: *And through the hands of the apostles many signs and wonders were done among the people* (Acts 5:12a).

Prayer

Father, my life lacks power. I realize that this is because my witness for You is half-hearted and lacking at the best of times. Fill me with the power of Your Holy Spirit, I pray, just like You did the apostles in the upper room. Set me on fire to share the good news. Amen.

Obedience to God was the hallmark of the apostles' lives.

Fearlessly proclaiming the gospel

Read Galatians 1:1–12

But I make known to you, brethren, that the gospel which was preached by me is not according to man. For I neither received it from man, nor was I taught it, but it came through the revelation of Jesus Christ. (Galatians 1:11–12)

What we need in these last days are people who are fearless when it comes to the gospel of Jesus Christ. It requires placing obedience to God above obedience to man. Paul, another mighty warrior of God, was a Pharisee until God met him on the road to Damascus. Paul said in Galatians 1:10: *For do I now persuade men, or God? Or do I seek to please men? For if I still pleased men, I would not be a bondservant of Christ.* Who are you trying to find favour with, my friend? Are you one of those guys who run with the hares and hunt with the hounds? Today you are in church weeping and asking God to give you another chance; and tomorrow you are back in the pub, drunk as a skunk with the rest of the gang.

You cannot be a bondservant of Jesus Christ and a man-pleaser. You have to take a stand one way or the other. Obedience to God means fearlessly proclaiming the gospel of Jesus Christ to other people. Too many men try and walk a tightrope between trying to please God and man at the same time. This is why their ministry comes to nothing. It is why they have no power. Acts 5:12a tells us: *And through the hands of the apostles many signs and wonders were done among the people.* The reason for their powerful ministry was because they pleased God and not man. They were passionate about obeying God and fearlessly proclaiming the gospel.

Too many people live lives of compromise. You cannot do this, my friend. It will come to nothing. If you are wondering why you are not experiencing blessing in your life and ministry; then take a moment to examine who you are obeying. It cannot be a blend between God and man. It has to be a 100% commitment to God. He wants all of you. He wants you to fearlessly proclaim His gospel. The power and blessing can only follow obedience. Make the decision today to fearlessly proclaim the gospel.

Prayer

Father God, I thank You for Your great love for me. I realize that the only response that is appropriate is for me to love and obey You in return. Help me to fearlessly obey You, proclaiming the gospel of Jesus Christ. I choose today to obey You rather than man. I want to please You and You only. Amen.

I must make the decision today to fearlessly proclaim the gospel.

Choosing to serve God and not man

Read Luke 16:1–13

"No servant can serve two masters; for either he will hate the one and love the other, or else he will be loyal to the one and despise the other. You cannot serve God and mammon." (Luke 16:13)

Our Scripture tells us that we cannot serve two masters. Matthew 12:30 further reinforces this: *He who is not with Me is against Me, and he who does not gather with Me scatters abroad.* Paul says in Romans 1:16a–b: *For I am not ashamed of the gospel of Christ, for it is the power of God to salvation for everyone who believes.* The power comes from not being ashamed of the gospel of Jesus Christ. Salvation is found only in Jesus Christ; He is the one and only way to heaven.

You need to make a decision today as to whether you are going to serve God or man. It is quite simple; if you choose to serve man then it is your choice, but God help you. Jesus is coming soon and you'll pay the price for your decision when He returns. You might choose to accuse me of preaching fire and brimstone. No, I am not, but I am committed to speaking the truth in love, my friend. This is why our television programme is called *Grassroots*; we are about getting down to the basics and telling it like it is. Our mandate is to preach the gospel.

You have heard the saying attributed to Edmund Burke: "The only thing necessary for the triumph of evil is for good men to do nothing". Every day our newspapers are filled with stories of the evil that man perpetrates. The only way to put a stop to it is for Christians to stand up and speak the truth about the Lord Jesus Christ. Then people will begin receiving a revelation of who God is. He is a God of love, but He is also a God of justice. In Acts 9, when Paul received a revelation of Jesus Christ, his life was changed. Ananias was part of that miracle because he obeyed the prompting of the Holy Spirit and went to see Paul. When people meet Jesus Christ they will stop murdering and plundering. We cannot serve two masters, my friends. We have to be committed to speaking the truth.

Prayer

Father, You have been speaking to me very clearly and plainly. I choose to no longer remain deaf. I choose to stand up and be counted. I choose to serve You and not man. Use me, I pray, to spread the message of Your gospel. Make me a blessing to others. I want to serve You wholeheartedly. Amen.

I cannot serve two masters; I have to choose between God or man.

Not compromising

Read Acts 20:17–38

"Therefore I testify to you this day that I am innocent of the blood of all men. For I have not shunned to declare to you the whole counsel of God." (Acts 20:26–27)

One of the things I am concerned about is the level of compromise that I see in the Christian church. Compromise not only breaks down the individual Christian's witness but it also breaks down the fabric of the church of Jesus Christ. I agree with those who believe that the Roman Emperor Constantine's conversion to Christianity and his subsequent legalization of Christianity was the beginning of compromise in the Christian church. It moved people away from making personal decisions to follow Jesus Christ towards obeying the authorities. The people ended up fearing and obeying Caesar instead of God. This is where the church became lukewarm and the Power departed. You cannot compromise; you cannot serve two masters. Are you trying to serve two masters today?

When people preach the Bible literally as it is written they often find themselves in trouble with the academics and the theologians. God's Word is straightforward, there is nothing complicated about it – everyone from fishermen through to educated doctors were able to understand the teaching of Jesus. I preach the Word of God literally; I believe the Bible exactly as it is written. We have to take a stand; compromising is not an option. Isaiah 59:19b says: *When the enemy comes in like a flood, the Spirit of the LORD will lift up a standard against him.* I want to encourage you to sign up for God's army: be salty; be controversial. You can be sure that if you preach the Word of God you will automatically be controversial.

Preaching the gospel as it stands in the Bible will get you into trouble with the religious people. It got Jesus into trouble; it also got the disciples, Paul and the other apostles into trouble. Did it stop them? No, it only made them more determined to preach the gospel without compromise. Do you stand up for what is right in your home? Do you take a stand in your workplace? When you are with your friends do you stand up for what is right? Don't compromise, my friend. You cannot obey God and compromise.

Prayer

Father, I worship You today. You are a great and mighty God – there is none like You. I stand in Your presence and lift my hands in surrender to You. I want to walk in Your ways. I want to stand tall for You no matter what situation I find myself in. Help me to never compromise but to always be obedient to Your Word. Amen.

I must take a stand at home, at work and when I am with my friends.

Believing in the truth

Read John 14:1–14

Jesus said to him, "I am the way, the truth, and the life. No one comes to the Father except through Me." (John 14:6)

It deeply concerns me that there are professors who don't believe the literal story of Jonah and the fish. They don't believe that Jonah stayed in the belly of the fish for three days and three nights. I want to tell you that he did; if the Bible says that he did, then he did. Some of these self-same theological professors are telling their students to disregard the Bible. To them it is only an "old fairy tale". When you start to do this then your faith is zero. Those professors won't lay hands upon the sick and pray that God will raise them up, because they don't believe that He heals. If you do not believe that Jesus is the way, the truth and the life then how are you going to have any power?

We need to take authority. People constantly phone me and I receive many emails from people asking me to please pray for them. I pray for everyone. What about those who don't get healed? I don't know; that's not my business. My job is to lay my hands upon the sick and pray the prayer of faith, asking God to heal them. This is what Jesus told His disciples to do: *And He said to them, "Go into all the world and preach the gospel to every creature … And these signs will follow those who believe: In My name they will cast out demons; they will speak with new tongues; they will take up serpents; and if they drink anything deadly, it will by no means hurt them; they will lay hands on the sick, and they will recover"* (Mark 16:15, 17–18).

The religious leaders who believe that as long as you lead a good life you will go to heaven have it all wrong. Good people don't go to heaven; believers go to heaven. Jesus is the way, the truth and the life. The Bible is clear on this: no one comes to the Father except through Him. Only sinners saved by grace are going to heaven.

Prayer

Father, I thank You and praise You for Jesus Christ, my Lord and saviour. Thank You, Jesus, that You are the way, the truth and the life. Thank You for saving me, a sinner. I am so grateful that You have redeemed me. Thank You that I am not going to spend eternity with You because of what I have done or will do, but because of what You have done for me. Amen.

I must believe God and His truth, not the devil and his lies.

Worshipping only the King of Kings

Read Daniel 3:8–30

"…our God whom we serve is able to deliver us from the burning fiery furnace, and He will deliver us from your hand, O king. But if not, let it be known to you, O king, that we do not serve your gods, nor will we worship the gold image which you have set up."
(Daniel 3:17–18)

We are saved through faith in Jesus Christ. We are saved to worship God and God alone. They crucified our saviour because He proclaimed that He was God. He died and rose again. If you go to Jerusalem you will find an empty tomb because He is alive! He is coming again for us, His bride. He is coming for those who will only serve God; for those who worship Him alone, the one and only living God.

Shadrach, Meshach and Abed-Nego were three young men who refused to worship anyone other than the living God. They lived in the days of Nebuchadnezzar, who was regarded by his subjects as a god. He made a statue of himself and proclaimed that his people were to worship his statue. Shadrach, Meshach and Abed-Nego refused to obey him. They would not bow down to a graven image. When he heard about it he was furious and told them that if they didn't repent he would throw them in the fiery furnace. They stood firm and told the king that their God was able to deliver them, but even if He didn't they would rather die than worship anyone other than the living God.

How's that for faith, folks? There are too many Christians serving God conditionally today. "Lord, if you give me my farm back, I'll serve you"; "Lord, if you bring my wife back, I will serve you"; "Lord, if you heal my daughter, I will serve you." This is not faith; faith is unconditional surrender. Shadrach, Meshach and Abed-Nego were thrown into the furnace. As the people watched they saw four people in the fire: Jesus was right there. God saved them. *Nebuchadnezzar spoke, saying, "Blessed be the God of Shadrach, Meshach, and Abed-Nego, who sent His Angel and delivered His servants who trusted in Him, and they have frustrated the king's word, and yielded their bodies, that they should not serve nor worship any god except their own God!"* (Daniel 3:28). What about you, my friend? Are you bowing down to graven images or are you only worshipping the King of Kings?

Prayer

Father God, I worship You today and I choose to serve You unconditionally. I will walk in Your ways and do Your will. I know that You can deliver me, but even if You should choose not to, I will faithfully serve You and do Your will. Amen.

Am I bowing down to graven images? Or am I only worshipping the King of Kings?

Trusting God in the midst of trials

Read Job 1:6–22; 13:15

Though He slay me, yet will I trust Him. (Job 13:15a)

J ob knew about trusting God in the midst of trials. After everything that happened to him, he was still able to say: *Though He slay me, yet will I trust Him*. This is faith. We can trust God in the midst of our trials. He did not let Shadrach, Meshach and Abed-Nego down when they stood in the fiery furnace. God did not let Job down when he had lost everything but his life. He will not let you down either – no matter what you are going through today. He is there with you in the midst of your trial.

I was a rebel. I was a sinner and I was going down for the last time. If it weren't for the Lord Jesus Christ, I would not be preaching God's Word today. I'd be lying in a gutter somewhere or I would be in a mental institute. When my little nephew fell off my tractor and I ran over him, killing him – I want to tell you that if I was a nominal Christian I would not have been able to handle it. The only thing that kept me alive was a living God. Jesus Christ was the one who said to me: "Angus, I am with you always." It was an accident but the devil was telling me that I was a fool; I had killed my brother's son. I had to make a choice. You have a choice today and the choice is quite simple: Are you going to trust God in the midst of your trial; or are you going to believe the devil and his lies?

In Hebrews 13:5b–6 the Lord promises us: *"I will never leave you nor forsake you." So we may boldly say: "The LORD is my helper; I will not fear. What can man do to me?"* You do not need to fear man. You do not need to fear death. Paul understood this when he said: *…so now also Christ will be magnified in my body, whether by life or by death. For to me, to live is Christ, and to die is gain* (Philippians 1:20b–21).

Prayer

Father, I rest my weary head upon Your breast today. You know my sorrow and hurt. You have seen my tears. Thank You that through everything You are with me – I know that You will never leave me nor forsake me. No matter what happens I trust in You to see me through. Amen.

I choose to trust God rather than to believe the devil.

Living a holy life

Read Daniel 6:1–28

The king spoke, saying to Daniel, "Daniel, servant of the living God, has your God, whom you serve continually, been able to deliver you from the lions?" (Daniel 6:20b)

One of my heroes in the Bible is a man named Daniel. He was a mighty man of God; he was a holy man. Holiness is the end product of obedience. Another way to say it is that obedience leads to holiness. Daniel was a man of prayer. Daniel prayed to the God of Israel every day with his curtains wide open. He was not ashamed of his God. Daniel's obedience to God did not start on the day that King Darius was tricked into signing a royal decree. It stated that anyone who prayed to any god other than him would die. No, Daniel's obedience started when he was a young man and he refused to eat the rich food offered to him by the king. Another important thing about living a life of holiness is that Daniel hung around with other people who were obedient to God. Two days ago we saw how three of his friends, rather than bowing down to Nebuchadnezzar, were thrown into the fiery furnace. It is important to choose your friends wisely.

When the decree went out Daniel could have quietly closed the curtains and prayed in secret. That was not his way; he would not disobey his God. King Darius loved Daniel and he was devastated when he realized what had happened. He didn't have a choice though and he had to carry out the decree. Then Daniel was thrown into the lion's den. *But the king spoke, saying to Daniel, "Your God, whom you serve continually, He will deliver you"* (Daniel 6:16b).

Earlier this month we looked at the apostles Peter and John. When they were directed to stop preaching the gospel they said: *"We ought to obey God rather than men"* (Acts 5:29b). In the morning the king rushed to the lion's den and he was so excited to find Daniel alive and well. The Lord had sent His angel to close the mouths of the lions. Daniel lived a life of obedience that led to him being a holy man. Are you living a life of obedience or compromise?

Prayer

Father, I thank You for the many mighty men in Your Word who are such a fine example of living lives of obedience to You. I realize that the only way to live a holy life is to live an obedient life. Father, forgive me that I so easily compromise when the going gets tough. Help me to stand tall and courageous for You. Amen.

Holiness is the end product of obedience.

Being a living sacrifice

Read Romans 12:1–21

I beseech you therefore, brethren, by the mercies of God, that you present your bodies a living sacrifice, holy, acceptable to God, which is your reasonable service. And do not be conformed to this world, but be transformed by the renewing of your mind, that you may prove what is that good and acceptable and perfect will of God. (Romans 12:1–2)

Have you ever studied a picture of the Temple and the Holy of Holies where the altar was? This was where Aaron, the high priest, would take the people's sacrifices and place them on the altar. On either corner of the altar were horns sticking out. For the next few days I want us to look at tying ourselves to the altar and what this means. I don't have to tell you that we are living in perilous times. Times are hard and tough. The devil accuses us; he tries to tell us that we are not going to make it, that we are hypocrites, liars and thieves. The devil has a go at me in much the same way that he does with you.

The Bible tells us that we have to work out our salvation with fear and trembling. We have to make sure that we run the race. It is not between you and your minister; it is not between you and your denomination or church. When all is said and done, my dear friend, at the end of the day it is between you and God. I learnt this some years ago when I had a massive heart attack. I lay on the ground and there was nothing I could do. You might remember that it was in the middle of a Mighty Men Conference. All the men prayed for me and God healed me; but at that moment when I lay on the grass it was me and God. There was no one else.

I want to encourage you to work on your relationship with Jesus Christ. In the same way you have to work on your marriage and other close relationships, so also you need to work on the most important relationship in your life. I want to weep when I hear people say that they do not trust Christians. Who told you to trust Christians anyway? You can only trust God. You cannot even trust yourself. You need to begin spending more time with God; you need to work on your relationship with Him.

Prayer

Father God, You have called me to present my body as a living sacrifice to You. Walking in obedience to You means that I do not hold anything back. Father, help me to make the most of the time that I have left. I realize that when all is said and done, it is only You and me – there is nothing and no one else. Amen.

I must work on my relationship with Jesus Christ.

Binding myself to the altar

Read Psalm 118:25–29

God is the LORD, and He has given us light; bind the sacrifice with cords to the horns of the altar. (Psalm 118:27)

H ave you ever noticed the Scripture that says you need to *bind the sacrifice with cords to the horns of the altar?* Who is the sacrifice and what kind of cords is the Psalmist talking about? You and I are the sacrifice, my friends. Romans 12:1 says: *…present your bodies a living sacrifice…* Paul says this is our reasonable service. God wants all of us – He wants wholehearted commitment from us. The cords that the Psalmist refers to are made up of love, forgiveness, faith, strength and hope in Jesus Christ. These cords will see you through when the accuser of the brethren tries to come up against you.

Our Scripture says that we should bind the sacrifice (ourselves) with the cords of love, faith, strength and hope to the horns of the altar. I love to watch cowboys roping their steers at rodeos. They rope them around their horns and then they loop the rope around the horn on their saddle, holding the animal in place. When they have done this then they bring the steer in and tie him up.

God says we must bind ourselves with cords to the horns of the altar. We must hang in there at all costs. If we are bound to the altar then it will not be so easy to move off the altar. We will be securely bound to the altar. When the devil comes to condemn us we will not fall for his lies. Obedience means believing what God says about you, rather than what the devil says. The Psalmist praises God saying: *God is the Lord, and He has given us light.* The light that we have is the Lord Jesus Christ. He is the light of the world. We no longer walk in darkness. We walk in obedience to God in the light of the Lord Jesus Christ. You are not to be conformed to this world but transformed by the renewing of your mind; this means that you focus on Jesus and not on the things of the world.

Prayer

Father God, thank You for this wonderful image of the altar and the cords of love, faith, strength and hope in Jesus Christ. Help me to place myself upon the altar and then bind the cords around me so that I cannot move off the altar. While I am on the altar, I know that the devil won't be able to touch me. I choose to obey You by believing You and not the enemy. Amen.

I am bound to the horns of the altar with the cords of love, forgiveness, faith, strength and hope.

Walking in freedom

Read Romans 8:1–11

There is therefore now no condemnation to those who are in Christ Jesus, who do not walk according to the flesh, but according to the Spirit. For the law of the Spirit of life in Christ Jesus has made me free from the law of sin and death. (Romans 8:1–2)

I read a beautiful story about a man who went to an outreach campaign that was held in a big tent. The preacher made an altar call and the man went forward. As he walked out of the tent the devil told him he was a liar and reminded him of all the sins he had committed. The man was totally dejected by the time he arrived home. He didn't give up though and the next night he went back to the big tent. The preacher preached another fiery message. Again he got up and he went forward. The sin fell off him; he was rejoicing and he was happy. He walked out of the tent and the devil did the same thing as the night before.

This continued for five nights. On the fifth night he took a hammer and a big wooden stake with him. When the altar call was made he went forward and he prayed the sinner's prayer for the fifth time. Then he took out the stake. He hammered the stake into the ground with the fourteen-pound hammer. Then he walked out. Somebody stopped him to ask why he had done this. He said, "I have nailed my colours to the mast. I have nailed my sin to the ground." The devil did not trouble him again that night. What that man did was bind himself to the horns of the altar. He declared that he was standing for God, therefore according to Romans 8:1: *There is therefore now no condemnation to those who are in Christ Jesus, who do not walk according to the flesh, but according to the Spirit.*

My dear friend, people often come to me and say, "Angus, I'm not sure God has forgiven me." If you have confessed your sin then He has forgiven you. He commands you to go and sin no more. Every day you need to remind yourself that you are forgiven. This is what I do. I remind myself that I am free because Jesus died for me on the cross of Calvary.

Prayer

Father, thank You that I do not stand condemned before You because of what Jesus did for me on Calvary. I am forgiven; my sins are washed away. Help me to walk in obedience to You every day. Help me to remain upon the altar. Thank You for my freedom in Jesus. Amen.

I am free because Jesus died for me on the cross of Calvary.

Trusting in God's forgiveness

Read Psalm 103:1–12

For as the heavens are high above the earth, so great is His mercy toward those who fear Him; as far as the east is from the west, so far has He removed our transgressions from us. (Psalm 103:11–12)

God has forgiven you! This is good news. Once you have confessed your sin, you must believe that God forgives you and does not remember your sins. When we forgive someone we must do the same thing; but we don't do this, do we? Let's be honest. We forgive somebody; then the next week when they make another mistake, we remind them of what they did the previous week. This is not forgiveness. When the Lord forgives, He forgets. Remember when the teacher wrote with chalk on the blackboard, and then erased it with a duster. It was gone forever and could not be brought back. This is how God forgives us. God casts our sins into the dam and puts up a big sign reading: "No Fishing".

Psalm 103:11–12 says: *For as the heavens are high above the earth, so great is His mercy toward those who fear Him; as far as the east is from the west, so far has He removed our transgressions from us.* Our sins are gone. If God doesn't go looking for our sins why do we? Tie yourself with the cords of love, forgiveness, faith, strength and hope around the horns and cling to the altar. I don't speak a lot about the devil because I don't believe in giving him prominence. However, I want to share something with you. He is alive, he exists, he is real and he is trying everything in his power to discourage you from following the Lord. This is the truth. He is two things: He is the father of all lies and he is the deceiver of the brethren.

If you listen to him he will kill you with his lies. He tries to erode the cords with which we tie ourselves to the altar. He tries to make us believe that God doesn't love us. He erodes our faith. If our faith is eroded then we lose our strength. If we do not have strength then our hope wanes. When the cords are weakened and severed we slip from the altar. Don't allow this to happen, my friend: be wise to his schemes.

Prayer

Father, You are a great and wonderful God. Your mercies are new every morning. Your grace is so amazing. Help me to walk in obedience to You, believing in You and what Your Word says to me. Thank You that You have removed my sins as far as the east is from the west. Amen.

God casts my sins into the dam and puts up a big sign reading: "No Fishing".

Staying close to God

Read Psalm 19:7–14

Let the words of my mouth and the meditation of my heart be acceptable in Your sight, O LORD, my strength and my Redeemer. (Psalm 19:14)

The lies of the enemy can only have power in your life if you allow them to. James 4:7 tells us: *Therefore submit to God. Resist the devil and he will flee from you.* If you resist him he has to flee from you. He cannot stay unless you allow him to. Watch what you say. If you speak negatively then you will not walk in victory. The Psalmist knew about this. He prayed: *Let the words of my mouth and the meditation of my heart be acceptable in Your sight, O LORD, my strength and my Redeemer* (Psalm 19:14). I pray this prayer every single day. Watch your words! What you say is what you get.

Up in the jungles of Central Africa the people believe in the witch doctor. His medicine is powerful amongst the people. Someone will approach the witch doctor and pay him to put a curse on another person. They will let the person know that they are going to die. If the person is not a Christian, a believer in Jesus Christ, then that person will believe the lies of the devil. They will lie down in their hut and they will die. No medical doctor, no medicine and no person can help them because they believe in their heart that they are going to die and so they do.

Tie the cords of love, forgiveness, faith, strength and hope in Jesus Christ around the horns of the altar and stay close to God. Believe His Word. Psalm 19:7–11 tells us: *The law of the LORD is perfect, converting the soul; The testimony of the LORD is sure, making wise the simple; The statutes of the LORD are right, rejoicing the heart; The commandment of the LORD is pure, enlightening the eyes; The fear of the LORD is clean, enduring forever; The judgments of the LORD are true and righteous altogether. More to be desired are they than gold, Yea, than much fine gold; Sweeter also than honey and the honeycomb. Moreover by them Your servant is warned, And in keeping them there is great reward.*

Prayer

Lord, my God, I am so grateful to You for Your love for me. It is so amazing that I don't have to fear anything or anyone as long as I remain close to You. Keep me on the altar of obedience, I pray. Amen.

I must stay close to God and believe His Word.

My attitude determining my altitude

Read Revelation 12:7–12

Then I heard a loud voice saying in heaven, "Now salvation, and strength, and the kingdom of our God, and the power of His Christ have come, for the accuser of our brethren, who accused them before our God day and night, has been cast down." (Revelation 12:10)

*T*he Barrier of Spears is a book about R. O. Pearse who climbed the Drakensberg Mountains. He had a heart disease and he had been told that he only had a limited amount of time before he died. He came out to South Africa and he started climbing the mountain peaks. He recklessly climbed sheer walls of rock and he jumped from ledges. He climbed peak after peak. He didn't die of his heart disease – he died when he was a very old man. Your attitude determines your altitude. If you lie down and believe you are going to die, then you will die.

If you believe you will never give up drinking, then you never will. If you don't believe you are going to be able to stop smoking marijuana or taking cocaine, then you won't shake the habit. I have good news for you, my friend. If you tie the cords of love, forgiveness, faith, strength and hope in Jesus Christ around the horns of the altar – if you say I am not going to let go until God blesses me – then you will come through. You will be able to ride out the storm. When the devil comes to accuse you and tell you that you will never make it, tell him where to go. You do what James 4:7 advises: *Therefore submit to God. Resist the devil and he will flee from you.*

He is a defeated foe: *Then I heard a loud voice saying in heaven, "Now salvation, and strength, and the kingdom of our God, and the power of His Christ have come, for the accuser of our brethren, who accused them before our God day and night, has been cast down"* (Revelation 12:10). He is the father of lies. Believe God and what He says about you. Numbers 23:19 says: *"God is not a man, that He should lie, nor a son of man, that He should repent. Has He said, and will He not do? Or has He spoken, and will He not make it good?"* Obedience is allowing your attitude to determine your altitude.

Prayer

Father God, salvation and strength belong to You. Today, I choose to allow my attitude to determine my altitude. I submit to You, Lord. Thank You for the cords of love, forgiveness, faith, strength and hope that bind me to Your altar. Amen.

As I tie the cords of love, forgiveness, faith and strength around me I will ride out the storm.

Being more than an overcomer

Read 1 John 5:1–13

For whatever is born of God overcomes the world. And this is the victory that has overcome the world – our faith. (1 John 5:4)

If you love Him you will do what He tells you to do. It doesn't matter what the outcome is or what the consequences are. As we close off this month I want to tell you that in order to be an overcomer you need to live a life of obedience. This will lead to you living an abundant life irrespective of what happens to you. An obedient life is a life filled with joy and peace. 1 Timothy 6:6 says: *Now godliness with contentment is great gain.*

If you are walking in obedience you have nothing to fear. Paul understood this when he said in Philippians 1:21: *For to me, to live is Christ, and to die is gain.* This is how we are meant to live. It is what we should be able to say. Can you pray today: "Lord, I am making a decision today to obey the greatest commandment in the Bible and that is to love You. Loving You means that I will obey You; and obeying You means that I have the key to eternal life."

Make a decision today to put whatever is holding you back from obeying God wholeheartedly aside. Ask God to give you the strength to be an overcomer. *"Come to Me, all you who labor and are heavy laden, and I will give you rest. Take My yoke upon you and learn from Me, for I am gentle and lowly in heart, and you will find rest for your souls. For My yoke is easy and My burden is light"* (Matthew 11:28–30). So often we try to bypass the obedience and the overcoming. We want the rewards without the sacrifice. The interesting thing is that you will find that surrendering to Jesus does not mean that you live an arduous life. No, my friend, remember: His yolk is easy and His burden is light. Submit to Him and become more than an overcomer, through Him who died to save you. There is no other way for a child of God to live other than in obedience. Choose obedience – choose life.

Prayer

My Father God, thank You that Your yoke is easy and Your burden is light. Thank You that You love me. I am so grateful that You fill me with Your Holy Spirit who enables me to walk in Your ways. There is nothing that I want more than to be an obedient overcomer. Amen.

Choose obedience – choose life.

MARCH

Now is the time ... to live by faith

Living by faith means ... having faith in God

Living by faith means ... abiding in the Word

Living by faith means ... believing in Jesus

Living by faith means ... fearlessly proclaiming Jesus Christ

Living by faith means ... Jesus is my hope of glory

Living by faith means ... I will overcome the world

Living by faith means ... praising God through my tears

Living by faith means ... abiding in God's grace

Living by faith means ... extending God's grace to others

Living by faith means ... trusting Jesus with what I have

Living by faith means ... giving God His glory

Living by faith means ... walking on water

Living by faith means ... trusting God despite the storm

Living by faith means ... walking by faith and not by sight

Living by faith means ... looking to Jesus

Living by faith means ... accepting my ways are not God's ways

Living by faith means ... experiencing God's love

Living by faith means ... following God into the unknown

Living by faith means ... putting my money where my mouth is

Living by faith means ... not remaining in a sinking boat

Living by faith means ... knowing Jesus

Living by faith means ... hearing the Word of God

Living by faith means ... leaving my comfort zone

Living by faith means ... forsaking everything and everyone

Living by faith means ... walking with the Lord of faith

Living by faith means ... not growing weary

Living by faith means ... being prepared to pay the price

Living by faith means ... doing what Jesus would do

Living by faith means ... fulfilling the Great Commission

Living by faith means ... persevering and enduring

Living by faith means ... enjoying the victory

Having faith in God

Read Mark 11:12–14, 20–24

So Jesus answered and said to them, "Have faith in God." (Mark 11:22)

You might ask me: "How do I grow in faith, Angus?" *So then faith comes by hearing, and hearing by the word of God* (Romans 10:17). When we begin spending time in God's Word, we will grow strong in faith. When our faith increases then the things of this world start fading. If you place your problems alongside the Word of God they will no longer assume gigantic proportions. You will not lie awake at night worrying about them. When viewed in the context of God's Word you will not be overwhelmed, and you will be able to see the challenges you face in proportion. Faith is the antidote to insomnia. It is also the antidote to fear. Not faith in faith, but faith in God and Jesus Christ, His Son.

God's Word is our manual for life. It has instructions for every facet of your life: if you follow God's Word then you will have nothing to worry about. The Bible tells you how to love your wife. It tells you how to treat the people who work for you. The Bible tells you how to treat those who are less fortunate than you are. If you follow God's manual and obey it then you will be filled with ever-increasing faith. You know what they say: "Success breeds success." The more you faithfully obey God's Word the more success you will have in every area of your life. This will breed more faith and you will want to obey God's Word even more. A good cycle will be created in your life. Why would you want to live in failure when you can live in the fullness of all that Jesus accomplished for you on Calvary?

You know, the longer I walk with the Lord the more I enjoy His Word. The Bible is still the best-seller in the world, did you know that? Yes, it always has been and it always will be. The Bible is called the good news because it encourages our faith; bringing freedom and life to all who obey it.

Prayer

Father God, I realize that it is only faith in You that will bring about change in my life. As I trust You more and more I will grow in my faith. Spending time in Your Word will teach me to walk in Your ways. I want to develop a positive cycle in my life. Thank You for Your Word. Amen.

The more you faithfully obey God's Word the more success you will have in every area of your life.

Abiding in the Word

Read John 8:31–36

Then Jesus said to those Jews who believed Him, "If you abide in My word, you are My disciples indeed. And you shall know the truth, and the truth shall make you free." (John 8:31–32)

J esus Christ has overcome the devil and He is seated in heaven at the right hand of the Father. He died on Calvary, rose again and ascended to heaven so that you can have faith in God. He says to you: *"He who believes in Me, as the Scripture has said, out of his heart will flow rivers of living water"* (John 7:38).

In order to believe in Him you need to have the Word inside of you. Jesus further promises us in Mark 11:22–24: *"Have faith in God. For assuredly, I say to you, whoever says to this mountain, 'Be removed and be cast into the sea,' and does not doubt in his heart, but believes that those things he says will be done, he will have whatever he says. Therefore I say to you, whatever things you ask when you pray, believe that you receive them, and you will have them."*

Freedom comes from abiding in God's Word. The more you abide in God's Word the more faith you will have. The more faith you have the more freedom you will enjoy. *Then Jesus said to those Jews who believed Him, "If you abide in My word, you are My disciples indeed. And you shall know the truth, and the truth shall make you free"* (John 8:31–32). When the religious leaders of Jesus' day heard Him talking about this freedom in John chapter eight they didn't understand what He was saying. Their reaction was that they didn't need anything. They were arrogant and proud, caught up in their sin. There are so many people today who are just like those religious leaders. They don't realize their need or their sin. *Jesus answered them, "Most assuredly, I say to you, whoever commits sin is a slave of sin. And a slave does not abide in the house forever, but a son abides forever. Therefore if the Son makes you free, you shall be free indeed"* (John 8:34–36). Don't hesitate come to Jesus today. Believe in Him, abide in His Word and He will set you free.

Prayer

Father God, I come to You today. I bow before You. I acknowledge my need of You. Forgive me, Lord, for the sins that I have committed. Cleanse me and wash me clean. I thank You that I walk in the freedom of Your Son, Jesus Christ. Thank You that I abide in Your Word, daily growing in my faith. Amen.

Don't hesitate but come to Jesus today. Believe in Him, abide in His Word and He will set you free.

Believing in Jesus

Read 1 John 5:1–15

For whatever is born of God overcomes the world. And this is the victory that has overcome the world – our faith. Who is he who overcomes the world, but he who believes that Jesus is the Son of God? (1 John 5:4–5)

Christianity in a nutshell is: believing that Jesus Christ is the Son of God. He is not one of the gods; no, He is God. He is God made flesh. He came down from heaven and He was born in a place called Bethlehem. That is correct. The first people who came to see Him were shepherds who had been out in the fields at night tending their sheep. They came with their flocks of sheep into the little cave where Jesus lay in the manger. It was in this lowly place that the shepherds found the Son of God who had taken on the form of a baby.

There is more evidence in history to prove that Jesus Christ walked on this earth than there is to prove Julius Caesar did. Why is it then that we doubt Him so easily? Some people go out of their way to try and disprove the Bible. I don't know why they don't just believe. The evidence is there wherever you go. We see evidence of Jesus in the elements, in nature and in people's lives. As you know I am a naturalist. My wife and I arise early in the morning. We often run with a flashlight because it is still so dark. As we run we see the glory of God wherever we look. We smell the fresh morning air sent especially for us to breathe in. I don't know how it is rejuvenated every night, but every morning it is fresh and brand new.

As I look up I see birds flying across the sky. On the farm there are eagles, geese and ducks; every one of them is shouting out that Jesus Christ is Lord! I think that you need to be blind not to see God in creation. I don't believe that there is such a thing as an atheist. Even in the Amazon jungle you will meet indigenous people who, although they have never heard the gospel, will tell you that there is a god. They just don't know His name yet.

Prayer

My Father God, I come into Your presence today bowing at Your feet. I proclaim with all of creation that Jesus Christ is Your Son. I lift my hands in praise and adoration to You. You are a great God. Thank You that I know You. Thank You that I can believe in Jesus Christ and have faith in Him. Amen.

Christianity in a nutshell is: believing that Jesus Christ is the Son of God.

Fearlessly proclaiming Jesus Christ

Read Acts 17:22–34

"… for as I was passing through and considering the objects of your worship, I even found an altar with this inscription: TO THE UNKNOWN GOD. Therefore, the One whom you worship without knowing, Him I proclaim to you: 'God, who made the world and everything in it, since He is Lord of heaven and earth, does not dwell in temples made with hands. Nor is He worshiped with men's hands, as though He needed anything, since He gives to all life, breath, and all things.'" (Acts 17:23–25)

Paul fearlessly addressed the Greeks in Athens, introducing them to the "Unknown God" to whom they had erected a statue. All Paul had to do was introduce them to Jesus Christ. This is what evangelism is all about, my friend, simply telling people about Jesus Christ. I have mentioned David Livingstone to you before. He travelled on expeditions into Africa. When he came to a village the first person he would ask to meet was the witch doctor. He wasn't fearful.

You see, David Livingstone had read 1 John 4:4 which says: *You are of God, little children, and have overcome them, because He who is in you is greater than he who is in the world.* If you are a believer and you are a man of faith, you have overcome the world. You don't have to be afraid of wizards, witches, witch doctors or mediums. You don't have to be afraid because they are imposters. We follow the one and only true God and His Son, Jesus Christ. All the power of heaven and earth is at our disposal. David Livingstone used to make an appointment to see the witch doctor. He didn't condemn the witch doctor or criticise him; instead Livingstone approached him with respect. He sat down and talked with him. The witch doctor would show him the roots that they used to cure a stomach condition. He would tell Livingstone about the bark of a particular tree that was used as prevention against the contraction of malaria. So they would sit and talk together. Only then would Livingstone begin to talk to the witch doctor about Jesus.

The witch doctor often responded by saying that he had been searching for Jesus all of his life. He would ask Livingstone to tell him more. The witch doctor would become the priest in his village, the bringer of the good news to his people. We don't need to fear anything in this world. The Lord says in 2 Timothy 1:7: *For God has not given us a spirit of fear, but of power and of love and of a sound mind.*

Prayer

Father, forgive me that so often I am fearful of what people will think if I speak about Jesus Christ. Help me to learn from David Livingstone and his technique when talking to people. Give me a love and an interest in people so that it will be easy for me to engage them. Amen.

You have been given a spirit of power and of love and of a sound mind.

Jesus is my hope of glory

Read Colossians 1

To them God willed to make known what are the riches of the glory of this mystery among the Gentiles: which is Christ in you, the hope of glory. (Colossians 1:27)

J esus is our hope of glory. This means that we can go wherever He tells us to go. We do not go into a place with the intention of condemning people. Rather we go in the name of the Lord Jesus Christ showing His love to the people we meet. Yes, there are certain places that the Lord will tell you not to go because the time is not right. That is fine. You need to be sensitive and obedient to Him. If you are walking by faith then God will speak to you. He will tell you what He wants you to do and where He wants you to go. There are other times the Lord will tell you that you must go somewhere because the people or a person needs help.

We once held a campaign in England. A young man with the most amazing facial tattoos that I have ever seen attended the meetings. In fact you could not see any of his skin because his whole face was tattooed. It was an unbelievable sight. It is easy to be critical of someone like that; we automatically want to pigeonhole them. However, that morning during the meeting he gave his life to Jesus Christ. The tears ran down his face as he spoke to me. He was born again. He still had the tattoos on his face but he had a new heart and a new life.

Who are those that overcome the world? They are those that believe that Jesus Christ is the Son of God. That is what it is all about; in fact that is all that it is about. I want to ask you today: "Are you walking around on eggshells?" You live your life trying not to upset "those" people; you don't go "there" and you are careful to avoid "that" group of people. Watch out! You have the Lord Jesus Christ in you. He is your hope of glory. You need fear nothing and no one. Share Jesus your hope of glory. Go in the presence and the strength of the Lord.

Prayer

Father, I ask that I may be filled with the knowledge of Your will in all wisdom and spiritual understanding; that I may walk worthy of You, Lord, fully pleasing You, being fruitful in every good work and increasing in the knowledge of You; strengthened with all might, according to Your glorious power, for all patience and longsuffering with joy; I give thanks to You, my Father. Amen.

Share Jesus, your hope of glory. Go in the presence and the strength of the Lord.

I will overcome the world

Read 1 John 5:1–13

For whatever is born of God overcomes the world. And this is the victory that has overcome the world – our faith. (1 John 5:4)

I f you are walking by faith then you will overcome the world. You have the victory. You don't have to be afraid of anybody or anything. Walk in love and the power of the Holy Spirit. How do we receive this faith that we are talking about? We receive faith first of all by spending time with God. People often ask me how I manage to make so many of the *Grassroots* programmes. The answer to this question is simple, my friend. I spend time with God. I close myself off in my prayer room, and in my closet I wait on the Lord. I do not write fancy sermons; I wait on God. The Lord tells me what it is that He wants me to tell His people. He gives me the message I am to share. It is such a privilege to be a messenger for the King of kings and the Lord of lords.

It is not faith in faith that will overcome the world, but faith in Jesus Christ. He is the saviour of the world. The older I grow the deeper I fall in love with Him. He's a friend who is closer than a brother. The bigger the waves, the fiercer the storms – the closer He is to me. The more I get to know Him the greater my faith becomes. It is our faith that will enable us to overcome the world. *For whatever is born of God overcomes the world.* **And this is the victory that has overcome the world – our faith** (1 John 5:4).

My friend, it doesn't matter what your problems or your needs are today; they may well be huge. No matter what you are going through you can know that Jesus is with you. He doesn't change. Hebrews 13:8 says: *Jesus Christ is the same yesterday, today, and forever.* Put your faith in Him. Do not put your faith in the government, the economy, your business, your job or in any person. You are only safe if your faith is in Jesus Christ. It is by faith that you will overcome the world.

Prayer

My Father, I come to You in the name of Jesus Christ, my Lord and saviour. Jesus, thank You that You have promised me that You will never leave me nor forsake me. As I walk in faith with You I overcome the world. Amen.

Do not put your faith in anyone or anything; you are only safe if your faith is in Jesus Christ.

Praising God through my tears

Read Psalm 30:1–12

…Weeping may endure for a night, but joy comes in the morning. (Psalm 30:5b)

As you read this beautiful psalm maybe you do so with tears running down your face. Even if you are not in the throes of grief at the moment you can probably relate to the sentiments of the Psalmist as he penned this psalm. How wonderful, though, that it is not only about experiencing sorrow. It is also a psalm that testifies to the goodness and faithfulness of our God.

> Sing praise to the LORD, you saints of His,
> And give thanks at the remembrance of His holy name.
> For His anger is but for a moment,
> His favour is for life;
> Weeping may endure for a night,
> But joy comes in the morning.
>
> Now in my prosperity I said,
> "I shall never be moved."
> LORD, by Your favour You have made my mountain stand strong;
> You hid Your face, and I was troubled.
>
> I cried out to You, O LORD;
> And to the LORD I made supplication:
> "What profit is there in my blood,
> When I go down to the pit?
> Will the dust praise You?
> Will it declare Your truth?
> Hear, O LORD, and have mercy on me;
> LORD, be my helper!"
>
> You have turned for me my mourning into dancing;
> You have put off my sackcloth and clothed me with gladness,
> To the end that my glory may sing praise to You and not be silent.
> O LORD my God, I will give thanks to You forever. (Psalm 30:4–12)

Living by faith means that you can smile through your tears. You know that you can trust your God no matter what comes your way. Take courage today. Turn to Him and not away from Him. He will turn your mourning into dancing.

Prayer

Thank You, Father, that You make my mountain stand strong in the midst of trouble. I trust in You today. I look forward to my glory singing praise to You forever. Amen.

The Lord clothes me with gladness.

Abiding in God's grace

Read Romans 1:13–25

For in it the righteousness of God is revealed from faith to faith; as it is written, "The just shall live by faith." (Romans 1:17)

ohn Newton wrote the beautiful hymn "Amazing grace". He was a man who knew all about grace. So also have many other mighty men of God, such as Martin Luther and John Wesley. They all discovered that *"the just shall live by faith"*. John Wesley and Martin Luther had been searching for God all of their lives. These men were educated theologians. Yet despite all their learning they could not find peace until the day dawned when they realized that "the just (the righteous) will live by faith". All of a sudden they were at peace even though it was the hardest time in their lives.

I can identify with this; the hardest time in my life is now. Despite this, I sleep better now than I ever have. The reason for this is that my faith isn't in my own ability or my circumstances. My faith is in Jesus Christ. Therefore the fiercer the storm or the bigger the test, the greater my faith grows. Romans 10:17 tells us how to grow our faith: *So then faith comes by hearing, and hearing by the word of God.* If you want more faith then spend more time with Jesus Christ; this is how you will receive more faith.

John Newton captained slave ships. I cannot think of anything worse or more terrible than taking poor people as slaves. He literally dealt in human flesh. Then Newton met Jesus Christ as his Lord and saviour. He repented of his sins and by faith he accepted that God had forgiven him. It would take years, but he ceased being a slave trader and became a preacher instead. As Newton lay dying he mumbled, "What a great sinner I am; but what a great saviour Jesus is." Newton understood grace:

Amazing grace! (how sweet the sound)
That sav'd a wretch like me!
I once was lost, but now am found,
Was blind, but now I see.

Have you come to the place in your life where you are experiencing the grace of God? Living by faith means that you abide in His grace.

Prayer

My Loving heavenly Father, I bow in Your presence. I lift my hands, my heart and my voice in praise and gratitude to Your wonderful name. Thank You, thank You for Your amazing grace that saved a wretch like me. What a saviour is Jesus my Lord! Amen.

Have you come to the place in your life where you are experiencing the grace of God?

Extending God's grace to others

Read Matthew 18:21–35

Then his master, after he had called him, said to him, "You wicked servant! I forgave you all that debt because you begged me. Should you not also have had compassion on your fellow servant, just as I had pity on you?' (Matthew 18:32–33)

There are two sides to the grace coin. The one side is us receiving grace from God. The converse side is us extending grace to other people. An acronym for G.R.A.C.E. is *God's riches at Christ's expense*. We can never do anything to deserve or earn God's favour. The only person who deserved God's favour was Jesus Christ. Grace is a wonderful, free and undeserved gift that God bestows upon us. The result of us receiving and living in God's grace should be that we in turn extend grace to other people. Instead of being critical and judgmental we should be kind and compassionate. It doesn't mean that we condone the sin, but rather it means that we love the sinner despite what they have done.

Sometimes we are called upon to extend grace to people who have wronged us. Our story today tells of a servant who owed his master a debt that he couldn't repay. The master graciously forgave him the debt. The man went out and came across a fellow servant who owed him money. When his debtor couldn't pay him, he threw him into prison. When the master heard about this he was furious. The result was that the ungracious servant was also thrown into jail. My friend, God is serious about expecting us to extend grace to others.

We are sinners saved by grace. We cannot hold things against other people. There are times when we will have to extend grace in faith. We have to trust God for the outcome. Grace is not cheap and there are times that it will cost us dearly to extend grace to another person. That is the whole point of grace – it was never meant to be cheap. It cost God everything to extend His grace to you and me. Therefore He understands when you are wrestling with a difficult situation and grace does not come easily to you. This is what living by faith is about. Ask God to help you and then trust Him to make it possible for you to extend grace.

Prayer

My Father God, I bow before You and give You thanks. I praise You for Your great and bountiful grace towards me. Help me, I pray, to be able to extend grace to other people; particularly those who don't deserve it. Help me to remember Your grace towards me even though I don't deserve it. Amen.

Ask God to help you and then trust Him to make it possible for you to extend grace.

Trusting Jesus with what I have

Read Matthew 14:13–23

Then He commanded the multitudes to sit down on the grass. And He took the five loaves and the two fish, and looking up to heaven, He blessed and broke and gave the loaves to the disciples; and the disciples gave to the multitudes. (Matthew 14:19)

How many times have you felt that you have nothing to offer God? You look at your finances, you look at your gifts and you look at your circumstances. You don't see anything that God can use. There are so many people who are caught up in what they don't have. They don't realize that God can take little and make it into much. Many people in our country have been disadvantaged. They have not received a good education. They do not have high-paying jobs. Many people are caught up in their circumstances and never lift their eyes to look beyond themselves.

This is a favourite trick of the enemy. He likes to keep us mired in our circumstances, feeling sorry for ourselves. When this happens our faith is stunted and we are disinclined to step forward and be used by God. Jesus was ministering to the crowds in Matthew chapter fourteen. They had been there listening to Him all day and they were getting hungry. The disciples suggested to Jesus that He send them home so that they could go away and feed themselves. In verse sixteen He told His disciples to give the people food. Their response was: *"We have here only five loaves and two fish"* (Matthew 14:17).

Jesus' response was: *"Bring them here to Me"* (Matthew 14:18). They had to take a step of faith and lift their eyes up from the five loaves and two fish. They had to focus on Jesus. After Jesus had blessed the loaves and fish He gave them back to His disciples. It took a further step of faith to begin handing out the fish and bread. The more they handed out the more there was to hand out. There was an abundance of food – more than enough. There were twelve baskets left over. Why do we struggle to trust God with what we have? He is not limited by what we have because He owns everything. He doesn't ask you to give what you don't have. Trust Him today with all that you have. Allow Him to multiply it for His glory.

Prayer

Father, forgive my unbelief, I pray. Help me to learn from this miracle that You performed. You can take what I have and use it abundantly to fulfil Your will and Your purposes. Help me to lift my eyes from myself and my inadequacies and focus them upon You and Your abundance. Amen.

Trust Him today with what you have. Allow Him to multiply it for His glory.

Giving God His glory

Read Matthew 14:22–33

Immediately Jesus made His disciples get into the boat and go before Him to the other side, while He sent the multitudes away. And when He had sent the multitudes away, He went up on the mountain by Himself to pray. Now when evening came, He was alone there. (Matthew 14:22–23)

f Jesus Christ is your Lord I want to tell you today that nothing can happen to you without His permission. I don't care how big the waves are. I don't care how big the storm is. If you trust Him with your life and you have faith in Him He will see you through. As you read the Scripture reading I hope that you allowed the Word of God to speak to your heart and your spirit. I always say that we should not be interested in the opinions of man; we must only be interested in the opinions of God. It is through His Word that He reveals His will to us, His children.

Jesus told His disciples to get into the boat and go to the other side of the lake while: *He went up on the mountain by Himself to pray* (Matthew 14:23b). He went to spend time with His Father. He was the perfect example to us. Jesus received His power from the time He spent with His Father. It was during these times that the Father told Him what to do. *Then Jesus said to them, "When you lift up the Son of Man, then you will know that I am He, and that I do nothing of Myself; but as My Father taught Me, I speak these things"* (John 8:28).

Jesus had just performed the amazing miracle of feeding the 5,000 (Matthew 14:13–21). Jesus knew that it was after His greatest successes that He needed to return to His Father and spend time with Him. The glory was His Father's. He didn't do anything outside of the will of His Father. This is a lesson that we can learn. How many times does the enemy do his best work with us after our greatest successes? Could this be because we have not returned to our Father to give Him the glory that is due His name? How many men have been destroyed and their ministry discredited because they have tried to take the glory that belongs to God alone? Don't ever take God's glory.

Prayer

My Father, I come to You and praise Your name. I am so aware of the temptation that there often is to take the credit and the glory for myself. I know that this is the enemy tempting me. Help me, I pray, to resist him. I bow before You, realizing that everything I am and everything I have comes from You. Amen.

I must give the Father the glory due to Him.

Walking on water

Read Matthew 14:22–33

So He said, "Come." And when Peter had come down out of the boat, he walked on the water to go to Jesus. (Matthew 14:29)

t is an amazing experience to stand on the shores of Galilee. One is filled with awe as you realize that so many of the experiences related in the Gospels took place on and around the Sea of Galilee. It is a small but very beautiful lake and on a clear day you can easily see over to the other side. It can also become treacherous very quickly, with a storm arising in no time at all. On the night the disciples were sailing over it this is exactly what happened. A terrible storm blew up and the waves crashed around them. The disciples thought they were going to drown.

Then they saw Jesus walking on the water towards them. Now, my dear friend, I want to ask you: Have you ever seen anybody walk on the water? I haven't! Peter, the big, impetuous fisherman; Peter, the doubter who would deny Jesus three times; Peter, the one who claimed that he would die rather than forsake Jesus, said: *"Lord, if it is You, command me to come to You on the water."* Jesus replied: *"Come."* Peter climbed out of the boat and began to walk towards Jesus. He had the faith to step out of the boat. The other eleven stayed put.

So often we want to play it safe. We are not prepared to take that step of faith. We hang back and we are spectators. We watch other people being used by God. We see other people accomplishing great things for God. We become envious and we feel left out. The truth is that God loves all His children equally. He wants to use all of us to do His work here on earth. He is not a respecter of persons. However, He can only use us if we are willing to be used. This requires that we be prepared to step out of the boat. We have to live by faith. Living by faith means that you are prepared to climb out of the boat and walk on water.

Prayer

Father, forgive my lack of faith, I pray. I spend so much time watching from the sidelines. I want to be used by You to do Your work here on earth. Fill me with Your Spirit, I pray. Give me power and strength to do Your will. Amen.

Living by faith means that you are prepared to climb out of the boat and walk on water.

Trusting God despite the storm

Read Matthew 14:22–33

So He said, "Come." And when Peter had come down out of the boat, he walked on the water to go to Jesus. But when he saw that the wind was boisterous, he was afraid; and beginning to sink he cried out, saying, "Lord, save me!" (Matthew 14:29–30)

We mock Peter and say: "Ah, but Peter slipped up." We forget that at least he was willing to climb out of the boat. Maybe there is a storm raging in your life. Like the disciples you are terrified. You need to remember that Jesus is standing in the midst of your storm; you are not alone. Maybe God told you to do something that required a step of faith. You were obedient to the call. It could be that you resigned your job and went into full-time ministry for the Lord. Possibly you began a new business because you believed that was what God was telling you to do. Maybe you recently married because God told you it was the right thing to do. On the other hand for you it might be something else completely.

You obeyed God but now the storm is raging and you are beginning to panic. The disciples obeyed Jesus when He told them to go over to the other side of the Sea of Galilee. In the midst of them obeying Him the storm arose. Jesus didn't abandon them; instead He walked out towards them on the water. Peter immediately responded when he realized it was Jesus. He climbed out of the boat and he began walking on the water towards Jesus. He was fine while he kept his eyes upon Jesus. The moment he looked away he saw the waves and he began to sink. He cried out to Jesus: *"Lord, save me!"*

And immediately Jesus stretched out His hand and caught him, and said to him, "O you of little faith, why did you doubt?" And when they got into the boat, the wind ceased. Don't you love this? Jesus immediately stretched out His hand. The moment Peter cried out Jesus was there. *And when they got into the boat, the wind ceased* (Matthew 14:31–32). Are the waves threatening to engulf you? Don't look to your circumstances because they will overwhelm you. Look to Jesus. Call out to Him and He will answer you.

Prayer

Father, today I choose to look to Jesus. I will not look at what is going on around me. It is only as I keep my eyes fixed upon Jesus that I can keep my focus. Jesus, like the disciples, I proclaim: *"Truly You are the Son of God"* (Matthew 14:33). My faith is in You, Lord. Amen.

Don't look to your circumstances because they will overwhelm you. Look to Jesus.

Walking by faith and not by sight

Read 2 Corinthians 5:6–15

For we walk by faith, not by sight. (2 Corinthians 5:7)

As you have followed these readings has God spoken to you through His Holy Spirit? Maybe you have come to realize that you are not living by faith. You have allowed circumstances, situations and your intellect to get in the way. As a result of this you are walking by sight rather than by faith. If you cannot see it, touch it or rationalize it then you don't believe it. When Peter got out of the boat to walk on the water towards Jesus his sight was actually a hindrance. This is why 2 Corinthians 5:7 says: *For we walk by faith, not by sight.*

Some of us are too clever for our own good. Now I am not being nasty or sarcastic when I say this. It is to our own detriment that we are so clever. Our minds and our intellect take precedence over our faith. We worry: What will happen if this doesn't work out? Where will we be if we cannot sell the produce we have grown? If we are turned down for the loan we have applied for then we are finished... The list of the things we can worry about and the questions we can ask goes on and on. The result is that we are left incapacitated: we become terrified, and we do nothing.

This is where faith comes into the picture. Faith goes to the market with a basket. Why? Because it is expecting to bring lots back. Faith laughs at impossibilities. So we must do what we can and then trust God for the rest. Verse eight of our reading tells us: *We are confident, yes, well pleased rather to be absent from the body and to be present with the Lord.* The result of walking by faith and not by sight is that we are confident. Isn't that wonderful? No matter what happens we know that God is in control. Can you say like Paul: *... we are well known to God* (verse 11b)? If you know God and He knows you then you have nothing to fear no matter what happens.

Prayer

My Father, I come before You in praise and worship. I lift my hands and exalt Your holy name. There is none like You. Thank You that You know me and because You know me I can know You in return. Help me to walk by faith, not by sight, I pray. Amen.

Faith goes to the market with a basket. Why? Because it is expecting to bring lots back.

Looking to Jesus

Read Matthew 14:13–33

And when the disciples saw Him walking on the sea, they were troubled, saying, "It is a ghost!" And they cried out for fear. But immediately Jesus spoke to them, saying, "Be of good cheer! It is I; do not be afraid." (Matthew 14:26–27)

Matthew chapter fourteen continues to teach us faith lessons. The disciples were sitting in the boat looking at Jesus, but they didn't recognize Him. They had spent so much time with Him and yet they mistook Him for a ghost. It was only when Jesus called out to them that they realized it was Him. My friend, you cannot look at the waves crashing around you and at Jesus at the same time. Either you are looking at Jesus or you are looking at the waves.

If you believe you are going to drown, then you will drown. If you stand looking at the waves for long enough then they will roll in and crash over your head. The waves are not your business by the way; you are not meant to concern yourself with them. Your job is to look to Jesus. If God has commanded you through Jesus Christ, His Son: "Come," then you had better go where He is telling you to go. If on the other hand He says: "Stay," then you had better stay and trust God to do the rest. Our problem is that we often spend too much time looking at the situation, then we become incapacitated by doubt and we do nothing. You know what they say: *The road to hell is paved with good intentions.* Tomorrow I am going to do this; and tomorrow I am going to do that. Yet you never do anything because you are not willing to climb out of the boat and operate by faith.

Paul encourages us in Hebrews 12:2: *looking unto Jesus, the author and finisher of our faith, who for the joy that was set before Him endured the cross, despising the shame, and has sat down at the right hand of the throne of God.* Nothing should have diverted Peter's attention from Jesus. He shouldn't have looked down, to the side or even behind him. He should have steadfastly kept his eyes fixed upon Jesus. If you have become distracted and are no longer looking to Jesus, turn your eyes upon Him now.

Prayer

Father God, I so easily become distracted. I look around me and I see all the reasons why I shouldn't do what You are telling me to do. I feel overwhelmed by the evidence. Please forgive me and help me to look only to Jesus who is the Author and Finisher of my faith. I know that I can do anything You ask me to through Jesus Christ Your Son. Amen.

If you have become distracted then turn your eyes back to Jesus now.

Accepting my ways are not God's ways

Read Matthew 14:22–33

But when he saw that the wind was boisterous, he was afraid; and beginning to sink he cried out, saying, "Lord, save me!" And immediately Jesus stretched out His hand and caught him, and said to him, "O you of little faith, why did you doubt?" And when they got into the boat, the wind ceased. (Matthew 14:30–32)

This is what is happening to many people today. We start out looking to Jesus and trusting God. We live and walk by faith. Then the storms hit and the waves roar. The presence of the world distracts us from focusing upon Jesus. We begin to question the logic of what God is doing or telling us to do. God's ways are not our ways. When God fed a crowd of 5,000 with two fish and five barley loaves, it didn't make sense.

I have experienced the same thing on my farm. Many a time I've planted a crop of maize in dry ground. Why? I have done it because God told me to do it. How did He tell me? He told me through His Word. Every time this happened, not a week after I planted the crop by faith, the rain began falling. The crop grew and we ended up with a bumper harvest. There is a saying that goes like this: *"He who hesitates is lost."* OK. You have to make up your mind about what you are going to do. Are you going to climb out of the boat, trusting God as you step onto the water? Keep your eyes on the Lord and keep walking? You'll be surprised how much ground you cover when you look to Jesus and remain focused upon Him. On the other hand, when you look to your circumstances you will begin to slip and you will fail.

As I mentioned before, the Bible says that Jesus immediately stretched out His hand when Peter cried out to Him and He caught Peter. Jesus didn't allow Peter to slip under the water; but Peter had to call out to Him and ask for help. If you are beginning to slip under the water, if the waves are threatening to close in over your head, then don't delay: Call out to Jesus today and He will immediately respond to you. He will not allow you to fall or to fail if you turn to Him. His ways are not your ways – live by faith.

Prayer

My Father God, I am grateful to You that Your ways are not the ways of man. I see things so one-dimensionally. Help me to trust You completely. I want to live and walk by faith, trusting You and not my circumstances. Amen.

If you call out to Jesus He will not allow you to fall or to fail.

Experiencing God's love

Read Romans 8:31–39

For I am persuaded that neither death nor life, nor angels nor principalities nor powers, nor things present nor things to come, nor height nor depth, nor any other created thing, shall be able to separate us from the love of God which is in Christ Jesus our Lord. (Romans 8:38–39)

The Lord is not out to punish us, folks. Please don't think that the Lord walks around with a big stick just waiting to beat us. His desire is to help you weather your storm. *Yet in all these things we are more than conquerors through Him who loved us* (Romans 8:37). He is there to help you realize your dream. He wants to glorify His Father through you. William Carey, the missionary, said: "Do great things for God and expect great things from God." He was a cobbler by trade. As you know he went to India to preach the gospel. He believed that he would be a great evangelist. You will also remember that his wife and his children died in India. Carey never led anybody to Christ. On the surface he appeared to be a failure. He went through his personal storm and he was sinking. It didn't seem as if the Lord cared.

Then he discovered the purpose for his being sent to India. God used him to translate the Bible from English into Bengali, Sanskrit, and many other tongues. Before that he didn't even realize that he had an incredible aptitude for languages. God gave him the ability to translate. Very often you don't realize why God sends you on a particular road until you arrive on the other side. Carey became the chief interpreter in the High Court of Delhi for the British government. He also ran a printing press that was second to none.

God has a purpose for your life. No matter where you find yourself or what is going on in your life at the moment, God loves you. This is the most important thing you need to know. In the midst of your storm He is there. He wants you to experience His love as real and tangible. Remember always *that neither death nor life, nor angels nor principalities nor powers, nor things present nor things to come, nor height nor depth, nor any other created thing, shall be able to separate us from the love of God which is in Christ Jesus our Lord* (Romans 8:38–39).

Prayer

Father God, I thank You today for Your love for me. It is a love that will not let me go no matter what happens. I am so grateful that nothing can separate me from Your love. Thank You that I am more than a conqueror because of Your love. Amen.

No matter where you find yourself or what is going on in your life at the moment, God loves you.

Following God into the unknown

Read 2 Corinthians 5:12–21

…and He died for all, that those who live should live no longer for themselves, but for Him who died for them and rose again. (2 Corinthians 5:15)

We mentioned David Livingstone earlier this month. I never tire of reflecting on the lives of these mighty men of God. Livingstone thought God had sent him to evangelize Africa. However, his main success was not converting people. What he did was set the world on fire. David Livingstone showed the world what God can do through one man who is committed by faith to following Him. The horrific slave trade was abolished because of Livingstone coming to Africa. He wrote letters home telling the British people what was happening on this Dark Continent.

I come from central Africa and David Livingstone's name is revered by black people all over Africa. His nickname was "the good man". All the towns in central Africa have been changed to African names (and that is as it should be). However, there is still a town called Livingstone. There is also a place in Malawi called Blantyre, the name of the little town in Scotland where Livingstone was born. Why do you think this is? It is because Livingstone walked by faith, not by sight. He climbed out of the boat and walked on the water. There was many a time that he felt as if he was sinking but he kept his eyes focused on Jesus Christ and the Lord saw him through. Livingstone died at the age of 60, mission accomplished. He was a few years younger than I am now.

Livingstone died in the middle of Africa all by himself, riddled with malaria and dysentery. The elders told the young boy looking after Livingstone that if he was suffering he was to call them. The boy became concerned because Livingstone had been on his knees praying next to his bed for such a long time. He went and called the old men. Livingstone had died on his knees praying to his saviour, Jesus Christ. Livingstone was a man who would not turn back no matter how bad the storm was.

Prayer

My Father God, in the midst of the storm there You are. I have nothing to fear. I can safely obey Your command to me. I have no interest in pleasing anyone else but You. Keep me faithful, I pray. Amen.

Are you someone who will not turn back no matter how bad the storm is?

Putting my money where my mouth is

Read Hebrews 11:1–10

But without faith it is impossible to please Him, for he who comes to God must believe that He is, and that He is a rewarder of those who diligently seek Him. (Hebrews 11:6)

I am a man of faith but there are times I that I say: "Lord, I don't know how You are going to do this." A few years ago I was due to preach the gospel to 2,500 men from all over the United Kingdom. I was unsure about whether I should go. The Lord had said "Go", but like Peter I was on the water and beginning to sink. The day before I was meant to leave my visa was declined. My son-in-law and I drove through to Pretoria, about 700 km away. We were there when the office opened. The lady said that I would never get a visa in time. I told her that I was meant to preach in England the following night.

To cut a long story short, the visa was issued. I drove all the way back home, said goodbye to my wife, and boarded a plane to Johannesburg for the connecting flight to the UK. Halfway to Johannesburg the pilot announced that there was a problem with the engine and he turned back. When we disembarked in Durban we were told they would put us on another plane. I told them that I had a connecting flight leaving for England. I asked the Lord: "What is happening here? I am sinking! Help me!" The Bible says that Jesus immediately reached out His hand to Peter. The plane was fixed within 15 minutes and we were on our way again. We landed at Oliver Tambo International Airport and I ran to catch my flight.

As I approached the boarding gate I realized that something was going to happen in Great Britain. It was one of the most amazing campaigns that I have ever had. I had the privilege of marrying twelve couples in one day. We saw people repenting and giving their lives to Jesus. I saw men standing up for the Lord. Why? Because the Lord said: "Get out of the boat." My friends, we have to put our money where our mouth is when it comes to walking by faith.

Prayer

My Father, You know the end from the beginning of everything. There is nothing that You cannot accomplish. Nothing is impossible with You. I can do anything You ask me to through Jesus Christ who strengthens me. Amen.

I have to put my money where my mouth is when it comes to walking by faith.

Not remaining in a sinking boat

Read Hebrews 13:1–17

"I will never leave you nor forsake you." So we may boldly say: "The LORD is my helper; I will not fear. What can man do to me?" (Hebrews 13:5c–6)

T he boat is sinking, my friend. The boat is riddled with wood rot. It is no longer safe to cling to the boat. The time has come to step out of the boat and begin to walk on the water. The people who are blithely sitting in the boat are going to get a nasty shock. God is calling His children to live a life of faith. He has the most amazing things that He wants to do through us, but He cannot do them while we are sitting in the boat. The boat is a false safety net. I say it often but it is true: The safest place for a child of God is in the centre of His will. Therefore the safest place is on the water. We need to walk the faith walk, my friend. God calls every one of His children to walk by faith, not just a select few. We do not have the option of being spectators on the sidelines – we have to participate in the faith walk.

It is not about how much money you have in the bank. Some of the richest men in the world crumbled when we experienced the financial crunch a few years ago. The largest banks in the world imploded. It is not about how healthy you are. How long does our health last? I also thought I had health until I experienced a heart attack.

One minute I was preaching my heart out and the next I was lying on the grass. Jesus healed me. I didn't get better; Jesus healed me and He gave me a new heart. You cannot rely on your health, your money or your reputation. The only person you can rely upon is the Prince of Peace. He is the One who says: *"I will never leave you nor forsake you."* So, I want to encourage you to climb out of the boat and walk on the water; don't look at the waves. God will see you through and you will fulfil your calling.

Prayer

Father, I step out of the boat now. I look to You as I walk forward. Thank You that You are ever before me. I am safe in Your will and Your purposes for my life. Thank You that You hold me in the palm of Your hand. Amen.

I want to encourage you to climb out of the boat and walk on the water; don't look at the waves.

Knowing Jesus

Read Hebrews 11:1–12

But without faith it is impossible to please Him, for he who comes to God must believe that He is, and that He is a rewarder of those who diligently seek Him. (Hebrews 11:6)

M any people whom I meet say to me, "Angus, I want more faith. I want to be able to run the race, finish the job and walk in the light that is so precarious at the moment. I want to walk a straight line; there seem to be so many ups and downs." Oswald Chambers, the author of *My Utmost for His Highest,* whose devotional I just love, stated: "The root of faith is the knowledge of a person." You don't receive faith by snapping your fingers or by waving a magic wand. You don't receive faith by listening to faith messages. You receive faith by knowing a person. Of course that person is Jesus Christ, the son of the living God.

Abraham was such a man. Abraham believed God and it was accounted to him as righteousness and he was called a friend of God. (We read this in James 2:23, Genesis 15:6 and Romans 4:3.) The reason it is mentioned so often is because you cannot please God without faith. *But without faith it is impossible to please Him, for he who comes to God must believe that He is, and that He is a rewarder of those who diligently seek Him.*

Look at verse eight of Hebrews chapter eleven: *By faith Abraham obeyed when he was called to go out to the place which he would receive as an inheritance. And he went out, not knowing where he was going.* Abraham didn't know where he was going but he knew Who was leading him.

Can you imagine somebody saying to you, "I want you to pack your bags and go?" And you say, "Where?" The second most traumatic thing a person experiences, after losing a loved one, is moving home. You can imagine how much faith it takes to move to an unknown destination. God told Abraham to go and he obeyed. This is why he was a "friend of God". It was not because he was a good man, but because he was an obedient man. He was a man who knew his God.

Prayer

My Father, I want to be known as Your friend. I want to be a man of faith. I realize that this will only happen as I get to know You better. I cannot live a life of faith if I do not know You. Amen.

Abraham was a "friend of God" – not because he was a good man, but because he was an obedient man.

Hearing the Word of God

Read Romans 10:1–21

So then faith comes by hearing, and hearing by the word of God. (Romans 10:17)

We know that ... *faith comes by hearing, and hearing by the word of God.* I am sure you can quote this Scripture in your sleep. However, do you really hear what God is saying to you when you read His Word? The Word of God is Jesus in print. So the more you get to know Jesus, the more faith you will have. Why? Because the root of faith is in the knowledge of a person. Romans 10:13 says: For *"whoever calls on the name of the Lord shall be saved."* The more time you spend with someone the more you get to know them. So if you never read the Bible and get to know Jesus through His Word you will never grow in faith.

The kind of hearing we are talking about is not a superficial hearing. It is a hearing with intent. It is a hearing based in experience. It is hearing that engenders a response from the hearer. Countless times through the Gospels Jesus says: *"He who has ears to hear, let him hear!"* There is a sobering verse in Romans 11:8. God persevered with His people for generation upon generation until eventually ...*"God has given them a spirit of stupor, eyes that they should not see and ears that they should not hear, to this very day."* The challenge to us today is to open our spiritual ears and hear what God is saying to us.

People often request prayer so that they can receive more faith. This is the wrong prayer to pray. We must pray that God will give us a hunger to read the Word. When you read the Word, then you will grow in faith. The better you get to know Jesus the more faith you will have. Romans 10:8–9 says: ... *"The word is near you, in your mouth and in your heart"* (*that is, the word of faith which we preach*): that if you confess with your mouth the Lord Jesus and believe in your heart that God has raised Him from the dead, you will be saved.

Prayer

Father God, I thank You for the wonderful privilege of having Your Word freely available to me. Forgive me that I spend so little time in Your Word. I realize that the root of faith is the knowledge of a person, Jesus Christ. Amen.

We must pray that God will give us a hunger to read the Word.

Leaving my comfort zone

Read Genesis 12:1–9

Now the LORD had said to Abram: "Get out of your country, from your family and from your father's house, to a land that I will show you. I will make you a great nation; I will bless you and make your name great; and you shall be a blessing." (Genesis 12:1–2)

Having a relationship with God and walking by faith will sometimes bring about separation from country and kin. This happened to Abraham. God told him to leave Haran and set out on a journey to a land that God would show him. Abraham obeyed because he knew God. If God said to you: "I want you to stop what you are doing and go to the Congo. I want you to start a mission settlement there." "I want you to resign your job and I want you to go to Bible College." "I want you to take time out and go into the desert and spend some time there." What would your answer be?

Oswald Chambers comments that nowadays it is not so much the physical separation, but rather the mental and spiritual separation that is so much harder for us. I had personal experience of this separation with my mother. She lived in Greytown about 15km away from us. It was just after Jill and I made a commitment to Jesus. We popped in to have a cup of tea with my Mom. I was sitting by the fire and my mother started crying. The tears ran down her face. I asked, "Mom, what is wrong?" In her broad Scottish accent she said, "Laddie, it is never the same any more." "What is not the same any more, Mom?" I thought there was something wrong with her. "Our relationship isn't the same." Then I realized what had happened. I had come to meet Jesus Christ as my saviour and my Mom wasn't a Christian.

There was a supernatural separation. I had joy and peace in my heart and she didn't. Straight away there was a buffer. I said to her, "Mom, I know what it is. We have met Jesus." She said "Aye, Laddie." I asked, "Wouldn't you like to meet Him as well?" She said she would and right there I led my mother to Christ. From that moment onwards our relationship was deeper and richer than it had ever been. There had been a separation that took place for just a moment, because we were with Christ and she was in the world.

Prayer

My Father, I realize that there are times that following You will take me out of my comfort zone. It can cause me to feel separation between myself and my loved ones. Help me to be faithful to You and gentle and compassionate to others at the same time. Amen.

Walking by faith will sometimes bring about separation from country and kin.

Forsaking everything and everyone

Read Luke 14:25–33

"And whoever does not bear his cross and come after Me cannot be My disciple. So likewise, whoever of you does not forsake all that he has cannot be My disciple." (Luke 14:27, 33)

Before I became a Christian I had many friends. However, after I became a Christian many of my friends deserted me. I didn't leave them. I will never forget: the day I gave my life to Christ I told my counsellors, "I don't want to lose any of my friends." They were old Christians and they just smiled and replied, "Don't worry, Angus, you won't have to leave them." I didn't; they actually left me.

When people came to my house I always made sure they had lots to drink and eat. I had an impressive liquor cabinet. Three months after coming to know the Lord I was convinced that alcohol was doing me and my family no good. I poured the contents of my liquor cabinet down the toilet and pulled the chain. Shortly after this we had a family over to dinner. I offered the man a drink – he had a choice of cola, fruit juice or lemonade. He looked at me as if I was insulting him. He had a cola but it was the last time that he ever came to my house. Prior to that evening I had regarded him as one of my closest friends. Natural separation happens and we have to be prepared to forsake everyone and everything. When you come to Jesus some people will love you and some people will hate you for the sake of the gospel.

Now Abraham went to an unknown destination. His was a physical separation because God told him to leave his home and go. Physical separation is hard enough, but I want to tell you that mental and spiritual separation can be even harder sometimes. I have seen young people commit to Christ. They have excitedly gone home to tell their parents and met with rebuke and ridicule. I have also seen a man make a commitment that his wife or girlfriend just doesn't understand. *"If anyone comes to Me and does not hate his father and mother, wife and children, brothers and sisters, yes, and his own life also, he cannot be My disciple"* (Luke 14:26).

Prayer

Father, this is a hard one. It is not easy when I am misunderstood and reviled for my faith. Yet I know, Jesus, that You were prepared to endure all this and so much more on Calvary so that I can be saved. I choose separation from earthly ties if that is what it takes to follow You. Amen.

Natural separation happens and we have to be prepared to forsake everyone and everything.

Walking with the Lord of faith

Read John 14:1–14

"Do you not believe that I am in the Father, and the Father in Me? The words that I speak to you I do not speak on My own authority; but the Father who dwells in Me does the works." (John 14:10)

D id you identify with the stories of the past few days? Maybe you are not very popular in your own home because of your relationship with the Lord. I am not suggesting that you must Bible-bash people. Don't do that. Don't leave Christian books on the coffee table with the hope that your loved one will read them – they won't. You must love them and pray for them. The time will come when they will come to you and say, "I want to have what you have." You can trust God with your loved ones. He loves them more than you can ever love them. The better you get to know Him the more you will understand this.

The root of faith is the knowledge of a person – Jesus Christ. They crucified Jesus for no other reason than that He proclaimed that He was God. Not because He was a thief and He stole money like the two thieves who were crucified on either side of Him. He was crucified for His faith. He said: *"I am One who bears witness of Myself, and the Father who sent Me bears witness of Me"* (John 8:18). *"He who has seen Me has seen the Father; so how can you say, 'Show us the Father?'"* (John 14:9b). When you go around telling people that Jesus is God they will hate you for the same reason that they hated God. That is the bottom line.

Don't worry, though, because Jesus says there is good news and it is this: *Consider it a sheer gift, friends, when tests and challenges come at you from all sides. You know that under pressure, your faith-life is forced into the open and shows its true colours. So don't try to get out of anything prematurely. Let it do its work so you become mature and well-developed, not deficient in any way* (James 1:2–4 *The Message*). So make sure that whatever you do is for His name's sake and not because you are being controversial or rebellious. Live by faith and the Lord of faith will walk with you.

Prayer

Father, I bow before You. I come in the name of Jesus Christ, Your one and only Son. Thank You, Jesus, that You bear witness to the Father. I want to walk the walk of faith with You, living every day to please You. Amen.

Live by faith, letting it do its work in your life.

Not growing weary

Read Isaiah 40:21–31

But those who wait on the LORD shall renew their strength; they shall mount up with wings like eagles, they shall run and not be weary, they shall walk and not faint. (Isaiah 40:31)

O swald Chambers says faith is not only about mounting up with wings like eagles. It is also about walking and not fainting. Faith has to have feet. Faith is a "doing" word. It is an action word. Faith is not about dramatic events or emotions. Faith is saying, "Lord, I love You and I am going to persevere. I will push through the rough and I trudge through the desert. I will not give up even though times are hard because I believe in You and what You have in store for me." If this is your attitude then the day will come when you will walk straight out of the desert and into a land of milk and honey, just like the Israelites did.

Faith is not a feeling; it is a fact. Consider 2 Corinthians 5:7: *For we walk by faith, not by sight.* There is a lot of bad teaching that finds its way into the church on this issue. Unfortunately there are people who say, "Come to Jesus and all of your problems will be over." Nowhere in the Bible does it say this. Come to Jesus unconditionally and Jesus will walk with you through the fire. This is why so many people become disillusioned; they believe a lie. They say, "I asked God and He didn't give me what I asked for." What did you ask God for?

Jesus said in 1 John 5:14–15: *Now this is the confidence that we have in Him, that if we ask anything according to His will, He hears us. And if we know that He hears us, whatever we ask, we know that we have the petitions that we have asked of Him.* This is the secret. We must ask according to God's will – not according to our wants. No matter what we are going through God will give us the strength to endure. *For He Himself has said, "I will never leave you nor forsake you"* (Hebrews 13:5b). This is His promise to us; this is why we mustn't grow weary. We must keep *… looking unto Jesus, the author and finisher of our faith* (Hebrews 12:2a).

Prayer

My Father, there are times that I grow so weary. I know that the place to find strength to carry on is at the foot of the Cross. It is there that I need to lay down my will. It is there that I need to find Your will for the situation I find myself in. Then I know that I can run and not grow weary. Amen.

Faith has to have feet.

Being prepared to pay the price

Read Job 1:13–22; 13:15

Though He slay me, yet will I trust Him. Even so, I will defend my own ways before Him.
(Job 13:15)

There can be no conditions attached to serving God. The moment you put the little word "if" in front of your response to something God tells you to do, you are in trouble. When you come to Jesus Christ you enter into a covenant with God. There is no place for the word "if" in this covenant. You cannot stand at the altar on your wedding day and say to your wife, "I promise that I will love you and I will take care of you if: you make my supper every night, wash my clothes, and look after the house." It is meant to be unconditional surrender. It is the same with our relationship with Jesus.

Job is our example in this matter. He lost everything and still he cried: *Though He slay me, yet will I trust Him* (Job 13:15a). This is the price that you have to pay for walking by faith. It is the price of heeding God's call to go to an unknown destination. It comes through your association with Jesus. When you become a Christian, my friend, there are certain things you must leave behind. You cannot go back to the same places you used to go to. You cannot frequent those places of sin because Jesus wouldn't go there. When you are not sure simply ask yourself this question: WWJD – What would Jesus do?

In other words, can the Lord sit down next to me when I drink, listen to ugly stories and watch blue movies and pornography? If I would be embarrassed then I have my answer: I mustn't go there or do that. Too many Christians spend their lives with one foot in the world and the other in the kingdom of God. It is not possible to live like this. This is not what living by faith means. Job's commitment was an all-out commitment. Even though he lost everything, he did not turn his back on God. His faith saw him through and in the end God rewarded him for his faith. Are you prepared to pay the price?

Prayer

Father, in the midst of my trials I hear You speaking to me. I know that my commitment needs to be a wholehearted commitment to You – no matter what happens. Help me to always ask the question: What would Jesus do? I can never go wrong if I do this. Amen.

Are you prepared to pay the price for your faith?

Doing what Jesus would do

Read Romans 6:12–23

Do you not know that to whom you present yourselves slaves to obey, you are that one's slaves whom you obey, whether of sin leading to death, or of obedience leading to righteousness? (Romans 6:16)

n the book *In His Steps* by Charles M. Sheldon the following story is told. A preacher was preaching to a rich congregation when an unkempt man staggered into the church. He collapsed and nobody knew what to do with him. They were in shock and they didn't know whether to pick him up or not. They were right out of their depth; out of their comfort zones. The pastor announced that those people who were serious about God should meet with him in the side room after the service. Only a handful of people attended the meeting. The pastor announced: "We are going to make an agreement with God. We are going to ask ourselves a question every time we have to make a decision. '*What would Jesus do?*'" It transformed their lives completely.

One of the people from the church was a newspaper tycoon. He owned a huge newspaper in America. The Sunday paper was their top grossing edition of the week. The tycoon asked himself the question: Would Jesus be in agreement with me putting a newspaper out on a Sunday? And he felt the answer was no. So he told his editor no more Sunday papers. The editor said, "We are going to go bankrupt." He stuck to his guns. Later the editor came in and said, "We have the scoop on a big story: The World Championship Boxing contest." In those days they boxed with bare knuckles, pummelling each other to a mess. There was no referee calling it quits. It was a gruesome and ugly thing. The fighters were affected for the rest of their lives.

The tycoon declined the story. Again the editor told him he would go bankrupt. Still he refused. He did nearly go bankrupt but then God restored his newspaper and it went right to the top. We have said before that living by faith is a very practical thing. It requires us climbing out of the boat. The question is: *What would Jesus do?* When you receive the answer be obedient and do it.

Prayer

Father, You have called me to live in obedience to You. Obeying You requires active faith. When You tell me to do something it means that I have to decide whether I will obey You or my own desires. I want to obey because obedience leads to righteousness. Amen.

What would Jesus do? When you receive the answer be obedient and do it.

Fulfilling the Great Commission

Read Mark 16:1–20

And He said to them, "Go into all the world and preach the gospel to every creature."
(Mark 16:15)

Another story from *In His Steps*: An opera singer was due to go to Europe to sing in some of the famous opera houses. She was riding in her carriage through the red-light area. From her carriage she noticed all the prostitutes as they gathered under the streetlights. The young opera singer got out and began singing to the prostitutes. Her friends who saw her standing on the street corner singing as they drove past couldn't believe what they saw. They believed that the beautiful young girl was wasting her talent on the prostitutes. But God used her to change them and turn their lives around.

The root of faith is found in the knowledge of a person. When you meet the person your life is going to be turned the right way up. God told Abraham to leave his homeland and go to another destination. It changed Abraham's life. God told Moses to take His people out of the land of Egypt and journey to Canaan, the land of milk and honey. In order to arrive at their destinations they had to travel through a desert place. Do you have clarity about what God is calling you to do? He has a purpose for each of us. We all have a part to play in fulfilling the Great Commission. If you don't yet know what part you are to play then it is time to come before Him and "listen with ears that hear" to what He is telling you to do.

Once you hear from God you have to step out of the boat. You have to be prepared to move out of your comfort zone and step forward in faith. Jesus died and rose from the dead. He appeared to His disciples and gave them the Great Commission. You and I are His modern-day disciples and we are entrusted with the good news of the gospel. Can you imagine what a difference it would make in this world if each day every Christian asked what Jesus would do – and then did it?

Prayer

My Father God, You sent Your Son. He died for my sins. He rose from the dead and He has made me a part of taking Your good news out to my world. Help me to listen carefully as You talk to me. Help me to ask the right questions and when I receive the answers, to obey. Amen.

Are you playing your part in fulfilling the Great Commission?

Persevering and enduring

Read Revelation 3:7–13

Because you have kept My command to persevere, I also will keep you from the hour of trial which shall come upon the whole world, to test those who dwell on the earth.
(Revelation 3:10)

Jesus continued, saying: *Behold, I am coming quickly! Hold fast what you have, that no one may take your crown. He who overcomes, I will make him a pillar in the temple of My God, and he shall go out no more* (Revelation 3:11–12a). Perseverance and faith are interchangeable; you cannot have one without the other. Oswald Chambers says in *My Utmost for His Highest* that *"perseverance is more than endurance"*. The Lord is telling us to hold fast because we are coming to the climax of the ages. My dear friend, don't lose your faith. What is faith? *Now faith is the substance of things hoped for, the evidence of things not seen* (Hebrews 11:1).

Don't lose your faith. If you lose your faith you have lost everything. The devil is speeding things up to such a degree that it is easy to start losing heart. When you begin to feel fearful the devil steps in. Depression, stress and anxiety creep up and the next thing is the contemplation of suicide and so on. That is from the pit of hell, I tell you. The Lord commands you to hold fast to your faith, He is coming quickly. Hold fast. Faith requires patience; you see, faith is not a speedy thing. Faith takes time. Abraham knew about faith. He waited a hundred years before the Lord fulfilled His promise to him.

I have yet to meet a man of faith who does not have patience. If you are one of those men who demand everything to happen now, then you probably have a way to grow in your faith. That is the world's way. Waiting upon the Lord takes time. The devil doesn't want you to take time out, to pray and to wait on the Lord. When you have big decisions to make don't allow yourself to be pressured or rushed. Take your time to hear from the Lord. Spend time in prayer and in His Word. He will come through and tell you what He wants you to do. When He speaks then be quick to obey.

Prayer

My Father God, You are so faithful to me. You are always there, You never leave me and You never forsake me. Help me to be faithful in return. I want to grow in my faith and I realize that the only way to do this is to patiently walk with You. Amen.

Take your time to hear from the Lord. Spend time in prayer and in His Word.

Enjoying the victory

Read 1 Corinthians 15:50–58

But thanks be to God, who gives us the victory through our Lord Jesus Christ.
(1 Corinthians 15:57)

We have spent this month talking together about what it means to "live by faith". My friend, now is the time – like never before – when the world needs to see men and women of faith. Time is running out. We have to stop play acting and get serious about God and our Christian walk. One of Jesus' shortest commands to us is: *"Have faith in God"* (Mark 11:22b). We find it so difficult to hand over the reins of our lives to God. We want to control everything. You cannot be in control and live by faith – it is not possible. Paul tells us in Romans 10:17: *So then faith comes by hearing, and hearing by the word of God.* If you want to grow in faith you must spend time with God in His Word.

Then Jesus said to those Jews who believed Him, *"If you abide in My word, you are My disciples indeed. And you shall know the truth, and the truth shall make you free"* (John 8:31–32). As we grow in faith we must abide in Jesus; the more we abide in Him the freer we will be. We need fear nothing and no one because: *For whatever is born of God overcomes the world. And this is the victory that has overcome the world – our faith. Who is he who overcomes the world, but he who believes that Jesus is the Son of God?* (1 John 5:4–5). Do not put your faith in anything or anyone other than Jesus. Hebrews 13:8 tells us: *Jesus Christ is the same yesterday, today, and forever.*

We lift our eyes from our circumstances and focus them upon Jesus. We step out of the boat, out of our comfort zones, and trust Him. When the storms and the waves threaten to drown us we know that Jesus is in control. We will have the victory no matter what comes our way. We will lift our hearts, our hands and our voices and declare: *But thanks be to God, who gives us the victory through our Lord Jesus Christ.*

Prayer

My Father God, I praise and worship You today. I lift my voice in adoration to You and to Jesus Christ, Your Son. Jesus, You are my wonderful Lord. You are the saviour of my soul. I choose today to walk in faith, trusting You no matter what happens in my life. Amen.

I am victorious through Jesus Christ, my Saviour.

APRIL

Now is the time to walk in humility

Humble yourself before the Lord

Read James 4:1–10

Humble yourselves in the sight of the Lord, and He will lift you up. (James 4:10)

Pride is as old as time itself. It was pride that caused Satan to be thrown out of heaven. One of the reasons that Eve ate of the fruit from the tree of the knowledge of good and evil was pride. Down through history we can list the names of people whose lives have been devastated by pride. This month we are going to look at the issue of pride. Together we will learn what it means for a child of God to walk in humility. We will examine the lives of some of the mighty men of God from the past, and how they dealt with pride in their lives. Now is the time for Christians to walk and live in humility.

Everywhere we look pride is the order of the day. Sadly even in the church pride seems to be rampant. There is often very little difference between the world and the church when it comes to pride. In James 4:10, the Lord Jesus says: *Humble yourselves in the sight of the Lord, and He will lift you up.* Humility is one of the most difficult virtues to achieve. The more God uses you, the humbler you need to be. It is not a natural thing for man to humble himself. It is hard for us because the natural inclination of our sinful natures is pride. Our "old self" does not want to die and we have to be constantly vigilant to bow in surrender to the Lord. Dying to self is not a one-off event; it has to happen every day of our lives.

The last thing to fade before you physically die and go to heaven is pride. In 1 Peter 5:5 God says, *Yes, all of you be submissive to one another, and be clothed with humility, for "God resists the proud, but gives grace to the humble."* Now as never before Christians must set an example of humility. So many of the problems we face in our country are caused by the pride of man. How are you doing in the pride department?

Prayer

My Father God, at the beginning of a new month I come before You and bow my knee in worship. Lord, I acknowledge that I so often stumble in the area of pride. Walking in humility is not a natural state for me. I pray that You will work in my heart and life through Your Holy Spirit to help me to walk humbly before You. Amen.

Now as never before Christians must set an example of humility.

The problem is "I"

Read Romans 7:7–25

For I know that in me (that is, in my flesh) nothing good dwells; for to will is present with me, but how to perform what is good I do not find. For the good that I will to do, I do not do; but the evil I will not to do, that I practice. Now if I do what I will not to do, it is no longer I who do it, but sin that dwells in me. (Romans 7:18–20)

P ride stubbornly keeps raising its ugly head. Paul understood this battle all too well. In our reading today he shares very candidly his fight with his flesh. In frustration he cries out: *For the good that I will to do, I do not do; but the evil I will not to do, that I practice.* Make no mistake, my dear friend, it is very hard. It is something that we need to work on daily. We need to persevere; we must not give up. Paul encourages us in Philippians 2:12: *Therefore, my beloved, as you have always obeyed, not as in my presence only, but now much more in my absence, work out your own salvation with fear and trembling.*

You cannot say "abracadabra" to pride and think that it will conveniently go away. Praying and believing alone will not make pride disappear in a puff of smoke. Pride is bred into the very fibre of our being. David says in Psalm 51:5: *Behold, I was brought forth in iniquity, and in sin my mother conceived me.*

The sin of pride resulted in Lucifer being cast out of heaven. He thought that he was equal to God. Isaiah 14:12–14 tells us: *"How you are fallen from heaven, O Lucifer, son of the morning! How you are cut down to the ground, you who weakened the nations! For you have said in your heart: 'I will ascend into heaven, I will exalt my throne above the stars of God; I will also sit on the mount of the congregation on the farthest sides of the north; I will ascend above the heights of the clouds, I will be like the Most High.'"* One third of the angels went with him (Revelation 12:9). Take a look again at Isaiah 14:12–14 and count the number of times the word "I" is used; in total five times in three verses. This is the root of all iniquity: The middle letter of the word pride is "I"; and the middle letter of the word sin is also "I".

Prayer

My Father, like the apostle Paul I bow before You today and cry – *O wretched man that I am! Who will deliver me from this body of death? I thank God – through Jesus Christ our Lord!* (Romans 7:24–25a). Jesus, You are the One who saves my soul. Help me to put pride to death today, I pray. Amen.

The middle letter of the word pride is "I"; and the middle letter of the word sin is also "I".

Doing it God's way

Read James 4:1–10

Therefore submit to God. Resist the devil and he will flee from you. Draw near to God and He will draw near to you. (James 4:7–8a)

T he same pride that caused Satan's downfall is still at work in the lives of humans today. Frank Sinatra, Old Blue Eyes – we all love his music – sang: *I did it my way*, but it didn't do him much, good did it? Doing it our way won't do you and me any good either. There is only one way to do it and that is God's way.

The Lord says, *Humble yourselves in the sight of the Lord, and He will lift you up* (James 4:10). God can only start to move in your life once you humble yourself. How are you doing right now? You might say, "Angus, I am so down at the moment, I cannot sink much lower." Maybe you should just sink down onto your knees after all: it is the safest place for you to be. That's right: when you are riding high and you are up on a pedestal it is easy for you to be knocked off. As the saying goes, "the higher you fly, the greater your fall". When you are on your knees you cannot fall any further.

I remember many years ago Christians in the West sent letters to the believers behind the Iron Curtain in Russia who were in prison for their faith. People wrote saying that they were praying for them to remain faithful to the Lord. The Russian Christians were in concrete boxes in solitary confinement. The Russian believers wrote back telling the Westerners not to pray for them, but rather to pray for themselves. They explained that where they were they couldn't fall into temptation because they had nothing but God. However, in the West it is so easy to fall and the easiest way to fall is as a result of pride. The well-known proverb says: Pride comes before a fall. The Bible puts it like this in Proverbs 16:18: *Pride goes before destruction, and a haughty spirit before a fall. The Message* Bible says: *First pride, then the crash – the bigger the ego, the harder the fall.* We need to keep ourselves humble.

Prayer

My Father, I come before You and bow at Your feet. I realize that it is on my knees that I am most likely to be humble. Through trial and error I realize that doing it my way does not work. I surrender to You, my Lord. I submit to You. Help me to do it Your way. Amen.

The bigger someone's ego, the harder they will fall.

The hallmark of a man of God

Read Proverbs 11:1–12

When pride comes, then comes shame; but with the humble is wisdom. (Proverbs 11:2)

When asked what the three greatest virtues of mighty men of God are, Martin Luther answered: "First, humility; second, humility; and third, humility." One of my heroes (I have told you about him many times; and I will talk about him again in the future), is Pastor William Duma. He was a Baptist preacher and he has long ago gone to be with the Lord. He grew up in the Hills of Umkomaas down on the South Coast of KwaZulu-Natal. He was a short man who wore glasses: definitely not a Rambo-like character, but very definitely a mighty man of God. The Lord used Pastor Duma to win countless souls for Himself.

God particularly used him in a healing ministry. People sent their handkerchiefs and scarves to him from America, Canada and all over the world. He laid his hands on the items and prayed the prayer of faith. He then posted the handkerchief or scarf back. The item was placed under the sick person's pillow and that person was healed. This is also in the Bible by the way. In Acts 19:12 we read that Paul did it: *...so that even handkerchiefs or aprons were brought from his body to the sick, and the diseases left them and the evil spirits went out of them.*

I remember one time William Duma was invited to preach at a very posh church. It was tradition in this church for the preacher to enter through the grand doors at the back of the church. He would then walk down the aisle to the front of the church where the altar was. The service started at nine o'clock and there was no sign of Pastor Duma. After ten minutes the minister went to look for him. He found Pastor Duma around the back of the church at the door the cleaning lady used to enter the church. When the minister enquired why he had come in the back way he answered, "Because I am a servant of the Lord." Humility is the hallmark of a man of God.

Prayer

My Father God, I thank You for the example of men such as Pastor Duma. Lord, I pray that You will help me to be known as a man who is characterized by humility. Fill me with the power of Your Holy Spirit in order for me to serve You better. Amen.

Humility is the hallmark of a man of God.

Show humility to all men

Read Titus 3:1–8

...to speak evil of no one, to be peaceable, gentle, showing all humility to all men. (Titus 3:2)

William Carey is another one of my heroes. As you know he was an Englishman who went to India to preach the gospel. He had many hardships there and as you will remember he didn't actually lead anyone to Christ. He was a humble man whom God used as an interpreter and to start a printing press. Carey was willing to lay aside his own ambitions and be used by God in the way that God wanted to use him. In humility he submitted to God's will and purposes for his life.

Carey came from humble beginnings. He was a cobbler by trade. Once, a man, trying to mock Carey, asked him, "Mr Carey, I believe you are a shoemaker by trade?" Carey replied, "No, sir, I am not a shoemaker. I cannot make shoes – I only repair them. I am a cobbler." I imagine that the man must have felt humbled after trying to make a fool of the man of God.

How would you have replied if you had been Carey? Would you be able to take the advice we find in Titus 3:2 ... *to speak evil of no one, to be peaceable, gentle, showing all humility to all men.* When someone pokes at you what do they find? A man filled with pride who will retaliate or a humble man who knows how to keep his own counsel? Believe me when I tell you that I am talking to myself as much as to you regarding this subject of humility. You know that if you kick a dead dog, it doesn't move. However, if you kick a sleeping dog, it will turn around and bite you. If we are dead to the "old self" then people will not be able to get a rise out of us; but if the "pride man" is still alive we will come back with a sarcastic reply. God commands us to show *all humility to all men.*

Prayer

My Father, it is all too easy for me to retaliate when I am prodded by someone. Thank You that You have saved me, through the washing of regeneration and the renewing of the Holy Spirit, whom You poured out on me abundantly through Jesus Christ, my saviour. Amen.

A humble man knows how to keep his own counsel. Show all humility to all men.

Pride versus wisdom

Read Proverbs 14:1–14

In the mouth of a fool is a rod of pride, but the lips of the wise will preserve them.
(Proverbs 14:3)

The saying "sticks and stones will break my bones, but words will never harm me" is simply not true. In fact, it works the other way around. Words can cause permanent damage; bones can heal from the sticks and stones. However, words said in anger can never be taken back. Words used to belittle or demoralize someone leave scars that often never heal. Although these scars are not visible, they are no less real than physical scars. Pride and arrogance expressed through words and actions can hurt people more severely than a broken bone ever could. Isaiah 9:9 tells of those who speak *in pride and arrogance of heart*. Pride is a heart matter; you can be sure that where there is pride there is a heart filled with arrogance.

Proverbs 10:19 says: *In the multitude of words sin is not lacking, but he who restrains his lips is wise.* It is better to keep silent if you cannot think of anything constructive to say. When we walk humbly in the Spirit then we will be able to say: *All the words of my mouth are with righteousness; nothing crooked or perverse is in them* (Proverbs 8:8). *Pleasant words are like a honeycomb, sweetness to the soul and health to the bones* (Proverbs 16:24).

You will not find pride and wisdom living side by side. They are at odds with each other. Each day we have the opportunity to choose how we will live. We can choose to be filled with God's Holy Spirit, praying: *Search me, O God, and know my heart: try me, and know my thoughts: And see if there be any wicked way in me, and lead me in the way everlasting* (Psalm 139:23–24 KJV). Our other option is that we can choose to walk according to the flesh and allow pride to rule our lives. Wisdom will count its words. Pride will wreak havoc wherever it goes. You can be a person who brings healing or someone who hurts and harms others. You cannot be filled with pride and be wise at the same time.

Prayer

My Father, I ask You to forgive me that so often my sinful nature chooses pride over wisdom. Search me, O God, and know my heart: try me, and know my thoughts: And see if there be any wicked way in me, and lead me in the way everlasting (Psalm 139:23–24). Help me to be humble, I pray. Amen.

You cannot be filled with pride and be wise at the same time.

The character of a new man

Read Colossians 3:12–25

Therefore, as the elect of God, holy and beloved, put on tender mercies, kindness, humility, meekness, longsuffering; bearing with one another, and forgiving one another, if anyone has a complaint against another; even as Christ forgave you, so you also must do.
(Colossians 3:12–13)

Fathers, watch how you speak to your children. Your words can either build them up or break them down. You can either give them confidence or you can make them believe that they will never be good enough. God loves us with an unconditional love. His love is not dependent upon how we perform. Our love for our children should be the same. Paul admonishes us: *Fathers, do not provoke your children, lest they become discouraged* (Colossians 3:21).

Your life is the most important testimony that your children will ever observe. As they watch you they will either be drawn to Christ or pushed away from Him. It is an awesome responsibility and not one that should be taken lightly. They will watch how you live: Out in the world and behind closed doors in your home. They will take note of how you talk to them, their mother and other people. How you react in difficult circumstances and under provocation are all lessons that you teach your children. You are the "watchman" for your family. Next month in preparation for Father's Day month – June – we are going to look at what it means to stand as the watchman for your family.

A man who is renewed in Christ, who has a heart filled with humility and gratitude to God for all that He has done for him, will in turn love and show grace to others. *But above all these things put on love, which is the bond of perfection. And let the peace of God rule in your hearts, to which also you were called in one body; and be thankful* (Colossians 3:14–15). Immerse yourself in the Word of God: *Let the word of Christ dwell in you richly in all wisdom…* (Colossians 3:16a). A new man, a real man, a humble man, a mighty man of God will speak words of love, encouragement and wisdom to his family, the people with whom he works, his friends and everyone with whom he comes into contact. Are you developing the character of a new man?

Prayer

My Father, thank You for new life in Christ. Forgive me for sometimes hurting those nearest to me when I allow arrogance to reign in my heart. I want to be a man worthy of my calling in Christ Jesus. Fill me with love, humility and wisdom, I pray. Amen.

Are you a renewed man in Christ, who has a heart filled with humility?

Humility is a virtue

Read 1 Corinthians 13

Though I speak with the tongues of men and of angels, but have not love, I have become sounding brass or a clanging cymbal. (1 Corinthians 13:1)

heard a story of a man in central Africa who commented to one of the British High Commissioners, "The problem with you people is that you think you are the best in the world." The Commissioner replied, "No, sir, we do not think we are the best in the world; we know we are the best." This attitude doesn't cut it with God. He says, *Humble yourselves in the sight of the Lord, and He will lift you up* (James 4:10).

Jesus watched the people of His day pushing themselves forward. So *He told a parable to those who were invited, when He noted how they chose the best places, saying to them: "When you are invited by anyone to a wedding feast, do not sit down in the best place, lest one more honorable than you be invited by him; and he who invited you and him come and say to you, 'Give place to this man,' and then you begin with shame to take the lowest place. But when you are invited, go and sit down in the lowest place, so that when he who invited you comes he may say to you, 'Friend, go up higher.' Then you will have glory in the presence of those who sit at the table with you. For whoever exalts himself will be humbled, and he who humbles himself will be exalted"* (Luke 14:7–11).

The "Jesus way" is to walk in love and humility. Paul advises us in 1 Corinthians 13:4d: *Love... is not puffed up.* We said that you cannot be both proud and humble at the same time. Likewise you cannot be loving and proud at the same time. Being puffed up (with pride), means that you will behave rudely, you will insist on your own way in everything and you will be easily provoked. As a child of God we walk in submission to God our Father, Jesus Christ His Son and the Holy Spirit. If you do not have love you have nothing. Humility is a virtue of a man of God.

Prayer

My loving heavenly Father, You have shown me in so many ways how much You love me. Help me to love people with Your love. Help me to be a man who prizes the virtue of humility. Amen.

The "Jesus way" is to walk in love and humility. If you do not have love you have nothing.

Humility before honour

Read Proverbs 15:14–33

The fear of the LORD is the instruction of wisdom, and before honor is humility.
(Proverbs 15:33)

I once read a book about Doctor Billy Graham, the evangelist (I know there are lots of people who do not like him, but then again there are many more who love him). I, for one, respect him greatly. He is a man who has walked the distance. He has been evangelizing longer than I have been alive and as you know I am not a youngster. His grandson told the story of how Billy Graham was visiting a town somewhere in America. One evening he had a couple of hours to spare, so he decided to contact some old people who had helped him with a previous campaign a few years earlier. He wanted to take them out for supper.

The grandson says that he will never forget his grandfather phoning these people. He made the phone call and when the person answered Billy Graham introduced himself, saying he wasn't sure if they remembered him. He explained that he had run a campaign in the town some years before. He told them that he wanted to take them out to dinner if they were free. Of course they knew who he was, but he was so humble that he genuinely thought they might not remember him.

This puts me in mind of Proverbs 15:33: *The fear of the Lord is the instruction of wisdom, and before honor is humility.* My friend, God uses people like Billy Graham. He came from humble beginnings – he was a dairy farmer's son. No matter how much fame he achieved Billy Graham never lost his humility. God has a problem with people who think they are somebody. Remember there is only one way to go when you become proud, and that is downward. Somebody or something will humble you if you do not humble yourself.

Prayer

My Father, thank You for the example of great men who have humbly served You all their lives. Jesus, You are the greatest example of humility. You humbled Yourself to die on the Cross of Calvary to save my soul. Thank You, Jesus. Amen.

Somebody or something will humble you if you do not humble yourself.

A spectator or an instrument

Read Psalm 18:1–30

With the merciful You will show Yourself merciful; with a blameless man You will show Yourself blameless; with the pure You will show Yourself pure; and with the devious You will show Yourself shrewd. For You will save the humble people, but will bring down haughty looks. (Psalm 18:25–27)

Robert Murray McCheyne, a Scotsman, was born in Edinburgh, Scotland. He died at the age of 29, mission accomplished, during a typhus epidemic. He was a man of piety and of prayer – a preacher, pastor and poet who wrote many letters. Despite his youth he had been praying and preaching for revival for a number of years. He worked in Dundee, a big city in the north-east of Scotland. God honoured his prayers and brought a mighty revival to Dundee. However, when the revival came, Robert Murray McCheyne was not even in Dundee. He was in Palestine, in Israel, preaching the gospel to the Muslims.

I love this quote from McCheyne: "I was but an adoring spectator rather than an instrument." He didn't even want to acknowledge how God had used him as an instrument in the revival that took place in Dundee. Folks, this is genuine humility. Too many Christians stand around wanting to be adoring spectators. To become an instrument means that you are willing to lay down your life for the master. It means saying, "God, use me wherever and however You want to; no limits and no conditions." Living a life like this means living a life of faith and humility. Often God is going to tell you to do things that go against human wisdom and logic. At times like this you need to know your God; you need to recognize His voice over and above all the other voices clamouring around you.

When you walk this kind of a "faith walk" with God there is no place for pride in your life. The "faith walk" makes you very aware of your dependence upon your God. You know that only He can do what He has called you to do. Jesus said in Matthew 19:26: *"With men this is impossible, but with God all things are possible."* God will not let you down my friends. Psalm 18:27 tells us: *For You will save the humble people, but will bring down haughty looks.*

Prayer

Father God, You are my Lord and my God. I humbly bow before You today. Lord, I want to be an instrument in Your service. I am tired of being a spectator, adoring You from the sidelines. Amen.

"I was but an adoring spectator rather than an instrument."

Honoured to be a servant

Read Matthew 20:20–28

"Yet it shall not be so among you; but whoever desires to become great among you, let him be your servant. And whoever desires to be first among you, let him be your slave – just as the Son of Man did not come to be served, but to serve, and to give His life a ransom for many." (Matthew 20:26–28)

Remember I quoted Martin Luther the other day who said that the three greatest virtues of men of God are: humility, humility and humility. *Humble yourselves in the sight of the Lord, and He will lift you up* (James 4:10). Those who are preachers or pastors are meant to be servants; yet some of us walk around thinking that we are better than other people. Instead we are meant to be washing the feet of the congregation. We are the ones who are supposed to be taking care of the unbeliever. What we often do instead is walk around with a lapel badge saying "I am somebody special". No! We are servants of the Lord.

On January 25th I told you a story that A. W. Tozer recounted of a young man and the prayer he prayed after his ordination. Tozer refers to him as a "minor prophet". I want to remind you again today of this prayer as it speaks directly to humility. "Oh Lord, I have heard Your voice and I was afraid. You have called me to an awesome task in a grave and perilous hour. You are about to shake the Nations and also Heaven that the things that cannot be shaken may remain. Lord, my Lord, You stooped down to honour me to be a servant. I humbly bow before You today. It is an honour to serve You. Amen."

Notice he says, *"Lord… You… honour me to be a servant."* No man can take this honour upon himself; God calls an individual to serve Him as a servant of the gospel of Jesus Christ. Isn't that beautiful! This young man went on to say: "They have rejected You, Master and it is to be expected that they will also reject me, your servant. I am prepared for it." Are you prepared for people to say all manner of evil about you for the sake of the gospel? There is only one way you will be able to withstand the opposition and that is if you walk in humility before your God.

Prayer

My Father, I bow before You in humility. I ask that You will forgive me for so often allowing myself to become puffed up with pride and a sense of my own importance. Help me to learn from the example of Jesus my saviour. Amen.

Lord, You have honoured me to be a servant.

Leaving all to follow Jesus

Read Luke 14:25–33

"If anyone comes to Me and does not hate his father and mother, wife and children, brothers and sisters, yes, and his own life also, he cannot be My disciple. And whoever does not bear his cross and come after Me cannot be My disciple." (Luke 14:26–27)

Some people are under the impression that if you come to Jesus you will all of a sudden be seen as a hero! It doesn't work like this in the kingdom of God; it actually works the other way around. Yesterday we saw that nobody can claim this honour; it is the Lord who calls you. Then when He has called you, you have to be prepared to be rejected, even sometimes by your own family and friends. Why? Because Jesus was also rejected by the people of His day. There are people who will say that you are overdoing it, and you don't have to be so radical for Christ – of course you do!

Listen as the minor prophet whom Tozer wrote about continues talking to the Lord: "My God, I will not waste time deploring my weakness, or my unfitness for the work. The responsibility is not mine, but Yours." Remember this; the responsibility is not ours but His, we are His servants. He further says, "You have said; 'I knew you, I ordained you and I sanctified you.' You also said; 'You shall go wherever I send you and whatever I command you, you will speak.' So who am I to argue with You or to question You or Your sovereign choice. The decision is not mine, Lord, it is Yours. So be it, Your will be done."

God is looking for humble servants who will get stuck in and help the sheep who are being attacked by savage wolves. The minor prophet says: "It is time, Lord, for the work to proceed, for the enemy has entered into Your pastures and scattered Your sheep, tearing them apart. False shepherds will abound denying the danger and laughing at the perils that surround the sheep. The sheep are deceived by these 'Hirelings' and follow them with touching loyalty, while the wolf closes in to kill them and destroy them. Oh Lord, please give me sharp eyes to detect the presence of the enemy." Are you willing to walk in humility and leave everything to serve God?

Prayer

My Father, help me, I pray, to humbly walk before You. Give me the courage to be prepared to leave everything to follow You. You are the One who calls me. I answer Your call and choose to walk in obedience to Your voice alone. Amen.

Are you willing to walk in humility and leave everything to serve God?

A humble servant of the Lord

Read 1 Peter 2:1–17

But you are a chosen generation, a royal priesthood, a holy nation, His own special people, that you may proclaim the praises of Him who called you out of darkness into His marvelous light. (1 Peter 2:9)

W e are to walk in humility. *But you are a chosen generation, a royal priesthood, a holy nation, His own special people, that you may proclaim the praises of Him who called you out of darkness into His marvelous light.* He has ordained us to be priests of the kingdom of God. You don't have to wear a dog collar; you don't need the title of pastor to be a servant of the Lord. You can be a farmer, a businessman, a factory worker or a college student. No matter what your profession or employment status you have an obligation. If you have made a commitment to Christ then you have a responsibility to care for God's sheep. The minor prophet in Tozer's book continued praying: "Lord, forbid that I should become a religious scribe and thus lose my prophetic calling." Wow! That is a powerful statement!

Tozer wrote this book, that I have been referring to over the past few days, some fifty or sixty years ago, but it is still so appropriate. He continues: "Save me from the curse that lies dark across the face of the modern clergy. The curse of compromise, of imitation, of professionalism. Save me from the era of judging a church by its size and its popularity or the amount of its yearly offerings. Help me to remember that I am not a religious manager but a prophet. Let me never become a slave to crowds." Folks, what do you feel as you read these words? It makes me shake in my boots!

In our reading today Peter says: *Beloved, I beg you as sojourners and pilgrims, abstain from fleshly lusts which war against the soul, having your conduct honorable among the Gentiles, that when they speak against you as evildoers, they may, by your good works which they observe, glorify God in the day of visitation* (1 Peter 2:11–12). Another way to say this would be that we are to walk in humility before our God and then we will automatically be a witness to both our fellow Christians and people in the world.

Prayer

Dear Father, thank You that You are not a respecter of persons. You have called each one of Your children to serve You in humility. You judge us not by our intellect, our education or our station in life. You judge us by how much we love You and whether we walk in obedience before You. Amen.

You don't need the title of pastor to be a servant of the Lord.

Keeping covenant with God

Read Psalm 25:1–15

The humble He guides in justice, and the humble He teaches His way. All the paths of the LORD are mercy and truth, to such as keep His covenant and His testimonies. (Psalm 25:9–10)

When I became a servant of the Lord I made a covenant with God. I promised Him that if I accepted an invitation to a church with only ten people and two weeks later I received an invitation to a church with thousands of people, I would not cancel the first appointment. You must never make a promise to God and not be prepared to keep it. One time I was invited to speak at a church. I was absolutely exhausted and I turned down the invitation. I needed to spend time with my wife and my children as I had hardly seen them due to my heavy schedule.

Two days later I received a telephone call inviting me to a city-wide crusade on the western side of South Africa. It was for the very same weekend that I had just declined the offer to preach in the other gentleman's church. As if this was not enough, there was an even bigger temptation. I particularly like Celtic music and one of my favourite singers is Robin Mark. I have always wanted to attend one of his concerts and hear him in person. A few months earlier I had been preaching in Ireland and I missed Robin Mark because he was in America at the time. The organizers of the crusade told me that Robin Mark was going to do all the praise and worship at the crusade and I was to be the guest speaker. I mean if you're a soccer fan that would be the equivalent of somebody giving you a seat right at the touch-line at Old Trafford, to watch Manchester United win the league.

I declined the invitation because I had said no to the other appointment. I had made a covenant with the Lord and there is no way that I could break that promise. I am a servant of the Lord and for me it is not about the crowds – it is about humbly bringing the gospel of Jesus Christ to people wherever the Lord leads me to do so.

Prayer

My Father God, You are a Holy God. You demand honesty from Your servants. Lord, I pray that You would help me to be faithful to all my promises to You. Help me to humbly serve You no matter what the temptations are that I face. Amen.

You must never make a promise to God and not be prepared to keep it.

The urgency of humility

Read 2 Corinthians 10:1–18

But "he who glories, let him glory in the LORD." For not he who commends himself is approved, but whom the Lord commends. (2 Corinthians 10:17–18)

I have been an evangelist for many years. I've seen Christian leaders crave publicity and the thrill of the crowds more than worldly performers do. This is a tragic thing. I've seen men stepping over each other in their attempt to rise to the top. God forbid that ever happens. Gentlemen, we are sons of the living God; we are not hirelings. We are not part of a show. We need to understand that we are involved in matters of life and death!

We need to be very careful of the devil's ploys to ruin our ministry and our calling. He will do anything he can to encourage us to chase after the crowds, publicity and money. Never forget God says: *Humble yourselves in the sight of the Lord, and He will lift you up* (James 4:10). The minor prophet continues talking to the Lord: "Save me from being in bondage to things." It must never be about things! It's always about people; we must never forget this.

"Let me not waste my days puttering around the house. Lay terror upon me, oh God, and drive me to the place of prayer; where I may wrestle with the principalities, the powers and the rulers of this darkness. Deliver me from over eating and late sleeping." How do you like this? Folks, we have to be disciplined soldiers! The way some of us behave you would think we were in a skirmish not a war. After this comes the judgment. "I accept hard work and small rewards in this life," the minor prophet prays. "I do not ask for an easy place. I shall try to be blind to the little ways that make life easier. If others seek the smoother path I shall try to take the hard way."

Prayer

Father, *though we walk in the flesh, we do not war according to the flesh. For the weapons of our warfare are not carnal but mighty in God for pulling down strongholds, casting down arguments and every high thing that exalts itself against the knowledge of God, bringing every thought into captivity to the obedience of Christ* (2 Corinthians 10:3–5). Amen.

We need to understand that we are involved in matters of life and death!

A humble soldier

Read Philippians 2:1–18

Therefore if there is any consolation in Christ, if any comfort of love, if any fellowship of the Spirit, if any affection and mercy, fulfill my joy by being like-minded, having the same love, being of one accord, of one mind. Let nothing be done through selfish ambition or conceit, but in lowliness of mind let each esteem others better than himself. Let each of you look out not only for his own interests, but also for the interests of others. (Philippians 2:1–4)

So often our lives are all about ourselves. "Woe is me! I need my rest. I need my time out." I have never read of the apostle Paul saying this to the Jews. On the contrary he said: *Yes, and if I am being poured out as a drink offering on the sacrifice and service of your faith, I am glad and rejoice with you all. For the same reason you also be glad and rejoice with me* (Philippians 2:17–18). I want to ask you today: are you being poured out as a drink offering?

Folks, stop worrying about yourself and start worrying about other people. Some of us are so concerned with this life and our own comfort. This doesn't mean that we mustn't look after ourselves. After all, our bodies are the temple of the Holy Spirit. I jog because I try and look after myself physically, but it must not become a god in my life! It is a means to an end. We can look beautiful on the outside but be rotting away on the inside. Our biggest enemy is ourselves, not the devil. We are soldiers of the cross. Paul had this advice for Timothy: *You therefore must endure hardship as a good soldier of Jesus Christ. No one engaged in warfare entangles himself with the affairs of this life, that he may please him who enlisted him as a soldier* (2 Timothy 2:3–4).

True abundance flows out of humble submission to God our Father. It is not about self and satisfying our own selfish desires. Jesus was our perfect example of humble leadership. He was God and yet in Philippians 2:5–8 we read: *Let this mind be in you which was also in Christ Jesus, who, being in the form of God, did not consider it robbery to be equal with God, but made Himself of no reputation, taking the form of a bondservant, and coming in the likeness of men. And being found in appearance as a man, He humbled Himself and became obedient to the point of death, even the death of the cross.*

Prayer

My Father God, You have called me to serve You as a good soldier of the cross of Jesus Christ. Help me to set aside my own felt needs and desires. Like Paul may I be willing to be poured out as a drink offering in the line of service for You, my Lord. Amen.

You therefore must endure hardship as a good soldier of Jesus Christ.

Walk humbly with your God

Read Philippians 1:1–24

For to me, to live is Christ, and to die is gain. (Philippians 1:21)

The minor prophet continues, "I am Thy servant to do Thy will and that will be sweeter to me than position or fame. I choose it above all other things on earth or in heaven. Though I am chosen by You for a high and heavenly calling, let me never forget that I am a man with all the natural faults and passions that plague the race of men. Fill me with the power of the Holy Spirit that I will go in Thy strength and tell of Thy righteousness. I will spread abroad the message of the redeeming love while my normal powers still endure. Then, dear Lord, when I am old and weary and too tired to go on, prepare for me a place above and make me to be numbered with Thy saints with Thy everlasting glory. Amen and Amen."

Is your desire to serve God with all your strength for as long as you can here on earth? Jesus promises us: "*In My Father's house are many mansions; if it were not so, I would have told you. I go to prepare a place for you. And if I go and prepare a place for you, I will come again and receive you to Myself; that where I am, there you may be also*" (John 14:2–3). This is our future but as long as we have breath we are to humbly serve God here on earth.

Paul put it this way: *… so now also Christ will be magnified in my body, whether by life or by death. For to me, to live is Christ, and to die is gain. But if I live on in the flesh, this will mean fruit from my labor; yet what I shall choose I cannot tell. For I am hard-pressed between the two, having a desire to depart and be with Christ, which is far better* (Philippians 1:20b–23). My friends, the driving force in our lives should be to walk humbly with our God, serving Him with all of our heart until He takes us home to be with Him.

Prayer

My Father God, I am humbled as I realize anew what an amazing privilege it is to know You and serve You. Thank You for choosing me to be one of Your servants. Lord, please keep me faithful and true to You until it is time for me to go home. Amen.

The driving force in our lives should be to walk humbly with our God, serving Him with all of our heart.

A contrite heart

Read Psalm 51

O Lord, open my lips, and my mouth shall show forth Your praise. For You do not desire sacrifice, or else I would give it; you do not delight in burnt offering. The sacrifices of God are a broken spirit, a broken and a contrite heart—These, O God, You will not despise.
(Psalm 51:15–17)

It saddens me beyond words when I hear of the casualties who fall by the wayside: men and women of God who are tripped up by the devil. Kathryn Kuhlman said that she never listened to what her fans or her critics had to say about her; because if she did they would have destroyed her. Tozer's minor prophet was not interested in the accolades of men either. At his ordination he realized that it was between him and God. Even though he was a young man he had the wisdom to realize that his ministry was between him and God. He was not going to be swayed by the crowd and whether they loved him or hated him. His desire was to do only what God instructed him to do.

In the Bible we see many examples of men who disobeyed God. Some of them repented of their sin and turned back to God. In His mercy and grace God forgave them. One such man who comes to mind is David. He was chosen by God when he was very young. He knew God and God knew him. God sent Samuel to anoint him as the future king of Israel (1 Samuel 16). David started off as a shepherd looking after his father's sheep. Being the youngest he was the one who was sent to deliver the food when his brothers were at war with the Philistines. God used David to slay the giant. Humbly and fearlessly he carried out God's instructions. There are many other examples of how God used David.

It is hard to believe that this same man who so passionately and fearlessly served God could be tripped up like he was with Bathsheba. God had to send Nathan, the prophet, to confront him (2 Samuel 12). David repented of his sin and God restored him. We read of his humble repentance in Psalm 51. Don't ever be lulled into a false sense of security my friend – this is just what the enemy wants. The walk of humility is a daily walk with God.

Prayer

My Father, I pray that You will protect me from the enemy and his wiles in my life. I do not want to be caught out. I realize that it is so easy to fall when I take my eyes off of You. Help me to remain humble and dependent upon You. Amen.

Don't ever be lulled into a false sense of security – this is just what the enemy wants.

Vanity and false humility

Read Colossians 2:1–19

Let no one cheat you of your reward, taking delight in false humility and worship of angels, intruding into those things which he has not seen, vainly puffed up by his fleshly mind, and not holding fast to the Head, from whom all the body, nourished and knit together by joints and ligaments, grows with the increase that is from God. (Colossians 2:18–19)

Paul warns the Colossians about being taken in by someone who is *taking delight in false humility and is vainly puffed up by his fleshly mind*. False humility and vanity are the exact opposite of humility. There are always those who will try to mislead God's people through philosophies and clever talk. Peter warns: *But there were also false prophets among the people, even as there will be false teachers among you, who will secretly bring in destructive heresies, even denying the Lord who bought them…* (2 Peter 2:1). I have often said that we are too clever for our own good. Why is it that we as humans always feel the need to add to God's Word? God's Word is so profound that the cleverest person will never be able to come to the end of studying it, but it is also so simple that someone who is not very well educated can understand it.

Paul says to the Colossians: *For I want you to know what a great conflict I have for you and those in Laodicea, and for as many as have not seen my face in the flesh, that their hearts may be encouraged, being knit together in love, and attaining to all riches of the full assurance of understanding, to the knowledge of the mystery of God, both of the Father and of Christ, in whom are hidden all the treasures of wisdom and knowledge* (Colossians 2:1–3). He encourages them and reminds them of what they have in Christ. *Now this I say lest anyone should deceive you with persuasive words* (Colossians 2:4).

We are not to judge, but on the other hand we are to act with discernment. You can quickly see if someone is acting out of vanity and false humility. You can see by the way they behave whether they are walking in authentic humility before God. Don't be deceived by clever words. Ultimately you are responsible for your own walk with God – so don't let someone else cheat you and lead you astray. Now as never before is the time to walk in humility.

Prayer

Father, I thank You for Your Holy Spirit who dwells within me. I thank You for the full assurance of understanding and all the treasures of wisdom and knowledge that I have at my disposal in Jesus Christ. Amen.

Don't be deceived by clever words.

Humble faithfulness

Read 2 Chronicles 30:13–27

But Hezekiah prayed for them, saying, "May the good LORD provide atonement for everyone who prepares his heart to seek God, the LORD God of his fathers, though he is not cleansed according to the purification of the sanctuary." And the LORD listened to Hezekiah and healed the people. (2 Chronicles 30:18c–20)

Hezekiah succeeded his father Ahaz as King of Judah. 2 Chronicles 28:22 says *… King Ahaz became increasingly unfaithful to the LORD*. Ahaz had closed down the temple and destroyed its contents. So when Hezekiah took over everything was in a shambles. He was only twenty-five years of age at the time and he reigned for twenty-nine years. *And he did what was right in the sight of the LORD, according to all that his father David had done* (2 Chronicles 29:2). The first thing that Hezekiah did was to call the Levites together; he told them that they were to reopen and repair the House of the Lord. They were to clean up and sanctify the temple so that sacrifices could once again be offered to God.

Remember I wrote a few days ago that we must be careful when we make a covenant with the Lord to keep it. Hezekiah said to the Levites, *"Now it is in my heart to make a covenant with the LORD God of Israel, that His fierce wrath may turn away from us"* (2 Chronicles 29:10). Hezekiah led the people of Israel back into worshipping God. He wiped out the wickedness and unfaithfulness of his father. *Thus Hezekiah did throughout all Judah, and he did what was good and right and true before the LORD his God. And in every work that he began in the service of the house of God, in the law and in the commandment, to seek his God, he did it with all his heart. So he prospered* (2 Chronicles 31:20–21).

Isn't this a wonderful verse? Hezekiah walked humbly before His God. He made amends for his wicked father. He led his people wisely, despite his youth. He followed God with all his heart and he prospered. My friends, we are not prisoners of our background. It doesn't matter what you come from. You make your own choices. You can choose to serve God wholeheartedly. Maybe you need to be the first person in your family who lives a life of humble faithfulness to God.

Prayer

My Father, I come to You today and give You praise that You are a great and wonderful God. You demand obedience and faithfulness from Your servants. Walking with You in humble faithfulness is the only path to prosperity and blessing. Amen.

Choose to serve God wholeheartedly in humble faithfulness.

Beware a heart filled with pride

Read 2 Chronicles 32:1–30

Then Hezekiah humbled himself for the pride of his heart, he and the inhabitants of
Jerusalem, so that the wrath of the LORD did not come upon them in the days of Hezekiah.
(2 Chronicles 32:26)

S
ennacherib, king of Assyria, came against Judah. Hezekiah realized that
Sennacherib's purpose was to make war against Jerusalem. He consulted with
his leaders and immediately put a plan in place to thwart Sennacherib. Hezekiah
did not become fearful because he knew his God. Listen to what he said: *"Be strong
and courageous; do not be afraid nor dismayed before the king of Assyria, nor before all the
multitude that is with him; for there are more with us than with him. With him is an arm of
flesh; but with us is the LORD our God, to help us and to fight our battles." And the people
were strengthened by the words of Hezekiah king of Judah* (2 Chronicles 32:7–8). He
knew his God. He lifted the eyes of his people from their circumstances to their God.

Sennacherib was no match for the Israelites and he was defeated and killed. It is
now that we see a subtle change taking place in Hezekiah's life. *And many brought gifts
to the LORD at Jerusalem, and presents to Hezekiah king of Judah, so that he was exalted
in the sight of all nations thereafter* (2 Chronicles 32:23). Notice the phrase – *he was
exalted in the sight of all nations thereafter.* Hezekiah was in trouble. He was no longer
walking in humble obedience and faithfulness to his God. He forgot his covenant. He
was taking God's glory.

*In those days Hezekiah was sick and near death, and he prayed to the LORD; and He
spoke to him and gave him a sign. But Hezekiah did not repay according to the favor shown
him, for his heart was lifted up; therefore wrath was looming over him and over Judah and
Jerusalem* (2 Chronicles 32:24–25). Fortunately Hezekiah came to his senses: *Then
Hezekiah humbled himself for the pride of his heart, he and the inhabitants of Jerusalem, so
that the wrath of the LORD did not come upon them in the days of Hezekiah* (2 Chronicles
32:26). Serving God is a serious matter, my friend; you cannot play games with Him.
Humbly serve Him with faithfulness and obedience, honouring your commitments to
Him.

Prayer

My Father, help me to learn a lesson from what happened to Hezekiah. Don't ever let
me allow my accomplishments to go to my head. Help me to remember that everything
good in my life is a gift from You. I need to give You the glory due Your name. Amen.

**Humbly serve Him with faithfulness and obedience, honouring your
commitments to Him.**

A life of humble obedience

Read Daniel 10:1–12

Then he said to me, "Do not fear, Daniel, for from the first day that you set your heart to understand, and to humble yourself before your God, your words were heard; and I have come because of your words." (Daniel 10:12)

D aniel's walk of faith did not start in the lions' den: No, it was the culmination of a life lived in humble obedience and faithfulness to God. As a young man Daniel was taken captive along with his friends Shadrach, Meshach and Abed-Nego. They were taken from their homes in Jerusalem to Babylon. Daniel and his friends were chosen to serve in the king's court. They were given the best food and the best education.

In Daniel 1:8a we read: *But Daniel purposed in his heart that he would not defile himself with the portion of the king's delicacies, nor with the wine which he drank.* God gave him favour with the chief of the eunuchs. God honoured his obedience and as we know he thrived on the simple diet that he ate. Even in the face of personal danger it was not an option for Daniel to stop praying and worshipping his God, as was his habit. He humbly submitted to God and trusted Him to do His will in his life. The king was very upset about Daniel being thrown into the lions' den. *But the king spoke, saying to Daniel, "Your God, whom you serve continually, He will deliver you"* (Daniel 6:16b). The next morning Daniel said to the king: *"My God sent His angel and shut the lions' mouths, so that they have not hurt me, because I was found innocent before Him…"* (Daniel 6:22a).

God used Daniel throughout his life to bring His messages to His people. In chapter ten Daniel receives these words of commendation: *"…from the first day that you set your heart to understand, and to humble yourself before your God, your words were heard"* (Daniel 10:12b). Psalm 10:17 says: LORD, *You have heard the desire of the humble; You will prepare their heart; You will cause Your ear to hear.* Daniel's life was firmly rooted in his relationship with his God. He was steadfast throughout his life. Daniel was able to say *"…but the people who know their God shall be strong, and carry out great exploits"* (Daniel 11:32b).

Prayer

My Father, I bow in Your presence. I ask You to help me to be consistent in my obedience and faithfulness to You. Lord, help me in Jesus' name to walk humbly before You. Lord, I want to know You like Daniel did. Amen.

The people who know their God shall be strong, and carry out great exploits.

Breaking the power of pride

Read 2 Chronicles 7:12–18

"...if My people who are called by My name will humble themselves, and pray and seek My face, and turn from their wicked ways, then I will hear from heaven, and will forgive their sin and heal their land." (2 Chronicles 7:14)

God has always demanded humility from His people. It is a condition of serving God. You can look throughout history and you will see countless examples of people who have fallen as a result of pride creeping into their lives. God spoke to the people of Israel in Leviticus 26:19 and He told them: *I will break the pride of your power; I will make your heavens like iron and your earth like bronze.* Whenever either a person or a group of people walk in pride there comes a time when they fall. This is why Proverbs 15:33 says: *The fear of the LORD is the instruction of wisdom, and before honor is humility.*

The Psalmist puts it like this: *The LORD lifts up the humble; He casts the wicked down to the ground* (Psalm 147:6). My friend, God does not share His glory. We must never forget who we are and who He is. *Behold, the Lord, The LORD of hosts, Will lop off the bough with terror; Those of high stature will be hewn down, and the haughty will be humbled* (Isaiah 10:33). In our reading God advised Solomon that He wanted the people to humble themselves. God said that if they did this in repentance then He would hear them, forgive them and heal their land.

He said something similar in the book of Jeremiah: *For I know the thoughts that I think toward you, says the LORD, thoughts of peace and not of evil, to give you a future and a hope. Then you will call upon Me and go and pray to Me, and I will listen to you. And you will seek Me and find Me, when you search for Me with all your heart* (Jeremiah 29:11–13). Our God is gracious and loving, but He is also just and righteous. Spend some time before the Lord today and ask His Spirit to search your heart. Is there pride in your heart? If there is then repent before God today, seek His face and ask His forgiveness – because if you don't He will break the pride of your power.

Prayer

My Father, as I bow my knee and my heart in Your presence today, search me, I pray. Shine the Light of Your Spirit into the dark recesses of my heart. Show up all the pride and haughtiness in me. Father, I want to walk before You in humility. I want a heart that is pure and filled only with love for You. Amen.

If there is pride in your heart then repent before God, seek His face and ask His forgiveness.

Jesus' teaching on humility

Read Luke 18:9–14

"I tell you, this man went down to his house justified rather than the other; for everyone who exalts himself will be humbled, and he who humbles himself will be exalted." (Luke 18:14)

J esus had a lot to say about humility. In His day the religious leaders were not known for their humility. They walked around very proud of their holiness and they thought that they were better than everyone else. I want us to look briefly at three instances that Jesus highlighted regarding humility. The first one is found in Matthew 18:1–4: *At that time the disciples came to Jesus, saying, "Who then is greatest in the kingdom of heaven?" Then Jesus called a little child to Him, set him in the midst of them, and said, "Assuredly, I say to you, unless you are converted and become as little children, you will by no means enter the kingdom of heaven. Therefore whoever humbles himself as this little child is the greatest in the kingdom of heaven."*

Even in Jesus' day people jostled for position. In Luke Jesus was at a dinner and He noticed how people were pushing to get the best seats at the table. He spoke to the people around Him saying to them: *"When you are invited by anyone to a wedding feast, do not sit down in the best place … go and sit down in the lowest place, so that when he who invited you comes he may say to you, 'Friend, go up higher.' Then you will have glory in the presence of those who sit at the table with you"* (Luke 14:8a, 10). Then Jesus hit them with the punchline. *"For whoever exalts himself will be humbled, and he who humbles himself will be exalted"* (Luke 14:11).

There were very few people lower than the tax collector in Jesus' day. He told this parable to the religious leaders who trusted in their own righteousness and despised other people. *"The Pharisee stood and prayed thus with himself, 'God, I thank You that I am not like other men – extortioners, unjust, adulterers, or even as this tax collector'"* (Luke 18:11). The tax collector on the other hand prayed: … *"God, be merciful to me a sinner!"* (Luke 18:13) Who do you think went home justified?

Prayer

My Father God, I come to You in the name of Jesus my saviour. Lord Jesus, I thank You that when You walked on this earth You gave me a number of lessons regarding humility. You left me in no doubt as to how I am to live before You. Help me to be obedient to Your teaching, I pray. Amen.

"…whoever humbles himself as this little child is the greatest in the kingdom of heaven" (**Matthew 18:4**).

Jesus our example of humility

Read Philippians 2:5–11

Let this mind be in you which was also in Christ Jesus … He humbled Himself and became obedient to the point of death, even the death of the cross. (Philippians 2:5, 8b)

Jesus is without doubt our ultimate example of living a life of humility. Paul in Philippians chapter two reminds us of this. He exhorts us to have the same mind that Jesus Christ had. Jesus was prepared to humble Himself to the point of death. Why? So that You and I can have eternal life. Jesus lived His whole life on earth being an example to us of what it means to walk in humility and obedience to God, our Father.

Jesus came to earth to do the will of His Father. When He became a man He was dependent upon His Father to give Him the power to do the work God had set out for Him to do. *Then Jesus answered and said to them, "Most assuredly, I say to you, the Son can do nothing of Himself, but what He sees the Father do; for whatever He does, the Son also does in like manner… I can of Myself do nothing. As I hear, I judge; and My judgment is righteous, because I do not seek My own will but the will of the Father who sent Me"* (John 5:19, 30).

Jesus' greatest test came in the Garden of Gethsemane. There He had to submit His will to the will of His Father. He had to accept His destiny to die on the Cross of Calvary to save us from our sins. If you have a few minutes read the portion of Scripture in Matthew 26:36–46 again. Three times Jesus prayed; and three times He submitted to the will of His Father. *"O My Father, if this cup cannot pass away from Me unless I drink it, Your will be done"* (Matthew 26:42b). When everything is said and done, the essence of humility is submission to the will of God. If you are walking in God's will, doing the things He is telling you to do, then you will be humble. You will know without a doubt that only He can do the things that He does through you. It is not you but Him.

Prayer

My Father God, thank You for Jesus Your Son. Jesus, thank You that You are my ultimate example of walking and living a life of humility before the Father. I want to follow Your example. Amen.

If you are walking in God's will, doing the things He is telling you to do, then you will be humble.

Paul – a servant's heart

Read 1 Timothy 1:12–17

This is a faithful saying and worthy of all acceptance, that Christ Jesus came into the world to save sinners, of whom I am chief. (1 Timothy 1:15)

The Paul who wrote to Timothy was a different man to the one in Acts chapter nine. He had been arrogant, believing wholeheartedly in his vendetta against the Christians. What made the difference in Paul's life? He encountered Jesus Christ on the road to Damascus. My friend, I was a different man before I met Jesus Christ in the little Methodist church in Greytown. My life changed direction and since then it has never been "business as usual".

Paul's life was radically changed. God had a specific plan and purpose for his life. The Lord said to Ananias: ... *"Go, for he is a chosen vessel of Mine to bear My name before Gentiles, kings, and the children of Israel. For I will show him how many things he must suffer for My name's sake"* (Acts 9:15–16). As we know Paul went through many trials in his service of the master. In Acts 20:19a he says, *"serving the Lord with all humility, with many tears and trials..."* He was spared very little; we read in 2 Corinthians of the vision Paul experienced and the thorn in the flesh that he received. Paul believed this thorn in the flesh was sent to keep him humble. *And lest I should be exalted above measure by the abundance of the revelations, a thorn in the flesh was given to me, a messenger of Satan to buffet me, lest I be exalted above measure* (2 Corinthians 12:7).

No matter what he went through Paul never wavered in his devotion to Christ or in his service to the church. He said to the Corinthians: *For though I am free from all men, I have made myself a servant to all, that I might win the more* (1 Corinthians 9:19). Paul served God in all humility and was able to say: *But by the grace of God I am what I am, and His grace toward me was not in vain; but I labored more abundantly than they all, yet not I, but the grace of God which was with me* (1 Corinthians 15:10).

Prayer

My Father, thank You for the example of Your servant Paul. Lord, it is an encouragement to me when I read and meditate upon the lives of great men who have served You in humble faithfulness. Father, keep me faithful, I pray. Amen.

But by the grace of God I am what I am, and His grace toward me was not in vain (1 Corinthians 15:10a).

Boasting in the Lord

Read Psalm 34

My soul shall make its boast in the LORD; the humble shall hear of it and be glad. (Psalm 34:2)

Yesterday we spoke about Paul and the example that he is to us with regard to living a life of humility. We looked briefly at 2 Corinthians chapter twelve regarding Paul's vision and his thorn in the flesh. He makes this statement in verses five and six: Of such a one I will boast; yet of myself I will not boast, except in my infirmities. For though I might desire to boast, I will not be a fool; for I will speak the truth. But I refrain, lest anyone should think of me above what he sees me to be or hears from me. Paul says in Galatians 6:14: But God forbid that I should boast except in the cross of our Lord Jesus Christ, by whom the world has been crucified to me, and I to the world.

This is the crux of the matter isn't it? We have nothing to boast about other than in *the cross of our Lord Jesus Christ.* No matter how many degrees we have, how much money we have or where we live – none of these things can be taken into eternity with us. They are things that if committed to Christ can be used in His service and for His glory. We must see them only as a means to an end – they must not define who we are. The only thing that can define us is our relationship with Jesus Christ. *Blessed is that man who makes the LORD his trust, and does not respect the proud, nor such as turn aside to lies* (Psalm 40:4).

For our boasting is this: the testimony of our conscience that we conducted ourselves in the world in simplicity and godly sincerity, not with fleshly wisdom but by the grace of God, and more abundantly toward you (2 Corinthians 1:12). God does not share His glory, my friend.

Everyone proud in heart is an abomination to the LORD (Proverbs 16:5a). As you come to the end of this month come to God and commit yourself to Him; covenant to walk in humility before Him.

Prayer

My Father, I come to You bowing before Your throne. I will not boast in anything other than the Cross of Jesus Christ, my Lord and saviour. I give You the glory, Lord. Help me to walk in humility. May I have a contrite heart that is filled with love for You. Amen.

I commit myself to God and covenant to walk in humility before Him.

A contrite and humble spirit

Read James 4:1–10

Draw near to God and He will draw near to you. Cleanse your hands, you sinners; and purify your hearts, you double-minded. Lament and mourn and weep! Let your laughter be turned to mourning and your joy to gloom. Humble yourselves in the sight of the Lord, and He will lift you up. (James 4:8–10)

During this past month we looked at David and the time in his life when he committed adultery with Bathsheba. He had to repent before God. We read his prayer in Psalm 51. We looked at the life of Hezekiah and how he humbled himself before God when he realized that he had sinned. There are instances in our lives when we have to come before God because of specific sin and ask His forgiveness. However, what we are really talking about today is having a lifestyle that is characterized by a contrite and a humble heart.

For thus says the High and Lofty One Who inhabits eternity, whose name is Holy: "I dwell in the high and holy place, with him who has a contrite and humble spirit, to revive the spirit of the humble, and to revive the heart of the contrite ones" (Isaiah 57:15). The Word also says to us: Seek the Lord, all you meek of the earth, who have upheld His justice. Seek righteousness, seek humility (Zephaniah 2:3a). So often there is not a lot of difference between the way that God's children and people in the world live. This is incredibly sad isn't it?

Paul, in 1 Timothy 6:4, says of people like this: He is proud, knowing nothing, but is obsessed with disputes and arguments over words, from which come envy, strife, reviling, evil suspicions. He continues: For men will be lovers of themselves, lovers of money, boasters, proud, blasphemers, disobedient to parents, unthankful, unholy (2 Timothy 3:2). Come before God today and make right with Him. Don't delay, my friend, because you don't know if there will be another chance. Purpose in your heart to walk before your God humbly with a contrite heart. We are called to be an example to the world around us. Through our lives we must show them what it means to humbly love our God and our fellow man. But He gives more grace. Therefore He says: "God resists the proud, but gives grace to the humble" (James 4:6).

Prayer

My Father, I come to You in Jesus' name. Father, I realize that You look at the heart and judge the measure of a man. You are not impressed by my outward appearance. Forgive me that so often I am more interested in working on the outside than I am on the state of my heart. Amen.

Purpose in your heart to walk before your God humbly with a contrite heart.

God's Word on humility

By humility and the fear of the LORD are riches and honor and life. (Proverbs 22:4)

always say that I am not interested in anyone's opinion – I am only interested in what God says. I have often said to you that you must not take my words as gospel. You must take God's Word as your ultimate authority. With this in mind let us allow God's Word to speak to us today on the subject of humility.

When pride comes, then comes shame; but with the humble is wisdom (Proverbs 11:2).

The LORD lifts up the humble; He casts the wicked down to the ground (Psalm 147:6).

A man's pride will bring him low, but the humble in spirit will retain honor (Proverbs 29:23).

Be of the same mind toward one another. Do not set your mind on high things, but associate with the humble. Do not be wise in your own opinion (Romans 12:16).

The lofty looks of man shall be humbled, the haughtiness of men shall be bowed down, and the LORD alone shall be exalted in that day (Isaiah 2:11).

For all that is in the world – the lust of the flesh, the lust of the eyes, and the pride of life – is not of the Father but is of the world (1 John 2:16).

The fear of the LORD is the instruction of wisdom, and before honor is humility (Proverbs 15:33).

Therefore, as the elect of God, holy and beloved, put on tender mercies, kindness, humility, meekness, longsuffering (Colossians 3:12).

… to speak evil of no one, to be peaceable, gentle, showing all humility to all men (Titus 3:2).

Arise, O LORD! O God, lift up Your hand! Do not forget the humble (Psalm 10:12).

LORD, You have heard the desire of the humble; You will prepare their heart; You will cause Your ear to hear (Psalm 10:17).

The humble He guides in justice, and the humble He teaches His way (Psalm 25:9).

Therefore humble yourselves under the mighty hand of God, that He may exalt you in due time (1 Peter 5:6).

Prayer

Father, I thank You for Your Word today. Lord, I am so grateful that You speak to me so clearly through Your Word. It is truly everything that I need for life and godliness. Help me, I pray, to be a doer of Your Word and not just a hearer of it. Amen.

God's Word is our ultimate authority on every subject.

A prayer of humble commitment

Read James 4:1–10

Humble yourselves in the sight of the Lord, and He will lift you up. (James 4:10)

I want to share something that was found nailed to the back of a door in a little hut in Zimbabwe. It was written by a pastor before he was arrested and put in jail. I ask you to read this poem and as you do, use it to re-commit yourself anew to living a life of humility consecrated to God.

I am part of the fellowship of the unashamed; I have Holy Spirit power. The die has been cast and I have stepped over the line. The decision has been made and I am a disciple of His. I won't backslide, let up, slow down or back away. My past is redeemed, my present makes sense and my future is secure. I'm finished and done with low living, sight-walking, small planning, smooth knees, colourless dreams, tamed visions, mundane talking, cheap living and dwarfed goals. I no longer need pre-eminence, prosperity, position, promotion or popularity. I don't have to fight; I don't have to be right. I don't have to be first. I don't have to be tops; recognized, praised, rewarded or even regarded.

I now live by faith, I lean on His presence, I walk by patience, I live by prayer and I labour with power. My face is set, my gait is fast, my goal is heaven, my road is narrow, my way is rough and my companions are few. My Guide is reliable and my mission is clear. I cannot be bought, compromised, detoured, lured or led away. I cannot be turned back, deluded or delayed. I will not flinch in the face of sacrifice or hesitate in the presence of the enemy. I will not ponder in the pool of popularity or meander in the maze of mediocrity. I won't give up, shut up or let up; until I have prayed up, paid up and preached up for the cause of Christ. I am a disciple of Jesus Christ; I must go on until He comes. I must give until I drop, I must preach until all know and work until He stops me; and when He comes for His own He will have no problem in recognizing me, my banner will be clear!

Prayer

My Father, I give You my heart, my life, my soul and everything that I am and have. Keep me humble and loving You, I pray. Amen.

"I won't give up, shut up or let up; until I have prayed up, paid up and preached up for the cause of Christ."

MAY

Called to be a watchman

Blowing the trumpet

Teaching your family to love God

The enemy is at the gate

Don't be caught napping

Be battle ready

A vigilant watchman

The courage to speak up

Walk your talk

Don't neglect your responsibilities

Evaluate your lifestyle

Do not become discouraged

Being different for Jesus

Empowered to be a watchman

Don't be ashamed

Are you hot or cold?

Speak out

God's ways are fair

A word from the Lord's mouth

Becoming a holy people

Godliness with contentment

Freedom from condemnation

The Son will set you free

Everything but nothing

What is God warning you about?

Jesus, the Way to freedom

Enter by the narrow gate

Keeping watch for the prodigal

We will serve the Lord

The watchman's armour

A watchman over my House

Called to be a watchman

Read Ezekiel 33:1–11

Again the word of the LORD came to me, saying, "Son of man, speak to the children of your people, and say to them: 'When I bring the sword upon a land, and the people of the land take a man from their territory and make him their watchman.'" (Ezekiel 33:1–2)

We are called by God to be watchmen. Watchmen over the House of Israel. What is the House of Israel and who makes up the House of Israel? The House of Israel is the fellowship of the believers and it is made up of the believers. If you are a follower of Jesus Christ then you are called to be a watchman. Especially the more mature Christians need to take on this task. Notice I didn't say "older" Christians, but rather the "more mature" Christians. Maturity is not a matter of age alone. We have an obligation. Our obligation is to make sure that the truth is spoken at all cost. Your obligation is to warn the young ones when the devil is lurking nearby. There are two levels on which we are to be watchmen. First and foremost in our own homes. We are to be vigilant, keeping guard over our family. Then secondly, we are to be watchmen guarding our broader Christian family.

You might say to me, if we were together, that your kids don't listen to you. That might be true – but you didn't listen to your parents either, did you? No matter whether they listen or not you still have an obligation to look out for them. You are the watchman guarding them. Call them by name, encourage them, spend time in the Word and pray for them. You have to look after your family: your wife and your children (and grandchildren when they come along). Your family comes first but after them you need to also look out for your staff and the people who work for you (and with you). Maybe you are a farmer, a businessman, a foreman, a manager, a teacher or even a student. Whatever your sphere of influence you have an obligation to be a Watchman over the House of Israel. If ever you needed to be a watchman – now is the time. We are approaching the climax of the ages and the great battle is poised to begin. Read our key text again – are you ready to be a watchman?

Prayer

My Father God, I come before You very aware of the challenge of Your Word to me and my responsibility to obey You. Help me to step up to the plate, Father. Help me to be a watchman worth my salt. Amen.

We are approaching the climax of the ages and the great battle is poised to begin – are you ready to be a watchman?

Blowing the trumpet

Read Ezekiel 33:1–11

"…when he sees the sword coming upon the land, if he blows the trumpet and warns the people, then whoever hears the sound of the trumpet and does not take warning, if the sword comes and takes him away, his blood shall be on his own head." (Ezekiel 33:3–4)

Verse three continues, *"…when he sees the sword coming upon the land, if he blows the trumpet and warns the people…"* What does Ezekiel mean when he talks about "blowing the trumpet"? First of all, what is the trumpet? The trumpet is the Word of God. The Word of God is our plumbline for life and living. You know that because I am a farmer I often refer to God's Word as my agricultural manual. It doesn't matter what your occupation is: God's Word is your manual – His Word will instruct you and tell you what to do and when to do it. No matter what the situation, no matter what the challenge, God's Word has the answers that you need.

Blowing the "trumpet" means sharing the truth of God's Word. It is not your truth or my truth that we are to share – no, it is God's truth. As you learn from His Word it is your duty to share the truths you learn with other people. We can share God in many different ways: through Christian television programmes, sermons, witnessing for God on the street and also in the workplace, to name but a few. This is the time to blow the trumpet, to warn the people of what is to come. Ephesians 4:15 instructs us: *but, speaking the truth in love,* [so that all] *may grow up in all things into Him who is the head – Christ.* This is the ultimate goal: that everyone will be mature in Jesus Christ, who is the head of the church.

"… then whoever hears the sound of the trumpet and does not take warning, if the sword comes and takes him away, his blood shall be on his own head." You are not responsible for people's reactions to the message of warning. You are only responsible for delivering it. All God asks from you is obedience to His command. God has told us that He is not interested in our sacrifices but rather in our obedience to Him. We need to be faithful to God first before anyone else. Divided loyalties will lead to compromise.

Prayer

Dear Lord, I bow before You and worship You. You are the great and mighty God; there is none like You. Help me, I pray, to be a faithful watchman who does not shrink back from blowing the trumpet of the truth of Your Word. Amen.

Be faithful to God first before anyone else. Divided loyalties will lead to compromise.

Teach your family to love God

Read Deuteronomy 6:1–9

"Hear, O Israel: The LORD our God, the LORD is one! You shall love the LORD your God with all your heart, with all your soul, and with all your strength." (Deuteronomy 6:4–5)

Being a watchman who blows the trumpet means you are to share God's Word with your family. It does not help if you are out saving the world and your own family is suffering. You are first and foremost a watchman over your own family. God calls you to blow the trumpet – do not shirk your responsibility to teach and instruct those in your family regarding the truth in God's Word.

One of the commands that speak about sharing God's Word with our families is found in Deuteronomy 6:4–9: *"Hear, O Israel: The LORD our God, the LORD is one! You shall love the LORD your God with all your heart, with all your soul, and with all your strength. And these words which I command you today shall be in your heart. You shall teach them diligently to your children, and shall talk of them when you sit in your house, when you walk by the way, when you lie down, and when you rise up. You shall bind them as a sign on your hand, and they shall be as frontlets between your eyes. You shall write them on the doorposts of your house and on your gates."* God is speaking here to the children of Israel, but it is just as relevant to us today. If you don't tell them how will they know?

As a parent it is your duty to give moral guidance to your children. You do this by example as well as by instruction. Again, God's Word is your manual – all the wisdom you need is to be found in the Bible. As a parent you cannot be silent on issues regarding appropriate dating. If you don't tell your children that God's Word forbids sex before marriage, who will? Not the world, that is for sure. You need to educate them regarding the dangers of drugs and drink. Fathers, you are the person who must teach your sons how to treat women. Abuse is as prevalent in the church as it is in the world – this is not how God wants us to live.

Prayer

My Father, I thank You for my family. I am so grateful for the wonderful privilege You have given me of being the watchman over my family. Each one is precious to me and I pray that You will help me to be faithful to You in carrying out my responsibilities towards them. Amen.

God's Word is your manual – all the wisdom you need is to be found in the Bible.

The enemy is at the gate

Read Ezekiel 33:1–11

"Say to them: 'As I live,' says the Lord GOD, 'I have no pleasure in the death of the wicked, but that the wicked turn from his way and live. Turn, turn from your evil ways! For why should you die, O house of Israel?'" (Ezekiel 33:11)

God tells us He has no pleasure in the death of the wicked. Peter says it like this in 2 Peter 3:9: *The Lord is not slack concerning His promise, as some count slackness, but is longsuffering toward us, not willing that any should perish but that all should come to repentance.* We are living in desperate times, my friend. Do you feel the urgency? There is no time for napping and sleeping. We must be about our Father's business, sharing the good news of the gospel of Jesus Christ with everyone we come into contact with.

As we said yesterday we have a primary responsibility towards our families to share God's Word with them. They need to be in no doubt about what it means to follow Jesus. Telling them is only one aspect of teaching them – the most important component is living the life. Lead by example. We are also called to be watchman over our friends. If you have a friend who is involved in doing something that is harmful to them it is your duty to warn them. You need to tell them what God's Word says regarding their situation. If they choose not to listen to you, well, there is nothing you can do about that. The important thing is you have told them. All you can then do is pray for them.

It is not God's choice that people should perish in their sins. This is why He sent Jesus to this world. *"For God so loved the world that He gave His only begotten Son, that whoever believes in Him should not perish but have everlasting life. For God did not send His Son into the world to condemn the world, but that the world through Him might be saved. … But he who does the truth comes to the light, that his deeds may be clearly seen, that they have been done in God"* (John 3:16–17, 21). We serve a God of love and grace. The enemy is at the gate and we need to turn to Jesus while there is still time.

Prayer

My Father, thank You for Your incredible love towards us as human beings. Jesus, thank You for Your sacrifice on Calvary. You died so that we can have eternal life. Father, thank You for Your grace and Your desire for all to be saved. Help me to faithfully share Your love with others. Amen.

The enemy is at the gate and we need to turn to Jesus while there is still time.

Don't be caught napping

Read Matthew 26:36–46

Then He came to the disciples and found them sleeping, and said to Peter, "What! Could you not watch with Me one hour? Watch and pray, lest you enter into temptation. The spirit indeed is willing, but the flesh is weak." (Matthew 26:40-41)

Some years ago God gave me a picture of a watchman and it really scared me. I arranged for someone to make a painting of the picture God had given me and then I hung it up in a church in Pietermaritzburg where I was preaching. The painting depicted an old medieval castle with big turrets and flags flying. There were many people inside the castle and they were all sound asleep. There was a watchman right at the top of the tower and he had a huge horn, a big trumpet. His job was to watch out for the enemy should they try to sneak up upon the castle. As soon as he saw the enemy approaching, he was supposed to blow the trumpet. Then everyone inside the castle would wake up, arm themselves and be ready to fight the enemy.

Do you know what happened? Yes, you have guessed correctly, the watchman fell asleep – sound asleep. The picture shows the enemy stealthily creeping up on the castle. Some of the enemy soldiers had placed ladders up against the castle walls. They were scaling the walls and entering the castle. The whole community who lived inside the castle were fast asleep. Thousands of the enemy were standing on their ramparts. All the while this was happening the watchman slept soundly.

What happened? The town was destroyed because one man couldn't stay awake. We saw the same thing happen with the three disciples that Jesus took with Him into the Garden of Gethsemane. They were supposed to watch and pray with Him. They were meant to be His watchmen, supporting Him in His time of need. They could not keep awake. Three times Jesus came back to them and each time they were asleep. What is happening in your life at the moment? God has called you to be a watchman. You are meant to keep watch over your family. It is your calling to protect them and to look out for them. Now is the time for you to be a watchman – don't be caught napping.

Prayer

My Father, I realize that the enemy is approaching – help me to be vigilant, I pray. I don't want to give him a foothold in my life or the lives of my family. Thank You for the power of Your Spirit who dwells within me. Empower me, I pray. Amen.

Keep a watch over your family – don't be caught napping.

Be battle ready

Read Ezekiel 33:1–11

"But if the watchman sees the sword coming and does not blow the trumpet, and the people are not warned, and the sword comes and takes any person from among them, he is taken away in his iniquity; but his blood I will require at the watchman's hand." (Ezekiel 33:6)

I f you don't have a regular quiet time with God then you are spiritually asleep. A watchman needs to be constantly alert. He can never rest on his laurels or become sluggish and slow. A soldier in the army has to keep fit and be alert at all times when he is on active duty. He has to train daily so that he will be battle ready at all times. Paul spoke to Timothy about being a good soldier. *No one engaged in warfare entangles himself with the affairs of this life, that he may please him who enlisted him as a soldier* (2 Timothy 2:4). On a spiritual level one of the ways we remain fit and healthy is by spending time with God in His Word and in prayer.

As a born-again Christian, if you love Christ as God, you have an obligation to warn people when you see them doing something that is totally outside of God's will. Our Scripture verse tells us that there are dire consequences if the watchman does not blow the trumpet in order to warn the people. We established that the trumpet is the Word of God – blowing it means we share what the Word says with other people. You will not be able to share God's Word, or warn people about the truth found in it, if you do not know what the Word says.

You have to warn people and if you don't our Scripture says: *"… his blood I will require at the watchman's hand."* This is a hard word isn't it? Being a watchman on the walls is a serious business, my friend. You have a sacred duty to protect those closest to you. You also have a further responsibility to the body of Christ as well. You cannot allow your fellow brothers and sisters to be misled or deceived – you have to be the "trumpet blower". Then after your fellow Christians you need to be sharing the good news of the gospel with people in the world. They need to hear it, and if you don't tell them, then who will?

Prayer

My Father God, I come to You in Jesus' name. Forgive my lethargy and disobedience. I pray that You will help me to be a vigilant, diligent, well-trained watchman who is always ready to blow the trumpet of truth. Amen.

You have an obligation to warn people when you see them doing something outside of God's will.

A vigilant watchman

Read Ezekiel 33:1–11

"But if the watchman sees the sword coming and does not blow the trumpet, and the people are not warned, and the sword comes and takes any person from among them, he is taken away in his iniquity; but his blood I will require at the watchman's hand." (Ezekiel 33:6)

We continue looking at this Scripture about the watchman in Ezekiel. I encourage you to take some time in God's presence and ask Him to speak to you through His Holy Spirit. Ask Him to help you to be a diligent watchman. Recommit your life to Him. Covenant to be obedient to the prompting of the Holy Spirit when He tells you to do or say something to someone. This Scripture that we have read again today is a hard Scripture. It is not easy being a Christian. It is not meant to be; it takes everything that we have. Why shouldn't it? After all it took everything that God and Jesus had in order to save us. Salvation is not cheap. Jesus died for us and He said: *"Greater love has no one than this, than to lay down one's life for his friends"* (John 15:13).

If you love people you will warn them. If you love your family you will be on your guard to protect them. The enemy is so subtle and he uses many different things to try and trip us up. One of the ploys he uses is to inveigle his way into the lives of people through social media. There are an ever growing number of options for people to communicate with each other. On the surface of it this would appear to be a good thing, but on another level it is a way for people to be led into temptation. Children and young people cannot be left without supervision when it comes to interacting on social media platforms. Parents, you need to know what your children are doing; you need to know with whom they are communicating.

It can be just as dangerous for adults. Too many men are falling into temptation on the Internet. There is an unlimited supply of pornography available at the touch of a button. This has caused untold heartache and damage to marriages and relationships. Be a vigilant watchman; be careful not to lose your testimony. Guard your own life and guard the lives of your loved ones.

Prayer

My Father, I thank You that Your Word tells me that greater are You who is in me than he who is in the world. I am grateful that I am not at the mercy of the enemy. Keep me faithful and vigilant, I pray. Amen.

Be a vigilant watchman; be careful not to lose your testimony.

The courage to speak up

Read Ezekiel 33:1–11

"But if the watchman sees the sword coming and does not blow the trumpet, and the people are not warned, and the sword comes and takes any person from among them, he is taken away in his iniquity; but his blood I will require at the watchman's hand." (Ezekiel 33:6)

A t some time or another in our lives I am sure all of us are guilty of not having spoken up when we should have. I will never forget something that happened when I was a young boy. I haven't spoken of it for many years. When I became a Christian I asked God to forgive me. At the time I was about eight or nine years old. I was sitting in the front passenger seat of my mother's motor car somewhere in central Africa, waiting for her to come out of the post office. A lady was walking on the pavement and a man came running from behind her. He stole her purse out of her bag and ran in the other direction. The woman turned around too late to see who it was. I didn't have the courage to open my mouth and shout out, "There he is: he's got your purse!" For years and years this bugged me. All that I needed to do was say, "Madam, there he is!" They could have caught him and she would have had her purse back, but I didn't have the courage.

My dear friend, if you see your friend in danger, if you see your friend keeping bad company, or if you see your friend doing something you know is not good for him, then please warn him. For God's sake do it! Romans 10:13–14 says: *For "whoever calls on the name of the LORD shall be saved." How then shall they call on Him in whom they have not believed? And how shall they believe in Him of whom they have not heard? And how shall they hear without a preacher?* There you have it, my friend: if you don't tell them who will?

You have an obligation as a believer. When you make a decision to follow Christ you become part of God's army. There is no place for passive soldiers; we are all on permanent active duty. Don't be guilty of not speaking up when the situation demands it – someone's life could depend upon it.

Prayer

My Father, I ask You to forgive me for the times when I have remained silent instead of speaking words of warning to people. You have given me Your Word: help me to use it to show people what Your will is for them. Amen.

Don't be guilty of not speaking up when the situation demands it.

Walk your talk

Read Ezekiel 33:1–11

"When I say to the wicked, 'O wicked man, you shall surely die!' and you do not speak to warn the wicked from his way, that wicked man shall die in his iniquity; but his blood I will require at your hand. Nevertheless if you warn the wicked to turn from his way, and he does not turn from his way, he shall die in his iniquity; but you have delivered your soul." (Ezekiel 33:8–9)

You cannot force somebody to repent and follow Jesus. What you can do though is point the way. Your responsibility is to live a life that is a good testimony to Jesus Christ. It doesn't help if you are always preaching to other people about how they should live, but you live exactly the way you want to. Your walk is just as if not more important than your talk. The two need to match each other. Ultimately each person has to make their own decision for Christ. So if someone decides against following Christ, it is on them, not on you. Your part is to share the good news of the gospel with them.

You can continue to pray for people, but you are not responsible for their choices. The same is true if you see someone who is sinning – you have to be a faithful watchman and warn them. You must faithfully "blow the trumpet". The Bible tells us that we must be – ... *speaking the truth in love,* [so that everyone] *may grow up in all things into Him who is the head – Christ –* (Ephesians 4:15). The object of our speaking God's Word to people is so that they can become mature in Christ. When we live and walk a life of maturity in Christ, the enemy will not be able to find a weak spot for his fiery darts to pierce our armour.

On the other hand you will be held responsible if you do not share the gospel with people or warn them when they are sinning. If you don't have the courage to speak out when you see someone going down the wrong road then you are responsible. You must warn them; you must gather your courage and say, "Listen, man: stop that nonsense!" If you don't warn the person and they fall, then it is your responsibility. As we have been saying, being a watchman is a grave matter; it is not to be taken lightly. We are busy with matters of life and death.

Prayer

My Father, I thank You for Your great and wonderful love to me. I realize that I have a responsibility to share Your good news with other people. Help me not to shrink back from my responsibility. Help me to be faithful to You and Your calling upon my life. Amen.

You have the answers and you have the responsibility to share them.

Don't neglect your responsibilities

Read Ezekiel 33:1–11

"Say to them: 'As I live,' says the Lord GOD, 'I have no pleasure in the death of the wicked, but that the wicked turn from his way and live. Turn, turn from your evil ways! For why should you die, O house of Israel?'" (Ezekiel 33:11)

There it is. God doesn't want any of us to perish. He has given us a responsibility. That responsibility is to tell people. My friend, this is why I do what I do. This is why we have our *Grassroots* television programme. I do what I do for no other reason other than I want to encourage people to "keep-on-keeping-on" for Jesus. People often challenge me for being too radical, too fundamental.

These same people will dangle a red herring in front of me; they challenge the fact that I teach that Jesus is the only Way. They don't like it that I talk about the day of judgment. Exception is taken to the fact that I teach that God is a good God, He is fair but He is also a just God who punishes sin. They often bring up the people in the Amazon who have never heard the gospel. What happens to them, they ask; will they be judged? Well, I believe God will judge each person according to their works. I honestly believe this.

The fact of the matter is, no matter what the red herrings are that you try and bring into the debate, you cannot get away from the truth. I believe that for those who know the truth and still resist God there is no hope. The only way people will be saved is if they are told. The only way they are going to hear is if we speak. As I have often said, this is not only the responsibility of preachers and church leaders; no, we are all responsible. The last few days we have been examining our responsibility to speak to the people in the world around us. However, I want to take you back to your own family. Remember that your role as a watchman starts there. Don't neglect those nearest and dearest to you. Make sure that they hear the gospel. Don't hesitate to speak out when you see your children starting down a wrong path. The old saying "Prevention is better than cure" is a true one.

Prayer

My Father, I worship before You. I accept my responsibility as a watchman who is called to blow the trumpet. I will warn those who are going the wrong way. Particularly I realize that I need to guard my family, looking after them and caring for them. Amen.

The old saying "Prevention is better than cure" is a true one

Evaluate your lifestyle

Read Hebrews 12:12–29

Therefore strengthen the hands which hang down, and the feeble knees, and make straight paths for your feet, so that what is lame may not be dislocated, but rather be healed. Pursue peace with all people, and holiness, without which no one will see the Lord: looking carefully lest anyone fall short of the grace of God... (Hebrews 12:12–15a)

I want to return to the topic of our "walk matching our talk". I encourage you to stop and examine yourself. We are often so busy living life and doing things for God that we don't stop to take stock of our lives. It is important to just pause for a while and evaluate where you are. You need to ask yourself some pertinent questions. As a watchman called by God, is my lifestyle matching up to my title? Do I deserve the title "man of God"? Am I a faithful watchman? It is vitally important that when your family looks at you they see a man who walks his talk. When the people you work with look at your life there must be nothing that they can point a finger at.

I want to remind you that it is not so much what you say that is going to influence people, but rather who you are and how you live. We cannot get away from this. I don't know how many times I have fallen short myself. You know it is very easy to sit here and mouth off, but it is much harder to live the life. We all fall short, including me. Romans 3:23 says: *for all have sinned and fall short of the glory of God.*

Our reading today exhorts us to be careful that no one falls short of the glory of God. *Therefore strengthen the hands which hang down, and the feeble knees, and make straight paths for your feet, so that what is lame may not be dislocated, but rather be healed* (Hebrews 12:12–13). This is our task as God's watchmen. We are meant to strengthen those who are weak. We must prevent those who are in danger of stumbling because their knees have become feeble, from falling. Don't allow your lifestyle to disqualify you from fulfilling your calling as a watchman on the wall. We are all human and when we fail we must be quick to repent and ask for forgiveness. Our lifestyle must not cause anyone to stumble.

Prayer

Father, I recognize that so often I fall short of Your standards. I fail to co-ordinate my life with my talk. Forgive me, I pray. Lord, today I repent before You. I want to be a faithful watchman who will not be disqualified from my calling. Amen.

Our lifestyle must not cause anyone to stumble.

Do not become discouraged

Read Hebrews 12:1–12

For consider Him who endured such hostility from sinners against Himself, lest you become weary and discouraged in your souls. (Hebrews 12:3)

The other thing that can disqualify us from fulfilling our calling as a watchman on the wall is when we allow the cares of this life to weigh us down. We can become so disheartened and burdened that we lose our joy. When this happens our senses become dulled and we are no longer alert to the approach of the enemy. It is one of his favourite tactics: to dishearten and discourage the Saints. My friend, are you discouraged and disheartened today? Are you spending more time looking around you than you are looking to Jesus? Hebrews 12:2 says: *looking unto Jesus, the author and finisher of our faith, who for the joy that was set before Him endured the cross, despising the shame, and has sat down at the right hand of the throne of God.*

Jesus is our example. He did not allow anything to distract or detract Him from His calling. He trusted completely in His heavenly Father. He believed implicitly that His Father would see Him through every trial. It was because of this unshakable belief that He was able to face the cross of Calvary. We are called to live above our circumstances. You cannot afford to be dragged down by what is going on around you. Keep your eyes upon Jesus – He is the *author* and the *finisher* of your faith. This is what sets us apart and makes us different. People need to be able to look at our lives and see how we handle difficult circumstances. Then they will be drawn to Jesus. We will then earn the right to speak into people's lives.

One of the wonderful gifts we have to offer the world around us is hope. Hope in Jesus Christ. Hope of a better life; hope of eternal life. *To them God willed to make known what are the riches of the glory of this mystery among the Gentiles: which is Christ in you, the hope of glory* (Colossians 1:27). This is the precious truth you have to share with the people around you.

Prayer

Father, I come to You in the precious name of Jesus Christ, my Lord and saviour. Jesus, thank You that You are my hope of glory. You are the one to whom I can turn no matter what happens in my life. Help me to share the hope that I have in You with everyone around me. Amen.

One of the wonderful gifts we have to offer the world around us is hope. Hope in Jesus Christ.

Being different for Jesus

Read Philippians 3:1–21

Brethren, join in following my example, and note those who so walk, as you have us for a pattern. (Philippians 3:17)

C an you honestly say that you are living a life that makes you different for Jesus? I am not speaking about being eccentric or weird. I am not referring to the way you dress. What I mean is, do people look at your life and say to themselves, "There is something different about that man." The kind of difference I am referring to is the kind that makes people desire to have what you have. That makes them want to be like you. This does not mean that you take the glory for yourself. It simply means that people recognize Jesus in you and they want Him too.

You are an example one way or the other. Either you are a good example of what it means to be a Christ follower or you are a bad example. Paul was able to say in our reading today: *Brethren, join in following my example…* Can you say the same thing to your sons and daughters, to the people you work with, to your friends? In 1 Thessalonians 1:6–7 Paul commends them: *And you became followers of us and of the Lord, having received the word in much affliction, with joy of the Holy Spirit, so that you became examples to all in Macedonia and Achaia who believe.* The apostle Paul understood his responsibility as a watchman. He understood what it meant to be a soldier of the cross. He lived his life as an example to the church of his day.

Don't let the enemy rob you of your testimony. Be on your guard. In order to be the kind of watchman we are talking about you need to be different. You cannot be lethargic. Looking at my bull terrier lying next to me fast asleep, I cannot help thinking that he is not much of a watchdog. A watchman cannot afford to sleep; he has to remain alert. He has to be different, an example to those around him. He has to be prepared to go the distance. We have an awesome responsibility as God's watchmen over the house of Israel.

Prayer

My Father God, I thank You that You speak to me so clearly through Your Word. I realize that I have to live the kind of life that is a good example to those within my area of influence. I want to be able to say to them, "Follow my example." I know I can only do this as I walk in the grace and power of Your Holy Spirit. Amen.

We have an awesome responsibility as God's watchmen over the house of Israel.

Empowered to be a watchman

Read Acts 1:1–11

"But you shall receive power when the Holy Spirit has come upon you; and you shall be witnesses to Me in Jerusalem, and in all Judea and Samaria, and to the end of the earth." (Acts 1:8)

All the disciples except for John died martyrs' deaths. They say Thomas was pierced with a spear and James, the brother of Jesus, was stoned. Paul, the greatest apostle in the Bible, was beheaded. Peter again was crucified; he asked to be crucified upside down because he didn't consider himself worthy of dying in the same manner that Jesus did. Why? What were their crimes? They weren't thieves or murderers. No – they were watchmen. Faithful watchmen over the house of Israel. They were committed to the task of sharing the truth of God's Word with their world – even if it meant death. It was not even an option for them to shirk from their calling.

They were not always like this though. After Jesus was crucified on Calvary they fell apart. They either ran away or, in the instance of Peter, denied Jesus. Only John remained at the foot of the cross, faithful to Jesus to the end. What changed them? The power of the Holy Spirit changed them. Jesus promised them the Holy Spirit. *"But the Helper, the Holy Spirit, whom the Father will send in My name, He will teach you all things, and bring to your remembrance all things that I said to you"* (John 14:26). *And being assembled together with them, He commanded them not to depart from Jerusalem, but to wait for the Promise of the Father, "which," He said, "you have heard from Me"* (Acts 1:4).

My friends, we too need the infilling of the Holy Spirit. We need His power to be at work in our lives. It is the Holy Spirit who will guide you. He will direct you and help you to understand God's Word. He will give you wisdom to know the right and best thing to do for your family. He will give you the courage to stand firm in your convictions. It is He who will give you the words to speak when you need to "blow the trumpet" of truth. If you lack power then ask God today and He will fill you.

Prayer

My Father, there are times that I feel so inadequate for the task of being Your watchman. I am weak and weary. I need Your power today. Fill me with Your Holy Spirit, I pray. Come upon me as You did upon the disciples in the upper room. Fill me with Holy Ghost power, I pray, so that I can faithfully do Your work. Amen.

If you lack power then ask God today and He will fill you.

Don't be ashamed

Read Romans 1:16–32

For I am not ashamed of the gospel of Christ, for it is the power of God to salvation for everyone who believes, for the Jew first and also for the Greek. (Romans 1:16)

B efore his conversion Paul was full of his own achievements. His pedigree was impeccable and there is no doubt that his attitude was arrogant. After he met Christ on the road to Damascus his whole life changed. The Holy Spirit told Ananias that Paul would suffer much for the sake of the gospel. Paul was tirelessly unashamed of the gospel. His life was dedicated to spreading the gospel of Jesus Christ and to the building up of the body of Christ.

There is no doubt that if anyone had the right to boast then it was Paul. In 2 Corinthians chapter eleven Paul defends his apostleship. He speaks about all the things that he endured for the sake of the gospel. In chapter twelve he goes on to speak about the vision that he had. Then he makes an amazing statement in verse six. *For though I might desire to boast, I will not be a fool; for I will speak the truth. But I refrain, lest anyone should think of me above what he sees me to be or hears from me* (2 Corinthians 12:6). Paul's talk lined up with his walk. He did not speak one thing and live out another. He was consistent in his example to the churches.

His courage came from knowing Jesus. He had a personal encounter with Him and it changed his life. He was not ashamed of the gospel. *For I am not ashamed of the gospel of Christ, for it is the power of God to salvation for everyone who believes, for the Jew first and also for the Greek* (Romans 1:16). Submission comes before power. If you are lacking in power then submit to the Holy Spirit; ask Him to fill you. Then go out and speak up for Jesus and the power will come. It is a bit like electricity. The power is there, but if you don't flick the switch to release the electricity the room will remain in darkness. The power comes when you are not ashamed. You cannot get the power first. Go out there and use what God has given you.

Prayer

My Father God, thank You for the example of the apostle Paul. I am so grateful that You encourage me through Your Word. I pray that as I open my heart to the infilling of Your Holy Spirit You will help me to boldly go out and proclaim Your truth. I want to be a watchman who is not ashamed of the gospel. Amen.

The power comes when you are not ashamed. Go out there and use what God has given you.

Are you hot or cold?

Read Revelation 3:14–22

"I know your works, that you are neither cold nor hot. I could wish you were cold or hot. So then, because you are lukewarm, and neither cold nor hot, I will vomit you out of My mouth." (Revelation 3:15–16)

n South Africa we have many security companies. The watchmen who are employed by these companies work 24-hour shifts. However, one of the most vulnerable times is normally in the early hours of the morning. I often jog in the early morning and in winter I have to wear a light on my head because it is still pitch dark. I often run past some buildings and I see the watchmen on guard duty. They have their jackets and scarves on to protect them against the cold. What are they doing? They are watching to make sure that thieves don't break into the houses or businesses to steal from them.

We have been reading from Ezekiel chapter thirty-three about us being watchmen over the house of Israel. Some years ago I visited England. I preached about what God intends a relationship between a man and a woman to be: Men love your wives; wives submit to your husbands; and God not condoning sex outside of marriage. As a result of this we had the privilege of marrying twelve couples in the UK. The news of this filtered back to South Africa and when I arrived home I had numerous phone calls. A journalist contacted me and said, "I have two questions: Is it alright to have sex before marriage and is it OK to live together before getting married?"

This is an example of where one, as a watchman, has to blow the trumpet of truth. This is not happening in the church today. There is too much compromise. Anything goes! If you look at Revelations 3:15–16: The Lord says: *"I know your works, that you are neither cold nor hot. I could wish you were cold or hot. So then, because you are lukewarm, and neither cold nor hot, I will vomit you out of My mouth."* Who is setting the standard in your home? Do you base your decisions on what God's Word says, or on popular opinion and the culture of the day? Are you hot or cold when it comes to implementing God's standards?

Prayer

My Father God, You have called me to be a watchman, a guard over my home and my family. Help me to make the not-so-popular decisions when it is necessary. Help me to stand true to Your Word and Your principles. Amen.

Are you hot or cold when it comes to implementing God's standards?

Speak out

Read Ezekiel 33:1–6

Again the word of the LORD came to me, saying, "Son of man, speak to the children of your people." (Ezekiel 33:1–2a)

I want to continue with our discussion of yesterday. I asked you the questions: Who is setting the standard in your home? Do you base your decisions on what God's Word says or on popular opinion and the culture of the day? Are you hot or cold when it comes to implementing God's standards? Too many people subscribe to the latest psychology fads instead of the Bible. The journalist I mentioned demanded to know on what grounds I claimed that people must not have sex outside of marriage. I told her that the Bible is clear that sex outside of wedlock is fornication. A lot of churches don't like to preach this because they are scared the congregation will up and leave. However we have been called to be watchmen over the house of Israel and the house of the Christians.

We have an obligation to speak the truth in love. I am not talking about being a policeman; I am talking about being a watchman. We are there to guard the fort. Our job is to guard the principles of the Word of God. We are obligated: first to God, secondly to our family and then to our community and our nation. It's quite simple: until you get married you may not sleep with anyone. It is not OK to live together before you get married. Absolutely not. Why? God made these laws. Not for Himself: He is God. He doesn't need any laws. He is the law. He made them for me and for you. He made them for our benefit.

If your toddler crawled towards an open fireplace and there was a roaring fire in the grate you wouldn't just sit back and say: "Don't do that because you are going to get burnt." You wouldn't watch the child climb into the fire and end up in hospital with third-degree burns. Of course not! You would pluck the child up out of harm's way. Our heavenly Father has rules and regulations so that people won't get burnt. We have to speak out so that people do not mess up their lives.

Prayer

My Father, I come to You in Jesus' name, thanking You for Your grace and mercy. Thank You for Your Word that is so clear about how You want us to live. Help me to be a faithful watchman fearlessly blowing the trumpet of truth. Amen.

We have to speak out so that people do not mess up their lives.

God's ways are fair

Read Ezekiel 33:12–20

"Yet you say, 'The way of the Lord is not fair.' O house of Israel, I will judge every one of you according to his own ways." (Ezekiel 33:20)

We are talking about being watchmen over the house of Israel. God has called you to be a watchman over your house and He has called me to be a watchman over my house. What happens if your children don't obey you? You've got to let them know: "This house is run according to the Word of God. Either you obey God's Word or you have to move on." I am speaking about grown-up children, of course. You don't give up because your children are not serving the Lord. You carry on serving Him, and you continue to pray for them every day. You trust God to honour your prayers. I promise you they will come back as long as you leave the door open. Be ready to welcome them with open arms and not condemnation when they do come back.

People often come to me wanting to know how to handle the fact that they are a Christian and divorced. My answer is always the same; make sure you don't ever do it again. God forgives, but you can't go on doing it. You've got to be accountable and that is where the watchmen come in. There is no place in the Bible where it says: Come to Jesus and all your problems will be over. This is a serious race we are in; it is not a practice run. You get one chance at this life. You're not going to have another opportunity. This is it. After this, it's the judgment.

There are consequences for the choices we make in life. So often you will hear people bemoaning the fact that God is not fair. This is what we saw in our reading today. *"Yet the children of your people say, 'The way of the Lord is not fair'"* (Ezekiel 33:17). The way of the Lord is eminently fair. The problem comes when we don't live according to His commandments and what His Word says. Help your children to understand and commit to God's laws and you will be doing the very best for them as their parent.

Prayer

My Father, I confess that You are a righteous, loving, just and fair God. You are full of mercy and grace to those who come before You with hearts that are humble and contrite. Lord, help me to make wise choices and to teach my loved ones to do the same. Amen.

Help your children to understand and commit to God's law.

A word from the Lord's mouth

Read John 3:1–21

"He who believes in Him is not condemned; but he who does not believe is condemned already, because he has not believed in the name of the only begotten Son of God." (John 3:18)

D o you know why I like the job I have of speaking and sharing the good news with you? I like it because it is not Angus Buchan's opinion; it is God's opinion. You can either believe it or reject it, but you cannot argue with it. God is clear about what He wants from us. Good people don't go to heaven; believers do. The Bible teaches this. I am a Christian, a follower of Jesus Christ, a believer, but I do not judge you. The Word judges you.

If you want a fulfilled, peaceful and fruitful life, do it God's way. There is no short cut. So the Lord says: *"... hear a word from My mouth and warn them for Me"* (Ezekiel 33:7b). Jesus loves you. He died for you. John 3:17–18 says: *"For God did not send His Son into the world to condemn the world, but that the world through Him might be saved. He who believes in Him is not condemned; but he who does not believe is condemned already, because he has not believed in the name of the only begotten Son of God."*

Jesus cannot give you any more than this. He loves you and because of this He has set some commandments in place. He says: "Do it My way and you will have a lovely life." If only we would learn that God's commandments have not been put there to restrict us, but rather to give us freedom. John 8:32 says: *"And you shall know the truth, and the truth shall make you free."* This is God's will for you – He wants you to live in freedom. Obedience to God's Word brings freedom. *"And this is the condemnation, that the light has come into the world, and men loved darkness rather than light, because their deeds were evil. For everyone practicing evil hates the light and does not come to the light, lest his deeds should be exposed. But he who does the truth comes to the light, that his deeds may be clearly seen, that they have been done in God"* (John 3:19–21).

Prayer

Father, I thank You that I know You. I am so grateful, Jesus, that You came to this world to die for me. Thank You that I am Your servant. Help me to faithfully share the good news with everyone that I meet today. Help me to warn them. I want to be a faithful watchman. Amen.

"Hear a word from My mouth and warn them for Me" (Ezekiel 33:7b).

Becoming a holy people

Read Hebrews 12:1–17

Pursue ... holiness, without which no one will see the Lord. (Hebrews 12:14)

O ur obligation as believers is to tell people the truth, to blow the trumpet. On day five of this month I shared with you about the picture God gave me of the medieval castle. The people inside the castle were sound asleep and so was the watchman on top of the wall. The enemy came over the walls and into the city and killed the people. In Ezekiel God is calling us to be watchmen who do not have the blood of other people upon our hands. Our job is to share God's truth; if we don't we are guilty.

Jesus said in Matthew 12:30: *"He who is not with Me is against Me, and he who does not gather with Me scatters abroad."* Why? Because when you are a Christian you cannot be neutral. Taking a stand makes me unpopular with certain people, and I don't mind, as long as it's because I stand by the Word of God. You don't have to be controversial when you are a Christian. You simply have to tell the truth, and automatically you become very unpopular in certain circles. The only thing that counts is that God is pleased with you.

Being a watchman does not mean you are a policeman. You do not walk around carrying a big stick, just waiting for the opportunity to catch your children out because they're not home on time at night. It's not about going around pointing out everyone's sins to them; no, it is telling them about the love of Christ. His love is so contagious that when people encounter it they don't want to go on sinning, because they don't want to hurt God. Remember the other day I told you about the twelve couples that I married in the UK. Well that day the sermon that I preached was from Hebrews 12:14 *Pursue ... holiness, without which no one will see the Lord.* What is holiness? Holiness is the end product of obedience. When we become obedient, we become holy. When we become a holy people, we become a righteous people in the sight of God.

Prayer

Father God, You have called me to live a life of obedience to You. Obedience leads to holiness and holiness to righteousness. Thank You that I stand before You in the righteousness of Jesus Christ, Your Son. Help me to faithfully share Your truth with others. Amen.

When we become obedient, we become holy.

Godliness with contentment

1 Timothy 6:1–16

But you, O man of God, flee these things and pursue righteousness, godliness, faith, love, patience, gentleness. Fight the good fight of faith, lay hold on eternal life, to which you were also called and have confessed the good confession in the presence of many witnesses. (1 Timothy 6:11–12)

Most people are looking for contentment and peace. Everywhere I go both rich people and poor people are searching. Whether they live in Africa or Europe, they are all asking: "What must we do to find peace?" 1 Timothy 6:6 says: *Now godliness with contentment is great gain.* When you are walking in righteousness, you are at peace. When you live outside of God's will you do not have peace. There is something inside of each of us warning us that things are not right. Once we come to Christ and make right with God, we will know great peace and joy.

God's will is like an umbrella. As long as you are under His umbrella, you are safe. When you step out from under the umbrella you are on your own. You step out from under His protection. It is not worth it, my friend. The anguish of mind and soul are poor rewards for living contrary to God's will for our lives. On the other hand the contentment, peace and joy experienced when we follow His ways are wonderful.

The house of Israel refers to the Christians, the believers. We are meant to be blowing the trumpet of truth. The most effective way to blow the trumpet is to live a life of righteousness before God and man. My friends, the divorce rate among Christians is said to be equal to that of the world. This is unacceptable, because God says that he hates divorce (Malachi 2:16). When you made a covenant with your spouse, you said, "Until death us do part." That stands! I am not here to condemn you; I am here to help you to be set free. The Lord is in the business of transforming people. He is in the business of making donkeys into racehorses. This is what He does for us. He took me when I was down and out and He gave me a new life. He wants to do the same for you. He wants to give you a life of contentment, peace and joy.

Prayer

My Father, I bow before You today. Thank You again for Your Word of warning to me. I want to always walk under the shelter of Your umbrella. Help me to faithfully share the true path to contentment, joy and peace with others. Amen.

The contentment, peace and joy of following His ways are wonderful.

Freedom from condemnation

Read Romans 8:1–11

There is therefore now no condemnation to those who are in Christ Jesus, who do not walk according to the flesh, but according to the Spirit. (Romans 8:1)

The gospel is the truth; it is the good news! The good news is this: If you do it God's way, you will live forever. The good news also states that if you do it God's way, you will be free of condemnation. Romans 8:1 says it so beautifully: *There is therefore now no condemnation to those who are in Christ Jesus, who do not walk according to the flesh, but according to the Spirit.* Furthermore the good news is that if you do it God's way, the following is true: *And we know that all things work together for good to those who love God, to those who are the called according to His purpose* (Romans 8:28). This is certainly good news!

As I have said, the Christian's job is not to be a policeman putting people in jail but rather to help set them free from prison. Free from the prison of what? The prison of condemnation! If you are not paying your income taxes, then it is my duty as a watchman to tell you that you have to pay them. You might respond that you cannot afford to pay them. My response to that would be that you cannot afford not to. The money does not belong to you; it belongs to the government. Jesus said: *"Render therefore to Caesar the things that are Caesar's, and to God the things that are God's"* (Matthew 22:21b). Do you understand what I am saying? When you do what is right you will see your business begin to prosper. God honours obedience. We have often looked at the Scripture in 1 Samuel 15:22b: *Behold, to obey is better than sacrifice…*

When you do things God's way you will find that things begin to come right in your life. It doesn't mean that as a Christian you will never know hardship, but it does mean that you can come before God with clean hands. You can bring your petitions before Him with confidence. You can live in freedom, without condemnation, knowing that you are doing things God's way.

Prayer

Father, thank You for the freedom that is mine in Christ Jesus, Your Son. Thank You that as I choose to do things Your way I can know complete freedom and liberty in Your presence. Help me to share this truth with others who need to be set free from their prisons. Amen.

Live in freedom, without condemnation, knowing that you are doing things God's way.

The Son will set you free

Read John 8:31–36

"Therefore if the Son makes you free, you shall be free indeed." (John 8:36)

J esus promised you …*if the Son makes you free, you shall be free indeed.* Are you enjoying this freedom that He promised you? Take an honest look at your life. If you call yourself a Christian, but are not living in this freedom, you need to ask yourself: Am I living my life God's way or my own way? If you are living God's way then you will have freedom and liberty irrespective of your circumstances. You can be locked in a physical prison and still know freedom and liberty. This freedom that we are talking about has nothing to do with your circumstances – it has to do with your heart.

As a watchman over the house of Israel it is your duty to share the freedom you have with those around you. You are not meant to keep the keys to this freedom for yourself. God has tasked you with a commission. It is to warn people about the impending danger of the enemy who wants to steal and pillage from them. I remind you again of Ezekiel 33:7–8: *"So you, son of man: I have made you a watchman for the house of Israel; therefore you shall hear a word from My mouth and warn them for Me. When I say to the wicked, "O wicked man, you shall surely die!' and you do not speak to warn the wicked from his way, that wicked man shall die in his iniquity; but his blood I will require at your hand."*

I don't want your blood on my hands, I love you too much. Ezekiel 33:9 says: *"Nevertheless if you warn the wicked to turn from his way, and he does not turn from his way, he shall die in his iniquity; but you have delivered your soul."* I have a responsibility, first to God and then to you, to tell you the truth. Once I've told you the truth, I can do no more. I cannot force you to follow after God. God created each of us with a free will to choose. What choices will you make today?

Prayer

My Father, thank You for giving me a choice. Help me to always choose Your way. I know that You love me. I know too that You are a just and righteous God. Keep me faithful to You. Help me to share Your freedom with others. Amen.

God created each of us with a free will to choose. What choices will you make today?

Everything but nothing

Read Mark 10:17–31

Then Jesus, looking at him, loved him, and said to him, "One thing you lack: Go your way, sell whatever you have and give to the poor, and you will have treasure in heaven; and come, take up the cross, and follow Me." But he was sad at this word, and went away sorrowful, for he had great possessions. (Mark 10:21–22)

One of the saddest stories in the Bible is that of the rich young ruler. He came from the house of Israel (in other words he was a believer). He came to Jesus looking for freedom. He wanted to know how he could have eternal life. He told Jesus that he had obeyed all the commandments from when he was a young boy. He attended the synagogue; he kept the law. It reminds one again of 1 Samuel 15:22a *"Has the LORD as great delight in burnt offerings and sacrifices, as in obeying the voice of the LORD?"* The rich young ruler was prepared to do all the outward things. He did these with great dedication. It is clear though that they didn't bring him peace and freedom. He was still longing for more.

When Jesus told him what he had to do to gain eternal life he was not prepared to do it. *"One thing you lack: Go your way, sell whatever you have and give to the poor, and you will have treasure in heaven; and come, take up the cross, and follow Me"* (Mark 10:21b). He turned away and left Jesus. The Scripture says: *But he was sad at this word, and went away sorrowful, for he had great possessions* (Mark 10:22). How tragic: The rich young ruler had everything, but at the same time he had nothing. What does this story teach us? Jesus wants us to be prepared to surrender everything to Him. We cannot hold anything back. It is all or nothing, my friend, as the rich young ruler learnt to his sorrow.

Maybe you are a pillar of your community. You might well be a leader in your church. Every time the church doors are open you are sitting in your pew; yet there are things you are witholding from the Lord. If this is the case then you are not going to know freedom. You are not going to enjoy the fruits of eternal life. Jesus says He wants 100 per cent of you. You cannot keep certain doors locked. He will accept nothing less than complete surrender.

Prayer

My Father God, I can identify with the rich young ruler. Lord, forgive me that so often I try to keep certain things back from You. I want to serve You, but I don't want to completely surrender to You. I know that I cannot continue to live like this. I surrender my all to You. Amen.

You cannot keep certain doors locked. He will accept nothing less than complete surrender.

What is God warning you about?

Read Ezekiel 33:1–11

Again the word of the LORD came to me, saying, "Son of man, speak to the children of your people, and say to them: 'When I bring the sword upon a land, and the people of the land take a man from their territory and make him their watchman, when he sees the sword coming upon the land, if he blows the trumpet and warns the people, then whoever hears the sound of the trumpet and does not take warning, if the sword comes and takes him away, his blood shall be on his own head. He heard the sound of the trumpet, but did not take warning; his blood shall be upon himself'" (Ezekiel 33:1–5a).

What is God warning you about today? Are there things that He is convicting you of that you know He wants you to stop doing? It might be pornography. You believe that nobody will ever find out. They will. We all know the saying: "Be sure your sins will find you out". Well, 1 John 1:6 puts it like this: *If we say that we have fellowship with Him, and walk in darkness, we lie and do not practice the truth.*

You need to burn the books. You need to stop going onto those internet sites. God is giving you a second chance. He is warning you. If you are having an affair then break it off, because if you don't you will be exposed. The devil won't expose you, God will, because He wants to save your soul. Paul even talks about this in 1 Corinthians 5:1–5: *It is actually reported that there is sexual immorality among you… And you are puffed up, and have not rather mourned, that he who has done this deed might be taken away from among you… In the name of our Lord Jesus Christ, when you are gathered together, along with my spirit, with the power of our Lord Jesus Christ, deliver such a one to Satan for the destruction of the flesh, that his spirit may be saved in the day of the Lord Jesus.* Take heed of the watchman blowing the trumpet of truth.

Prayer

My Father, I bow in repentance before You today. Forgive me, I pray. Help me to turn away and leave my sin behind me. Amen.

My Father, forgive me that I have not been a faithful watchman. I have not blown the trumpet of truth for my friend who is sinning. Give me the courage to share the truth of Your Word with him. Amen.

Take heed of the watchman blowing the trumpet of truth.

Jesus, the Way to freedom

Read Matthew 5:27–32

"And if your right hand causes you to sin, cut it off and cast it from you; for it is more profitable for you that one of your members perish, than for your whole body to be cast into hell." (Matthew 5:30)

Jesus says that it is better to go to heaven with one eye and one hand rather than to go to hell with two hands and two eyes. Jesus warns, but He doesn't force. Think back to a day or two ago and the story of the rich young ruler. He came to Jesus with a question and Jesus gave him the answer. When the young man chose to turn away and reject what Jesus was telling him to do, Jesus did not run after him. Jesus was sad that he chose to walk away, but He didn't stop him. Jesus didn't call him back and offer him a compromise. He didn't tell him it was OK for him to sell half of his goods. No, the young man had to make the choice; it was all or nothing.

It is the same with us. Jesus died to save us. Through His death on Calvary He gave us everything we need. 2 Peter 1:3 says: … *His divine power has given to us all things that pertain to life and godliness, through the knowledge of Him who called us by glory and virtue.* Jesus does not bargain with us. He doesn't have to, because He is God. He lays it out for us in His Word: "This is the way I want you to walk," and then it is up to us to choose. Proverbs 2:13 says you can … *leave the paths of uprightness to walk in the ways of darkness;* or you can … *walk in the way of goodness, and keep to the paths of righteousness* (Proverbs 2:20).

Jesus said to him, "I am the way, the truth, and the life. No one comes to the Father except through Me" (John 14:6). My friend, Jesus is the only way to freedom. You need to choose freedom for yourself, then you need to make sure that you tell other people how to get it too. You cannot force them to choose Jesus and freedom, but you can give them the option, by telling them. After that it is up to them.

Prayer

Cause me to hear Your loving kindness in the morning, for in You do I trust; cause me to know the way in which I should walk, for I lift up my soul to You (Psalm 143:8). Amen.

Choose freedom for yourself, then you need to make sure that you tell other people how to get it too.

Enter by the narrow gate

Read Matthew 7:7–14

"Enter by the narrow gate; for wide is the gate and broad is the way that leads to destruction, and there are many who go in by it. Because narrow is the gate and difficult is the way which leads to life, and there are few who find it." (Matthew 7:13–14)

I f we are to be watchmen on the walls blowing the trumpet of truth we need to make sure that we know what the Word of God says. We cannot be giving people the wrong message and misleading them. For instance you cannot say that you love Jesus Christ, and then tell people that there are many different ways to get to heaven. According to God's Word all roads do not lead to heaven. There is only one way that leads to heaven and that is through Jesus Christ, the Son of the living God.

Jesus cautioned us in Matthew 7:13–14: *"Enter by the narrow gate; for wide is the gate and broad is the way that leads to destruction, and there are many who go in by it. Because narrow is the gate and difficult is the way which leads to life, and there are few who find it."* One of the most controversial Scriptures is the one that we looked at yesterday in John 14:6: *Jesus said to him, "I am the way, the truth, and the life. No one comes to the Father except through Me."* People don't like this Scripture; it offends them. They get upset, but it is the truth.

If you want to live a victorious life, one that is filled with purpose, then you have to give Jesus Christ your best. Not second best, not the part that is left over, but your very best. I have told you before: He is a jealous God. He says: *"For I, the Lord your God, am a jealous God"* (Exodus 20:5b) and *"for you shall worship no other god, for the LORD, whose name is Jealous, is a jealous God"* (Exodus 34:14). When you hear a man say: "I love Jesus plus…", there is a problem. If you love Him you have to give Him everything and obey His commandments. You are called as a watchman over the house of Israel (the house of the believers). Don't send people mixed messages, my friend. Make sure that you spend time in God's Word so that you can blow the trumpet of truth accurately.

Prayer

My Father, I want to be a watchman worth my salt. I know that in order to share Your Word accurately I need to spend time with You, in Your Word. Help me to give You my best, not what is left over. Help me to make time for You, so that I can know You more. Amen.

Spend time in God's Word so that you can blow the trumpet of truth accurately.

Keeping watch for the prodigal

Read Luke 15:11–52

"But when he was still a great way off, his father saw him and had compassion, and ran and fell on his neck and kissed him." (Luke 15:20b)

The Lord wants transparency from us: so when you become a Christian, you must become transparent. We must wear our hearts on our sleeves, so that people can see what we are about. If you tell someone the truth and they won't listen, there is nothing more you can do apart from praying for them. If you have a rebellious child who will not listen to you, pray for them and love them. Tell them that the door is always open, as long as they are willing to adhere to God's conditions. They are welcome to come home any time, once they have made the choice to begin living by God's rules.

Jesus told the beautiful story of the prodigal son in Luke chapter fifteen. The prodigal son's father never gave up on his son. If we trust and pray, God will bring our prodigal child home too. They will come back and ask for forgiveness. Don't despair and don't give up, whatever you do. Persevere in your prayers and trust in God. This is what a faithful watchman does – he doesn't leave his post because it gets hard. He stays on guard. In the story of the prodigal son it is clear that the father was looking out for his son, waiting for him to come home. Our Scripture says, *But when he was still a great way off, his father saw him…* His father did not forget what he looked like. He faithfully kept guard, watching to see when his son would return.

The father showed his son unconditional love. He didn't hold his sins against him. The son asked for forgiveness and the father forgave him. Too many parents become bitter, hardening their hearts against their prodigal children and also against God. Learn from the father in our story today. Remain strong, keep your testimony, stay on guard and continue to be a faithful watchman worthy of your calling. This is the greatest example that you can set your children. You are a watchman first and foremost over your own household.

Prayer

My Father, You know how much it hurts to see my child not serving You. You know the pain of a father's heart. Keep me faithful to You through this season of my life. Help me to set the example of what it is to be a faithful watchman over my family. Amen.

Be a faithful watchman worthy of your calling. This is the greatest example that you can set your children.

We will serve the Lord

Read Joshua 24:14–28

And the people said to Joshua, "The LORD our God we will serve, and His voice we will obey!" (Joshua 24:24)

W e've got to stand firm. We have to maintain the standards of God's Word at all costs. This will make you unpopular with certain people. For instance if you are at a work function and part of the entertainment is watching "blue movies", what do you do? Do you keep quiet because you don't want to upset the status quo? You don't want to offend the bosses? You are supposed to be a watchman over the house of Israel. You are obligated to stand up and walk out of that pub or wherever it is. Maybe you are too scared to speak up because you could lose your job. Would you rather lose your job or your salvation?

I am asking you today: when the chips are down, who will you serve? I want an honest answer from you before God. We have a saying at Shalom, *Come what may, I will follow the Lord.* Joshua put it this way to the Children of Israel in Joshua 24:15b: *"But as for me and my house, we will serve the LORD."* I want to advise young parents to start early. When your baby is still crawling, begin to bring them up in the fear of the Lord. Proverbs 22:6 says *Train up a child in the way he should go, and when he is old he will not depart from it.*

I have a growing number of grandchildren, but I can honestly tell you that I would hate to be a young parent today. There was enough nonsense going on when I was younger, but I am amazed when I see what young parents today have to put up with. They really need God's wisdom to bring their children up. As a father it is imperative that you are a good watchman over your home. You need to bring your family up in a way that honours God. You need to know His Word so that you can accurately blow the trumpet of truth. Then you will be able to say: "I and my family, we will serve the Lord."

Prayer

My Father, I want to bring my family up in a way that is honouring to You. I commit myself to Your principles and Your Word. I pray that You will give me wisdom and grace. Give me unconditonal love. Give me the resilience to stand against popular culture. I and my family, we will serve You. Amen.

You need to bring your family up in a way that honours God.

The watchman's armour

Read Ephesians 6:10–20

Finally, my brethren… Put on the whole armor of God, that you may be able to stand against the wiles of the devil. (Ephesians 6:10a, 11)

As a watchman you need to be prepared at all times for the attack of the enemy. You cannot afford to let your guard down. Soldiers in an army constantly train and increase their skills. They have to do this, so that should the day come and their country goes to war, they will be ready. It does not help if they allow themselves to become unfit and sluggish. It is too late to start training when the enemy is already approaching or attacking. It is the same with us. We have to be battle ready at all times. Paul gives us a picture in Ephesians chapter six of how God's watchmen are meant to gear up for battle.

I want you to spend time today asking God to help you to use these articles of armour in your life. Don't go out to face the battles of the day without being fully clothed and protected. This armour will keep you alert and battle ready; it will protect you as you face the enemy. You will be ready for his attacks. Paul says we should put them on so that we can … *be strong in the Lord and in the power of His might* (Ephesians 6:10b). You do not face the battle alone. It has been said that the reason the soldier doesn't have armour on his back is because he is meant to be on the offensive, moving forward. God has your back – He will protect you. Ephesians chapter six doesn't speak about running away from the enemy – it speaks about facing him head on.

Shielded by God's armour you must protect your family. Paul says: *For we do not wrestle against flesh and blood, but against principalities, against powers, against the rulers of the darkness of this age, against spiritual hosts of wickedness in the heavenly places.* It is a bloody battle out there, but we are not unarmed; we are not unprepared. *Therefore take up the whole armor of God, that you may be able to withstand in the evil day, and having done all, to stand* (Ephesians 6:12, 13).

Prayer

My Father, thank You that You have not left me without protection as I face the battle. Help me to appropriate each piece of the the armour You have given me. Help me to stand firm. Make me a worthy watchman who blows the trumpet of truth faithfully. Amen.

We have to be battle ready at all times.

A watchman over my House

Read Ezekiel 33:1–20

"So you, son of man: I have made you a watchman for the house of Israel; therefore you shall hear a word from My mouth and warn them for Me." (Ezekiel 33:7)

We have the awesome responsibility of being called to be a watchman by God. First, we are a watchman over our family, then the body of Christ, the church. We are also a watchman over those we work with and the people who work for us. Then we are called to guard our communities and our nation. Our charge is to blow the trumpet of truth. We are to warn people and share God's love and His laws with them. First and foremost, we have to ensure that we are living a life worthy of our calling in the Lord. You cannot go around telling other people how they should live if you are not living right yourself. Your greatest area of influence is in your own home. You are called to love your wife and your children. You set the example of what it means to be a watchman who lives true to his calling.

God has given us all we need to be able to do this. We have His Word. He has given us His Holy Spirit, who guides us and leads us into all truth. We looked at the armour of God in Ephesians chapter six yesterday. This is the protection that God has developed and given to us so that we do not face the enemy defenceless. We are told to: *Stand therefore, having girded your waist with truth, having put on the breastplate of righteousness, and having shod your feet with the preparation of the gospel of peace; above all, taking the shield of faith with which you will be able to quench all the fiery darts of the wicked one. And take the helmet of salvation, and the sword of the Spirit, which is the word of God.* Lastly Paul says, *praying always with all prayer and supplication in the Spirit, being watchful to this end with all perseverance and supplication for all the saints* (Ephesians 6:14–18). Take up God's armour and stand firm as a watchman over the House of Israel. *If God is for us, who can be against us?* (Romans 8:31).

Prayer

My Father, this has been an amazing month. Thank You for the calling You have placed upon my life to be a watchman over the house of Israel. Thank You for my family, for the church, for my community and my country. Keep me faithful as I share Your truth with those You have entrusted to me. Amen.

If God is for us, who can be against us?

JUNE

Now is the time ... to be a spiritual leader

Needed – spiritual role models

Whom can we imitate?

Don't back the wrong jockey

Imitate me, as I imitate Christ

A new creation

Set your feet upon the rock

He will establish your steps

Imitating Christ

Let your yes be yes

Repent and be filled with the Spirit

Freedom in Jesus

Looking forward…

Qualifications for spiritual leadership

God looks upon the heart

Guarding your heart

Servant heart

The greatest must be the least

Know who you are in Jesus

Jesus the servant leader

Following Jesus' example

A spiritual leader is humble

Love your enemies

Coming back from failure

Be compassionate

Count your words

The spirit of Elijah

Prophet, priest and king

Absence makes the heart grow fonder!

Your primary responsibility

A servant heart

Needed – spiritual role models

Read Philippians 4:4–9

The things which you learned and received and heard and saw in me, these do, and the God of peace will be with you. (Philippians 4:9)

People are searching for role models in this world. Especially young folks need mentors they can look up to. They want to know how they are going to get through this life, yet there are so few spiritual fathers to help them. Spiritual fathers are desperately needed in these last days – men whose lifestyle others can copy, men who can be emulated. We need men whom we can look up to. It is so sad that we all too often hear of so-called spiritual fathers falling – men in leadership who sin and as a result lose their testimony, bringing disgrace upon the Lord.

Paul had been coaching and teaching the Philippians. In his letter he instructs them: *Finally, brethren, whatever things are true, whatever things are noble, whatever things are just, whatever things are pure, whatever things are lovely, whatever things are of good report, if there is any virtue and if there is anything praiseworthy – meditate on these things.* Then he concludes with our key text: *The things which you learned and received and heard and saw in me, these do, and the God of peace will be with you* (Philippians 4:8, 9).

If you want to be a good runner, then get alongside a world champion sprinter and train with him. If you want to be a good rugby player, then play with a Springbok rugby player. If you want to be a good farmer, find a successful farmer who is making lots of money to mentor you – not a farmer who is going bankrupt. In order to succeed you need to imitate somebody who is successfully doing what you want to do. Otherwise you will fail. Paul lived out what he taught; therefore he was able to tell the Philippians to emulate him, to do the things they saw him do. They were to speak the way he spoke. He was their example of what it meant to be a spiritual leader. I wonder how many of us can truthfully invite people to say and do the things we do; to live the way we live?

Prayer

My Father, I thank You for Your Word to me today. Once again, Lord, You are speaking to me. I realize that You are calling me to be a spiritual leader whom people can look up to. I have a responsibility to walk my talk. Amen.

I wonder how many of us can truthfully invite people to live the way we live?

Whom can we imitate?

Read Philippians 4:4–9

The things which you learned and received and heard and saw in me, these do, and the God of peace will be with you. (Philippians 4:9)

We will spend another day in Philippians chapter four. You will notice this year we are spending more time in some portions of Scripture. We aren't always moving to a different portion each day. It is important for the Word of God to take root in our lives. It needs to settle into our hearts, our spirits and our minds. We need to meditate upon it. Psalm 119:103 says: *How sweet are Your words to my taste, sweeter than honey to my mouth!* God's Word is our manual for life.

It would appear that the worse things get – the uglier people become and the more ungodly they behave – the cooler they are considered to be. For instance look at some of the young film stars who become caught up in all kinds of sin and immorality. You read about them taking overdoses of drugs and dying. Sadly this is an all-too-common occurrence. They do this because they are emulating someone. After all, we all imitate someone. The question is: whom do you choose to imitate? On the other hand, are you the kind of person that someone else can imitate? Paul didn't start out as someone you would choose as a role model. He persecuted the Christians; he hunted them down, had them arrested and persecuted. He was the person who guarded the coats of the men who stoned Stephen to death in Acts: *And the witnesses laid down their clothes at the feet of a young man named Saul* (Acts 7:58b).

A while later Paul met Jesus Christ and he was a changed man. He fell in love with Jesus. His life was radically different after his encounter with Jesus. He became an imitator of the Lord Jesus Christ. He lived like Jesus and for Jesus. This is why he could invite the Philippians to imitate him. It wasn't because he was so good, but because Jesus in him was the answer. Ultimately there is only one person whom we can imitate. His name is Jesus Christ and He is the Son of the living God.

Prayer

My Father, I thank You for Your Son, Jesus Christ, my Lord and saviour. Jesus, I bow before You and worship You today. You are everything to me. I realize that as long as I keep my eyes focused upon You I need never stumble or fall. Amen.

Ultimately there is only one person whom we can imitate. His name is Jesus Christ.

Don't back the wrong jockey

Read 1 Corinthians 4:6–21

Therefore I urge you, imitate me. (1 Corinthians 4:16)

A very wealthy American with a net worth of around 250 million US dollars was asked what his secret was for making so much money. They wanted to know what had made him successful. You know what his answer was? He told them that when he looked at buying a company he was not interested in the financial statements. He said that he "backed the jockey and not the horse". He looked at the CEO of the company. He met the staff. Once he had done this he made his decision whether to buy the company or not. This man was a multi-millionaire. He was an economist, with a brilliant brain. He wanted to meet the men, because he knew that is where the power is.

This month we are looking at becoming a spiritual leader. In order to become a spiritual leader you need to develop spiritual character. You need to follow someone who is going to take you to the finish line. Sometimes the problem, especially with young people, is that they follow the wrong person. That is why they land up down a cul-de-sac. A cul-de-sac is a road that comes to a dead end. When you land up in a cul-de-sac you have to make a U-turn. Then you have to go all the way back to the beginning and start again. Some people seem to spend their whole lives going down cul-de-sacs. They continually back the "wrong jockey".

Again we turn to the apostle Paul: *I do not write these things to shame you, but as my beloved children I warn you. For though you might have ten thousand instructors in Christ, yet you do not have many fathers; for in Christ Jesus I have begotten you through the gospel. Therefore I urge you, imitate me. For this reason I have sent Timothy to you, who is my beloved and faithful son in the Lord, who will remind you of my ways in Christ, as I teach everywhere in every church* (1 Corinthians 4:14–17). The world needs spiritual leaders who can be role models for others.

Prayer

My Father, I realize that as a human being my judgment is often flawed. I tend to look at the outward appearances of people. You look at the heart. Help me to learn from You. I want to be the kind of role model that other people can look up to. Make me a spiritual leader who brings honour to You. Amen.

The world needs spiritual leaders who can be role models for others.

Imitate me, as I imitate Christ

Read 1 Corinthians 11:1–12

Imitate me, just as I also imitate Christ. (1 Corinthians 11:1)

Fathers, you are role models for your children. You are the head of your home. You are the authority figure. You are the one that they watch. They look to see how you handle situations. You cannot talk one thing and live another in front of your family. They will notice and they will call you on it. You cannot expect your children to behave one way if you behave another. I want to tell you this is scary stuff. It might shock you to know that this scares me. I know that I am a rotten sinner inside. I know there is nothing good in me. However, I know that the one I am following and imitating is perfect.

It might seem outrageous of Paul, who after all was only a man like you and me, to say, "imitate me". In other words: do exactly what I do. He says: *Imitate me, just as I also imitate Christ*. He could say this because he could also say, "I am doing what God does". As Christians we should all be able to say: *Imitate me, just as I also imitate Christ*. However, there are very few of us who can say this because our lives do not match up with what we are saying. I have a real heart for young people. Young people are the future of our nation: the future of this world. So many times they are disappointed by the way adults behave. If you are a young person don't follow man, follow God.

Fathers, your son is not going to do what you tell him to do. Your son is going to do what you do. I have seen this time and time again. I have two sons; both of them are farmers. This is not a coincidence, because I am a farmer. One of my daughters has married a farmer. The other daughter has married a forester. These too are not coincidences. Your children will not do what you tell them to do. They will do what you do. What kind of an example are you?

Prayer

My Father, I realize that I am the book that my children read every day of their lives. Help me to live in such a way that I can say to them: *Imitate me, just as I also imitate Christ*. Amen.

Your children will not do what you tell them to do. They will do what you do.

A new creation

Read 2 Corinthians 5:12–20

Therefore, if anyone is in Christ, he is a new creation; old things have passed away; behold, all things have become new. (2 Corinthians 5:17)

Yesterday I asked you, "What kind of an example are you?" I want to continue talking about this today. If you smoke you cannot tell your children not to. They won't believe you when you tell them it is bad for their health and that they will not succeed at sport. As sure as I am sitting here, they will smoke. They will smoke because they are imitating you. Maybe you are having an affair and you think nobody knows; I am telling you your kids will know about it. Yes they will. And guess what? As soon as they grow up they will do exactly the same. If you beat up your wife, sir, I can tell you right now your sons will grow up to be wife beaters. Even if they detest you and hate you for doing it to their mother, they will do it.

I have seen these things many times as I have counselled people. If you have a drinking problem, sir, look at your ancestors and you will soon discover where it comes from. This may all sound very negative, but unfortunately we have to face up to the truth. Last month we spoke about the watchman blowing the trumpet of truth. I love you too much to keep silent about these things, my friend. I am so pleased to tell you today that there is good news. You don't have to live like this. It doesn't matter what your heritage is. Maybe you were not blessed to have a godly heritage. That is alright. You can cut the past off. You can make a new beginning. You can start a new heritage.

2 Corinthians 5:17 says: *Therefore, if anyone is in Christ, he is a new creation; old things have passed away; behold, all things have become new.* We can cut off those spiritual roots. We can cut them off in the name of Jesus Christ and you can start afresh. This is the good news. You don't have to continue committing the sins your forefathers did. You are a new creation in Christ Jesus.

Prayer

My Father, I give You thanks and praise for Your amazing grace to me. Thank You that it doesn't matter where I come from, only where I am going. I want to begin a new tradition of righteousness and holiness in my family. Amen.

It doesn't matter what your heritage is. You can start a new tradition.

Set your feet upon the rock

Read Psalm 40

He also brought me up out of a horrible pit, out of the miry clay, and set my feet upon a rock, and established my steps. He has put a new song in my mouth – Praise to our God; many will see it and fear, and will trust in the LORD. (Psalm 40:2–3)

The Scripture we read yesterday in 2 Corinthians 5:17 is one of my favourite Scriptures. Before Jesus made me a new creation I was a drinking man; I smoked and I had a foul mouth. What brought about the change? I found someone I could imitate. His name is Jesus Christ, the Son of the living God. He changed my life and He also changed the life of each one of my family. My children don't smoke and they don't drink. They all love Jesus Christ. Not because of what I told them, no sir; hopefully because of the change they saw in my life.

You will no doubt be familiar with the saying, "Words are cheap, but money buys the whiskey". I shouldn't use a saying like that, should I? Maybe not, but we are talking about real issues. What this saying means is: don't talk about it, do it. Nike's slogan – "Just do it" – expresses the same thing. Another one you will know is: "Put your money where your mouth is". My friends, God has reached down from heaven and He has given you everything you need to live a Godly life. If you are in a horrible pit, if you are mired in the mud today then reach out to Him. Don't spend another minute there.

Psalm 40 is a beautiful piece of Scripture that speaks to us about God's grace and mercy. He will hear your cry. *Blessed is that man who makes the LORD his trust* (Psalm 40:4a). Come to God today. Allow Him to set your feet upon the rock, Jesus Christ. Let Him establish your steps. In place of the foul language He will put a new song in your mouth. You will sing praises to your God. The result of this change in your life will be that many will see it and they will come to know the Lord. They too will trust in Him. You can rewrite your own story as well as the story of your family today. Come to Jesus and let Him make you a new creation.

Prayer

My Father, I come to You in the precious name of Jesus, my saviour and Lord. Father, thank You for Your grace and wonderful mercy towards me. You have promised me a firm road upon which to walk. You have given me Your Word that You will put a new song in my mouth. I am so grateful to You. Amen.

Allow Him to set your feet upon the rock, Jesus Christ. Let Him establish your steps.

He will establish your steps

Read Psalm 40

He also brought me up out of a horrible pit, out of the miry clay, and set my feet upon a rock, and established my steps. (Psalm 40:2)

I want you to read Psalm 40 again today because you need to take special note of where it says *"and established my steps"*. Having established steps speaks of dependability, integrity, doing what you say you are going to do, being honourable and being trustworthy. These are all characteristics of a spiritual leader. Too many guys promise the world and never deliver on their promises. They are going to do this and they are going to do that. I want to tell you something, gentlemen: some of your wives are not submitting to you because you don't deliver the goods.

You are always promising to fix up the house, but you never do it. You promise to attend your child's sports day, but you are never there. Then you wonder why your wife doesn't respect you and she doesn't submit to you. She doesn't respect you because you don't deserve it. We need to get real. Christianity is a real faith. It is not a religion. It is a way of life. Jesus is asking you today, are you worth imitating? This is a heavy one. Are you really worth imitating? You can only say by the grace of God I am.

To be worth imitating you need to be a man whose steps are established. Your word needs to be your bond. You need to stand by your principles no matter what the consequences. When you become this kind of a man you will begin to see the change in your marriage, your family, your business, your career and your social circle. Not everyone will like what they see, because we know that the devil is out to get us when we stand up for Jesus. My friend, upsetting the devil is the least of your worries, I promise you. If you want to be a spiritual leader then you need to be someone worth imitating. You need to be the watchman blowing the trumpet of truth. This means that you stand for truth as well as declaring truth.

Prayer

My Father, I want to be a man whose steps are established. Someone on whom people can rely. I want to be a spiritual leader to my family and those within my area of influence. Help me to walk my talk, I pray. Amen.

You need to be a man whose steps are established. You need to stand for truth as well as declare truth.

Imitating Christ

Read John 14:15–31

Jesus answered and said to him, "If anyone loves Me, he will keep My word; and My Father will love him, and We will come to him and make Our home with him." (John 14:23)

When I came to Jesus Christ I was at the end of my tether. I couldn't go on any longer. I had tried to imitate many different people and every single time I was disappointed. Then one day I met a person. Not a religion. Not a faith. No: I met a person. His name is Jesus Christ. So many young people share with me that the leaders they have looked up to have fallen and failed them. They have either divorced their wives, been found with their "fingers in the till", or gone off on some tangent or other. I want to tell you this: I didn't give my life to a preacher. I didn't give my life to a denomination; nor for that matter to a religion. No, sir, I gave my life to a man. His name is Jesus Christ and He has never ever once in all the years let me down.

If you read the Gospels of Matthew, Mark, Luke and John, you will read about Jesus' lifestyle and it is certainly worth imitating. You never hear about Him beating up a woman or molesting a child. He never took money from the poor. In fact He took money from the rich and gave it to the poor. He looked after the little ones. He cared for the widows and the orphans. Remember he told the story about the old widow and the rich man bringing their offerings to the temple. The rich man wanted everybody to see him as he put his big sack of gold in the offering bag. On the other hand the widow was ashamed because she only had a brass farthing to put in the bag. Jesus said the woman gave more to the kingdom of God than the rich man.

Who are you looking up to? Jesus will never fail you, He will never disappoint you and He will never forsake you. One thing I have learnt about Jesus as I have come to know Him is that He is not a liar. I want to imitate Jesus.

Prayer

My Father, I thank You that I can come into Your presence in Jesus' name. Jesus, thank You that You are my example in all things. Thank You for the life You lived on earth. Thank You that in Your Word I can clearly read and understand how You want me to live. Help me to imitate You by keeping Your commandments. Amen.

Jesus will never fail you, He will never disappoint you and He will never forsake you. I want to imitate Jesus.

Let your yes be yes

Read Matthew 5:33–37

"But let your 'Yes' be 'Yes,' and your 'No,' 'No.' For whatever is more than these is from the evil one." (Matthew 5:37)

One of the biggest problems when it comes to spiritual character is people telling lies. In the past I was taken to task because I tended to exaggerate. This was not a joke; it was very real. If I said it was 1,000, it was actually 500. If I said it was 500, it was fifty. My mom and dad told me I did this as a child. I have had to address this tendency of mine. As you know there is no such a thing as exaggeration. What I was actually doing was lying. There is truth and then there are lies. There is nothing in the middle. You know what? Sooner or later your lies will find you out. I have had to repent of telling lies.

Who are you imitating, I ask you? This is the burning question about spiritual character. As a small boy I remember that a farmer's word was his bond. When someone told a farmer that he wanted to buy his entire maize crop – 100 hectares of maize, averaging 6 tons a hectare, which is 600 tons of maize, at 2,000 rand a hectare – the farmer would stretch out his hand and they would shake on it and it would be a deal. The buyer told the farmer that he would come back in the winter, when the farmer had harvested the crop, to collect the maize he had purchased. He paid the money up front and walked away; no contracts were signed, no lawyers, nothing – only their word.

My dear friend, this is spiritual character; it shows trustworthiness and honour. A gentleman's agreement. You rarely see this any more and yet this is what people need to see. If you say you will do something, you must do it. If you don't want to do it, don't say you will. Honour your word and God will honour you. Remember if you are a man of character you will … *let your "Yes" be "Yes," and your "No," "No."* If you live like this you will honour your Father.

Prayer

My Father, I ask You to forgive me that so often I lie and then pass it off as "exaggerating". You have spoken to me today through Your Word. Help me, I pray, to be a man whose "yes is yes" and whose "no is no". Amen.

If you say you will do something, you must do it. Honour your word and God will honour you.

Repent and be filled with the Spirit

Read 1 John 1:1–10

If we confess our sins, He is faithful and just to forgive us our sins and to cleanse us from all unrighteousness. If we say that we have not sinned, we make Him a liar, and His word is not in us. (1 John 1:9–10)

Maybe as you read this you are feeling that you have made a mess of your life. You have been a bad example to your children. You have not treated your wife as you should have. At work you have also been a bad example to your staff. If this is the case then you know what you must do: Yes, that is right, you must repent. What does it mean to repent? Repentance means starting again. No matter how bad things are it is never too late to repent. This is the good news of the gospel.

I remember an old Methodist minister, whose name was Tom Parker. He and his wife, Gladys, came from Yorkshire. One day as he stood in front of his congregation he realized that he was dry and he had nothing more to preach. He hadn't met with the Holy Spirit and so he was just going through the motions. On that day he humbled himself in front of his congregation. He got down on his knees at the altar and he started to weep. He asked the congregation to pray for him. All the people gathered around him and laid their hands on the old man. They prayed for him and he was filled with the Holy Spirit. His ministry changed from that day forward and he became a dynamic man of God. Tom Parker had more of an impact on my life than most other people have had.

What about you today, sir? Are you making an impact on your family? If not, come before God in repentance. It is time for you to make a new start. Admit your sins and your failures to God. Kneel in His presence. Meet with His Holy Spirit. Allow Him to fill you with His power and His purpose. Walk in the Spirit day by day and He will lead you into all truth. He will restore your witness and help you to maintain it no matter what the temptation. Don't settle for second best. Be a man who has spiritual character, a man worth imitating.

Prayer

My Father, I come before You and I repent today. Forgive me, I pray, for… I thank You that Your Word says that if I confess my sins You will forgive me and cleanse me from all unrighteousness. Fill me with Your Holy Spirit so that I can walk in Your ways. Amen.

Meet with His Holy Spirit today. Allow Him to fill you with power and with purpose.

Freedom in Jesus

Read Galatians 5:1, 16–26
Stand fast therefore in the liberty by which Christ has made us free, and do not be entangled again with a yoke of bondage. (Galatians 5:1)

In June we celebrate Father's Day. We honour our fathers. Men, what has been your reaction as you have been reading the devotionals this month? During May we looked at what it means to be a watchman called by God to guard your family. This month so far we have been looking at spiritual character. Maybe you are a man who by God's grace is enjoying a rich and full spiritual life. You have an ongoing, growing relationship with Jesus. You walk each day in the Spirit. You are human and have your faults like every man, but your heart is for God. You have a good, solid marriage and a family you are proud of and for which you are grateful to God.

On the other hand you may be someone who has made many mistakes and you have not managed to overcome them. Your life is not going well and you are at the end of your tether. Your marriage is in crisis and your family is in turmoil. As I have told you many times, I know what you are going through. I have been there. Or it could be that you love God but you come from a bad heritage. You have not had good role models. You constantly fall back into patterns you learnt growing up. You want to live differently but don't seem to be able to break the bonds.

My friends, if you fall into the first category, give God the glory and continue to enjoy Him. If you fall into either of the other categories – hear me today – it can stop now. Come to God. Repent. Turn from your sin. Cut off the influences of the past and choose to follow Jesus only. From today onward we are going to look at how you can build into your life so that you can become the spiritual leader you are meant to be. It doesn't matter what your past has been like; Jesus is the one you must imitate. Which category do you fall into and what are you going to do about it?

Prayer

My Father, thank You for Your grace and mercy. I bow in Your presence. I am so grateful that I can come to You just as I am. I thank You for Jesus, my saviour. Thank You that I can make a clean start. I love You, Lord, and thank You for Your love for me. Amen.

It doesn't matter what your past has been like; Jesus is the one you must imitate.

Looking forward ...

Read 2 Timothy 2:1–19

And the things that you have heard from me among many witnesses, commit these to faithful men who will be able to teach others also. (2 Timothy 2:2)

If you are a man who is able to thank God for a life that is orderly and functioning according to God's principles, then I have a word for you today. You need to find a man who is struggling and help him. Jesus may be the only one that we can imitate, but you have a responsibility to share God's goodness with others. You need to share the life lessons you have learnt. You need to share God's principles with someone who has not had your opportunities. Pray and ask God to show you someone to approach. Then befriend them and walk alongside them. Pray for them. Be a watchman over them. Blow the trumpet of truth: share God's Word with them. If you haven't done this before, I promise you, it will be one of the most rewarding things you will ever do.

If you are someone who has messed up, or someone who, because of a bad heritage, is struggling to get it right, then I want you to find a mentor. Pray and ask God to show you a man of God whom you can approach to mentor you. When God shows you whom, then go to that person and ask him to walk with you and teach you what God has taught him. A word of caution here. Remember the responsibility for your relationship with the Lord always rests first and foremost with you. No one else can take responsibility for it. However, you can learn a lot from someone who has walked further down the road than you have.

Jesus is and always will be the one that you imitate. So don't expect that your mentor will be perfect. He is a man like you are. However, the relationship that you can enjoy will be a blessing to both of you. You will have the opportunity to see how someone deals with life using Scripture as their manual and how the Holy Spirit leads them in all things. We are the body of Christ; we are meant to be there for each other.

Prayer

My Father, thank You that I am a part of Your body of believers. I am so grateful that I do not have to walk alone. I have Jesus, I have Your Holy Spirit and I have my brothers in Christ. Help me to be open to learning from others. Amen.

Pray and ask God to show you a man of God whom you can approach to mentor you.

Qualifications for spiritual leadership

Read Matthew 4:18–22; Mark 2:13–14; 3:13–19

Then He said to them, "Follow Me, and I will make you fishers of men." They immediately left their nets and followed Him. (Matthew 4:19–20)

What does it take to qualify as a spiritual leader? If we look at Jesus' leadership team we get a good understanding of God's requirements. As you read the Gospels you see how Jesus went about the process of choosing His team. It is interesting because He didn't do it in the same way that we probably would. As the head of a corporation, if you were choosing your top management team, you wouldn't in all likelihood choose any of the men that Jesus chose. None of them would qualify. If you were choosing the leadership for your church then you probably wouldn't choose any of them either. This leads us to wonder what is it that God looks for when He chooses spiritual leaders.

Clearly it is not perfection, nor is it education. It is not superior intellect and it certainly isn't based on class, social standing or how much money you have. So what does He look for? If you look at the calling process of each of the disciples there are a few things they have in common. Jesus called them and they responded. They were willing to drop everything and follow Him. They left their jobs, they left their homes; they left everything behind to follow Him. It certainly didn't make them perfect. They continually messed up. They made mistakes and ultimately they all fled when Jesus was arrested and crucified (all excepting John of course).

You might think they were the ultimate failures, but Jesus knew what He was doing. After His resurrection and ascension, the Holy Spirit came. Each of these men was baptized and filled with the Spirit. They went out and they changed their world. Jesus' faith in them was not misplaced. He knew exactly what He was doing. He has the same belief in you. What qualifies you as spiritual leadership material? Your willingness to heed Jesus' calling on your life. Your decision to follow Him and your wholehearted obedience to Him and His will for your life. These are the qualifications for being a spiritual leader – do you pass muster?

Prayer

My Father, thank You for speaking into my life today. I am so encouraged when I look at Your criteria for spiritual leadership. I choose to heed Your call today. I give myself wholeheartedly over to Your will for my life and the life of my family. I want to serve You faithfully. Amen.

Wholehearted obedience to Jesus and His will for your life qualifies you to be a spiritual leader.

God looks upon the heart

Read 1 Samuel 16:1–13

But the LORD said to Samuel, "Do not look at his appearance or at his physical stature, because I have refused him. For the LORD does not see as man sees; for man looks at the outward appearance, but the LORD looks at the heart." (1 Samuel 16:7)

Have you ever looked at somebody and wondered why God chose them for a particular task? Our human inclination is to question what God sees in that person. The truth is God does not judge the way we judge. In our reading today we clearly see this. He tells Samuel very clearly, the Lord does not see as man sees. God knows only too well that man looks at the outward appearance. God says to Samuel that He looks at the heart. When God looks at your heart what does He see?

Does He see someone who loves Him above everything and everyone else? He is a jealous God and He doesn't want anything or anyone else to be more important to us than He is. David loved God; he knew God. While tending his father's sheep he had plenty of time to grow in his relationship with God. He learnt to trust God. He knew that God would protect him and keep him safe. Trusting God meant that he was willing to obey God even in the face of great odds. This is why he could face Goliath.

You can hide the contents of your heart from most people if you try hard enough. Well, you can do it for a certain period of time, anyway. You know the saying: "You can fool some of the people some of the time, but you cannot fool all of the people all of the time." Jesus has this to say about the matter: "*A good man out of the good treasure of his heart brings forth good; and an evil man out of the evil treasure of his heart brings forth evil. For out of the abundance of the heart his mouth speaks*" (Luke 6:45). When we are under pressure what is inside of our heart usually comes spilling out. Do you trust God when the chips are down, when the pressure is on? Is He the one that you turn to? One of the marks of a true spiritual leader is showing grace under fire.

Prayer

My Father, I am always amazed at Your faith in me. You see way beneath the surface. Thank You that You look at my heart. It is what You see inside that makes the difference. Father, help me to trust You no matter what happens. Amen.

One of the marks of a true spiritual leader is showing grace under fire.

Guarding your heart

Read Proverbs 4:20–27

Keep your heart with all diligence, for out of it spring the issues of life. (Proverbs 4:23)

I t is from the heart that both good and evil stem. We act upon what is in our hearts. Therefore it is of vital importance that we learn to guard our hearts. It is an important principle for spiritual leaders to learn. When you fill your mind with God's Word then your heart will be pure. Proverbs puts it like this: *My son, give attention to my words; incline your ear to my sayings. Do not let them depart from your eyes; keep them in the midst of your heart; for they are life to those who find them, and health to all their flesh* (Proverbs 4:20–22).

In Jeremiah 17:9 we read: *"The heart is deceitful above all things, and desperately wicked; who can know it?"* Your heart cannot be relied upon to make wise decisions of its own volition. Matthew 15:19 says: *"For out of the heart proceed evil thoughts, murders, adulteries, fornications, thefts, false witness, blasphemies."* Paul warns us in 2 Timothy 2:22: *Flee also youthful lusts; but pursue righteousness, faith, love, peace with those who call on the Lord out of a pure heart.* We must keep God's Word hidden in our hearts. When God's Word is our plumbline for living, then we will know the right thing to do; our hearts and our minds will be "talking the same language". *Your word is a lamp to my feet and a light to my path* (Psalm 119:105).

What comes out of your heart: curses, unbelief and pessimism; or praise, faith and optimism? Hatred, gossip, slander and malice; or love, joy, peace and encouragement? Matthew 12:35 says: *"A good man out of the good treasure of his heart brings forth good things, and an evil man out of the evil treasure brings forth evil things."* These are the choices that are before you today. If you want to be a spiritual leader to your family, to your fellow believers and the people with whom you work, you need to guard your heart. From it flows either life or death. Which do you choose today?

Prayer

My Father, I open my heart to You today. Shine the light of Your Spirit into every corner of it. Illuminate those things that need to go. Help me to faithfully hide Your Word in my heart so that it will be my plumbline for all I desire, think, say and do. Amen.

If you want to be a spiritual leader you need to guard your heart.

Servant heart

Read Matthew 20:20–28

"And whoever desires to be first among you, let him be your slave – just as the Son of Man did not come to be served, but to serve, and to give His life a ransom for many."
(Matthew 20:27–28)

The disciples had once again got it all wrong. Who can blame them? As you look around the world today (and sadly we cannot exclude the church), men who are in leadership often seem to be out for their own gain. As you know, I have nothing against money and success. I am grateful to God that He has seen fit to give me and my family success. However, our success is never to be at the expense of other people or the ministry. In other words you do not serve God in order to feather your own nest.

Serving God means that you surrender everything to Him. Your hopes, your dreams and your aspirations – you lay them at the foot of the Cross. You become the least. He is the one who will raise you up and bless you as He sees fit. The mother of the sons of Zebedee asked Jesus if her sons could sit on either side of Him in heaven. Jesus replied that with great honour comes great sacrifice. Naturally the other disciples were peeved when they heard about this. Jesus used the situation as an opportunity to teach them a lesson about spiritual leadership.

He points out to them that the rulers of this world lord it over those who are under them. This is not how a spiritual leader behaves. A true spiritual leader is one who has a servant's heart. Jesus says, *"…whoever desires to become great among you, let him be your servant"* (Matthew 20:26b). In other words you are a leader for the purpose of serving. God calls you first and foremost to be a servant leader to your family. You are meant to model for your wife and children what the heart of a servant leader looks like. Remember your children will imitate you. They will either grow up with a heart to serve God and others or they will grow up thinking that the world owes them. It is up to you, so set a Godly example for your family to follow.

Prayer

My Father, I thank You that You have given me a clear blueprint of what it means to be a servant leader. Jesus, thank You for Your example. Help me to walk in Your ways following in Your footsteps. You have given me everything I need for life and godliness. Amen.

Your children will imitate you; they will either have a servant's heart or they will think that the world owes them.

The greatest must be the least

Read Luke 9:46–48; 22:24–30

"For he who is least among you all will be great." (Luke 9:48c)

A s you can see from our reading today the disciples spent quite a lot of time discussing their positions. One of the principles that Jesus wanted them to learn was what it meant to be a servant leader. It was important because once He returned to heaven they would be His hands and feet on earth. Jesus used everyday situations and occurrences to illustrate His lessons to His disciples. In this instance He used a small child who was standing nearby.

"...*Whoever receives this little child in My name receives Me; and whoever receives Me receives Him who sent Me*" (Luke 9:48). Children were not considered particularly important so this was a revolutionary statement that Jesus was making. He concluded the statement with the words "... *For he who is least among you all will be great*" (Luke 9:48c). He must have really had their attention. What does this say to you and me as we seek to discover and implement what it means to be spiritual leaders? Jesus was the Son of God. He was one with the Father, part of the Trinity; but He came to earth to be the ultimate servant leader.

Jesus showed us not only through what He said but also by His actions what it means to be the least. A few days ago we looked at the fact that servant leadership is a matter of the heart. It starts in the heart, not in the head. Jesus came to earth to do the will of His Father. We are on this earth to do the will of our Father too. We have been commissioned to share the good news of the gospel of Jesus Christ. First in our own homes and then with the world. It is true to say that the gospel is "caught" rather than "taught". In other words, it is how you live and not what you say that will either draw people to Jesus, or push them away from Him. Examine your heart today and make a new commitment to walk humbly before your God as a servant leader.

Prayer

My Father, I realize that as a human being I am often caught up in the issues that do not matter. I strive to be recognized, to succeed to "be somebody". None of this is Your way. You have called me to walk a different road – a road of servanthood. Give me the heart to go with my calling. Amen.

Examine your heart and make a new commitment to walk humbly before your God as a servant leader.

Know who you are in Jesus

John 13:1–17

Jesus, knowing that the Father had given all things into His hands, and that He had come from God and was going to God, rose from supper and laid aside His garments, took a towel and girded Himself. (John 13:3–4)

J esus is the greatest leader the world has ever known. Leaders can either be a force for good or for evil. They can either leave the world a better place than they found it, or they can leave untold misery and suffering behind them. Leaders are not always accessible to the people. Some of them expect to be treated in a special way. They are often put on a pedestal and revered by their followers. Unfortunately this happens all too often in the church as well.

However, this is not the kind of leader that Jesus was. He is our ultimate example of what it means to be a spiritual leader. He was God of the universe, but He was a servant leader. He came to do the will of His Father and to reveal the Father to mankind. He said that if you have seen Me you have seen the Father. So we can assume that the Father too has a servant heart. Jesus demonstrated this servant heart to us in John chapter thirteen.

Jesus, knowing that the Father had given all things into His hands, and that He had come from God and was going to God (John 13:3). Jesus knew who He was. His self-worth did not come from what people thought of Him; it came from His Father in heaven. My friends, if you are looking to people to validate you then you will be in trouble. Either you will compromise your principles to please them so that they will like you, or you will become discouraged and defeated when people criticize and condemn you for being "radical". A servant leader needs to find his validation in Jesus. You must serve God faithfully, sharing His truth with people. Jesus taught His disciples that being a servant leader meant knowing who they were in Him. We must fulfil our calling without fear or favour. God is the only one we have to please. You will find that when your eyes are fixed on Jesus, knowing who you are in Him will become a part of your DNA.

Prayer

My Father, I am so grateful that I do not need to prove anything to anyone. I am who I am in You. I am answerable only to You. As I walk with You, learning from You day by day, my servant heart will become obvious to the people around me. In You I have everything that I need. Amen.

When your eyes are fixed on Jesus, knowing who you are in Him will become a part of your DNA.

Jesus the servant leader

Read John 13:1–17

"For I have given you an example, that you should do as I have done to you. Most assuredly, I say to you, a servant is not greater than his master; nor is he who is sent greater than he who sent him. If you know these things, blessed are you if you do them." (John 13:15–17)

Jesus knew that the Father had given all things into His hands and that He had come from God and was going to God. So He arose from the supper table, laid aside His garments and girded Himself with a towel. The disciples must have been perplexed and wondered what He was about to do. They probably whispered amongst themselves, "Whatever is the Lord doing now?" Jesus poured water into a basin and He started to wash His disciples' feet, and then He wiped them with a towel. Have you ever washed someone's feet? My friend, if you have then you know it's a very humbling experience. I think it is more humbling for the person having their feet washed than for the one doing the washing, though.

Jesus didn't warn them that He was going to wash their feet. They had been travelling all day, walking along the dusty, dirty roads. They were filthy and they were sweaty. The other disciples were probably too taken aback to say anything, so they simply submitted, allowing Jesus to wash their feet. However when Jesus came to Peter it was a different story. You know Peter: he was rarely at a loss for words. He objected strongly to Jesus washing his feet. I am sure his intentions were good; he didn't want Jesus humbling Himself in this way. On the other hand Peter was proud and he possibly didn't want to be humbled either.

Peter said to Him, "You shall never wash my feet!" Jesus answered him, "If I do not wash you, you have no part with Me." Simon Peter said to Him, "Lord, not my feet only, but also my hands and my head!" (John 13:8–9). Peter always went over the top didn't he? … *Jesus knew that His hour had come that He should depart from this world to the Father, having loved His own who were in the world, He loved them to the end* (John 13:1). Jesus didn't have much longer with His disciples. This was one of the last opportunities that He had to demonstrate servant leadership to them.

Prayer

My Father, You sent Jesus to this world to teach me what servant leadership looks like. It is a humbling experience to realize that so often I get it wrong. Help me, I pray, to follow the example of my master. Amen.

Peter was proud and he possibly didn't want to humble himself.

Following Jesus' example

Read John 13:1–17

"If I then, your Lord and Teacher, have washed your feet, you also ought to wash one another's feet. For I have given you an example, that you should do as I have done to you." (John 13:14–15)

Jesus said some really important things to His disciples in John chapter thirteen. He asked them a question in verse twelve: *"Do you know what I have done to you?"* He then went on to answer His question: *"You call Me Teacher and Lord, and you say well, for so I am. If I then, your Lord and Teacher, have washed your feet, you also ought to wash one another's feet"* (John 13:13–14). Jesus then delivers the crux of the lesson He wants them to learn about spiritual leadership and what it means to have a servant's heart. He says, *"For I have given you an example, that you should do as I have done to you. Most assuredly, I say to you, a servant is not greater than his master; nor is he who is sent greater than he who sent him."* Jesus finishes off by saying to them (and to us), *"If you know these things, blessed are you if you do them"* (John 13:15–16, 17).

During the first part of this month we learnt that Jesus is the one we are to imitate. We are blessed if we come from a godly heritage where we had good role models. If we come from a heritage where there weren't good role models it's OK; Jesus is our ultimate role model. Everything we need to know He has told us in His Word. When He was teaching His disciples, He was also teaching us. So, my friend, the bottom line is that you have no excuse. You cannot use your background as a reason for not getting it together. That is not good enough.

Jesus pulled together a ragged assortment of men and poured His life into them for three years. When He left them they had everything they needed to continue His work here on earth. Once the Holy Spirit had come upon them they went out in power and changed their world. Jesus wants you to go out and change your world. Be the man He saved you to be. Be a spiritual leader with a servant's heart.

Prayer

My Father, thank You that I have all that I need to be what You have called me to be. Jesus, thank You for Your example. I heed the call. I choose to follow You. I choose to be a spiritual leader who has a servant's heart just like You have. Amen.

Be the man He saved you to be. Be a spiritual leader with a servant's heart.

A spiritual leader is humble

Read 1 Peter 5:1–11

"God resists the proud, but gives grace to the humble." Therefore humble yourselves under the mighty hand of God, that He may exalt you in due time. (1 Peter 5:5b–6)

We have to humble ourselves, but as you know this is a difficult thing to do. In fact it is hard for most men, no matter where they come from, or who they are. Jesus understood this and that is why He washed the disciples' feet. He gave them a lesson in what it means to be a servant leader. Being a servant leader means that you humbly allow others to minister to you, as well as you ministering to them. It is most times more difficult to be the receiver than to be the giver.

1 Peter 5:5 does some plain speaking to us: *"God resists the proud."* There you have it. We need to humble ourselves, so that God can raise us up. As soon as you fold your arms and declare: "Nobody is going to do that for me!" the Lord says, "OK, you carry on. I am here for you when you come to your senses." Friends, please don't do this. I did it for too long. There is no time left: We need to humble ourselves. Maybe you have a problem with your rebellious son. Your pride has been hurt and you decide not to speak to him again. Why not, sir? One more time might be all that he needs. When you speak to him, do you shout at him, are you criticizing him or do you tell him that you love him? You can love the boy, but hate what he is doing; but you cannot hate the boy. He is your son! I am telling you, you will see a difference if you humble yourself. Then God can step in.

A spiritual leader has to have a humble heart. If you want to be a true servant leader you cannot be filled with pride. Peter goes on to say: ... *all of you be submissive to one another, and be clothed with humility* (1 Peter 5:5a). Jesus has promised that He will exalt you in due time. Trust Him. He will not let you down, no matter what happens.

Prayer

My Father, Jesus was a true servant leader. Forgive me that I so often let my pride get in the way of my being humble. Help me to submit to others. Help me to clothe myself in humility. Lord, You know some of the issues that I am facing in my life. Give me faith to trust Your timing and Your purposes for me. Amen.

Jesus has promised that He will exalt you in due time.

Love your enemies

Read Matthew 5:38–48

"But I say to you, love your enemies, bless those who curse you, do good to those who hate you, and pray for those who spitefully use you and persecute you, that you may be sons of your Father in heaven." (Matthew 5:44–45a)

Have you ever thought about the fact that Jesus washed Judas Iscariot's feet? That's right – He didn't skip over him. Jesus knelt down before Judas and washed his dirty, smelly feet; knowing full well that within a few hours he would betray Him. Would you be able to wash someone's feet when you know they're about to stab you in the back? When Judas left the dinner he went straight to the high priest and sold Jesus for thirty pieces of silver. Could you bring yourself to wash the feet of someone you know is going to betray you and be partly responsible for your death?

Jesus did this for every person who has ever been born, as well as for all those not yet born. He did it for Judas Iscariot. Romans 5:7–8 puts it so well: *For scarcely for a righteous man will one die; yet perhaps for a good man someone would even dare to die. But God demonstrates His own love toward us, in that while we were still sinners, Christ died for us.* God didn't wait for us to become perfect. He didn't wait for us to sort out all our issues. No, while we were still sinners, Christ died for us. Isn't this amazing and wonderful? Stop right now and thank Him for His grace and favour towards you.

As a spiritual leader you need to have the same attitude towards your enemies that Jesus had towards Judas Iscariot. He tells us in Matthew 5:46a: *"For if you love those who love you, what reward have you?"* It doesn't take spiritual character to love the people who love you in return; that is easy. It is loving those who do not love you that shows your mettle as a spiritual leader. It may be your wife or one of your children. It could be a relative. Often it may be someone you work with or even a fellow brother or sister in Christ. Whoever it is who "has it in for you", you have to love them as Jesus loves you.

Prayer

My Father, today I sit at your feet and I am amazed all over again at Your great love for me. I do not deserve Your love. Nothing I do will ever be enough to be worthy of Your love. It is a free gift. Help me, I pray, to offer this same love to those in my life who are difficult to love. Amen.

Whoever the person is who "has it in for you", you have to love them as Jesus loves you.

Coming back from failure

Read Luke 22:24–34

And the Lord said, "Simon, Simon! Indeed, Satan has asked for you, that he may sift you as wheat. But I have prayed for you, that your faith should not fail; and when you have returned to Me, strengthen your brethren." (Luke 22:31–32)

Jesus had just finished celebrating the Last Supper with His disciples. In John chapter thirteen, at this same event Jesus modelled humility by washing their feet. Despite the lesson on humility Jesus taught them they got into a discussion about who was the greatest. Jesus told them: *"Most assuredly, I say to you, a servant is not greater than his master; nor is he who is sent greater than he who sent him. If you know these things, blessed are you if you do them"* (John 13:16–17). It is in the midst of all of this that Jesus turns to Simon Peter and says to him: ... *"Simon, Simon! Indeed, Satan has asked for you, that he may sift you as wheat. But I have prayed for you, that your faith should not fail; and when you have returned to Me, strengthen your brethren"* (Luke 22:31–32).

Wow, Peter is upset. He cannot imagine betraying Jesus. After all, he loves Him. Jesus tells him that he will deny Him three times before the cock crows. It happened exactly as Jesus said it would. Peter denied Jesus twice and the Scripture says: *Peter then denied again; and immediately a rooster crowed* (John 18:27). Do you think that possibly Peter's failure was ultimately the making of him? It made him the man we meet in Acts. Even though he failed, God did not hang Peter out to dry. In fact, even before he failed, Jesus had reassured him that He was praying for him. Jesus said to Peter, *"... and when you have returned to Me, strengthen your brethren."*

What about you, my friend? Have you failed God? Have you disappointed your loved ones? Well, I have good news for you today. If you come back to God and repent, He will forgive you. He will give you another chance. He will help you to become the spiritual leader you are meant to be so that you can serve others. Return to Jesus today and strengthen your family and your brethren. Coming back from failure is not optional; it is a requirement.

Prayer

My Father, thank You that You never let go of me. Nothing surprises You or takes You unawares. I accept Your invitation to return to You. Forgive me, I pray. Cleanse me, fill me and use me in Your service and in the service of others. Amen.

Coming back from failure is not optional; it is a requirement.

Be compassionate

Read Luke 24:1–12

But Peter arose and ran to the tomb; and stooping down, he saw the linen cloths lying by themselves; and he departed, marveling to himself at what had happened. (Luke 24:12)

P eter had betrayed Jesus. He didn't believe that he could ever do such a thing but it happened and he had to live with the consequences. Can you imagine what the disciples must have felt like during those three days that Jesus was in the tomb? The three women came to the tomb to look for Jesus but the tomb was empty. Then they saw Jesus and ... *he said to them, "Do not be alarmed. You seek Jesus of Nazareth, who was crucified. He is risen! He is not here. See the place where they laid Him. But go, tell His disciples – and Peter – that He is going before you into Galilee; there you will see Him, as He said to you"* (Mark 16:6–7). Did you notice that? Jesus said, go and tell My disciples and Peter. He mentioned Peter by name.

He did this because he knew Peter would never respond out of his own. He had let the Lord down so badly. The women returned and told the disciples. Luke says: *And their words seemed to them like idle tales, and they did not believe them.* Not Peter though. *Peter arose and ran to the tomb.* He didn't need a second invitation. *...he departed, marveling to himself at what had happened* (Luke 24:11, 12). Peter believed. He responded to Jesus' compassion. Can you imagine what it must have meant to Peter when the women returned and relayed the message they had received; when they told Peter that his name had been mentioned specifically?

This is compassion. Jesus knew Peter's need and He reached out in compassion and met his need. A spiritual leader is one who shows compassion to other people: reaching out, building up, restoring and uplifting. If you know of someone who has lost their way, why don't you reach out to them today? It could be that all they are waiting for is someone to invite them back; someone to let them know that they haven't been forgotten, even though they have failed. After all wouldn't you want someone to do that for you?

Prayer

My Father, I am so grateful to You for Your compassion and love towards me. Help me to show the same compassion to other people who are in need. Show me someone to whom I can reach out and extend your compassion. Amen.

A spiritual leader shows compassion: reaching out, building up, restoring and uplifting.

Count your words

Read Proverbs 10:8–21

In the multitude of words sin is not lacking, but he who restrains his lips is wise.
(Proverbs 10:19)

t is not by accident that the most difficult place to maintain your testimony is in your own home. So often it is in the place where we should be the safest that we experience the greatest testing. If you are in a relationship where there is frequent strife it is very difficult. It doesn't matter who is responsible for the friction; if there is discord in your home then you as the spiritual leader of your home need to do something about it. It doesn't help to play the blame game. God has made you the head of your home. With this comes responsibilities as well as privileges; you cannot have the one without the other.

Often the place to start dealing with strife is by curbing your tongue. Our Scripture says it very succinctly: *In the multitude of words sin is not lacking, but he who restrains his lips is wise.* A home where the parents are constantly arguing and taking cheap shots at each other is no place to bring up children in the fear of the Lord. How do you expect your children to grow up and follow Jesus if you are not setting a proper example at home? We said earlier this month that your children will imitate you. Either they will copy your good behaviour or they will copy your bad behaviour, but copy you they will.

Don't allow the enemy to rob you of the privilege you have of setting the tone in your home. You, as the spiritual leader, are the one who shows your sons what it means to love and respect a woman. How you treat your wife shows your daughters the kind of man they should look out for when they grow up. Don't abdicate your position. The devil will use strife to try and chase you away from your home. Take charge of it. Ask God to help you to change the pattern. Start a new tradition in your family. Take your place as the spiritual leader in your home.

Prayer

My Father, in the midst of all the strife and turmoil I come to You. Lord, forgive me for so often taking the easy way out and emotionally withdrawing. I am so good at this. Help me to learn to keep quiet and not react to negativity. I choose today to change the narrative in my home. I will be a positive example to my family. Amen.

Your children will copy your good behaviour or they will copy your bad behaviour, but copy you they will.

The spirit of Elijah

Read Malachi 4:1–6

"Behold, I will send you Elijah the prophet before the coming of the great and dreadful day of the LORD. And he will turn the hearts of the fathers to the children, and the hearts of the children to their fathers, lest I come and strike the earth with a curse." (Malachi 4:5–6)

Before Jesus returns the spirit of Elijah will be poured out; it is the same spirit that John the Baptist had. The spirit of Elijah is going to turn fathers to their sons and sons to their fathers. It has already started happening. I see it everywhere I go. There is a growing sense of urgency. Jesus had a sense of urgency regarding His mission. *Jesus said to them, "My food is to do the will of Him who sent Me, and to finish His work."* He continued saying: *"Do you not say, 'There are still four months and then comes the harvest'?"* (John 4:34, 35a). In other words, don't say there is plenty of time – there isn't.

"Behold, I say to you, lift up your eyes and look at the fields, for they are already white for harvest! And he who reaps receives wages, and gathers fruit for eternal life, that both he who sows and he who reaps may rejoice together" (John 4:35b–36). The time is now! Jesus was pointing out to His disciples that the harvest was ready. They should not waste time, or procrastinate, thinking that tomorrow is another day. The day is here; the day is now. We are living in exciting times. God is in the business of restoration.

You are the spiritual leader of your family. God is wanting – no, expecting – you to take your rightful place as the head of your family. You are to lead the way so that your family will follow you in service to Jesus. You are to teach your sons what it means to be a spiritual leader. You are to teach your daughters what it means to have a spiritual head who looks out for them. You are to love your wife as the Bible instructs you to love her. When you are behaving as the spiritual head of your home then God will be able to bring blessing upon your family. Don't, whatever you do, abdicate your responsibilities. We are living in the last days and abdication is not an option that is open to you.

Prayer

My Father, You have promised me that You will enable me to fulfil my calling. You will not ask me to do anything that You cannot accomplish through me. I submit to You and Your Spirit. Fill me, I pray. Give me wisdom and everything I need to be the spiritual head of my home. Amen.

When you are behaving as the spiritual head of your family God will be able to bring blessing upon your family.

Prophet, priest and king

Read Malachi 4:1–6

"Behold, I will send you Elijah the prophet before the coming of the great and dreadful day of the LORD. And he will turn the hearts of the fathers to the children, and the hearts of the children to their fathers, lest I come and strike the earth with a curse." (Malachi 4:5–6)

We need to prepare for the coming of the Lord now. Why? Because God is turning fathers to their children and children to their fathers. My dad was a very special man. As you know, I had the privilege of leading him to Jesus before he died. We were brought up in a strict Scottish home; very similar in many ways to a traditional Afrikaans upbringing. In our home two things were never discussed: one was politics and the other was religion. They were just not spoken about. These topics were considered to be private.

In those days it was my mother who would encourage me to pray, read my Bible and attend church, not my dad. That is all changing now. Today things are different. God is raising up men to be the spiritual leaders in their home. The priest, the prophet and the king, as the Bible says. What is the priest? The priest is the one who leads the family into the presence of God. As the prophet he is the one who determines the direction in which the family will go. As the king he is the one who supplies the food, clothing and education for his children.

When I see a lady looking very beautiful and well dressed, I know she has a husband who loves her and is taking his rightful place in the home. When I see a lady who is unkempt and unhappy, I know her husband is not fulfilling his role in the family. If the husband is taking up the role in his family, if he is disciplining his children properly, he will only have to speak once and they will listen. This will take a lot of pressure off his wife. Friends, I am sharing my heart here. I get so disillusioned when I go into Christian homes and see the children running wild. Doing whatever they want to do. Mothers running after them, fathers looking embarrassed. No discipline whatsoever, the children totally out of control. This is not a witness for God.

Prayer

My Father, You have called me to be priest, prophet and king in my home. Help me to take this responsibility seriously. Fill me with Your Spirit so that I can be everything you want me to be. Amen.

God is raising up the men to be the leaders in their home. The priest, the prophet and the king.

Absence makes the heart grow fonder!
Read Hebrews 13:5 and 2 Corinthians 12:9

Travelling back from the USA after an intensive preaching tour with our team we are so looking forward to seeing our loved ones again, especially our precious wives.

Many years ago as a young farmer God called me to preach the Gospel. He spoke to me almost audibly through His Holy Spirit and asked me three distinct questions while driving in my farm pick-up. I was on my way to book the town hall in a neighboring town for my first ever preaching campaign.

1. "Are you prepared to be a fool for me?" I responded, "That's easy, Lord, since I am a fool anyway".

2. "Are you prepared for men to say all evil about you for My name's sake?" Once again I answered, "Yes, Father, I shall do it for You". However, I am only now really starting to understand the meaning of that request!

3. "Are you prepared to see less of your family for My name's sake?" I distinctly recall that request like it was just yesterday and with hot tears running down my cheeks and driving into that little country town I clearly remember replying, "Lord Jesus, I do not know if I have the strength to do this for You because I get so very homesick, being a Farmer and being used to coming home each night as the sun sets to be with my beloved family.

I knew the Father knew exactly what I was talking about; He had to allow His only begotten Son to leave Him for thirty-three years! Then I distinctly remember the Father saying to me through His Spirit in the depths of my heart, "My grace is sufficient. For you my strength is made strong in weakness."

And so, as I fly home over the oceans of the world in this big silver bird back to my beloved wife and family, having done my bidding for King Jesus in a far off country with my team, just like weary soldiers we go home rejoicing in the great victory of seeing the lost saved, healed, restored and made into new creatures in Christ Jesus!

We are so looking forward to seeing our loved ones again, and the old adage "absence makes the heart grow fonder" becomes such a reality to us yet again. But then again we would not have had it any other way , because to be in God's perfect will is sheer peace and joy.

Prayer

Father God, please forgive me for always seeming so ungrateful for the wonderful privilege that You have given me to preach Your Gospel to the lost and hurting of this world. I really am so fulfilled and grateful for the call You have seen fit to put on my life, but it is just that I do miss my family. And I do know that You are more able to look after them, take care of their needs than I ever could, so thank you, Lord Jesus. Amen.

Your primary responsibility

Read Deuteronomy 6:1–9

"And these words which I command you today shall be in your heart. You shall teach them diligently to your children, and shall talk of them when you sit in your house, when you walk by the way, when you lie down, and when you rise up."
(Deuteronomy 6:6–7)

Where do you stand today? Have you received the spirit of Elijah? God is turning the hearts of the fathers to the children, and the children to the fathers. You need God's empowering to fulfil your role as the spiritual leader in your family. If your children are to respect you then you must live your life in a way that will earn their respect. You cannot tell your children to go to church and then never go yourself. You cannot tell them not to drink alcohol, but you drink heavily. You cannot expect your children not to smoke if you smoke. This is where the problem arises. Your children will not do what you tell them to do. They will do what you do. I have seen it countless times. It is actually quite scary to watch your children emulating you.

Remember earlier this month we spoke about how our children will imitate us. They are either going to imitate us for good or for evil. As the spiritual leader of your home you have a responsibility to set a godly example for your children to follow. My children are all grown up. They're married and have children of their own. I watch my sons and how they conduct themselves. Sometimes I am happy and sometimes I am embarrassed by what I see, because I see myself exactly replicated in what they are doing or not doing.

What about you today? Our greatest obligation is to make sure that our children are serving God. What does it profit a man if he gains the whole world and he loses his family? Mark 8:36 says: *"For what will it profit a man if he gains the whole world, and loses his own soul?"* The Scripture says soul not family, but isn't it the same thing? It profits a man absolutely nothing. You see, when you get to heaven one day God's going to ask you only one question: Where is your family? Not "How many souls have you led to Christ?" Your family is your primary responsibility; nothing else is more important.

Prayer

My Father, help me to be tireless in my efforts to bring my children up in a way that is pleasing to You. Above all I pray for their souls that they will make a commitment to follow You. Help me to be a faithful example and to persevere in praying for each one of them. Amen.

When you get to heaven one day God's going to ask you only one question: Where is your family?

A servant heart

Read Philippians 4:4–9

The things which you learned and received and heard and saw in me, these do, and the God of peace will be with you. (Philippians 4:9)

We are going to end this month with the same Scripture that we read at the beginning of it. Being a spiritual leader is all about having a servant heart. You can quite possibly be a leader in the world and not have a servant heart. However, in the kingdom of God anyone who genuinely qualifies as a spiritual leader has to be a servant. We see this in Jesus' life. He came to serve. He is the King of the universe, but yet He took it upon Himself to be a servant to all. He performed the ultimate act of service by dying on the cross of Calvary to take away our sins.

It is because of what He has done for you that you can be an effective servant leader. He has given you everything you need to be a good role model to your children. It doesn't matter if you do not have a godly heritage through your earthly family. If you are a child of God then you have a heavenly heritage; and you cannot get a godlier heritage than that. So there are no excuses. Take some time today to reflect back over the lessons that God has taught you this past month. Look at your life and ask the Holy Spirit to show you the areas where you need to shape up better. Then ask Him to come into those areas and renew you.

Take time today to pray for your wife. Bring her before the Lord and ask Him to bless and prosper her in every aspect of her life. Bring your children individually before God. Recommit them to Him. Seek His will regarding each of them. Ask God to help you and make you the husband and father He wants you to be. As we have often said, your children will not do what you tell them to do; they will do what they see you doing. Establish a Godly heritage in your family. Begin today to establish a legacy that your children can be proud of and God will approve of.

Prayer

My Father, I thank You that I don't have to do this on my own. You have given me everything that I need to serve You. You will continue to give me wisdom and insight each day. You will show me Your will. You will direct my paths. Bless my family, I pray. Thank You for them and the wonderful privilege I have of serving them. Amen.

Begin today to establish a legacy that your children can be proud of and God will approve of.

JULY

Now is the time ... to be God's man

A man for such a time

A man called by God

A man who fears God, not man

A man who speaks the truth

A man with a destiny

A man trusting God's provision

A man of faith

A man of his word

A man who doesn't just talk

A man who repairs the altar

A man who has the spirit of Elijah

A man just like me

A man serving God wholeheartedly

A man who knows peace

A man of prayer

A man who follows God

A man of God speaks faith

A man of God is always alert

A man cared for by his God

A man who hears God's voice

A man who lives by faith

A man who obeys

A man serving a merciful God

A man who is faithful

A man of power

A man who asks in faith

A man filled with power

A man who goes the distance

A man who believes in miracles

A man without limits

A man for these times

A man for such a time

Read Genesis 41:37–57

"…Can we find such a one as this, a man in whom is the Spirit of God?" (Genesis 41:38)

T his is a question that we can well ask today: *Can we find such a one as this, a man in whom is the Spirit of God?* We are entering the second half of this year. We began a journey together in January. At the start of this journey we discussed our calling to be ambassadors for Jesus Christ. We are living in the end days. Now is the time of God's favour upon those who obey Him. *Behold, now is the accepted time; behold, now is the day of salvation* (2 Corinthians 6:2b). We have been called to spread the good news of the gospel to our world. As you have been moving through this year how are you doing as an ambassador for Jesus?

Obedience is the key to unlocking blessing in our lives. God is looking for men who will obey Him, no matter what, in these last days. In February we spent the month looking at what it means to be a man who walks daily in obedience to His God. As men of God we are called to live by faith. *For whatever is born of God overcomes the world. And this is the victory that has overcome the world – our faith. Who is he who overcomes the world, but he who believes that Jesus is the Son of God?* (1 John 5:4–5). Who are you putting your faith in: the world or in Jesus? James 4:10 tells us to: *Humble yourselves in the sight of the Lord, and He will lift you up.* Our calling is to be humble servants of the Living God.

We are called by God to be watchmen over the house of Israel – we are called to guard our families and the body of Christ, the church. Our duty is to blow the trumpet of truth, warning people about the approach of the enemy and what he is trying to do in our lives. Last month we spent time discovering what it means to be a spiritual leader; we discovered that one of the defining characteristics of a spiritual leader is servanthood.

Prayer

My Father, the only way I can be a man who will live as You want me to live is if I am filled with Your Holy Spirit. Lord, fill me and use me, I pray, in Your service, in the service of Your people and in the service of Your world. Amen.

As you review this year so far, what kind of a man are you turning out to be?

A man called by God

Read 1 Samuel 9:1–16

And he said to him, "Look now, there is in this city a man of God, and he is an honorable man; all that he says surely comes to pass. So let us go there; perhaps he can show us the way that we should go." (1 Samuel 9:6)

You are called to be a man of God, my friend; I am called to be a man of God. Now is the time of God's favour. Now is the time of salvation. Our job is to carry out God's bidding and bring His message to this world. He has chosen us as vessels of His grace and mercy. We are to go into all the world spreading the gospel of Jesus Christ. It starts in your own home, ministering to your family. Then it moves out in ever-widening circles to include your brothers and sisters in Christ, your friends, your work colleagues and then the rest of the world.

Jesus' last command to us before He died was: *"All authority has been given to Me in heaven and on earth. Go therefore and make disciples of all the nations, baptizing them in the name of the Father and of the Son and of the Holy Spirit, teaching them to observe all things that I have commanded you; and lo, I am with you always, even to the end of the age."* Amen (Matthew 28:18a–20). This month we are going to look at what it means to be a man of God. We will look at the lives of two men of God: Elijah and Elisha. Together we will allow the Holy Spirit to lead us into all truth as we study God's Word.

There is no excuse for any of us not to take up our calling as men of God. In 2 Peter 1:3 we read: *His divine power has given to us all things that pertain to life and godliness, through the knowledge of Him who called us by glory and virtue.* The key to unlocking the power of God in our lives is getting to know Jesus more and more every day. God's Holy Spirit within us will lead us and guide us; He will empower us to do the task that has been set before us. We have everything we need to live as men of God and fulfil our destiny.

Prayer

My Father, thank You for loving me. Thank You for saving me. I come before You grateful for all Your goodness to me. I want to be Your man. I want to serve You faithfully. I want to be useful to You and fulfil my destiny. Amen.

We have everything we need to live as men of God and fulfil our destiny.

A man who fears God, not man

Read 1 Kings 18:1–19

Then it happened, when Ahab saw Elijah, that Ahab said to him, "Is that you, O troubler of Israel?" And he answered, "I have not troubled Israel, but you and your father's house have, in that you have forsaken the commandments of the LORD and have followed the Baals." (1 Kings 18:17–18)

We will begin with examining one of my heroes in the Bible. His name is Elijah the Tishbite. King Ahab was a terrible tyrant. He was one of Israel's worst kings ever. He dominated Israel through violence and oppression, causing much fear among the people. However, there was one man whom King Ahab had tremendous respect for and that was Elijah the Tishbite. Elijah lived his life in obedience to God. He did what God told him to do without fear or favour towards any man, even the king of Israel.

God told Elijah to go and present himself to the king. When Ahab saw Elijah coming he asked him: *"Is that you, O troubler of Israel?"* From his answer it is clear that Elijah was not scared of Ahab: *"I have not troubled Israel, but you and your father's house have, in that you have forsaken the commandments of the LORD and have followed the Baals."* He told Ahab "straight", as we would say. Apparently Elijah was described as the "hairy man with the leather belt". He was the predecessor of John the Baptist. The same spirit that was in Elijah was also in John the Baptist. It is this same spirit that will turn the fathers to their sons and sons to their fathers. We looked at this briefly last month.

If ever our world and particularly our nation needed this spirit, it is now. We need to see reconciliation between fathers and their sons. And these are the days of Elijah and we know that the Lord Jesus Christ is coming back very soon. Isn't it true that so often we allow the fear of man to stop us from doing the will of God? We know that God is telling us to talk to someone, but we make all kinds of excuses not to do so. Remember that you are called to be a watchman blowing the trumpet of truth. If not now then when, my friend? Now is the time for you to be God's man. Take that step of faith and obey Him today.

Prayer

My Father, in the midst of all the clamour and noise around me, help me to hear Your voice. I choose today to obey You no matter what. I want to be Your man for this hour. Empower me through Your Holy Spirit I pray. Amen.

Now is the time for you to be God's man. Take that step of faith and obey Him today.

A man who speaks the truth

Read John 1:1–28

He said: "I am 'The voice of one crying in the wilderness: "Make straight the way of the Lord,"'" (John 1:23)

There are a lot of similarities between John the Baptist and Elijah. They both wore a leather belt. Both of them spent a great deal of time in the wilderness and up in the mountains speaking with God, fasting and praying. Neither of them touched strong drink; in other words they never drank alcohol. They both were holy men. It is also interesting that both of them lived during a time when there was a wicked king ruling over Israel. In Elijah's time it was King Ahab, and in John the Baptist's time it was King Herod.

Herod, like Ahab, ruled with fear and with violence. However, the Bible tells us that Herod had a lot of respect for John the Baptist; he actually liked him. King Herod did not actually want to kill John the Baptist. However, the woman whom Herod called his wife hated John the Baptist because he had exposed her. It is no different today. When a man of God with a backbone stands up and calls sin by its name there are those who take exception to it and will try to cause trouble. Both Elijah and John the Baptist were men like this.

Herod had taken his brother's wife as his own wife. John the Baptist came in from the wilderness and he rebuked King Herod for doing this. There was a big banquet and Herodias got her daughter to ask for John's head on a platter. Herod didn't want to do it but he could not go back on his word. You can be sure that if you stand up for Jesus Christ, my dear friend, you will be hated. You will be despised and you will not be loved. The bottom line is if you want to be a man of God, you cannot be indifferent. There is no way that you can claim that it is not your business. God's business is your business. It is as simple as that. He expects you to stand up for what is right, even if it is at the expense of your own life.

Prayer

My Father, in the midst of a wicked and crooked generation I want to stand tall as Your man. Help me to stand firm and never shrink from the truth – no matter how uncomfortable it is. Give me a love for people so that I will speak from a heart filled with love and compassion. Amen.

He expects you to stand up for what is right, even if it is at the expense of your own life.

A man with a destiny

Read 1 Kings 17:1–7

Then the word of the LORD came to him, saying, "Get away from here and turn eastward, and hide by the Brook Cherith, which flows into the Jordan. And it will be that you shall drink from the brook, and I have commanded the ravens to feed you there." (1 Kings 17:2–4)

Elijah was a man for whom things were either black or white. There were no grey areas. He gave all or nothing. Elijah was either in or he was out. We need more men like this today. D.L. Moody was one of the greatest evangelists who ever lived. He spoke to a hundred million people during the course of his life and this was before radio and television. Moody came from America to Britain and he began preaching what he thought was going to be a short campaign. He continued preaching for three years. Whole trains full of people followed him from station to station. The end result was that revival broke out. D.L. Moody said, "If man has nothing bad to say about you; you can be assured that the Lord Jesus has nothing good to say about you."

You don't have to run around trying to find enemies when you preach the truth. The Bible will condemn, but it also sets people free. Certainly you don't have to go out of your way to be controversial. All you have to do is preach the truth and you will be controversial. Why? Because Jesus was controversial. I am telling you we need more men like Elijah today. Our world needs them more than ever before. God is looking for men who are ready to put their life on the line.

The time for procrastinating is past. You cannot sit quietly on the sidelines any longer. We are at a crossroads: either we must stand up and be counted as God's men, or we must slink away from our calling. You have to choose the direction you will take. What is happening in your life today? Elijah knew exactly who he was, he knew where he was going and he knew in which direction his destiny lay. It has been said that the world stands aside for a man who knows where he is going. What about you, my friend? Where are you going? What is your choice going to be today?

Prayer

My Father, I give You praise today. You have called me and I respond to Your call upon my life. I have no desire to procrastinate or shirk back from Your calling. Give me Your words that I am to speak. Show me what You want me to do and I will do it. Amen.

It has been said that the world stands aside for a man who knows where he is going.

A man trusting God's provision

Read 1 Kings 17:8–16

"For thus says the LORD God of Israel: 'The bin of flour shall not be used up, nor shall the jar of oil run dry, until the day the LORD sends rain on the earth.'" (1 Kings 17:14)

I n verses two to four God told Elijah to go and sit by the Brook Cherith. There God fed him until the brook dried up. Then God told him to go to the widow. God took care of all Elijah's needs, both physical and spiritual. All Elijah had to do was trust God and do what He told him to do. God told him to go to the widow and ask her for food. It is interesting that God chose this poor widow who had so little. She was preparing to make the last meal for her and her son. All their food was finished and they were literally going to starve to death after their last meal.

When Elijah asked her for bread, he was asking her for everything. It was all she had. The request came with a promise: if she fed him, her bin would not run out of flour and her jar would not run out of oil. This was an incredible promise. She chose to believe Elijah, and God, true to His Word, kept His promise. There are lessons for us in this story. Elijah could have questioned God sending him to a widow who had nothing: Why not send him to people who had food to spare? He had to trust God that He knew what He was doing. The widow certainly had to trust that God would make good on His promise. She chose to obey and gave up the last of her food.

Neither of them second-guessed God. They chose to trust Him and God did as He said He would. What about you, my friend? What is God asking you to do today? As you look at your situation you may not be able to see logic in it. Maybe you cannot understand what God is planning on doing. You only know that He is calling you. Obey Him. Trust Him. He will not let you down. If He is telling you to do something He will make it happen. His ways are not our ways.

Prayer

My Father, thank You for the encouragement of this portion of Scripture today. Lord, I know that if You can undertake for Elijah You can do the same for me. I know that You can take little and turn it into much. Nothing is impossible for You. Amen.

If He is telling you to do something He will make it happen. His ways are not our ways.

A man of faith

Read 1 Kings 17:17–24

Then the woman said to Elijah, "Now by this I know that you are a man of God, and that the word of the LORD in your mouth is the truth." (1 Kings 17:24)

God kept His promise and the flour and the oil never ran out. As long as there was no rain and the drought continued, the widow had food to feed herself and her son. One day her son became ill and he died. She immediately went to Elijah. He didn't hesitate: he immediately took the boy and laid him before the Lord. There was no doubt in Elijah's mind that God could bring the boy back from the dead. God did just that and the boy was revived and healed. Elijah didn't doubt God or His ability to heal the boy. The woman said these wonderful words to Elijah: *"Now by this I know that you are a man of God, and that the word of the LORD in your mouth is the truth."*

What she was saying to Elijah was that his talk matched up to his walk. He was not all talk and no action. Too many Christians are exactly the opposite. They have an awful lot to say but neither their actions nor their lifestyles match up with their talk. You cannot fool people forever, my friend. If you are not genuine it will become evident. God is looking for authenticity from us. He looks at our hearts. We have spoken many times about how God looks at the heart. How He is not interested in our sacrifices. No: what He wants is a contrite heart; He wants repentance; He wants us to walk humbly before Him.

God is looking for men who want to have the spirit of Elijah. Men who will not be scared to stand up and be counted. He wants men who will fight injustice, who will not put up with the immorality and depravity of our society. God wants to see a breed of men who will not be compromised no matter what the temptation facing them. The only way we will fulfil these criteria is if we walk in the Spirit, if we know our God and we follow in Jesus' footsteps. God is looking for men of faith.

Prayer

My Father, I want to be Your man no matter what the cost. I thank You that You provide for me in miraculous ways. Help me never to doubt You. I want to be a man who does not compromise on the truth no matter what is happening around me. Amen.

God wants to see a breed of men who will not be compromised no matter what the temptation facing them.

A man of his word

Read 1 Kings 17:1; 18:1–16

And Elijah the Tishbite, of the inhabitants of Gilead, said to Ahab, "As the LORD God of Israel lives, before whom I stand, there shall not be dew nor rain these years, except at my word." (1 Kings 17:1)

After Elijah delivered the message to King Ahab that there would be no rain for "these" years, God told him to go into hiding. Ahab wanted to kill him, so God sent him off into the wilderness and He took care of Elijah there. Three years passed and the Lord told Elijah to go back to Ahab with another message. Ahab had been searching everywhere for Elijah. He was angry about the drought and he wanted to punish Elijah. On his way to Ahab Elijah met Obadiah, the King's servant. Obadiah feared the Lord. However, he was not happy to see Elijah because he knew that the king wanted Elijah dead. He was worried that if he told the king that Elijah wanted to see him, and then Elijah disappeared again, the king would kill him.

At this point, Obadiah reminds Elijah that he saved one of the prophets of the Lord when Jezebel ordered them all to be killed. Elijah gives Obadiah his word – he will not disappear; he definitely wants to speak to the king. Elijah reassures Obadiah: *"As the LORD of hosts lives, before whom I stand, I will surely present myself to him today"* (1 Kings 18:15). Elijah is a man of his word. Remember what the widow said to him: *that the word of the LORD in your mouth is the truth* (1 Kings 17:24b). Are you a man of your word? If we are men of God then our word has to be our bond.

Today too many people lack integrity. It is a very sad thing that the days of a handshake sealing a deal are gone. The spirit of Elijah is being poured out – that means that we will have the same spirit as the one that Elijah had. This means: no compromising; faith in God to provide for us; obedience no matter what the cost. Now is the time for the men of God to stand up and be counted. There is no time for fear. We are in warfare. As God's watchmen we must blow the trumpet of truth.

Prayer

My Father, I give You praise. I lift my hands in worship to Your holy name. I have one desire today and that is to be Your man for the hour we live in. Pour the spirit of Elijah out upon me, I pray, so that I can minister in the power of Your Holy Spirit. Amen.

Are you a man of your word? If we want to be men of God then our word has to be our bond.

A man who doesn't just talk

Read 1 Kings 18:17–24

"Then you call on the name of your gods, and I will call on the name of the LORD; and the God who answers by fire, He is God." (1 Kings 18:24)

Elijah the Tishbite never apologized to anybody for his belief in God. He knew that His redeemer lives. I want to tell you today, I know that my redeemer lives. Do you know who your redeemer is, and that He lives? If you are not sincere people will see right through you, my friend. The Bible tells us that our eyes are the window of our heart. When I preach I like to look into people's eyes; because people's eyes tell me a story. They either tell me that the person believes what I am preaching or that they don't believe what they are hearing.

Mount Carmel is where the battle took place between my hero and 450 ambassadors of the devil. A battle that must have shaken heaven and earth. One man of God against 450 adversaries: I say those are pretty good odds. What about you? I feel a little sorry for the 450. Apparently the Israeli army looks up to Elijah as a mentor. When we were in Israel Jill and I went off the beaten track and climbed right up to the top of Mount Carmel.

On top of Mount Carmel, one man took God's Word literally. Take a lesson from Elijah and be who you say you are. Don't talk with a forked tongue: if you love God act like you love Him. One day a man said to me, "Angus, preach so that we can see you." In other words, don't only talk with your mouth; talk with your life and with your actions. This is what God is looking for in these last days. Not men who can spout their mouths off in church and then go out and live like the devil for the rest of the week. Let's start looking at what we are saying. Remember that old hymn: *Stand up, stand up for Jesus, ye soldiers of the cross?* Are you standing up for Jesus today? Does the world know to Whom you belong?

Prayer

My Father, You have called me to be a faithful witness to You. Please keep me strong and committed to You and the cause of Your kingdom. Help me so that my talk and my walk match up with each other. Amen.

Are you standing up for Jesus today? Does the world know to Whom you belong?

A man who repairs the altar

Read 1 Kings 18:25–30

Then Elijah said to all the people, "Come near to me." So all the people came near to him. And he repaired the altar of the LORD that was broken down. (1 Kings 18:30)

Whenever Israel had an ungodly king they destroyed the altar of the Lord. They broke down the place of worship. This was an act of disrespect towards God. The altar was an important instrument in worship – it was where the people came to make their sacrifices to God. It was an important symbol for them. Every time a godly king came into power he would restore the altar and worship practices would resume. What we see Elijah doing on Mount Carmel is very important. Our Scripture says: *Then Elijah said to all the people, "Come near to me." So all the people came near to him. And he repaired the altar of the LORD that was broken down.*

The altar had been broken down and Elijah repaired it. He did it in the presence of all the people of Israel. He included them in the act of rebuilding the altar. Elijah was claiming back authority on behalf of the godly people of Israel. This would have spoken powerfully to them. Today we don't have physical altars upon which we make sacrifices. Romans 12:1 tells us: *I beseech you therefore, brethren, by the mercies of God, that you present your bodies a living sacrifice, holy, acceptable to God, which is your reasonable service.* The Lord requires of us that we present ourselves as a living sacrifice to Him.

Romans chapter twelve goes on to say: *And do not be conformed to this world, but be transformed by the renewing of your mind, that you may prove what is that good and acceptable and perfect will of God* (Romans 12:2). Has the altar of your life been broken down? Maybe things have happened in your life that have caused you to move off the altar of sacrifice. If this is the case then the first step towards becoming a man of God is to repair the altar. God is not interested in the things you do for Him. He is interested in your being 100 per cent committed to Him. If your altar has been broken down then take time to restore it today.

Prayer

My Father, forgive me, I pray. I realize that I have moved off of the altar of sacrifice. My life is no longer what it should be. I have made choices that have broken down my altar of sacrifice. Today I want to rebuild it. I want to give You my all. Thank You for Your mercy and grace. Amen.

If the altar of your life has been broken down then take time to restore it today.

A man who has the spirit of Elijah

Read 1 Kings 18:30–40

And it came to pass, at the time of the offering of the evening sacrifice, that Elijah the prophet came near and said, "Lord God of Abraham, Isaac, and Israel, let it be known this day that You are God in Israel and I am Your servant, and that I have done all these things at Your word. Hear me, O Lord, hear me, that this people may know that You are the Lord God, and that You have turned their hearts back to You again." (1 Kings 18:36–37)

Elijah stood on Mount Carmel with the 450 prophets of Baal and all the people of Israel. He said: "Today we'll see who God is." When you do this God comes on board! Some time ago there was a drought in Australia. Australian farmers were committing suicide as they faced the worst drought in living memory. Now, folks, I want to clarify something before I go on with this story: it has nothing to do with me; it has to do with the prayer of faith. It has to do with God's people when they repent. We travelled to Western Australia. Together with the farmers we repented and we came before God. We asked God to forgive us. Then we left and flew back to South Africa. After I arrived back I read in the newspapers that it was raining not only in Western Australia, but throughout the whole country! I want to tell you: God answers prayer, but He only answers *The effective, fervent prayer of a righteous man…* (James 5:16b).

You need to make a decision about where you stand. God is not looking for Christians in word only. He does not want fair-weather Christians, whose commitment to Him is dependent on how things are going. When things are going well then it is, "Praise God! Hallelujah!" However, when things are tough it is, "God, where are You: Why have You rejected me?" Folks, this is not the way to serve God! Elijah served God unconditionally, and when he called out to God, God heard his prayers and answered him.

I'll tell you one thing, when Elijah walked into a place everyone knew what he stood for. This is what we need today: more men like Elijah. God is pouring out the spirit of Elijah upon His people today. He is turning the hearts of fathers towards their children and the hearts of children towards their fathers. Are you the kind of man who is standing in line to receive this outpouring today? Now is the time – don't delay – come back to God today.

Prayer

My Father, I repent before You. I know that I have become sidetracked by so many things over the past while. Forgive me, I pray. Restore to me the joy of my salvation. Fill me with Your Spirit and Your power. Amen.

Are you the kind of man who is standing in line to receive the outpouring of the spirit of Elijah today?

A man just like me

Read James 5:13–18

The effective, fervent prayer of a righteous man avails much. Elijah was a man with a nature like ours, and he prayed earnestly that it would not rain; and it did not rain on the land for three years and six months. And he prayed again, and the heaven gave rain, and the earth produced its fruit. (James 5:16b–18)

E lijah was not a maverick. He did not do his own thing – the Bible clearly tells us he followed God's instructions. In 1 Kings 18:36b Elijah prays: *"Lord God of Abraham, Isaac, and Israel, let it be known this day that You are God in Israel and I am Your servant, and that I have done all these things at Your word."* Elijah is carrying out God's instructions. This is what gives him the power. It is not his will but God's will that he is fulfilling. You might think to yourself, "Well it was OK for Elijah. He was a special man. He was a prophet of God." No, my friend. James tells us: *Elijah was a man with a nature like ours.* So you cannot use that as an excuse.

God told him to pray that it wouldn't rain; he prayed and it didn't rain. Then God told him it was time to pray for the rains to come; he prayed and it rained. We often try and complicate matters of faith. The Bible is our manual (you know that I say this all the time). In the Word of God we have all the information we need to conduct our lives successfully. All we have to do is know what the Word says and then act upon it. God honours our obedience. All through Scripture you find evidence of God answering the prayers of men who lived in obedience to Him.

It is no different today, my friend – God honours obedience. Remember one of my favourite quotes from Scripture (I hope that by now you know it off by heart and you live by it). *"…to obey is better than sacrifice, and to heed than the fat of rams"* (1 Samuel 15:22b). Did you notice the word "heed"? It means to give careful attention to. Give careful attention to the Word of God today. If you want to be a man of God for this hour in which we are living then obeying and heeding are prerequisites that you cannot ignore.

Prayer

My Father God, I am encouraged by Your Word today. The fact that Elijah was a man just like I am means that if I walk in Your ways then You can use me too. Keep me faithful, I pray. I realize that being used by You comes as a result of obeying and heeding Your Word. Amen.

Obeying and heeding are prerequisites that the man of God cannot ignore.

A man serving God wholeheartedly

Read 1 Kings 18:20–40

So Ahab sent for all the children of Israel, and gathered the prophets together on Mount Carmel. And Elijah came to all the people, and said, "How long will you falter between two opinions? If the LORD is God, follow Him; but if Baal, follow him." But the people answered him not a word. (1 Kings 18:20–21)

The children of Israel had not only lost their focus but they had also lost their purpose. They had forgotten who they were. Their weakness allowed them to be worn down by King Ahab's cruel reign. The Israelites forgot that their God was king of the universe; they forgot that He was greater than any earthly king. God had made a covenant with them; He has never forgotten or forsaken that covenant. However, the people of Israel were a fickle people.

Elijah challenged them: *"How long will you falter between two opinions?"* They had no response. They stood there passively. You can see their passivity: Ahab summoned them and they came. They had become used to doing as they were told. They no longer knew what they believed. Elijah, a man filled with passion, couldn't handle this. In his frustration he said: *"If the LORD is God, follow Him; but if Baal, follow him."* In other words "act like men": take a stand one way or the other. Their response was: *not a word.* How sad is that? You cannot be passive when it comes to Jesus. They just stood there as if they were waiting for someone to make up their minds for them.

Sadly, too many Christians are like this. They have become weighed down by the cares of this world. Their sins are passivity and compromise. These people do not make any waves; they stand quietly on the sidelines waiting to see what will happen next. This is not an option for a passionate man of God; he has to be prepared to put himself out there. Elijah was prepared to risk everything. He had faith in the God of Israel. If God said so then it was good enough for Elijah. The challenge goes out to you today: *"How long will you falter between two opinions? If the LORD is God, follow Him; but if Baal, follow him."* You cannot remain neutral, my friend. Today is the day – choose whom you will serve. If you choose God then serve Him wholeheartedly.

Prayer

My Father, today I step away from the crowd who are standing on the sidelines. I step onto the path of total commitment to You. I leave behind the things that have hindered me and made me a passive Christian who doesn't know what he stands for. I want to do Your will above everything. Amen.

Choose whom you will serve. If you choose God then serve Him wholeheartedly.

A man who knows peace

Read Judges 6:1–27

Now Gideon perceived that He was the Angel of the LORD. So Gideon said, "Alas, O Lord GOD! For I have seen the Angel of the LORD face to face." Then the LORD said to him, "Peace be with you; do not fear, you shall not die." So Gideon built an altar there to the LORD, and called it The-LORD-Is-Peace. (Judges 6:22–24a)

What did Elijah say to the prophets of Baal? Let's see who God is – let's put Him to the test. The Bible clearly says, don't tempt the Lord your God. However, testing is a different matter. You can test the Lord your God. When you do this it is called putting out a "fleece" before the Lord. Gideon did this: He said, "Lord, tomorrow morning, if it's wet all around this fleece, but the fleece itself remains dry, then I'll know that I've heard from You." That's exactly what happened. Gideon was just like you and me. He still didn't believe God and he said, "Lord, one more time please, tomorrow morning I want it to be dry all around the fleece but the fleece itself must be wet." Sure as anything, that's exactly what happened and then Gideon knew God had spoken to him. Gideon built an altar there and called it The-Lord-Is-Peace.

Too many people run after prophets to find out what the Lord is saying. Don't be lazy. If you want to hear from God then go to God Himself. Seek the Lord in prayer, seek Him through His Word and He will show you what to do. He will tell you if you should go to Australia or stay in South Africa. He will give you guidance as to whether you should sell your farm or buy another one. God will tell you when it is the right time to get married or whether you should wait. Whatever it is you need to know – ask God! He will tell you what to do and He will give you the peace that comes with knowing and doing His will.

Getting back to Elijah: it was as important for the children of Israel to witness God on Mount Carmel as it was for the prophets of Baal. The Israelites needed to be shocked out of their apathy. If you are only going through the motions when it comes to your Christian walk, then it is time for you to be shocked out of your apathy.

Prayer

My Father, I come before You today. Thank You that I can bring all my concerns and questions to You. I know that as I spend time in Your Word and in Your presence You will guide me and direct my paths. I build an altar to Your name, and that name is The-Lord-Is-Peace. Amen.

He will give you the peace that comes with knowing and doing His will.

A man of prayer

Read James 5:13–18

The effective, fervent prayer of a righteous man avails much. Elijah was a man with a nature like ours, and he prayed earnestly that it would not rain; and it did not rain on the land for three years and six months. And he prayed again, and the heaven gave rain, and the earth produced its fruit. (James 5:16b–18)

The spirit of Elijah is so relevant to the times we are living in. Ask God by His Spirit to lead you and guide you into the truths in His Word. Elijah was a man of prayer. There is no doubt about that. You don't just wake up one morning and start praying for it not to rain for several years. Elijah had spent many hours in God's presence. He knew His God. He knew that He could trust God. This kind of faith comes from knowing someone intimately. I want you to consider three questions. How intimately do you know God? How much time do you spend in His presence? And when last have you done great exploits for Him?

Faith is faith. Elijah was a man of faith. He didn't see anything with the naked eye but he knew he was going to see fire from heaven. The prophets of Baal weren't too sure about their god. What was the difference between them and Elijah? Elijah had a relationship with his God; the prophets of Baal didn't have one with their gods. You know what happened on top of Mount Carmel – you have read the story several times this month. God showed up and proved He was God. He did the impossible and no one on that mountain could dispute the results. If you want God to answer your prayers you need to spend time with Him. You need to exercise your "prayer muscles", as it were.

Our text says: *The effective, fervent prayer of a righteous man avails much.* If you want to remain righteous before God you need to keep short accounts of your sins. Be quick to repent. Come before God and ask Him to cleanse you. Persevere in prayer: don't give up. Pray according to God's will. It is His will be done, not your will be done. As the Elijah spirit is poured out in our generation we will see God doing great exploits through His people. To be used of God requires submission to His will and obedience to His voice.

Prayer

My Father, help me to hear Your voice above all the clamour and noise around me. Keep me focused and concentrated on You no matter what the circumstances are that I find myself in. Make me a man of prayer; one who is righteous and fervent. Amen.

To be used of God requires submission to His will and obedience to His voice.

A man who follows God

Read 1 Kings 18:30–40

"Hear me, O LORD, hear me, that this people may know that You are the LORD God, and that You have turned their hearts back to You again." Now when all the people saw it, they fell on their faces; and they said, 'The LORD, He is God! The LORD, He is God!'" (1 Kings 18:37, 39)

Remember Elijah's words to the Israelites? *"If the LORD is God, follow Him; but if Baal, follow him" But the people answered him not a word* (1 Kings 18:21b). They wouldn't take a stand. I guess they had many different reasons for not responding. I am sure there were some of them who still believed in their hearts; but they were too scared to speak up. Then there were others who had become discouraged and they had given up on their faith.

Some were probably angry with God for not coming through for them. They had become worn down by the daily problems they faced living under a wicked dictator who cared nothing for the people. There were even those who had given up on their faith in the God of Abraham, Isaac and Jacob; they had thrown in the towel and joined the Baal worshippers. Can you imagine what it must have been like to be one of the crowd on Mount Carmel that day? I am sure that besides Elijah there was no one expecting a miracle from God. Elijah wanted the people to experience God that day. He wanted to see their faith in God renewed. Hence his prayer: *"Hear me, O LORD, hear me, that this people may know that You are the LORD God, and that You have turned their hearts back to You again."*

After God showed Himself to the children of Israel on Mount Carmel they responded as follows: *... they fell on their faces; and they said, "The LORD, He is God! The LORD, He is God!"* (1 Kings 18:39) Where are you in your walk with the Lord? Do you fit into one of the categories of the people standing on Mount Carmel? Maybe you have your own category. Have you lost your hope and become discouraged? Remember Jesus' words to Thomas: *"... because you have seen Me, you have believed. Blessed are those who have not seen and yet have believed"* (John 20:29). Where do you stand today? You do not have the option to *"answer not a word"*. Silence is also an answer.

Prayer

My Father, I realize that so often I am one of those people who stand on the sidelines not being willing to make a commitment. Forgive me, I pray. Breathe the spirit of Elijah into me so that I can be filled with fervour for You. Amen.

Where do you stand today? You do not have the option to *"answer not a word"*. Silence is also an answer.

A man of God speaks faith

Read 1 Kings 18:41–46

Then Elijah said to Ahab, "Go up, eat and drink; for there is the sound of abundance of rain."
(1 Kings 18:41)

E lijah's job was not completed after the fire came down on Mount Carmel. There was still the matter of the drought to be sorted out. *Then Elijah said to Ahab, "Go up, eat and drink; for* there is *the sound of abundance of rain."* Elijah spoke these words of faith when there was not a cloud in the sky. Elijah went back up to the top of Mount Carmel and began to pray. He sent his servant to look towards the sea. The servant came back and reported: *"There is nothing."* Now what would you have done if that had been you? You told the king that the drought was about to end and nothing was happening.

Elijah, being a man of prayer and understanding that God's ways are not our ways, did not stop praying. After all, God had told him the drought was going to end. So as I often say: "If God says it, I believe it." For Elijah it was as simple as that. God said it, so he believed it. *Then it came to pass the seventh time, that he said, "There is a cloud, as small as a man's hand, rising out of the sea!" So he said, "Go up, say to Ahab, 'Prepare your chariot, and go down before the rain stops you'"* (1 Kings 18:44). Then God broke the drought.

When you read about this event doesn't it fill you with fervour and gratitude to God? Fervour that He would fill you with the same spirit that Elijah had so that you too can do exploits for Him. Gratitude because He is the same God today that He was in Elijah's day. His power is as potent today as it was then. There is nothing that is impossible for God, my friend. What is it that you need to believe Him for today? Seek His will, find out how He wants you to pray, and then don't stop until you see the cloud in the sky. A man of God is not swayed by circumstance or his surroundings; no, he speaks faith.

Prayer

My Father, I bow in Your presence today. I am awed at Your greatness: there is none like You. I pray that You will show me Your will and how I should pray for the situation that I am facing. Give me Your heart on this matter and then help me to faithfully pray it into being. Amen.

A man of God is not swayed by circumstance or his surroundings; no, he speaks faith.

A man of God is always alert

Read 1 Kings 19:1–10

And when he saw that, he arose and ran for his life, and went to Beersheba, which belongs to Judah, and left his servant there. (1 Kings 19:3)

t is hard to believe that this is the same man that we met in chapter eighteen. How did Elijah go from being a mighty man of valour to someone who would run away because of a woman's threats? He stood up to King Ahab and told him that it wouldn't rain for several years. He faced 450 prophets of Baal on Mount Carmel and then destroyed them. In faith he told the king that it would start raining again and it did. Yet when one woman threatens to kill him he turns tail and literally runs for the hills. What happened and what can we learn from Elijah's experience?

Elijah was plain worn out. His defences were low and he didn't take time to restore himself. We need to make sure that we look after ourselves. It is important to eat properly and to get enough sleep. Whenever we experience a spiritual high we need to be extra vigilant. In the same way you need food and rest you need to feed yourself spiritually as well. Take time in the Word and in prayer – allowing God to restore you. The devil knows when we are at our weakest and he waits to get a hold of us. 1 Peter 5:8 puts it like this: *Be sober, be vigilant; because your adversary the devil walks about like a roaring lion, seeking whom he may devour.*

In May we looked at being called to be a watchman. On day 30 we spoke about putting on the full armour of God. This is our protection against the wiles of the enemy. Read Ephesians 6:10–20 again and ask God to help you to put each piece of armour on. Isn't it wonderful that God does not leave us without help? He speaks clearly to us through His Word, giving us everything we need to live a strong life for Him. If a man like Elijah could be caught short then so can you and I. Don't be complacent. Guard your heart and your mind at all times.

Prayer

My Father, thank You for this warning. I realize that the only way I can be safe is by living close to You. Thank You that You don't leave me at the enemy's mercy. You have given me everything I need to live the life You have called me to live. Keep me strong, I pray. Amen.

If a man like Elijah could be caught short then so can you and I. Guard your heart and mind at all times.

A man cared for by his God

Read 1 Kings 19:1–10

And there he went into a cave, and spent the night in that place; and behold, the word of the LORD came to him, and He said to him, "What are you doing here, Elijah?" (1 Kings 19:9)

Elijah was in a bad way: *But he himself went a day's journey into the wilderness, and came and sat down under a broom tree. And he prayed that he might die, and said, "It is enough! Now, LORD, take my life, for I am no better than my fathers!"* (1 Kings 19:4). He was feeling very sorry for himself. It is a wonderful thing to witness God's care and concern for Elijah. God knew exactly what Elijah needed. He needed to refresh himself. Elijah slept and then God sent an angel to bring him food and drink. Then Elijah slept again; and again the angel brought him more food and drink. Elijah was restored physically – he was able to go forty days to Mount Horeb on the strength he gained from that food.

However, Elijah was not restored emotionally or spiritually yet. When he arrived on Mount Horeb he went to hide in a cave. God found him and said to him: *"What are you doing here, Elijah?"* Elijah was feeling very sorry for himself indeed. *"... I have been very zealous for the LORD God of hosts; for the children of Israel have forsaken Your covenant, torn down Your altars, and killed Your prophets with the sword. I alone am left; and they seek to take my life"* (1 Kings 19:9–10). Elijah is sitting up on the mountain having a pity party.

What about you, my friend? Have you been "disappointed" by God? Was there something you were trusting Him for; and either it didn't come to pass or, when it did, you felt let down because it didn't turn out as you expected? Are you sitting on top of your own Mount Horeb, in your cave, feeling sorry for yourself? God hasn't forgotten about you – He knows where you are. He is standing before you today and asking you: *"What are you doing here?"* God will never leave you or forsake you. He never makes a mistake. So whatever put you in the cave He has the answer. Stand at the mouth of your cave and watch the Lord pass by.

Prayer

My Father, I come before You. I know that You are a great God. Forgive me for doubting You. Forgive me that I have taken my eyes off You and placed them on my circumstances. How grateful I am that You will never leave me or forsake me. Amen.

Are you sitting on top of your own Mount Horeb, in your cave, feeling sorry for yourself?

A man who hears God's voice

Read 1 Kings 19:11–18

…and after the fire a still small voice. So it was, when Elijah heard it, that he wrapped his face in his mantle and went out and stood in the entrance of the cave. Suddenly a voice came to him, and said, "What are you doing here, Elijah?" (1 Kings 19:12c–13)

When Elijah arrived on top of Mount Horeb the Lord asked him: *"What are you doing here, Elijah?"* He answered the Lord: *"I have been very zealous for the LORD God of hosts; for the children of Israel have forsaken Your covenant, torn down Your altars, and killed Your prophets with the sword. I alone am left; and they seek to take my life"* (1 Kings 19:9–10). This is not the confident man who confronted a king and the 450 prophets of Baal. Isn't it wonderful how gracious God is to Elijah? He tells Elijah to go and stand on the mountain before the Lord.

First God sends a terrifying storm that rocks the mountain – but God isn't in the wind. There follows an earthquake and then a fire – but God is in neither of them. Lastly there is a rustling, a small still voice – and there is God. Isn't this beautiful? Elijah had witnessed God's great power when He had swooped down from heaven and consumed the sacrifice on top of Mount Carmel. Now God is showing Elijah that He is also the gentle, still, small voice. Elijah needed to encounter God in this intimate way. He needed God to soothe his spirit. He needed to be refreshed and renewed. Elijah had to stop and listen – it was then that he could hear God's voice again.

Wherever you find yourself today, take time to stop and listen for the still small voice of God. Elijah had to stop running before he could hear from God. You too need to come to a place of rest and then wait and listen for the voice of the Lord. As you wait for Him, He will come to you. He will answer and He will direct you. So often we cannot hear His voice because there is so much noise and activity going on in our lives. God does not always reveal Himself through the razzmatazz; very often it is in the quietness that we hear Him best. Find your quiet place and listen to Him today – let Him share His heart with you.

Prayer

My Father, in the midst of all the hustle and bustle of life I have lost out on hearing from You. Today I choose to quiet myself in Your presence. As I wait on You please reveal Yourself to me. I need to hear Your voice, Lord. Amen.

Find your quiet place and listen to Him today – let Him share His heart with you.

A man who lives by faith

Read Hebrews 11:1–3, 32–40

And what more shall I say? For the time would fail me to tell of … the prophets: who through faith subdued kingdoms, worked righteousness, obtained promises, stopped the mouths of lions, quenched the violence of fire, escaped the edge of the sword, out of weakness were made strong, became valiant in battle, turned to flight the armies of the aliens. (Hebrews 11:32–34)

How are you doing when it comes to having faith in God? You might say to me: Angus, I believe in God, in Jesus Christ, His Son, and in the Holy Spirit. That is good, I am glad you do. However, what I am really asking you is, do you have faith? We have spent the past twenty days looking at a mighty man of faith. I hope that you are as encouraged by Elijah as I am. His faith encourages me, but I am also encouraged by his humanity.

It is a wonderful thing that God gives us glimpses of the humanness of our biblical heroes. Even though Elijah did valiant exploits for God he still had his moments of frailty and failure. The other wonderful thing, and it is such a blessing to me, is that God didn't desert him in his moment of weakness. No, God was right there bringing him back in line with His will again. So, my friend, where do you stand today? If you are weary and heavily laden take courage. God is still on His throne. He hasn't gone anywhere. He is watching over you and loving you through your difficulties.

If you are facing what seem to be insurmountable problems at the moment then take heart; you serve a God for whom nothing is impossible. Spend time in His Word; it is filled with accounts of God doing what is humanly impossible. Seek His face and when He speaks to you obey Him. So often our problem is that we want God to say what we want to hear. We don't want to obey Him unquestioningly. We want to maintain partial control over our lives and circumstances. It doesn't work like that. Either you obey God or you don't. If you aren't prepared to obey then He cannot help you. His is the still small voice calling you. So again I ask you: How are you doing when it comes to having faith in God? *Now faith is the substance of things hoped for, the evidence of things not seen* (Hebrews 11:1).

Prayer

My Father, I bow in Your presence, Lord. You have spoken directly to my heart today. I lay my burdens at the foot of the Cross and, Lord, I choose not to pick them up again. I am listening to You, Lord, and I am ready to obey You. I trust You and You alone. Amen.

Now faith is the substance of things hoped for, the evidence of things not seen.

A man who obeys

Read 1 Kings 19:11–21

So he departed from there, and found Elisha … who was ploughing with twelve yoke of oxen before him … Then Elijah passed by him and threw his mantle on him. And he left the oxen and ran after Elijah … (1 Kings 19:19–20)

God had Elijah's attention again. He came out of his depressive state and listened to God's instructions to him. God had a list of things that Elijah was to do. There is nothing vague about God's communication with Elijah. It is in verse seventeen that we see Elisha's name mentioned for the first time. *It shall be that whoever escapes the sword of Hazael, Jehu will kill; and whoever escapes the sword of Jehu, Elisha will kill.* Notice that Elijah immediately sets out to do as God has instructed him.

Elijah finds Elisha ploughing in his father's field. He throws his mantle on Elisha. What is Elisha's response to this? He leaves his father's oxen and runs after Elijah. On day thirteen in June we looked at what the qualifications are for a spiritual leader. We said the following: "What is it that God looks for when He chooses spiritual leaders? Clearly it is not perfection, nor is it education. It is not superior intellect and it certainly isn't based on class, social standing or how much money you have. So what does He look for? If you look at the calling process of each of the disciples there are a few things they have in common. Jesus called them and they responded. They were willing to drop everything and follow Him. They left their jobs, they left their homes; they left everything behind to follow Him.

We see the same pattern repeated with the calling of Elisha. He dropped everything, said his goodbyes to his family and verse twenty-one tells us: *Then he arose and followed Elijah, and became his servant.* Do you have this kind of faith in God? When He calls you and tells you to do something do you obey Him immediately, no questions asked? This is what it means to be a man of faith. God is looking for men like Elijah and Elisha, who will do His bidding and be used by Him to change our world. Are you such a man? If so, then come before God today and commit yourself afresh to Him.

Prayer

My Lord and saviour, I kneel at Your throne today in surrender to You. Lord, I hear You calling and I am answering Your call. Use me, I pray, in whatever way You want to. Amen.

God is looking for men like Elijah and Elisha, who will do His bidding and be used by Him to change our world.

A man serving a merciful God

Read 1 Kings 21:17–29

And the word of the LORD came to Elijah the Tishbite, saying, "See how Ahab has humbled himself before Me? Because he has humbled himself before Me, I will not bring the calamity in his days..." (1 Kings 21:28–29)

King Ahab and Elijah encounter one another again. It is clear from verses seventeen to twenty-six that God was very angry with Ahab. God spoke to Elijah and gave him a message for Ahab. He was the watchman on the wall. He was the one who blew the trumpet of truth for Ahab, warning him of impending doom and destruction. Elijah was not afraid of Ahab. He spoke the message that God gave him boldly. Elijah's first duty was obedience to God, not man.

When Ahab heard Elijah's message he reacted as follows ... *he tore his clothes and put sackcloth on his body, and fasted and lay in sackcloth, and went about mourning* (1 Kings 21:27). He realized that God meant business. He had plenty of experience of the fact that when God said something He did it. I am sure he still vividly remembered the drought and the Mount Carmel experience. So Ahab repents before the Lord. The Lord tells Elijah: *"See how Ahab has humbled himself before Me? Because he has humbled himself before Me, I will not bring the calamity in his days."* God is merciful to Ahab.

My friend, we serve a merciful God. He is a just God, but He is also a loving and merciful God. Are you in a place in your life where you feel things are hopeless? Maybe you have made mistakes and the consequences are threatening to overtake you. Come to God today. Repent before Him, confess your sins and He will be merciful to you. Maybe you know someone who needs to hear a Word from the Lord. Pray for them and if God leads you then go to them. Be the watchman blowing the trumpet of truth for them. Help them to see the error of their ways and the fact that we have a loving, merciful God who will forgive them if they turn to Him. Now is the time for the spirit of Elijah to manifest in our midst. The spirit of Elijah is a restoring spirit, one that brings people back together; one that brings healing and reconciliation.

Prayer

My Father God, I thank You for Your mercy today. I am so grateful that You do not treat me the way I deserve to be treated. You look at me through eyes of love. I come before You and pray for Your forgiveness and restoration in my life. Amen.

The spirit of Elijah is a restoring spirit, one that brings healing and reconciliation.

A man who is faithful

Read 2 Kings 2:1–6

But he said, "As the LORD lives, and as your soul lives, I will not leave you!" So the two of them went on. (2 Kings 2:6b)

Elisha followed Elijah faithfully. In 1 Kings chapter twelve we saw Elijah calling Elisha to follow him. He threw his mantle over him. Elisha left everything and he followed Elijah. In our reading today we see that Elijah is coming to the end of his life. It is time for him to depart. Elijah wants to leave Elisha behind but he refuses to be parted from him. Three times Elisha says to Elijah, "I will not leave you." He is determined to be faithful to the end. He knows that Elijah is going to heaven and he doesn't want to miss the last hours with his mentor. Elisha patiently learnt from Elijah.

Elisha proved himself to be a man who could be trusted. He proved himself faithful to the end. He had one desire and that was to serve God and to be used by God. He understood patience because he came from a farming background. He understood about preparing the soil, sowing and tending the crops. He knew that reaping could only take place once the crop was ripe and ready. Elisha learnt from his mentor Elijah. He did not waste a minute.

My friend, are you faithful in the small things as well as the big things? Faithfulness is not a characteristic that is generally held in high regard today. Too many people break their promises. People do not believe in perseverance and patience: we live in an instant society. Are you faithfully obeying and following God? What are you trusting Him for today? I hope it is something "God-sized" that only He can do. If God has laid something on your heart then don't stop until He has accomplished it. Remain faithful. Remain resolute and persevere until you see the evidence of what God has promised you. *God is faithful, by whom you were called into the fellowship of His Son, Jesus Christ our Lord* (1 Corinthians 1:9). He will never let you down. The question is, will you remain faithful to Him to the end? Can you say with Elisha, "I will not leave you"?

Prayer

My Father, I thank You and worship You today. Fill me with Your Holy Spirit I pray. Help me to persevere and be patient; and to never give up. Keep me faithful to the end I pray. Amen.

He will never let you down. The question is, will you remain faithful to Him to the end?

A man of power

Read 2 Kings 2:1–18

And so it was, when they had crossed over, that Elijah said to Elisha, "Ask! What may I do for you, before I am taken away from you?" Elisha said, "Please let a double portion of your spirit be upon me." (2 Kings 2:9)

Elisha received the mantle or the cloak symbolizing the anointing and the power of God from Elijah. Just before he was taken up into heaven Elijah asked Elisha what he wanted. If you think about it he could have asked for anything. What he asked for, though, was a double anointing of Elijah's spirit. He wanted twice as much power as Elijah had had. It was because he was faithful and persistent that God gave it to him. Elijah responded to his request as follows: *So he said, "You have asked a hard thing"* (2 Kings 2:10a). With great power comes great responsibility.

In 2 Kings we read that God used Elisha to perform exactly double the number of miracles, signs and wonders that Elijah did. Why? Simply because Elisha asked God in faith. Have you asked God for anything recently? If you haven't then maybe it is the reason you haven't received anything. There is no quick fix with Christianity, my dear friend. It is a lifestyle. You don't arrive, but rather carry on growing from one degree to another. Then when God sees your heart He will trust you with precious things such as a mantle of God.

He wants men who have a tender heart; men who have a heart for those who are lost, and men who have a heart for the hungry, the poor and the needy. God will use your compassion, love and brokenness to part the Jordan River in your life. You might ask: "Why does God use some people, and He doesn't use others?" God used Elisha, but He didn't use the forty prophets, after all they were all good men. Maybe the forty prophets weren't prepared to follow hard after Elijah, come what may. Come what may, we will follow You, Lord, to the end. It doesn't matter what happens; it doesn't matter what doesn't happen: we are going to follow You. Elisha was sure of his calling. He was steadfast in his pursuit of God. If you want to experience God in new and powerful ways then you too need to steadfastly pursue God.

Prayer

My Father, I want to have the same spirit that Elijah and Elisha had. Help me to be prepared to walk the distance. Keep me faithful and true to You. Amen.

If you want to experience God in new and powerful ways then you too need to steadfastly pursue God.

A man who asks in faith

Read 2 Kings 2:9–15

He also took up the mantle of Elijah that had fallen from him, and went back and stood by the bank of the Jordan. Then he took the mantle of Elijah that had fallen from him, and struck the water, and said, "Where is the LORD God of Elijah?" And when he also had struck the water, it was divided this way and that; and Elisha crossed over. (2 Kings 2:13–14)

The Jordan River is not just a stream. It is a fast-flowing, deep river. You cannot simply wade across it. Elisha stood by the bank of the Jordan River and: *Then he took the mantle of Elijah that had fallen from him, and struck the water, and said, "Where is the LORD God of Elijah?" And when he also had struck the water, it was divided this way and that; and Elisha crossed over.* Where is the Lord God of Elijah? Maybe you are asking this same question today. Where is He? Where is the Lord? Where are the miracles, the signs and the wonders? The Lord God of Elijah was waiting for Elisha to call upon Him; and when he called, God answered by parting the Jordan River. In the same way God is waiting for modern day Elishas to call upon Him.

James 4:2c says: *Yet you do not have because you do not ask.* I have learnt this the hard way, my dear friend. If you don't ask, you don't receive. What is the difference between Elisha and us? Nothing, we are all human beings. We have blood running through our veins; Elisha had blood running through his veins. So what makes the difference? The difference is quite simple: forty prophets said to Elisha, "Leave the man of God." Elisha replied: "I will not leave him." Until I receive his mantle, I am going to pursue him. Some of us have given up. You ask once and you don't receive, then you give up. The only difference between us and Elisha is that we haven't asked God for anything in faith.

It is no good asking God for something if you don't believe that you will receive it. What is the point? If you ask the Lord to bless your crop and then when nothing happens your attitude is "Oh well, I didn't think it would happen anyway", that is not faith! Hebrews 11:1 says: *Now faith is the substance of things hoped for, the evidence of things not seen.* Ask God for something in faith today.

Prayer

My Father, I am standing by my own Jordan River. Forgive me that I have been asking "Where is God?" when all the time You are right here. Today I come before You and I ask You in faith to… Lord, I believe that You will answer me. Thank You. Amen.

The difference between us and Elisha is that we haven't asked God for anything by faith.

A man filled with power

Read 2 Kings 2:1–14

Then he took the mantle of Elijah that had fallen from him, and struck the water, and said, "Where is the LORD God of Elijah?" And when he also had struck the water, it was divided this way and that; and Elisha crossed over. (2 Kings 2:14)

How are we to pray for the sick? In the name of Jesus of Nazareth, you find out what the problem is and you address it. Then by faith you speak into the life and situation of the person. Unfortunately, this is not happening and this is why we don't see the Lord God of Elijah moving among us. The Lord God of Elijah is waiting for the new Elisha to call upon Him. Many young men come to me and they ask, "Uncle Angus, I want you to pray over my hands. I want to lay my hands upon the sick. I want to see the sick recover. I want to see miracles." I reply, "I won't pray for your hands, I will pray that God will break your heart, so when you see sick people you will begin weeping for them." You know, sometimes not being sick, you don't really understand what the person is going through.

It was only after I literally stood at the gates of heaven that I came to understand the shortness of time. Now when a person tells me that he has had a heart attack, I can understand what he has been through. I thought I could before. Does that mean that we have to get sick before we can show compassion? Not at all. However, it does mean that we need to get down there where it is happening. We need to get down there where it counts, into the dust, into the dirt, into the gutter along with the person we are ministering to. Then we can call out to God.

We are always asking God for power. We ask Him for the baptism of the Holy Spirit. Why? So we can walk around town with three stripes declaring we have arrived now? No, friends: God gives you gifts, He gives you the anointing and He gives you the power so that you can use them to glorify His Son. That's all. And to see people come to full maturity in Christ. Have you witnessed the God of Elijah recently?

Prayer

My Father, I pray that You will give me a heart of compassion for those who are sick and in need. Help me, Father, that I will not be after power for power's sake. Use me to glorify Your Son, Jesus Christ, every day. Amen.

God gives you gifts, the anointing and the power so that you can use them to glorify His Son.

A man who goes the distance

Read Matthew 7:1–12

"Ask, and it will be given to you; seek, and you will find; knock, and it will be opened to you. For everyone who asks receives, and he who seeks finds, and to him who knocks it will be opened." (Matthew 7:7–8)

We need to ask God to supply our needs. This is what Matthew 7:7 tells us: *"Ask, and it will be given to you; seek, and you will find; knock, and it will be opened to you."* You can come boldly before the throne of grace today and ask God for the things you have need of. Or you can say: "I am so tired, I am so weary, I am so cross, I am so despondent, I am so sad, I cannot do anything." If this is where you are today then go back into your closet and pray. Ask God to refresh you, to strengthen you. None of us can accomplish anything but for the grace of God.

If you want to be used by the Lord, you need to understand that the world will ridicule you. Are you prepared for this? If you answer "not really", then God cannot use you in the same way that He used Elijah, Elisha and all the other men of God who have been persecuted for their faith. The testing is becoming more severe than in times gone by, because it is more subtle now. To stand up in public and speak the truth in love takes a lot of courage, my friend. God is not about to give you this responsibility if you are not prepared to do it. "Take the world, but give me Jesus" is a beautiful hymn written by Fanny Crosby. When you have a heart like this, oh man, things suddenly begin to happen.

Wherever I travel in the world I see people turning to God. We need to reach out to people, in love. We must join arms with our fellow preachers and build them up. We need people who will speak the truth. The signs and wonders will follow those who preach the Word. Jesus said: *"Heal the sick, cleanse the lepers, raise the dead, cast out demons. Freely you have received, freely give"* (Matthew 10:8). We are preaching the same gospel message today that was preached in the time of Jesus.

Prayer

My Father God, I bow in Your presence. Lord, I want to be Your man. First and foremost before anything else I want to do Your will and Your bidding. Give me the courage to go the distance. Amen.

Speak the truth and the signs and wonders will follow.

A man who believes in miracles

Read 2 Kings 3:1–20

And he said, "Thus says the LORD: 'Make this valley full of ditches.' For thus says the LORD: 'You shall not see wind, nor shall you see rain; yet that valley shall be filled with water, so that you, your cattle, and your animals may drink.'" Now it happened in the morning, when the grain offering was offered, that suddenly water came by way of Edom, and the land was filled with water. (2 Kings 3:16–17, 20)

One genuine miracle equals a thousand sermons. I have seen it before. When people don't want to listen to what you have to say, you pray the prayer of faith and something happens. Almost instantaneously there is no longer a need to talk. There are no words to explain it when a man who is in a wheelchair stands up and walks after you have prayed a simple prayer. Even the atheists can recognize God at work when they see it with their own eyes. It has happened to me, up in Mozambique. I have told you the story before. There was a woodchopper who had a pin through his leg which made it stiff. I prayed the prayer of faith and God healed him. As a result 5,000 Muslims came to the front to accept Jesus. Up until then I could have preached the best sermon of my life and they wouldn't have been interested.

So I hear your question: "Where is the Lord God of Elijah?" He is waiting for modern day Elishas to call upon Him. That is why Jesus said: *"But seek first the kingdom of God and His righteousness, and all these things shall be added to you"* (Matthew 6:33). Elijah said there would be no rain and there was no rain in the land. Then Elijah said it would rain and it did. Folks, when you pray in this way you get an instantaneous response from the Word. By the way I am not a name it and claim it person. I have my feet on the ground. I am an ordinary farmer.

However, I want to tell you I know that *Jesus Christ is the same yesterday, today, and forever.* This is what Hebrews 13:8 tells us. I also know that the blood flowing through my veins is the same blood that flowed through Elijah's veins. If Elijah said there would be no rain there was no rain; when he called fire down from heaven, the fire came down. You had better believe it, my friend. Do you have Elijah's blood in your veins?

Prayer

My Father, I thank You that You are the same God who did mighty exploits through Elijah. I am Your child and You give that same power to me. Help me to surrender to You so that You can use me in the same way You used Elijah. Amen.

The blood flowing through my veins is the same blood that flowed through Elijah's veins.

A man without limits

Read 2 Kings 4:1–7

So Elisha said to her, "What shall I do for you? Tell me, what do you have in the house?" And she said, "Your maidservant has nothing in the house but a jar of oil." (2 Kings 4:2)

People know that there is a God, and I believe in these last days, according to my Bible, the outpouring of the Holy Spirit will be greater than in the former days. So be ready to be used by God. Call upon the Lord God of Elijah and expect great things from God. If you expect nothing, you receive nothing. So I want to encourage you to start calling upon the Lord. The Lord has often used me to pray for rain in situations where there has been a drought. Yesterday we saw God using Elisha to bring water into the valley of Edom. It didn't even have to rain for God to provide water in this situation.

Today we see in our reading that God provides for the widow. Elisha says to her: *"What shall I do for you?"* Then he asks her: *"…what do you have in the house?"* She answers him: *"Your maidservant has nothing in the house but a jar of oil."* Over the past few days we have been talking about asking God for what we need. God is asking you today: *"What shall I do for you?"* You might feel that you have nothing to offer God. This is not true, my friend. God will use whatever we have to do His work. It is not about what you have or don't have. The truth is God has everything. You only need to be the vessel through which He works.

The widow had only one jar of oil left. She believed and acted upon Elisha's command to *"Go, borrow vessels from everywhere, from all your neighbors – empty vessels; do not gather just a few."* As long as there was capacity the oil came. It only stopped when the widow said: *"There is not another vessel." So the oil ceased* (2 Kings 4:3, 6b). This is thrilling – as long as we have capacity God will use us. There are no limits – we are the ones who place the limits on what God does through us. He is asking you today: *"What shall I do for you?"*

Prayer

My Father, I come before You thankful that You are a God who knows no limits. I realize that the limits are with me. Increase my faith, I pray. I want to be a man who is used by You. Amen.

He is asking you today: *"What shall I do for you?"*

A man for these times

Read 2 Kings 4:38–44

But his servant said, "What? Shall I set this before one hundred men?" He said again, "Give it to the people, that they may eat; for thus says the LORD: 'They shall eat and have some left over.'" So he set it before them; and they ate and had some left over, according to the word of the LORD. (2 Kings 4:43–44)

Friends, I want to tell you something now. Don't be too critical when you see miracles happening; instead, accept and believe. There might be some things that you are not happy about. Keep quiet and see what God is going to do, because God is going to do it anyway. I remember when my wife and I were baptized with the Holy Spirit. We attended the meeting with a dear friend, who today is still a dear friend. However he is a very studious man, an intellectual. He went with a notebook and a pen. I went with my mouth wide open, I was so thirsty. The Holy Spirit filled me with His spirit, He gave me a beautiful new language, and He gave me peace and power. The same thing happened to my wife, Jill. My friend left with a notebook full of notes and nothing else.

You have a choice to make today. I have a choice to make. It is very simple: Either we will be men who choose to believe what the Word says or we will choose not to believe. There are no half measures; it is all or nothing. Elijah was a man who was 100 per cent sold out to God. This was why God could use him like He did. Elijah was a man just like us. He also had his weak moments. However, he was sold out to God. Elisha received a double portion of the spirit that was upon Elijah because that is what he asked God for. So God used him in an even greater way than He did Elijah.

The choice is yours today. As you think back over this past month, what has God been saying to you? Come before Him today and sit in His presence. Ask Him to fill you afresh with His Holy Spirit. Now is the time of His favour. God is pouring out the spirit of Elijah. Now is the time for you to be used by God. It is up to you to choose to be God's man for this hour.

Prayer

Father, thank You for Elijah and Elisha. Lord, I pray that You will give me the same anointing, the same mantle, so that I can strike the Jordan River in my life. Divide it left and right so that I can walk through on dry land. Give me the faith to press on no matter what. I ask this in Your precious name. Amen.

Now is the time for you to be used by God. It is up to you to choose to be God's man for this hour.

AUGUST

Trust with all your heart

Trust in God alone

Mistrust destroys

Inquire of the Lord

When you are betrayed

Remember the name of the Lord

In whom is your expectation?

How do I grow in faith?

Faith comes by hearing

Faith in action

Faith has feet

Walk by faith

Faith is not a feeling

Our heavenly hope

Our faithful God

Persevering faith

Patient faith

A lesson in patience

Men of patience

The obedience of faith

Faith in the God who hears

The covenant of faith fulfilled

A different spirit

Learn the patience of faith

The patience of Job

The wisdom of faith

The birth of faith

The progression of faith

The maturing of faith

The obedience of faith

The provision of faith

Trust with all your heart

Read Proverbs 3:1–12

Trust in the LORD with all your heart, and lean not on your own understanding; in all your ways acknowledge Him, and He shall direct your paths. (Proverbs 3:5–6)

This is our key text for the month of August. What does it mean to trust in the Lord with all your heart? Do you think there is a link between trusting God with all your heart and loving Him with all your heart? *Jesus said to him, "'You shall love the LORD your God with all your heart, with all your soul, and with all your mind'"* (Matthew 22:37). Surely you cannot trust someone if you do not love them and you cannot love them if you do not trust them. It therefore follows that you cannot love and trust someone you do not know. Knowledge is the key that unlocks the door to faith and love. So before I ask you if you trust God with all your heart, I want to ask you, do you know Him? I am not talking about a superficial level of knowledge.

Many people know about God. They even believe that there is "a higher being". They believe in "the man up there". My friend, you cannot know God if you do not know His Son, Jesus Christ. Jesus said in John 14:7: *"If you had known Me, you would have known My Father also; and from now on you know Him and have seen Him."* In John 14:6: *Jesus said to him, "I am the way, the truth, and the life. No one comes to the Father except through Me."* If knowledge is the key that unlocks the door to faith and love, then Jesus is the door through which you have to pass in order to know the Father. As Jesus said, if you know Him then you know the Father.

Where do you stand with Jesus, my friend? Is He your Lord and saviour – can you call God your Father because you know His Son, Jesus Christ? This is the basis from which we launch our journey of discovery into what it means to trust God with all your heart. *Trust in the LORD with all your heart, and lean not on your own understanding...* Where do you stand today?

Prayer

My Father, thank You that I am Your child and that I know You because I know Jesus Christ, Your Son. This month I pray that You will teach me through Your Spirit what it means to trust You with all my heart. Amen.

Knowledge is the key that unlocks the door to faith and love.

Trust in God alone

Read Proverbs 3:1–12

Trust in the LORD with all your heart, and lean not on your own understanding; in all your ways acknowledge Him, and He shall direct your paths. (Proverbs 3:5–6)

n whom are you placing your trust: in God or in man? I hope that like me you have people in your life whom you feel you can trust. It is wonderful if you do. My best friend is my wife, Jill. I trust her. The young men who work with me making our *Grassroots* programmes are more than co-workers: they are my sons in the Lord and I trust them. However, at the end of the day I cannot trust man because I cannot trust myself; my friend, our flesh is so weak. This is why our key text says: *Trust in the LORD with all your heart…* The verse continues saying *… lean not on your own understanding.* Then you come to a pivotal point in the verse: *In all your ways acknowledge Him.* What does Proverbs say will be the result if you do this? *He shall direct your paths.*

We don't go in for formulas, but this is definitely God's recipe for living a successful life. You know, many people come to see me for counselling and prayer; many others write to me and you are welcome to write too, if you like. Sometimes these people question why God has allowed certain things to happen to them. Very gently, with much love, I have to explain to them that it isn't God who did it. If they search their hearts then most times they will have to admit that they trusted in a person or an organization. They trusted man's word instead of trusting in God alone. They took bad advice and now they are reaping a bad crop. Praise God though that it doesn't end there.

The Lord says in 1 John 1:9: *If we confess our sins, He is faithful and just* (because He was crucified for you and for me) *to forgive us our sins and to cleanse us from all unrighteousness.* Then we can move on again. I have been in this place many times and so have you. Come before God today and ask Him to forgive you and to restore you.

Prayer

My Father, I realize that I have looked everywhere but to You for guidance, Lord. Forgive me, I pray. I don't blame anyone but myself. I know what Your Word says and I disobeyed. Forgive me, restore me and lead me in Your ways. Help me to trust in You alone. Amen.

Trust in the LORD with all your heart – this is definitely God's recipe for living a successful life.

Mistrust destroys

Read 1 Samuel 22:6–23

Then Saul said to him, "Why have you conspired against me, you and the son of Jesse…" So Ahimelech answered the king and said, "And who among all your servants is as faithful as David…" (1 Samuel 22:13a,14a)

M istrust and jealousy destroy relationships. As we have already said, you cannot put your trust in anyone other than God. He is the only one who will never let you down. What about you? In whom are you placing your trust today? In 1 Samuel 22 we read about Saul's envy and jealousy of David. King Saul wanted to kill David, and yet David loved Saul. It is a terrible thing what jealousy can do to you. I have seen marriages totally destroyed because of jealousy. In so many relationships instead of people looking to God they look to each other. This means that you place too much pressure on your loved one; too much responsibility. When they do something that you do not like you panic because your trust is in them instead of in God.

Your partner and your children are given to you for a season. You have to entrust your relationships to God. We are responsible for our children, of course we are, but they do not belong to us. It is so sad when you see a young person who wants to leave home and the parents are hanging on. We have got to release our children. You can trust God with your children, my friend. The Bible tells us in Genesis 2:24: *Therefore a man shall leave his father and mother and be joined to his wife, and they shall become one flesh.* We are privileged to have our children live close to us geographically. However, when they walked out the gate the day they got married, their mom and I were no longer number one in their lives. You have to release your children.

You have to trust in God and you have to look to Him to provide for all your needs no matter what they are. Commit your responsibilities and relationships to Him and they will become so special to you. *Trust in the LORD with all your heart, and lean not on your own understanding; in all your ways acknowledge Him, and He shall direct your paths* (Proverbs 3:5–6).

Prayer

My Father, forgive me that so often I put my trust in myself or in other people. I expect too much from people and then they let me down. I know that because of my sinful nature it is difficult for me to have pure relationships. It is only when I allow You to love through me that I am able to be all that I need to be. Amen.

You have to trust in God and you have to look to Him to provide for all your needs.

Inquire of the Lord

Read 1 Samuel 23:1–5

Therefore David inquired of the LORD, saying, "Shall I go and attack these Philistines?" And the LORD said to David, "Go and attack the Philistines, and save Keilah." But David's men said to him, "Look, we are afraid here in Judah. How much more then if we go to Keilah against the armies of the Philistines?" Then David inquired of the LORD once again. (1 Samuel 23:2–4)

David learnt from a young age to put his trust in God. When he was out in the fields looking after his father's sheep it was God who protected him against the lion and the bear. He learnt to know his God as he sat alone in the fields. We said that you cannot trust someone you do not love. You also cannot love and trust someone you do not know. David knew his God. So it stood to reason that later in his life he placed his trust first and foremost in God. Who are you placing your trust in today? Who do you look to for security? In our reading David was advised that the Philistines were attacking the people in a town called Keilah.

At that time David was fleeing from Saul and he had 600 men with him. He was trying to stay out of Saul's way. Saul wanted to kill him because he was jealous of David. Saul believed that David wanted his throne, but this was not true. Saul was also jealous because his son, Jonathan, and David were best friends. So Saul, the King of Israel, was determined to kill David. When David heard that the Philistines were attacking Keilah he inquired of the Lord to find out what he should do. *Therefore David inquired of the LORD, saying, "Shall I go and attack these Philistines?"*

He did not inquire from other people. He did not take the word of his men, even though I am sure he trusted them. No, he inquired from the Lord and the Lord answered him and told him what to do. The Lord told him to go and David defeated the Philistines. David came and he settled in Keilah until word reached Saul that he was there. My friend, you have no one but yourself to blame if you choose to listen to man instead of God. Learn a lesson from David today and place your trust in God first and always; He is the one who will never let you down.

Prayer

My Father, in the midst of difficult decisions help me to keep my head. Help me not to be swayed by the opinions and solutions offered by people. Instead let me listen to You and You only. Amen.

Place your trust in God first and always; He is the one who will never let you down.

When you are betrayed

Read 1 Samuel 23:6–13

Then David said, "Will the men of Keilah deliver me and my men into the hand of Saul?" And the LORD said, "They will deliver you." (1 Samuel 23:12)

David was in an awful position. He'd defended and saved the inhabitants of Keilah, defeating their enemy for them. He and his men had chased the Philistines out of the town. He'd put his own life and the lives of his men at risk. Now when he needed the men of Keilah to protect him they were ready to hand him over to Saul. David must have felt betrayed and hurt when God revealed this to him. Again we see that David does not depend upon man. He doesn't assume that the people of Keilah will come through for him. No: he turns to God to ask God what to do. God doesn't desert David; He tells him that his life is in danger.

So David and his 600 men fled into the wilderness and when Saul arrived, David was long gone. 2 Samuel 22:31 tells us: *As for God, His way is perfect; the word of the LORD is proven; He is a shield to all who trust in Him.* There are lessons for us to learn from this experience of David's. Have you been in the place where someone whom you have helped out and been there for has betrayed you? I know I have and it is not an easy pill to swallow. Our natural reaction is to feel hurt and rejected. We either want to retaliate or we want to lash out and hurt the person back. Vengeance is not ours, my friend.

In October we are going to look at the theme "Vengeance belongs to the Lord". Suffice it to say now that either you believe God is in control of your life or you don't believe it. This is the choice you have to make. If God is in control then you trust Him to work all things out for your good. No man can do anything to you that God cannot use to His glory and honour. Don't trust people; trust God. If this is how you live then it will be a lot harder for people to disappoint you.

Prayer

My Father, in the midst of heartache and disappointment You alone are the one that I trust. I know that You are my shield. Nothing and no one can touch me as long as I stand firmly in Your will for my life. Amen.

No man can do anything to you that God cannot use to His glory and honour.

Remember the name of the Lord

Read Psalm 20:1–9

Some trust in chariots, and some in horses; but we will remember the name of the LORD our God. (Psalm 20:7)

The world believes that "God helps those who help themselves". Living by this maxim means that people do all manner of things to advance themselves. They lie, cheat, climb over the backs of other people and they do not care who is hurt in the process. This is the way of the world. There is a lot of pressure on us to conform to these standards. If you are a Christian and you know God, then this is not the way that you live. If you love Him and trust Him then you will not need to resort to these tactics to get ahead. People may ridicule you, they may think you are soft and they may even use this against you. However, your trust is not in man; your trust is in God.

The Psalmist knew what he was writing about when he penned Psalm 20. He begins the psalm with these comforting words: *May the LORD answer you in the day of trouble; may the name of the God of Jacob defend you; may He send you help from the sanctuary, and strengthen you out of Zion.* No matter what you're facing in your life right now go to your God. Lay it before Him; inquire of Him how He wants you to handle it. Don't trust in people or yourself. There are times when life is hard; things happen that we feel we don't deserve and we are not sure how to cope with. It is in these very situations that we need to *… know that the LORD saves His anointed; He will answer him from His holy heaven with the saving strength of His right hand* (Psalm 20: 1–2, 6).

Psalm 20 tells us that the end result of trusting God is that *He [will] grant you according to your heart's desire, and fulfill all your purpose. We will rejoice in your salvation* (Psalm 20:4–5a). The second half of verse eight says that we will remain standing upright. Remember the name of the Lord and you will come through victorious because God will not forsake you.

Prayer

My Father, I call upon Your name today. I ask You to help me. I am not looking to man or the methods of this world to overcome. I am looking to You. Restore the joy of my salvation to me. Lead me in Your ways and make me stand upright in Your presence. Amen.

Remember the name of the Lord and you will come through victorious – God will not forsake you.

In whom is your expectation?

Read Psalm 62:1–12

My soul, wait silently for God alone, for my expectation is from Him. (Psalm 62:5)

Placing expectations on people sets you up to be disappointed. Do you find yourself in the position where you are disappointed because something you were expecting has not happened? Are you disappointed because someone who either promised you something or from whom you expected something has not come through? Often we place unreasonable expectations upon our children, trying to live vicariously through them. We expect them to make our hopes and dreams come true. You do not have the right to do this, my friend.

Too many people walk around depressed and angry due to unmet expectations. Maybe you feel that you have been overlooked at work. You were expecting a promotion. You feel you have earned the promotion and yet someone else was favoured over you. What do you do with this disappointment? This is what Psalm 62 is talking about when it says: *He only is my rock and my salvation* (Psalm 62:2a). You cannot be disappointed if your expectation is in God. If you are trusting Him then you will know that He is in control of whatever happens in your life.

Nobody can keep the door closed if God wants to open it for you. He has a plan and a purpose for your life. The problem is often that we have a different plan to His and we want Him to bless our plan. Find out what His plan is for you and then walk in it. Trust and obedience go hand in hand. Remember the hymn "Trust and obey": *But we never can prove the delights of His love until all on the altar we lay; for the favour He shows, and the joy He bestows, are for them who will trust and obey. Trust and obey, for there's no other way to be happy in Jesus, but to trust and obey.* Our psalm puts it like this: *Trust in Him at all times, you people; pour out your heart before Him; God is a refuge for us* (Psalm 62:8). The bottom line is that we will only be happy when our expectation is in the Lord.

Prayer

My Father, I come before You today and thank You for Your faithfulness towards me. Forgive me that I often place my expectations upon people and things rather than upon You. I realize that this is why I so often face disappointment. Amen.

The bottom line is that we will only be happy when our expectation is in the Lord.

How do I grow in faith?

Read Hebrews 11:1–12

Now faith is the substance of things hoped for, the evidence of things not seen. But without faith it is impossible to please Him, for he who comes to God must believe that He is, and that He is a rewarder of those who diligently seek Him. (Hebrews 11:1, 6)

My favourite subject, as you know, is faith. I want to ask you the question: what constitutes faith? Many people whom I meet tell me they want more faith so that they can run the race and finish the course that God has set for them. They want to walk in the light that is so precarious at the moment. Oswald Chambers in *My Utmost for His Highest* wrote that: "The root of faith is the knowledge of a Person." Developing faith is not an instantaneous thing. You cannot wave a magic wand and receive faith. Faith is not something you receive by listening to faith messages. No, you don't. You grow in faith by knowing a person. That person is Jesus Christ, the Son of the living God.

Abraham was a man who had faith. *And the Scripture was fulfilled which says, "Abraham believed God, and it was accounted to him for righteousness." And he was called the friend of God* (James 2:23). In fact it is mentioned two more times in the Bible that Abraham believed in God (Genesis 15:6 and Romans 4:3). I believe the reason for this is that you cannot please God without faith. Hebrews 11:6 tells us: *But without faith it is impossible to please Him, for he who comes to God must believe that He is, and that He is a rewarder of those who diligently seek Him.*

Verse eight goes on to tell us: *By faith Abraham obeyed when he was called to go out to the place which he would receive as an inheritance. And he went out, not knowing where he was going.* In faith Abraham left his home and went to an unknown land. He trusted God. He believed God. Why? He did this because he knew God. What is God telling you to do today; and what is holding you back? If you know God then you will trust Him. It is as simple and as complicated as that, my friend. You cannot trust someone you don't know – so the question is, how well do you know Him?

Prayer

My Father, I want to know You more; this is the prayer and desire of my heart. I want to know You the way Abraham did, so that I can follow You wholeheartedly, trusting You in all things. Amen.

You cannot trust someone you don't know – so the question is, how well do you know Him?

Faith comes by hearing

Read Genesis 12:1–9

"Get out of your country, from your family and from your father's house, to a land that I will show you. I will make you a great nation; I will bless you and make your name great..." So Abram departed as the LORD had spoken to him. (Genesis 12:1b–2, 4a)

S top for a moment and think about what it was like for Abraham. Imagine being told to pack up and leave a farm that had been in your family for several generations. God's command to Abraham came with a promise. God said to Abraham, obey Me and I will bless you. Obedience had to come first though, then the blessing followed. It is the same with us, my friend. God wants to bless us, but we have to be prepared to trust Him and obey Him first. You cannot have blessing without faith and obedience.

They say that the second most traumatic thing you can experience is moving home. Most times when we move we know where we are going. Abraham didn't even know where he was going. Abraham was not called a friend of God because he was a good man; no, it was because he was an obedient man – he was a man of great faith. The Word tells us: *So then faith comes by hearing, and hearing by the word of God* (Romans 10:17). We know this don't we? This is part of our problem; we have become blasé and complacent. Yet James 1:22 says to us: *But be doers of the word, and not hearers only, deceiving yourselves.* This is a very important warning for us.

The Word of God is Jesus in print. So the more you get to know Jesus, the more faith you will have. Why? Because the "root of faith is in the knowledge of a Person" – Jesus Christ. The more time you spend with your spouse, the more you will get to know them. So if you never read the Bible you will never have faith. The Word of God is all about Jesus. *In the beginning was the Word, and the Word was with God, and the Word was God. He was in the beginning with God. All things were made through Him, and without Him nothing was made that was made. In Him was life, and the life was the light of men* (John 1:1–4).

Prayer

My Father, I know that You are not interested in lip service. I want to obey You and trust You. I realize though that I will not be able to do this unless I know You. Amen.

The "root of faith is in the knowledge of a Person" – Jesus Christ.

Faith in action

Read Luke 9:23–27

Then He said to them all, "If anyone desires to come after Me, let him deny himself, and take up his cross daily, and follow Me." (Luke 9:23)

A relationship with God sometimes in and of itself causes separation. What does this mean? It means that sometimes when you get to know the Lord you end up in a situation of separation. You see, that is what happened to Abraham. He had to leave his home and he had to travel to another destination. Abraham had to walk by faith, trusting God to fulfil His promise to him. Now when you come to know the Lord as your personal saviour and you walk by faith it can cause you to be in a situation where you experience separation.

God may call you as a missionary to a foreign country to start a work there. He might tell you to resign your job and attend Bible college. The Holy Spirit might convince you of a wrong relationship that you have to put an end to. Following Jesus requires sacrifice; it requires taking up your cross and following Him. It involves denying yourself. Sometimes the separation occurs because friends who were part of your old life no longer want to be friends with you. They no longer consider you to be any fun.

It can be that at work you have to be the one who walks away from the raunchy conversation. You cannot join the guys down at the pub for the all-nighter. Being able to do this involves trusting God. You need to know Him; you need to be sure that you believe that He knows what is best for you. You have to be prepared to trust Him no matter what. People might tell you that you are crazy – who gives up everything to go off into the unknown to serve God? You are in good company: Abraham did and he has been known as a friend of God ever since. Is that how you would like God to refer to you? If so, walk in obedience to Him, trusting Him above everyone and everything else in your life. *"If anyone desires to come after Me, let him deny himself … and follow Me."*

Prayer

My Father, thank You that You are the only one that I can trust. No matter what happens You will never leave me or forsake me. Help me to be obedient to Your voice as You direct me. Amen.

Walk in obedience to Him, trusting Him above everyone and everything else in your life.

Faith has feet

Read Isaiah 40:25–31

But those who wait on the LORD shall renew their strength; they shall mount up with wings like eagles, they shall run and not be weary, they shall walk and not faint. (Isaiah 40:31)

Most of us will never be called upon to go to a far country to spread the gospel. Your mission field is right within your own family. It is within your own home. The place you work is a fertile mission field. Oswald Chambers said that nowadays it is not so much physical separation but mental and spiritual separation that is so much harder. What he meant by this is exactly what we spoke about yesterday. Sometimes it is more difficult being a witness for Jesus within your own family than it would be to go across the seas and do mission work. This is why the root of faith is the knowledge of a person.

The more you get to know the Lord Jesus the more passionate you will become about Him. Jesus was passionate about His mission on this earth. His mission was to save you and me. The Pharisees and the Sadducees of Jesus' day hated Him. Why? Because of His faith. He made the claim that He was God in the flesh. As you know they didn't like that. So they crucified Him. When you go around telling people that Jesus is God they hate you for the same reason that they hated Him. This is the bottom line.

Jesus said in Luke 21:17: *"And you will be hated by all for My name's sake."* Jesus also said in Matthew 5:11: *"Blessed are you when they revile and persecute you, and say all kinds of evil against you falsely for My sake."* So make sure that it is for His name's sake and not because you are being controversial or because you are being rebellious. Be humble, but walk in faith and the Lord of faith will walk with you. Oswald Chambers tells us that faith is not mounting up with wings like an eagle. It is walking and not fainting. Faith has to have feet; it is a "doing" word. Faith requires action. You don't always feel like it, but this is where the love and the obedience come in.

Prayer

My Father, thank You for the promise in Your Word that assures me that if I wait on the LORD I shall renew my strength. I shall mount up with wings like eagles. I shall run and not be weary. I shall walk and not faint. Amen.

You don't always feel like it, but this is where the love and the obedience come in.

Walk by faith

Read 2 Corinthians 5:1–8

For we walk by faith, not by sight. (2 Corinthians 5:7)

Faith is not hearing music from heaven or seeing flashes of lightning, nor is it hearing bells ringing. Faith is saying "Lord, I love You and I am going to go for it. I will keep going no matter how tough it gets. No matter how rough the road. I will walk through the desert. No matter how hard things become I believe in You and in what You have in store for me." Then one day you will walk straight out of the desert into a land of milk and honey like the Israelites did. You need to walk the talk. This is why James 2:20 says: *But do you want to know, O foolish man, that faith without works is dead?*

Faith is not a feeling; it is a fact. *… we walk by faith, not by sight.* Unfortunately there is a lot of bad doctrine in the church. There are those who teach that if you come to Jesus all of your problems will be solved. Nowhere in the Bible will you find a Scripture that says this. What it does say is that you must come to Jesus unconditionally and He will walk tirelessly with you. Isaiah 40:28c promises us: *The Creator of the ends of the earth, neither faints nor is weary.* It is a tragedy that so many people become disillusioned because of bad teaching. Jesus doesn't promise you a bed of roses; but He does promise you: *"I will never leave you nor forsake you"* (Hebrews 13:5b).

Too many people try to bargain with God: "Lord, if You give me … I will follow You." There can be no conditions. The moment you introduce the little word "if" into a covenant, it is no longer a covenant. When you commit to Jesus it is all or nothing. Learn a lesson from Job. He said: *Though He slay me, yet will I trust Him* (Job 13:15a). If you find yourself in a place where you have been bargaining with God come before Him and repent today. The only choice is to walk by faith.

Prayer

My Father, I love You and I am going to go for it. I will keep going no matter how tough it gets. No matter how rough the road. I will walk through the desert. No matter how hard things become I believe in You and in what You have in store for me. Amen.

Faith is not a feeling; it is a fact. The only choice is to walk by faith.

Faith is not a feeling

Read Hebrews 11:1–12

Now faith is the substance of things hoped for, the evidence of things not seen. For by it the elders obtained a good testimony. (Hebrews 11:1–2)

We cannot rely upon our feelings: they are fickle. One day we feel good and positive, the next we feel down in the dumps and despondent. If you watch the news on television or listen to the radio you will hear daily things that can make you feel depressed. The level of anxiety and fear in South Africa has reached epidemic proportions. People of all cultures are under pressure and concerned about the future. If you base your faith upon your feelings then you will live a "yo-yo" Christian life. One day you will be strong and filled with faith and optimism. The next you will be in despair and filled with fear. We don't have to live like this. In fact I will go so far as to say you cannot be a Christian and live like this.

If you read through Hebrews chapter eleven you will see that the people of faith who are listed there believed God in the midst of dire circumstances. Many of them faced personal loss, even death in some instances. They were faced with a choice: To believe, or not to believe. It was black and white; there were no grey areas. In all these people's lives God was only able to undertake great things for them because they chose to believe. They chose to walk by faith. My friends, the closer we get to the end times the more vital faith is going to become.

Faith has to be practised. It is based in the knowledge of a person. Get to know Jesus. I don't mean making the decision to follow Him. That is the first step. You will only get to really know Him if you spend time with Him. Spend time in His Word, in prayer and listening to Him. The closer you get to Him the more your faith will increase. The more your faith increases the less you will be swayed by your feelings and what is going on around you.

Prayer

My Father, I come before You to thank You for Jesus. Thank You for Your Word and that I can know You through Your Word. I want to walk in faith and not be swayed by what is happening around me. Fill me with Your Spirit and Your strength. Amen.

The more your faith increases the less you will be swayed by your feelings and what is going on around you.

Our heavenly hope

Read Hebrews 11:1–16

These all died in faith, not having received the promises, but having seen them afar off were assured of them, embraced them and confessed that they were strangers and pilgrims on the earth. (Hebrews 11:13)

Where is your treasure stored? Listen to what Jesus had to say about this: *"Do not lay up for yourselves treasures on earth, where moth and rust destroy and where thieves break in and steal; but lay up for yourselves treasures in heaven, where neither moth nor rust destroys and where thieves do not break in and steal. For where your treasure is, there your heart will be also"* (Matthew 6:19–21). Do you think that this could be part of our problem? Do we have too much invested in our life on earth and not enough invested in our heavenly home?

Jesus also had this to say about heaven: *"Let not your heart be troubled; you believe in God, believe also in Me. In My Father's house are many mansions; if it were not so, I would have told you. I go to prepare a place for you. And if I go and prepare a place for you, I will come again and receive you to Myself; that where I am, there you may be also"* (John 14:1–3). We spend so much of our time worrying about material things. Don't get me wrong – it is important to provide for your family. The Word tells us that this is our duty. However, my friend, how much do we need? So many people are spending all of their waking hours chasing after keeping up with their neighbours.

My friend, you need to evaluate your lifestyle before God. As you know I am not opposed to success or money. What I am saying is that these things are not to be our motivation for living. Jesus has called us to live a far more exciting life than this. The people mentioned in Hebrews chapter eleven died in faith, never receiving the promise – but they believed and were prepared to die for that belief. Don't live a second-class life, my friend. You are a child of the King. You have a mansion waiting for you. Live your life in the fullness of this knowledge. Living by faith is the key to our heavenly hope.

Prayer

My Father, thank You for the promise of heaven. Thank You that my final destination is not this earth. Help me to live my life in the light of this knowledge. I am so thankful to You that I have a heavenly hope. Amen.

Living by faith is the key to our heavenly hope.

Our faithful God

Read Deuteronomy 7:1–9

"Therefore know that the LORD your God, He is God, the faithful God who keeps covenant and mercy for a thousand generations with those who love Him and keep His commandments." (Deuteronomy 7:9)

The reason that you and I can confidently live by faith is because we serve a faithful God. No matter what happens in your life you can depend upon God. *... know that the Lord your God, He is God, the faithful God...* This is why you have nothing to fear. This is why no one can harm you. This is why you can live the life of a conqueror. You serve a faithful God. He has promised to never leave you or forsake you. No matter what happens He walks beside you. He is there on the good days and He is there on the very worst days. He is a covenant-keeping God. Have you ever stopped to fully comprehend what this means? I am not talking about something that is academic. It is not an intellectual thing – no, God's faithfulness is the most precious commodity that you have.

God's faithfulness keeps us going; it gives us hope. We are precious to God. Let's read again what He has to say about the way He feels about us: *"For you are a holy people to the LORD your God; the LORD your God has chosen you to be a people for Himself, a special treasure above all the peoples on the face of the earth. The LORD did not set His love on you nor choose you because you were more in number than any other people, for you were the least of all peoples; but because the LORD loves you, and because He would keep the oath which He swore to your fathers"* (Deuteronomy 7:6–8a).

How do you feel when you read these words? This is God speaking to you, reassuring you of how He feels about you. When we come to the place of really understanding in our spirits what the faithfulness of God means to us then we can begin to live above our circumstances. You can rejoice because you are not at the mercy of the things happening around you. You can rise above your circumstances because you have your faithful God walking beside you.

Prayer

My Father, I thank You for Your faithfulness towards me. As I look back over my life I realize anew that You have always been there. No matter what has happened You have loved me and cared for me. I give You praise for this today. Thank You that I can live by faith because You are faithful. Amen.

You can rise above your circumstances because you have your faithful God walking beside you.

Persevering faith

Read Revelation 3:1–11

"Because you have kept My command to persevere, I also will keep you from the hour of trial which shall come upon the whole world, to test those who dwell on the earth. Behold, I am coming quickly! Hold fast what you have, that no one may take your crown."
(Revelation 3:10–11)

I want us to spend some time talking about the perseverance of faith. Oswald Chambers writes in his book *My Utmost for His Highest* that patience is even more than endurance. God calls us to persevere with patience. Chambers is not talking about the gritted teeth kind of endurance. It is the kind of endurance that rests in the knowledge that you know God is in control of your life. Remember what he wrote about faith: "The root of faith is knowledge of a Person." If you want to know the secret of perseverance this is it. The better you know Jesus, the closer you are to Him, the easier it will be for you to patiently endure.

The Lord is telling us to hold fast because we are coming to the climax of the Age. My dear friend, don't lose your faith. If you lose your faith you have lost everything. In fact it is possible you could lose your sanity. The reason I say this is because the devil is increasing the pressure to such a degree that it would be easy to start losing heart. If you are not grounded in your faith you are in danger of becoming fearful and anxious; it is then that the devil steps in. This leads to depression and even worse things such as the contemplation of suicide. Our mental institutions are full of people who have lost hope. This is from the pit of hell, I tell you.

The Lord encourages us to persevere. He promises that if we persevere He will keep us from the hour of trial which shall come upon the whole world, to test those who dwell on the earth. What do we have to look forward to at the end of the journey? Revelation 2:10c tells us: *Be faithful until death, and I will give you the crown of life.* As we said the other day, this world is not where it ends for us. Heaven is our destination; there we will reign with Jesus – this is the end goal of persevering faith.

Prayer

My Father, I worship You. Thank You for Your Words of exhortation and encouragement to me today. Give me grace, I pray. Help me to have a persevering faith. I want to know Jesus more and more so that my faith will grow stronger each day. Amen.

Be faithful until death, and I will give you the crown of life (**Revelation 2:10c**).

Patient faith

Read Colossians 1:1–14

...that you may walk worthy of the Lord, fully pleasing Him, being fruitful in every good work and increasing in the knowledge of God; strengthened with all might, according to His glorious power, for all patience and longsuffering with joy. (Colossians 1:10–11)

We are going to examine the patience of faith together. You see, faith is not an instant thing. Faith takes time. I have yet to meet a man of faith who does not have patience. Are you one of the guys who has bought into the world's belief that everything must happen now? You know how it goes: "If you buy this car today we will give you 25 per cent off." "Well, can I just think about it?" "No, there is nothing to think about because tomorrow the price will go up again." My dear friend, the next time the salesman says this to you, reply: "Don't worry, I will come back tomorrow." I can assure you tomorrow it will still be 25 per cent off.

The devil doesn't want you to take time out to pray and to wait on the Lord for wisdom. When I have big decisions to make I do not allow myself to be rushed into them. No matter how much pressure people try to place upon me, I wait on the Lord. This is the patience of faith. It is in His time. Not my timing or the timing according to someone else's agenda.

Oswald Chambers says you and I are like a bow and arrow. The bow has to be fully stretched before the arrow can be released. Maybe you are at the place where you feel that you cannot take much more. You feel as if you are going to snap. No, you are not going to snap because God is not going to allow you to. The reason He is stretching you is because He wants the arrow to hit the mark. Maybe you don't know where you are going or what you should do; but He does. He has the bow and arrow in His hands and He is directing it toward His target. He is telling you to be patient, to hang on. Of course, when the Lord lets the arrow go it hits the target spot on; and the patience of faith is rewarded.

Prayer

My Father, I realize that patience is one of the most difficult virtues to cultivate. It goes against my normal inclinations. Yet, I also realize that once again it comes down to knowledge of You; because if I know You I will trust You; if I trust You I will have patience. Amen.

I have yet to meet a man of faith who does not have patience.

A lesson in patience

Read Hebrews 11:1–12

Now faith is the substance of things hoped for, the evidence of things not seen.
(Hebrews 11:1)

Faith is to believe what you cannot see; but the reward of that faith is to see what you believe. I have experienced this not once but time and time again. If there is one thing that agriculture and farming have taught me, it is patience. It takes many years of patience and perseverance to build up a beef herd. In fact you are talking generations. I am talking about animals: the cows, the calves and the bulls. You need to breed new, different strains of animals to eventually breed the perfect animal. There is skill, yes; there is hard work, absolutely; but there is also patient faith. You must look to the future, believing that you will achieve the desired outcome.

The same is true with a maize crop: it doesn't grow overnight. It takes a full nine months from the time you start preparing your land until the time you begin harvesting. It takes the patience of faith. Faith is not a "hey presto" thing; you don't snap your fingers or wave a wand. Faith is not about naming and claiming what you want. You seek the will of God. Once He has spoken to you and told you what He wants you to do, then you do it. You are obedient to His voice, no matter what.

Then you keep doing what God has told you to do. You do not look at the circumstances around you. You are not swayed by peer pressure or the opinions of people. You remain faithful to God's voice. You patiently wait for Him to fulfil His will and His promise in your life. You will not be able to do this if you do not have a growing relationship with Jesus. We have said several times and I say it again: "The root of faith is a relationship with a Person." When you know Jesus you will recognize and know His voice speaking to you. The better you get to know Him, the easier it will be to patiently wait for Him to fulfil His Word to you.

Prayer

My Father, You teach me in so many different ways. I realize that patience is a commodity in short supply in the world today. Help me to know You, to know Your will and then to patiently trust You to fulfil Your will and promises in my life. Amen.

The better you get to know Jesus the easier it will be to patiently wait for Him to fulfil His Word to you.

Men of patience

Read James 1:1–8

Knowing that the testing of your faith produces patience. But let patience have its perfect work, that you may be perfect and complete, lacking nothing. (James 1:3–4)

Throughout the Bible we read about men of patience: those men to whom God made a promise or gave an instruction. Not one of them accomplished the task or received the promise in a hurry. Some of them never ever saw the fulfilment of what they believed God for, but they continued trusting and believing Him. When Abraham was seventy-five years old God told him to leave his homeland and go to a far country. In faith Abraham obeyed God, took his wife, his servants and his livestock, and left.

One of the promises that God made to Abraham was that He would make him into a great nation. God told Abraham that his descendants would number more than the stars in the heavens. *Then He brought him outside and said, "Look now toward heaven, and count the stars if you are able to number them." And He said to him, "So shall your descendants be"* (Genesis 15:5). Abraham was an elderly man already. Galatians 3:6 tells us: *… Abraham "believed God, and it was accounted to him for righteousness."*

Years and years passed after God made this promise to Abraham. Abraham had to walk by faith; he had to believe God even though he didn't see the results. Abraham learnt many lessons as he walked his faith walk. It was important for Abraham to learn these lessons before God fulfilled His promise to him. Then, when the time was right, God did exactly what He said He would do. My friend, has God promised you something? Did God tell you many years ago that something would happen in your life? Are you patiently believing or have you become disheartened and disillusioned? If you have then you need to take stock today. Make some time to be alone with God. Repent of your unbelief. Go before Him and ask Him to confirm His Word to you. Then recommit yourself to walking the faith walk with Him. Make a decision of your will that you will cultivate a lifestyle of patient faith. Don't look to the circumstances around you; look to God.

Prayer

My Father, I am so aware that I have allowed myself to become discouraged and sidetracked. Forgive me, I pray. Help me to get back on track. I want to live a lifestyle characterized by patient faith. Amen.

Cultivate a lifestyle of patient faith. Don't look to the circumstances around you; look to God.

The obedience of faith

Read Hebrews 11:1–12

By faith Noah, being divinely warned of things not yet seen, moved with godly fear, prepared an ark for the saving of his household, by which he condemned the world and became heir of the righteousness which is according to faith. (Hebrews 11:7)

God gave Noah a task to do that required a huge step of faith. Man had become very wicked. *So the LORD said, "I will destroy man whom I have created from the face of the earth, both man and beast, creeping thing and birds of the air, for I am sorry that I have made them." But Noah found grace in the eyes of the LORD … Noah was a just man, perfect in his generations. Noah walked with God* (Genesis 6:7–9). God decided to use Noah to save mankind from extinction.

God told Noah to build an ark because a flood was coming upon the earth. This had never happened before. Everyone ridiculed Noah, but it didn't deter him. He believed God and in faith he built the ark according to God's exact instructions. Can you imagine God telling you to do something like this? Would you have the faith to trust Him or would you bow to peer pressure? God is looking for men like Noah today, those who will trust Him for the seemingly impossible. The result of Noah's obedience and faith was that he and his family together with the animals were the only ones who were saved when the flood came. Noah and his family, together with the animals, spent forty days and forty nights in the ark. Then, when the water had subsided, God told them to leave the ark.

When they came out of the ark Noah built an altar to offer a sacrifice to the Lord. God had provided for this sacrifice by sending seven of every clean animal into the ark. God plans ahead, my friend; trust Him to know exactly what you will need to fulfil His purpose in your life. Noah's sacrifice was acceptable to God and He said: *"While the earth remains, seedtime and harvest, cold and heat, winter and summer, and day and night shall not cease"* (Genesis 8:22). Then God made a covenant with Noah and He sent a rainbow as a sign of that covenant.

Prayer

My Father, You are a covenant-keeping God. You are faithful to Your promises. I know that I can trust You. Lord, I lay my life upon Your altar. I pray today that my life will be a sweet-smelling sacrifice to You. Amen.

God is faithful to those who believe and obey Him.

Faith in the God who hears

Read Exodus 3:1–15

And the LORD said: "I have surely seen the oppression of My people who are in Egypt, and have heard their cry because of their taskmasters, for I know their sorrows. (Exodus 3:7)

Moses was a man with a destiny. The fact that he was alive was a miracle of God's grace and protection. Moses was an introvert – he did not really like the limelight. He had a speech impediment and he was used to being behind the scenes in the desert looking after his father-in-law's sheep. One day God interrupted his life and appeared to him in a burning bush. ... *God called to him from the midst of the bush and said, "Moses, Moses!" And he said, "Here I am."* God gave Moses a massive assignment. *"Come now, therefore, and I will send you to Pharaoh that you may bring My people, the children of Israel, out of Egypt"* (Exodus 3:4, 10).

Moses didn't want to do it. *But Moses said to God, "Who am I that I should go to Pharaoh...?"* God promised Moses: *So He said, "I will certainly be with you..."* Then *Moses said to God, "Behold, I am going..."* (Exodus 3:11a, 12a, 13a New American Standard). What we see here is: the encounter with God, the call of God and the response to God. My friend, have you had an encounter with God? Has He told you to do something? If so, what has your response been? Moses was reluctant but once he accepted that God had called him he obeyed God. He stepped out in faith and did as God had commanded him.

Moses lived a remarkable life of faith. It required a huge step of faith to believe that God could free the children of Israel from their slavery. They had been in captivity for hundreds and hundreds of years. The Lord used a man who was willing to believe Him. Moses was a man with the same weaknesses that we have – but he was a man of faith. Moses trusted and he obeyed. God hasn't changed – He is the same miracle-working God who called Abraham, Noah and Moses. Today He is calling you. Are you living a life of patient faith or are you stuck in Egypt too scared to take the first step towards freedom?

Prayer

My Father, how absolutely amazing You are. I am so filled with awe and wonder as I read the stories of these great men of faith. You are the same yesterday, today and forever. You have not changed. Help me to be obedient to Your calling upon my life and to develop a patient faith. Amen.

God hasn't changed – He is the same miracle-working God who called Abraham, Noah and Moses.

The covenant of faith fulfilled

Read Exodus 6:1–8

"I will take you as My people, and I will be your God. Then you shall know that I am the LORD your God who brings you out from under the burdens of the Egyptians. And I will bring you into the land which I swore to give to Abraham, Isaac, and Jacob; and I will give it to you as a heritage: I am the LORD." (Exodus 6:7–8)

This is a beautiful story of the patience of faithfulness. God made a promise to Abraham. He told him: *On the same day the LORD made a covenant with Abram, saying: "To your descendants I have given this land, from the river of Egypt to the great river, the River Euphrates – the Kenites, the Kenezzites, the Kadmonites, the Hittites, the Perizzites, the Rephaim, the Amorites, the Canaanites, the Girgashites, and the Jebusites"* (Genesis 15:18–21). The Israelites landed up in captivity through lack of faith in God. They chose not to believe Him; they chose to disobey and do things their own way. However, when God makes a covenant, He never forgets it and He never goes back on it.

For some 450 years the Israelites were in captivity to the Egyptians. They were enslaved. When the time was right God acted according to the covenant He had made with Abraham. Do you see the far-reaching effects of Abraham's faith in God? Today you and I are the beneficiaries of Abraham's belief in God. God always keeps His covenant, my friend. He will never let you down. The key is to wait in patient faith for Him to do what He has said He will do. Don't grow weary; don't give up. Keep the faith.

Sadly, too many of God's children are living their lives enslaved to the things of this world. God has promised us an inheritance that cannot be lost or tarnished; yet we choose, like the prodigal son, to go after the flesh pots of Egypt – until we find ourselves eating the pigswill of this world. If you have become lost along the way, today is your chance to return to your covenant-keeping Father. He waits for you with open arms. Come back to Him; reaffirm His voice speaking to you and what He has said. Then take a step of obedient faith. Choose to wait with patient faith, actively serving and believing Him as You wait for Him to fulfil His Word to you. Follow the examples of Abraham, Noah and Moses.

Prayer

My Father God, You are a faithful, covenant-keeping God. You never forget and You never go back on Your Word. Forgive my unbelief, I pray. Help me to walk in obedience and to wait with patient faith for You to fulfil Your Word to me. Amen.

Choose to wait with patient faith, actively serving and believing Him as You wait for Him to fulfil His Word to you.

A different spirit

Read Numbers 14:11-25

"But My servant Caleb, because he has a different spirit in him and has followed Me fully, I will bring into the land where he went, and his descendants shall inherit it." (Numbers 14:24)

Time and again the Israelites disobeyed, complained and distrusted God. That whole generation died in the desert. Why? Because they didn't have patience. They didn't trust God. They constantly questioned: "Why haven't we got food? Why haven't we got water? Why haven't we got clothes? When are we going to get there?" In the end, only two men from the original number crossed over the Jordan into Canaan – Joshua and Caleb. Why? Because they had a different spirit. They chose to believe God when all the others chose disbelief. They saw beyond the present circumstances and looked with the eyes of faith. Joshua and Caleb's patient faith bore fruit.

The patience of faith. Do you have patience, my friend? How are you doing in this department? Are you prepared to wait for what God has promised you? He will not let you down. If God has made you a promise it will come to fruition. The choice is yours: you can either choose to wait patiently or you can make your own plan. I have often mentioned Pastor William Duma. He never made a decision without seeking the council of His Father first. Once he was invited to go to Israel, all expenses paid, along with two other pastors. The other two pastors immediately accepted the invitation. Pastor Duma said, "Can I give you an answer tomorrow? I have to first ask my Lord whether I can go." The Lord said he could go, but he asked Him first.

How many times do we do things spontaneously when we should wait on God? I am finding in my own life that I have to wait on God like never before. I have been faithfully preaching the gospel for thirty years. Now after all this time God has begun opening the door of opportunity at Shalom like I would never have dreamed of thirty years ago. The patience of faith. Thrust yourself into God's hands; believe that His timing is perfect. Hold fast until He comes. What kind of a spirit do you have?

Prayer

My Father, increase my faith, I pray. Help me to patiently wait on You. I realize that everything that I have comes from You. Teach me to patiently and joyfully wait upon You. Amen.

Thrust yourself into God's hands; believe that His timing is perfect.

Learn the patience of faith

Read Romans 15:1–13

For whatever things were written before were written for our learning, that we
through the patience and comfort of the Scriptures might have hope. (Romans 15:4)

S ome thirty years ago there was a man named Piet Uys. He was a schoolteacher
in the northern part of South Africa. He decided to show his school pupils that
Jesus Christ is alive and that He honours faith. Piet took his whole class, about
twenty of them, on a three week holiday all over South Africa. They took no money
with them and trusted God to pay for everything. They stood with their rucksacks on
the side of the road and waited for God to provide. They went all around South Africa
and God fed them, provided accommodation and showed them all kinds of things "on
the house", as it were. They didn't spend a cent.

One night they landed up at our home. I will never forget it. Piet taught my boys
how to catch bass fish and prepare the fish properly. They built a fire and grilled the
fish; we had an amazing meal that evening. Then Piet, a very mature Christian, took
up his guitar and began playing for us. He prophesied over Jill and me. This took place
more than thirty years ago. He told us: "Angus and Jill, the Lord has a plan for your life.
He doesn't want to tell you what the plan is now, because if He did you will not be able
to contain it. It would frighten you to death, because you are not mature enough; and
you are not strong enough to take it. I am telling you, if you keep walking by faith, if you
keep the patience of faith, God is going to use you like you would never believe." Piet
Uys, if you ever read this, I want you to know it is happening.

If twenty years ago I had become tired and thrown in the towel it would never
have come to be. If I had demanded that God "deliver the goods or the show is over",
the deal would have been off. You see, you cannot dictate to God. You can ask Him but
you can't demand.

Prayer

*Now may the God of hope fill you with all joy and peace in believing, that you may abound
in hope by the power of the Holy Spirit* (Romans 15:13). Amen.

You see, you cannot dictate to God. You can ask Him but you can't demand.

The patience of Job

Read Job 13:1–15

Though He slay me, yet will I trust Him. Even so, I will defend my own ways before Him. (Job 13:15)

Job uttered the words: *Though He slay me, yet will I trust Him.* Despite this Job reached the point where he began thumping the table; he wanted to see results. His patience was growing thin. His farm was gone, he had lost his children and his money, and he was sick. He sat on the ash heap. Maybe this is where you are at the moment – on the ash heap covered in sores and boils. You are desperate for answers. God told Job to stand up like a man and talk to Him if he wanted answers. God continues telling Job that He wants to ask him a couple of questions. God wants to know where Job was when the earth was formed. Does Job know where the spring is in the middle of the ocean where the water comes out? Does he know how the sun rises in the morning and sets in the evening or how the stars were placed in the sky?

God goes on and on and Job grows quieter and quieter. I want to ask you, do you know the answers to these questions today? No, you don't; you might think you do, but you have no idea. Scientists will tell you: the more they find out the more they realize how little they know. The same is true of doctors, surgeons and specialists. I love doctors, but a doctor can only tell you what is wrong with you and prescribe medication; he cannot heal you. Only God can heal you. We are God's creation. We become impatient because we don't get what we want when we want it.

Job came to understand the greatness of his God. In Job 42:5–6 he says, *"I have heard of You by the hearing of the ear, but now my eye sees You. Therefore I abhor myself, and repent in dust and ashes."* Do you need an encounter with God today where you will see Him clearly for who He is – the God of the universe, who has everyone and everything under His control?

Prayer

My Father, I bow in repentance before You. Like Job, I know who You are, I know of You, but I am not seeing You clearly. Give me a fresh vision and open my eyes to see You clearly. Amen.

Do you need an encounter with God today where you will see Him clearly for who He is?

The wisdom of faith

Read Psalm 40

I waited patiently for the LORD; and He inclined to me, and heard my cry. He also brought me up out of a horrible pit, out of the miry clay, and set my feet upon a rock, and established my steps. (Psalm 40:1–2)

t is not a foolish man who has faith: it is a wise man. Rather it is a foolish man who continues to question his Creator. The Word says: *"And this is eternal life, that they may know You, the only true God, and Jesus Christ whom You have sent"* (John 17:3). Isn't this beautiful? When you know God you don't have to ask why. "The root of faith is the knowledge of a Person." You see, this is the thing: when you spend time with God you get to know His personality and His character; you learn that He will never do anything to harm you. He loves you too much. *"Greater love has no one than this, than to lay down one's life for his friends"* (John 15:13).

The greatest thing I can ever do for you, my friend, is to give you my life. I can't give you any more than that. This is what Jesus Christ did for you and for me on the cross of Calvary. While we were still in our sin. This is the miracle. The Bible even says that a good man will die for another good man, but you won't find a good man dying for somebody who is evil. Jesus died for you and me. We need to exercise the patience of faith because I am telling you what God has promised us is going to come to pass.

Something else that is imminent is the second coming. Jesus Christ is coming back sooner than you think. Live with all of your heart and give Jesus everything you have to give. Then when you die you will rest with Him. This is the patience of faith. Our psalm tells us: *Blessed is that man who makes the LORD his trust ... You are my help and my deliverer; do not delay, O my God* (Psalm 40:4a,17b). The Word also tells us: *So then faith comes by hearing, and hearing by the word of God* (Romans 10:17). Do you know your God? Are you a wise man who understands the wisdom of faith?

Prayer

My Father, thank You that You sent Your Son Jesus Christ to this world to save me. I praise You for Your love and faithfulness to me. I thank You that I can rest in You. I want to know You more and more. Amen.

Do you know your God? Are you a wise man who understands the wisdom of faith?

The birth of faith

Read Matthew 13:31–32, 17:14–21

"I say to you, if you have faith as a mustard seed, you will say to this mountain, 'Move from here to there,' and it will move; and nothing will be impossible for you." (Matthew 17:20b)

Abraham is known as the father of the faith. However, there was a progression in Abraham's faith walk with God. The more Abraham got to know God the more he trusted Him. I hope that as we look at this progression over the last few days of this month you will be blessed and encouraged in your own faith walk with God. In Genesis chapter twelve we read of God's call to Abraham. He tells him to pack up his family and his possessions and start walking to a new place. Abraham obeys God and does as He is told. In verse one God tells Abraham: *"Get out of your country, from your family and from your father's house."* God told him to get away from his family, but Abraham took Lot with him.

Then when Abraham and his group passed through Egypt we see that he uses Sarah in order to protect himself from the Pharaoh. God steps in and deals with the situation. In chapter thirteen Abraham and Lot part ways. If bringing Lot was a mistake God doesn't hold it against Abraham – He reaffirms His promise to Abraham, promising to give him more descendants than the dust of the earth. God was committed to Abraham and his faith walk. My friends, you need to realize that you are not in this faith walk alone. God is committed to walking it with you, in the same way He walked with Abraham. In chapter fifteen we see Abraham having his "conversion" moment. *And he believed in the LORD, and He accounted it to him for righteousness* (Genesis 15:6).

Even after this experience Abraham's faith had not reached maturity. He was still on a faith journey with God. It is important that you realize this as you evaluate your walk of faith with the Lord. Faith is like a mustard seed – you have to plant it. It is like a muscle – you have to use it. You need to practise faith. The better and deeper you get to know Jesus the easier it will be to trust Him.

Prayer

My Father, I thank You for Your faithfulness. I am so grateful that I am not alone on this journey of faith. Thank You that You are as committed to me as You were to Abraham. Lead me step by step, day by day. Lord, I plant my mustard seed; water and nurture it, I pray. Amen.

The better and deeper you get to know Jesus the easier it will be to trust Him.

The progression of faith

Read Genesis 16:1–16

Then she called the name of the Lord who spoke to her, You-Are-the-God-Who-Sees; for she said, "Have I also here seen Him who sees me?" (Genesis 16:13)

W hen Abraham left Ur he was seventy-five years old. Sarah, his wife, was sixty-five. Eleven years later God had still not made good on His promise to them. Sarah was now seventy-six and Abraham was eighty-six. Sarah decided that God needed some help and Abraham agreed to go along with her plan. So Abraham had a son with Sarah's maid, Hagar. As you can imagine that did not have a good outcome. Why? Because they disobeyed God. This was not God's plan. Abraham was disobedient and he had to bear the consequences of that disobedience.

Sarah drove Hagar away after she conceived Abraham's child. Hagar fled into the wilderness. God found her beside a spring of water. That day Hagar had an encounter with God. He revealed Himself to Hagar and made her a promise. Why did God do this? He did it because He is a covenant-keeping God and He made a covenant with Abraham. Hagar's reaction to her encounter with God was a beautiful one filled with meaning for you and me. God revealed Himself to her as El Roi – the God who sees. God saw everything she had been through. He understood her predicament. God told her to go back to Sarah and to serve her. He also told her that He would bless her son.

There would be consequences for the actions but that did not mean that God would not be there with them while they walked through them. It is no different with us, my friend. God loves you. He has made a covenant with you through the death and resurrection of His Son, Jesus Christ. God is committed to you. He is your El Roi – He is your God who sees. Whatever the situation is that you find yourself in right now – He is in it with you. Maybe you cannot see your way through it – but He can. You need to trust Him today. Hagar obeyed God and went back to Sarah. Whatever it is that God tells you to do, obey Him. He will see you through the situation.

Prayer

My Father, today I stop right here and I build an altar to Your name: El Roi – my God who sees. Thank You that You see everything clearly, even though for me it is all murky and muddled. I am trusting You. Help me to find my way out of this situation. Amen.

Whatever it is that God tells you to do, obey Him. He will see you through the situation.

The maturing of faith

Read Genesis 17:1–19

Then Abram fell on his face, and God talked with him, saying: "As for Me, behold, My covenant is with you, and you shall be a father of many nations. No longer shall your name be called Abram, but your name shall be Abraham; for I have made you a father of many nations." (Genesis 17:3–5)

Abraham encountered God in a new way. Up until that time Abraham believed in God. He was willing to obey God and he left his home for God. Each year he got to know God better. Each year he trusted God a little more. This whole month we have been saying that faith is rooted in the knowledge of a person. Abraham spent two and a half decades getting to know his God. One day God took Abraham to a new level of relationship with Himself. He gave Abraham a new name. Up until that day he had been known as Abram. God told him that his name would change to Abraham. God breathed His Spirit into Abraham.

This was the coming of age of Abraham's faith. It didn't mean that there wouldn't be other hurdles to climb. In fact the greatest test of Abraham's life lay ahead of him still. On that day Abraham entered a new dimension in his experience with God. The Lord had been maturing Abraham throughout the twenty-five years. Now Abraham had reached the place where he was ready to receive the promise that God had made to him in Genesis chapter twelve. I hope this is ringing bells for you, my friend. Abraham wasn't perfect; in fact, he made lots of mistakes along the way during the twenty-five years. However, he learnt his lessons, he remained faithful, he grew in his knowledge of God and his faith increased. Until one day God saw that Abraham was ready to receive the promise.

Abraham could be trusted with the fulfilment of the promise. You need to continue to faithfully follow God. Keep obeying Him; learn the lessons He wants to teach you each day. Grow in your knowledge of Him. Allow Him to breathe His Spirit into you and baptize you with His Spirit. Ask Him to give you a new name of faith. Then one day, when the timing is right, He will look at you and He will say: *"Is anything too hard for the LORD? At the appointed time I will…"* (Genesis 18:14).

Prayer

My Father, You are a great and wonderful God. Your faithfulness reaches from generation to generation. You are the same God that Abraham served. Father, fill me with Your Spirit today. Reach down and breathe Your Spirit into me. Empower me to walk in faith with You. Amen.

Allow Him to breathe His Spirit into you and baptize you with His Spirit. Ask Him to give you a new name of faith.

The obedience of faith

Read Genesis 21:1–8

And the LORD visited Sarah as He had said, and the LORD did for Sarah as He had spoken. For Sarah conceived and bore Abraham a son in his old age, at the set time of which God had spoken to him. (Genesis 21:1–2)

Twenty-five years after God first promised Abraham that He would make him a great nation He gave him his first child. In Genesis 18:14 (a year before Isaac was conceived) God says to them: *"Is anything too hard for the LORD? At the appointed time I will return to you, according to the time of life, and Sarah shall have a son."* This is the first time that God puts a time period to the promise; and He fulfils it to the day. God wanted to be sure that everyone would realize that only He could do this thing. Man had no hand in it. Sarah was too old to have a baby. It was a God thing. Throughout the twenty-five years leading up to Isaac's birth God had been teaching Abraham faith lessons.

Isaac grew to be a fine young man and then the day came that God put Abraham to the ultimate test. *Then He said, "Take now your son, your only son Isaac, whom you love, and go to the land of Moriah, and offer him there as a burnt offering…"* (Genesis 22:2). Can you imagine it? God asks Abraham to do the unthinkable. Why would God give and then take away? Isn't that the first thing you would be tempted to ask if this happened to you? For any parent this must surely be the ultimate test of faith. I want to ask you: do you think if God had fulfilled His promise to Abraham five or ten or fifteen or even twenty years after he left Ur that he would have been able to obey God? Do you think Abraham's faith would have been strong enough to do this thing? No, my friends; I doubt it.

Do you see the lesson here? God's timing is perfect. He is never a second too early nor a second too late. What was Abraham's response? Yes, you have it – he obeyed immediately. He didn't question; he didn't argue. Abraham knew that he could trust his God. The root of faith is the knowledge of a person.

Prayer

My Father, I am so in awe as I come before You today. You are a God of love, compassion and faithfulness. Your faithfulness reaches down throughout time. It envelops me, holding me in the circle of Your love for me. Help me to trust You with what You have given me. Amen.

God's timing is perfect. He is never a second too early nor a second too late.

The provision of faith

Read Genesis 22:1–18

But Isaac spoke to Abraham his father and said, "My father!" And he said, "Here I am, my son." Then he said, "Look, the fire and the wood, but where is the lamb for a burnt offering?" And Abraham said, "My son, God will provide for Himself the lamb for a burnt offering." So the two of them went together. (Genesis 22:7–8)

A braham trusted God implicitly. He had no guarantee that God would not make him go through with sacrificing Isaac. The old Abram would have tried to make a plan of his own. The new Abraham trusted in his God to do what was best for him and his son. Up the mountain they went. They prepared the altar and Isaac was placed upon it. Abraham was about to carry out God's instructions when God stopped him. *And He said, "Do not lay your hand on the lad, or do anything to him; for now I know that you fear God, since you have not withheld your son, your only son, from Me." Then Abraham lifted his eyes and looked, and there behind him was a ram caught in a thicket by its horns. So Abraham went and took the ram, and offered it up for a burnt offering instead of his son. And Abraham called the name of the place, The-Lord-Will-Provide* (Genesis 22:12–14a).

God provided and Abraham's place as the father of faith was secured for all eternity. This is what made Abraham a friend of God: his total commitment, obedience and faith in God. I hope that what you have come to understand over this past month, and particularly the past few days, is that this was a process. It was a journey. It was a life lived getting to know God. It is the same with you and me, my friends. It is one day at a time. It is choosing as each situation presents itself to trust God rather than yourself or someone else. This is what grows faith – knowing God, knowing Jesus Christ, His Son, and walking in the power of the Holy Spirit.

We will end with the same verses we began the month with: *Trust in the LORD with all your heart, and lean not on your own understanding; in all your ways acknowledge Him, and He shall direct your paths* (Proverbs 3:5–6). Have you grown in your faith over the past thirty days? Come before Him and tell Him.

Prayer

My Father, I bow before You. I lift my hands in praise and worship of Your holy name. I stand in Your presence and I give You praise that You are my God who provides for my every need. You give me everything that I need. I can totally rely on and rest in You. You will never let me down. Amen.

And Abraham called the name of the place, The-LORD-Will-Provide (Genesis 22:14a).

SEPTEMBER

Now is the time ... to be a prayer warrior

The secret place

A mighty warrior

The words of my mouth

Making time for prayer

Jesus our example

Where was Jesus?

Martha and the secret place

Four days late, but always on time

Where is your secret place?

An encounter in the secret place

The Lord of hosts

A time to mourn

The importance of solitude

A Sabbath rest

The Lord is my shepherd

What makes a prayer warrior

My food and drink

A strong, powerful warrior

Put on the whole armour

Our weaponry

The belt of truth

The breastplate of righteousness

Spreading the gospel of peace

Taking up the shield of faith

Wearing the helmet of salvation

Wielding the sword of the Spirit

Lord, teach us to pray

Praying to your Father

Give us this day, our daily bread

A persistent prayer warrior

The secret place

Read Psalm 91

He who dwells in the secret place of the Most High shall abide under the shadow of the Almighty. I will say of the LORD, "He is my refuge and my fortress; my God, in Him I will trust." (Psalm 91:1–2)

O ver the past few years I have spent a fair amount of time in airports around the world. I am constantly amazed as I watch travellers scurrying around. So many people on their way from somewhere en route to somewhere else. We live in a world of constant motion that never stops. Is it any wonder that people are more stressed than ever before? We see unprecedented acts of aggression and anger being perpetrated. People need to slow down. They need a secret place where they can shelter, where they can come to rest and regroup. This month we are going to talk about prayer and being a prayer warrior.

One of the steps to being a prayer warrior is having a secret place. A place where you can get away from the world and connect with God. In your secret place you can find refuge and solace when life is becoming too much. It is the place you can go to when you are hurt. There you can withdraw to find guidance. It is in the secret place where only you and your Father are that you can hear from Him. He can tell you His thoughts. You can seek His counsel and you can intercede for your loved ones. God will share His heart with you as you spend time in His Word, listening to Him in the secret place.

Being a prayer warrior is not about physical prowess, but rather about spiritual prowess. We have battles to fight and a war to win. In order to be successful we need to receive our orders from our Commander-in-Chief. As we learnt when we looked at the life of Elijah, God doesn't always talk through the thunder; very often He speaks in the still small voice. It is in the secret place that you will meet with Him and hear Him speak. Take a few minutes in your secret place as you begin this new month. Recharge your batteries. Tune up your spiritual antennae and wait on your Father.

Prayer

My Father, I come to You at the start of this new month. I want to know You more. I want a deeper relationship with You. I desire above all else to walk in Your will and Your ways. I know that it is through spending time with You in the secret place that I get to know You. Amen.

Being a prayer warrior is not about physical prowess, but rather about spiritual prowess.

A mighty warrior

Read 1 Samuel 17:2–37

Moreover David said, "The LORD, who delivered me from the paw of the lion and from the paw of the bear, He will deliver me from the hand of this Philistine." And Saul said to David, "Go, and the LORD be with you!" (1 Samuel 17:37)

I know that we have mentioned the story of David and Goliath earlier this year, but we never stop learning from God's Word. It is our guide, our manual for all of life. You can read the same story and there is always more you can learn from it – that is because it is alive. Hebrews 4:12 tells us: *For the word of God is living and powerful, and sharper than any two-edged sword, piercing even to the division of soul and spirit, and of joints and marrow, and is a discerner of the thoughts and intents of the heart.* I want us to look at the story of David and Goliath from the perspective of the men in the army of Israel.

They were all strong men who were trained to be soldiers. They were not cowards; they knew what they were doing when it came to battle. Despite this, the day they faced an enemy bigger than them they didn't know what to do. All their battle plans and strategies didn't work. Can you imagine them meeting together and trying to figure out how they were going to defeat Goliath? The more they thought about it the less they believed they could do it. What was the one thing they omitted to do? They didn't consult their Commander-in-Chief. You don't read anything about them going before God to ask Him how they should defeat Goliath.

David, on the other hand, spent a lot of time in his secret place with God. Out in the fields there was no one but God, him and the sheep. When the bear and the lion attacked him God told him what to do. He obeyed and his faith was strengthened. So when it came to Goliath David's natural reaction was to turn to God. God told him what to do and he simply obeyed God. My friend, God has the answer to every situation. There is no giant too big for Him. It is in your secret place that He will give you His game plan.

Prayer

My Father, I realize that I spend so much time making my own plans and not nearly enough time in consultation with You. It is no wonder that I am running from the Goliaths in my life. Amen.

There is no giant too big for Him. It is in your secret place that He will give you His game plan.

The words of my mouth

Read Psalm 19

Let the words of my mouth and the meditation of my heart be acceptable in Your sight, O LORD, my strength and my Redeemer. (Psalm 19:14)

There is an enormous amount of power in the spoken word. When you pray and speak out your thoughts in prayer you are releasing that power. You need to find your secret place and then go there to communicate with the Lord. Where do I find a secret place, you might ask me? Maybe you live in a block of flats on the seventh floor, in the middle of a city. Or it could be that you are a student living in a dormitory.

The truth is you can have a secret place wherever you are – it is not the physical location that matters. Your secret place is in your heart, so the Lord will meet with you wherever you are. You can be in the middle of the busiest station in Tokyo and you can close your eyes and go to that place. Maybe you need to try visualizing a secret place. I am not talking about anything weird so relax – I am a Christian, through and through.

The point is that even when you are busy or travelling you need to be able to go to your secret place. Having a personal ritual of being able to visualize yourself there can help you. For instance when I am away from Jill, I often feel lonely and I miss home. When this happens, wherever I am (it could be in a hotel or at an airport), I simply close my eyes and I visualize walking next to the stream at home or sitting down next to it. Once I have done this I have a talk with the Lord. I tell Him about my loneliness, how I am missing Jill and the family. Then in my spirit man He reassures me that He has everything under control at home. It is at those times that the Lord reaches down; He renews and refreshes me for the next part of my journey. Do you have a secret place? If not, then today is the day that you need to take the first steps towards creating one.

Prayer

My Lord, *Let the words of my mouth and the meditation of my heart be acceptable in Your sight, O LORD, my strength and my Redeemer.* Amen.

If you don't have a secret place then begin by taking the first steps towards creating one.

Making time for prayer

Read Psalm 91

"Because he has set his love upon Me, therefore I will deliver him; I will set him on high, because he has known My name. He shall call upon Me, and I will answer him."
(Psalm 91:14–15a)

Every mighty man or woman of God spends time with Him. This is the way you grow in your relationship with God. I have often said it to you, but I will say it again: He wants the first fruits of your day. You can meet with God anywhere, anytime in your secret place – however, you need to have regular times when you come before God at the beginning of the day as well. I guess you could say that the other times during the day are top-up times. It is in the early morning that God gives us our marching orders for the day ahead. It is in the morning hours that we need to be in our secret place listening to Him.

William Carey, of whom I have often spoken, was a man of prayer. William Carey's secret place was his rose garden where he tended his rose bushes. There he cried and laughed while he sought God's counsel. Maybe his secret place helped keep him sane when he was really hard pressed. John Wesley's mother, Susanna Wesley, had nineteen children (although not all of them survived to adulthood). She had her quiet time sitting by the fire. She pulled her apron over her head and then she prayed to God. When she did that her children knew that Mom was in her secret place speaking to Jesus and she was not to be disturbed.

Martin Luther was one of the busiest men on this planet. He said, "The busier I get, the earlier I get up in the morning." We tend to do it the other way around: when we get busier we cut back on our quiet time. You have an important meeting so you rush into the office to prepare. It is in the secret place that He will rejuvenate your spirit man. In the secret place God will give you clear direction for your day. He will give you the strategy you need for that important meeting. Spending time with God in your secret place is the most vital part of your preparation for the day ahead.

Prayer

My Father, I give You praise for Your faithfulness to me. Lord, forgive me that so often I do not make the time to be with You. Show me where my secret place should be and then help me to make the time to be with You there. Amen.

Spending time with God in your secret place is the most vital part of your preparation for the day ahead.

Jesus our example

Read Mark 1:29–39

Now in the morning, having risen a long while before daylight, He went out and departed to a solitary place; and there He prayed. (Mark 1:35)

No one had more demands on His time than Jesus did. He only had three years to accomplish His ministry. Every day, all day people were clamouring for His attention. He travelled with twelve men by His side. Yet the first priority in Jesus' life was withdrawing to His secret place to spend time with His Father. In Matthew 6:6, just prior to giving us the Lord's Prayer, He says: *"But you, when you pray, go into your room, and when you have shut your door, pray to your Father who is in the secret place; and your Father who sees in secret will reward you openly."*

It was during these times that Jesus received His Father's instructions regarding what He was to do. Have you ever wondered how Jesus decided who to heal and who not to heal? He didn't heal every sick person on the earth while He was here. His choices weren't random: His Father told Him what to do and what He was to say. *"The words that I speak to you I do not speak on My own authority; but the Father who dwells in Me does the works. Believe Me that I am in the Father and the Father in Me"* (John 14:10b–11a). Time and again we see Jesus withdrawing to His secret place to be with His Father. I don't think that their time together was only about what Jesus was to say and do. I am sure it was an opportunity for Jesus to just be in His Father's presence – simply being together.

There is no doubt that it was these times that gave Jesus His strength to carry on. It was during these times that He was rejuvenated for the task ahead of Him. What about you, my friend? Do you find solace and joy in the presence of Your Father? Do you sit at the feet of Jesus receiving from Him? If your life is lacking power and you are wondering why, maybe this is your answer. Withdraw to your secret place and meet with your Father.

Prayer

My Father, I take my example from Jesus, Your Son and my saviour. I come into Your presence. I rest in You. I wait upon You. I thank You for the privilege of being able to be with You. Amen.

If you are lacking power, withdraw to your secret place and meet with Your Father.

Where was Jesus?

Read John 11:1–27

…"I am the resurrection and the life. He who believes in Me, though he may die, he shall live. And whoever lives and believes in Me shall never die. Do you believe this?" (John 11:25–26)

A re you in the position where you have been calling on the Lord and it seems as if He is not hearing you? Sometimes your situation is desperate and Jesus seems to be somewhere else. This is how Mary and Martha felt. They were Jesus' friends. He had visited in their home and the Word tells us, *Now Jesus loved Martha and her sister and Lazarus* (John 11:5). Yet when Lazarus became sick and word was sent to Jesus He didn't drop everything and immediately rushed to their side. In fact Jesus waited until four days after Lazarus had died before He made His way to Bethany. By this time Mary and Martha had given up hope that Jesus would come to help them. They were hurt and disappointed.

If Jesus loved them as He said He did then why would He put them through this? When He was told that Lazarus was sick Jesus said: *"This sickness is not unto death, but for the glory of God, that the Son of God may be glorified through it"* (John 11:4). Martha came out of the city and met Jesus along the road. *Now Martha said to Jesus, "Lord, if You had been here, my brother would not have died. But even now I know that whatever You ask of God, God will give You"* (John 11:21–22). This encounter between Jesus and Martha is important – we will talk more about it tomorrow.

Jesus tells Martha that her brother will rise and she thinks He is referring to the resurrection. *Jesus said to her, "I am the resurrection and the life. He who believes in Me, though he may die, he shall live. And whoever lives and believes in Me shall never die. Do you believe this?"* This question is key: Do you believe? Martha answers: *"Yes, Lord, I believe that You are the Christ, the Son of God, who is to come into the world"* (John 11: 25–26, 27). Even though it had all gone wrong, even though her brother was dead, Martha believed. Martha was willing to entrust her situation to Jesus.

Prayer

My Father, thank You for Your faithfulness. Thank You that You are always there, no matter what is happening in my life. Help me to believe. Help me to trust You with every aspect of my life, even when I don't understand what is happening. Amen.

Martha believed and she was willing to entrust her situation to Jesus.

Martha and the secret place

Read Luke 10:38–42

And Jesus answered and said to her, "Martha, Martha, you are worried and troubled about many things. But one thing is needed, and Mary has chosen that good part, which will not be taken away from her." (Luke 10:41–42)

M artha is what we would call a "control freak". She was a workaholic. She didn't know how to sit still. She was always on the go. When Jesus came to visit she would busy herself preparing the meal and seeing that the house was in order. She made sure that everything was just so – to the point that she wore herself out. Then she began to feel resentful. Her sister Mary, on the other hand, only wanted to sit at Jesus' feet and spend time with Him. Mary understood about the "secret place" straight off. She knew that there was nothing more important than spending time with Jesus, whom she loved.

Mary also instinctively knew that Jesus was not interested in what she could do for Him. She realized that He wasn't interested in her works. Jesus wanted her to spend time with Him. To sit in the secret place talking and listening to Him. When Martha rebuked Mary for not helping her, *Jesus answered and said to her, "Martha, Martha, you are worried and troubled about many things. But one thing is needed, and Mary has chosen that good part, which will not be taken away from her."* This was the day that Martha learnt about the secret place. She learnt that Jesus was interested in her spending time with Him, not doing stuff for Him.

When she spent time with Him He would tell her what it was that she was to do. She didn't have to run around wearing herself out. Martha simply needed to abide in her secret place with Jesus. It was because Martha had learnt this that she was able to spontaneously answer Jesus when He asked her if she believed: *"Yes, Lord, I believe that You are the Christ, the Son of God, who is to come into the world"* (John 11:27). Martha knew Jesus – not in a superficial way, but in an intimate way. Martha had spent time in the secret place with Jesus; and as a result even in the midst of sorrow and great trial she trusted Him.

Prayer

My Father, I realize that so often I too run around serving You. I become so busy that it is easy to forget to slip into my secret place with You. I know that this is the reason that I sometimes feel worn out. As I sit before You today, refresh me, I pray. Amen.

Martha had spent time in the secret place with Jesus; and as a result she trusted Him.

Four days late, but always on time

Read John 11:28–44

And Jesus lifted up His eyes and said, "Father, I thank You that You have heard Me. And I know that You always hear Me, but because of the people who are standing by I said this, that they may believe that You sent Me." (John 11:41b–42)

J esus was totally at peace because He knew exactly what time He had to be at Lazarus' tomb, and exactly what He had to do. Why? Because the Most High God, His Father, had told Him in the secret place. Jesus received His instructions and He carried them out to the letter. When they approached the tomb Jesus was moved by the sorrow of his friend. The Bible says simply: *Jesus wept* (John 11:35). Some of the Jews who were standing around said: *"Could not this Man, who opened the eyes of the blind, also have kept this man from dying?"* (John 11:37). My friend, you need to know that there will always be those who will doubt and question God.

Jesus did not take time to answer them. He simply moved ahead with the plan that His Father had given Him. He asked them to remove the stone from in front of the tomb. Don't you love Martha? (She is ever practical, even in her renewed spiritual state.) She reminded Jesus that after four days there was going to be a stench when the tomb was opened. Jesus in turn reminded her: *"Did I not say to you that if you would believe you would see the glory of God?"* (John 11:40). Isn't that precious? Jesus was keeping Martha on track. He did not allow her to revert to her old self: the controlling, organizing-everyone Martha. He reminded her about the secret place and what the better choice was.

This story is about so much more than the miracle of Lazarus being raised from the dead. It is about God being glorified in the midst of impossible circumstances. It is about two women learning that they could trust Jesus no matter what happened in their lives. It is about one woman, Martha, learning to wait at the feet of Jesus. She learnt to spend time in her secret place. She learnt to come to peace and rest. She learnt that by listening to and obeying Jesus she could accomplish so much more than she could on her own.

Prayer

My Father, I thank You for Your love for me. I am so grateful that You take the time to teach me Your ways. You show me what it is that You want me to do. Help me to make the time to meet with You. I want to know You and trust You. Amen.

Martha learnt that by listening to and obeying Jesus she could accomplish so much more than she could on her own.

Where is your secret place?

Read Psalm 91

He who dwells in the secret place of the Most High shall abide under the shadow of the Almighty. I will say of the LORD, "He is my refuge and my fortress; my God, in Him I will trust." (Psalm 91:1–2)

We spend so much time fretting and worrying. Jesus had something very specific to say about worry. *"Therefore I say to you, do not worry about your life…"* Which of you by worrying can add one cubit to his stature? *"Therefore do not worry, saying, 'What shall we eat?' or 'What shall we drink?' or 'What shall we wear?' Therefore do not worry about tomorrow, for tomorrow will worry about its own things"* (Matthew 6:25a, 27, 31, 34a). The best solution for worry is the secret place. That's right: time in the secret place is the antidote to worry. You cannot worry when you are sitting at Jesus' feet. Mary knew this and Martha learnt it.

God is your provider. He is Jehovah-Jireh. Where is your secret place? You can have more than one – because your secret place is wherever you withdraw in order to be with Jesus. The location can change, but the secret place stays the same. I have quite a few secret places. One is saddling up my horse, Big Stuff, and riding him out into the fields. I switch off completely and I am alone with God. Something else that I do is early in the morning, before the sun rises, I have my quiet time; then I put on my running shoes and I go for a jog. Often in winter I run with the moon, because the sun takes so long to rise. While I am running I start talking to the Lord. It is beautiful and invigorating running through pockets of air that alternate between warm and cool. It is a wonderfully exhilarating time for me and it is often during these times that God gives me my messages.

So, my friend, if you are stressed out and worried about everything under the sun, stop for a moment. Withdraw to your secret place. Spend time sitting at Jesus' feet and hear what it is that He has to say to you. Often what He has to say to you is far more important than what you have to say to Him.

Prayer

My Father, I come to You today to sit at Your feet. Still my troubled spirit, I pray. Help me to settle down so that I can hear You speak to me. Teach me Your ways. Share Your heart with me. Fill me with Your Spirit. Amen.

Time in the secret place is the antidote to worry. You cannot worry when you are sitting at Jesus' feet.

An encounter in the secret place

Read Psalm 91

He who dwells in the secret place of the Most High shall abide under the shadow of the Almighty. I will say of the LORD, "He is my refuge and my fortress; my God, in Him I will trust." (Psalm 91:1–2)

W hen I was younger I often fasted and prayed up in the Drakensberg Mountains, about one hour west of Shalom. One day in mid-summer I took my rucksack and a bottle of water and I started to walk right up to the top of the mountain. I sat quietly; because it was in the middle of the week there was no one else up there. I simply sat with the Lord, having a good talk and a cry. I rejoiced in Him.

I was a little late starting back down the mountain. In the afternoons it normally rains and as I watched big black thunder clouds rolled in. It was the most amazing sight, my friend, as I stood looking down on the clouds beneath me. I watched as a full-blooded storm rocked the mountainside. There was thunder and lightning below me. I crept into a little cleft in the mountainside and I sat there watching the storm play out below me. I was totally dry as I sheltered in my secret place.

After about an hour the clouds parted and the sun came out. The streams ran down the side of the mountain. I began walking – no rushing or panicking – down the mountain singing praises to God. I had an encounter with the Lord that I have never forgotten. You see, if you are too busy you will never experience something like that. Our natural inclination is to run through the storm and get injured. This is how people get into trouble in the mountain. This is true spiritually, as well. When we encounter a storm in our lives we must shelter under the shadow of the Most High. God promises: *"Because he has set his love upon Me, therefore I will deliver him; I will set him on high, because he has known My name. He shall call upon Me, and I will answer him; I will be with him in trouble; I will deliver him and honor him. With long life I will satisfy him, And show him My salvation"* (Psalm 91:14–16).

Prayer

My Father, in the midst of the storm You are my shelter; You are my anchor; You are my harbour. I have nothing to fear as long as I am hiding in You. Answer me, deliver me, honour me and satisfy me, I pray. Amen.

When we encounter a storm in our lives we must shelter under the shadow of the Most High.

The Lord of hosts

Read Psalm 46

God is our refuge and strength, a very present help in trouble. The LORD of hosts is with us. The God of Jacob is our refuge. Be still, and know that I am God. (Psalm 46:1, 7, 10a)

t is in the secret place that you will meet the Lord of hosts. The Hebrew word for the Lord of hosts is Jehovah Sabaoth. This name of God carries the image of a mighty military commander, one who can summon rank upon rank of protective powers at a mere word. All creation is under God's control and obeys His sovereign command. The Lord of hosts has at His disposal the entire created universe with which to accomplish His purposes. All creation fights on behalf of the Lord of hosts. God employs this ultimate power that He has over the universe on behalf of us, His children.

My friend, when last has God shown Himself strong on your behalf? If it has been a while it is certainly not because He has lost power. Indeed no; His power remains the same for all eternity. The problem lies with us. In order to access His power we need to know Him. We cannot know Him if we do not spend time with Him. It is in the secret place that you will become acquainted with Jehovah Sabaoth. It is there that the God of Jacob will be your refuge. Jesus also referred to the solitary place. *Now in the morning, having risen a long while before daylight, He went out and departed to a solitary place; and there He prayed* (Mark 1:35).

If you are facing difficulties and problems that seem insurmountable, then you need the Lord of hosts to show Himself mighty on your behalf. Withdraw today to a solitary place where you can spend time with Him. Bring your situation before Him. Lay it at His feet. Place your burden at the foot of the Cross. *"Come to Me, all you who labor and are heavy laden, and I will give you rest. Take My yoke upon you and learn from Me, for I am gentle and lowly in heart, and you will find rest for your souls. For My yoke is easy and My burden is light"* (Matthew 11:28–30).

Prayer

My Father, the Lord of hosts. I come before You and lay my burdens at the foot of the cross. Jehovah Sabaoth, I ask You to show Yourself strong on my behalf today. Amen.

The Lord of hosts has at His disposal the entire created universe with which to accomplish His purposes.

A time to mourn

Read Matthew 14:1–14

So he sent and had John beheaded in prison. When Jesus heard it, He departed from there by boat to a deserted place by Himself. (Matthew 14:10, 13a)

Jesus was God, but He was also a man. So when He heard that His cousin, John the Baptist, had been beheaded by King Herod, He was devastated. The Bible says that when Jesus heard the news *He departed from there by boat to a deserted place by Himself.* Jesus' first reaction in His grief was to withdraw to a solitary place to be with His Father. He knew that it was His Father who would comfort and console Him. When you face grief, my friend, you need to wait on God, take time and pause. Ecclesiastes 3:4 tells us – There is *a time to mourn.*

If you are mourning the loss of a loved one take the time to come apart and be quiet. The answer is not to lose yourself in activity or in a big crowd. Jesus mourned His cousin. Jesus knew He would see John in heaven, very shortly in fact – within three years; but He missed Him and took time to mourn him. As a Christian do you give people the space to mourn? Or do you tell them to pull themselves together and to read the Word of God? We can be very insensitive sometimes. Telling someone who has lost a loved one that all things work together for good and therefore they should be rejoicing is not helpful. Of course if they are a Christian they know this. They know that God is in control. Hopefully they know their loved one is with Jesus.

However, they still need time to mourn. They need time to express their sadness. If Jesus needed time to do this, then surely so do we. So, my friend, if you are mourning today, if you are hurting, go to Jesus. Sit in the presence of your Father God. Allow Him to comfort you. Find refuge in His arms. He will allow you to simply be. No one will be able to comfort you like your Father will. As you wait in the solitary place with Him, He will give you the courage to carry on.

Prayer

My Father, thank You that You understand me like no one else does. With You I am able to be myself. I can open up allowing You to comfort me and love me. You know how much I am hurting. You know that I am confused and scared. I lay it all before You. Amen.

As you wait in the solitary place with Him, He will give you the courage to carry on.

The importance of solitude

Read Luke 5:1–16

So He Himself often withdrew into the wilderness and prayed. (Luke 5:16)

The busier you are the more important it is for you to have times of solitude with the Lord. You cannot run on empty. If you are at a place in your life where nothing is making sense any more – you need solitude. If you are a businessman running a large company and you have lost the passion for what you are doing – you need solitude. If you are a minister and you are running dry spiritually – you need solitude. Have you noticed in the passages of Scripture we have been reading this month that the busier Jesus' ministry became, the more time He spent in solitude with His Father? Jesus was God of the universe yet He took on the form of a man. As a man He needed time with His Father.

We have often mentioned that it was during these times that His Father told Him what to do and when to do it. God will do the same for you, my friend. We do not need to struggle along. I could not do what I do but for the times of solitude with my Father. Whether it is about what to preach or making decisions regarding the ministry, I need to hear from my Father. Don't try to do it alone – you will fail. If you need to make decisions about your business, then come before your Father and ask Him what you should do. He has a plan and He will share the plan with you.

Our society values activity. We are encouraged from an early age to be productive. This is all well and good, but we have failed to learn the art of quietness. John Ruskin said: *No music is music unless there is a pause.* Music doesn't flow on and on. There are pauses between the verses. Each instrument pauses and then continues according to the score. Music ebbs and flows; pausing at the appropriate moment and then picking up again. Our lives are like this too. We cannot keep going indefinitely; we need to stop – refuel – then carry on again.

Prayer

My Father, I have spent so much time rushing around. I have been on a treadmill. I often feel like I don't know how to step off it. Help me today to take that step and come into a quiet place with You. Amen.

We cannot keep going indefinitely; we need to stop – refuel – then carry on again.

A Sabbath rest

Read Genesis 1:1–2:3

Thus the heavens and the earth, and all the host of them, were finished. And on the seventh day God ended His work which He had done, and He rested on the seventh day from all His work which He had done. Then God blessed the seventh day and sanctified it, because in it He rested from all His work which God had created and made. (Genesis 2:1–3)

Sometimes I actually think we believe we have more energy, power and stamina than God. God created the heavens and the earth in six days. Then on the seventh day He rested. God commanded the Israelites: *"Work shall be done for six days, but the seventh is the Sabbath of rest, holy to the LORD"* (Exodus 31:15a). We see the reason for this command to rest in verse seventeen of the same chapter: *"It is a sign between Me and the children of Israel forever; for in six days the LORD made the heavens and the earth, and on the seventh day He rested and was refreshed."* You need to be refreshed; this is why the Sabbath day should be a day of rest.

I don't know which day you call the Sabbath day. I celebrate Sunday, but that does not make any difference. Paul says it can be any day of the week. The Seventh-Day Adventists celebrate Saturday. So what? The question is what does your Sabbath day – your day of rest – consist of? It saddens me when I hear of Christians going to the mall on their day of rest. For so many people their day of rest is busier than any other day of the week. They never stop as they try to raise a family and hold down a job in order to put bread on the table. On their day of rest there is so much work to be done around the house. They are running on empty.

No wonder that people become depressed, have nervous breakdowns and burn out. The antidote is taking time out. Jesus, the busiest man in the world, made time. What about us? Exodus tells us that God instituted a day of rest not because He wanted to impose a rule or regulation upon us; but rather because He gave us the gift of a day upon which we could be refreshed. You will find that if you take time to refresh yourself then you will be better able to handle the stresses and strains of life.

Prayer

My Father, I ask You to forgive me that I have been blindly stumbling along. I realize that I have not heeded Your Word to me. Lord, I am not coping and I realize that it is because I have disobeyed Your command to take a day of rest. Amen.

God gave us the gift of a day upon which we could be refreshed.

The Lord is my shepherd

Read Psalm 23

The LORD is my shepherd; I shall not want. (Psalm 23:1)

Our theme this month is "Now is the time to be a prayer warrior". When one thinks of being a warrior you think of action, don't you? About getting out there and doing the business. Yet we have spent most of the first half of the month talking about what would appear to be inactivity. We have been speaking about withdrawing to a secret place, finding a place of solitude where you can meet with God. A warrior needs to receive their orders from their commanding officer. This is what we have been discussing together. It is in the place of solitude, in the secret place that we receive our orders.

The most important part of prayer is listening. God loves to hear us talk to Him. We can tell Him anything and everything, but He loves it even more when we are prepared to sit and listen to what He has to say to us. So often our prayer time is all about rushing in, delivering the grocery list and then rushing out again. Then we wonder why God doesn't answer; why we don't hear from Him. He is only too willing to talk to us, but are we prepared to listen? Psalm 23 is probably one of the best known and most loved portions of Scripture. It is about resting, finding contentment. It is about trusting and knowing that God is in control.

We live in uncertain times. People are fearful of the future. Psalm 23 is the solution to this fear. The Lord is your shepherd, my friend. He will guard you, He will care for you and He will lead you all the way home. You need fear nothing as long as you are following Him. Don't become sidetracked by the storms of life. Spend time with your Father in the secret place and you will constantly be refreshed and restored. His promise to you in verse six is that: *Surely goodness and mercy shall follow me all the days of my life; and I will dwell in the house of the LORD forever.*

Prayer

My Father, I come before You. Thank You that You are my shepherd and I want for nothing. You restore me and lead me in the paths of righteousness. I rest in You, my shepherd. Amen.

Spend time with your Father in the secret place and you will constantly be refreshed and restored.

What makes a prayer warrior?

Read Ephesians 6:10–18

Finally, my brethren, be strong in the Lord and in the power of His might. Put on the whole armor of God, that you may be able to stand against the wiles of the devil.
(Ephesians 6:10–11)

A warrior needs certain support structures to make him successful. When an army goes to war they will not be successful if they do not have a support structure behind them. They need uniforms and boots. The army has to have weapons and artillery. Water and food are important as well. They need to spend time training and honing their skills for battle. Then the commander-in-chief of the army needs to know what he is doing. He needs a battle strategy. It benefits an army greatly if they have a secret weapon at their disposal. Our theme for this month is – *"Now is the time to be a prayer warrior"*.

The word "warrior" usually conjures up images of action, doesn't it? Yet we have spent a lot of time talking about withdrawing to a secret place and spending time in solitude with God. We have been speaking about resting and taking refuge. Is this at odds with the idea of being a prayer warrior? Not at all. Where do you think our training happens? It happens in the secret place, when we spend time with our commander-in-chief. We learn the skills of battle through the Word of God. God's Word is food to our Spirit. Jesus gives us rivers of living water. Our weapons and armoury are mighty to bring down principalities and powers. Our uniform is the armour of God. Our secret weapon is God's Holy Spirit empowering us.

It all starts with receiving our strategy from our commander-in-chief. This is not a one-off occurrence. We return regularly for updates, to hear what He has to say to us. He gives us our orders and our mission. The place where He passes on His orders is in the secret place. As we have said several times this month this is where Jesus withdrew to receive His orders from His commander-in-chief. We are going to take a few days to examine our armour and some of the support structures that God has put in place for us.

Prayer

My Father, I bow in Your presence with awe and gratitude. I thank You for Your faithfulness and love toward me. I want to be a prayer warrior who does mighty exploits for You. I rest in Your presence and bow at Your feet. Amen.

God gives us our orders and our mission. The place where He passes on His orders is in the secret place.

My food and drink

Read John 6:22–40

And Jesus said to them, "I am the bread of life. He who comes to Me shall never hunger, and he who believes in Me shall never thirst." (John 6:35)

S o much of our lives are consumed by the process of gathering sustenance for our physical bodies. We work at least five days a week to earn the money to put food on the table for our families. While this is good and noble, because it is your God-given task to provide for your family, never forget that God is your provider. Our reading today follows on from the feeding of the 5,000. As you know Jesus withdrew to be in a solitary place with His Father. However, the people whom He had fed wanted more of the same – so they followed Him expecting and hoping for another miracle.

Jesus made the following statement when He realized what the crowd wanted: *"Do not labor for the food which perishes, but for the food which endures to everlasting life, which the Son of Man will give you, because God the Father has set His seal on Him"* (John 6:27). As God's warrior your focus is not consumed only by the temporal, because you realize that there is a bigger picture. You look to Jesus, the bread of life, to provide your sustenance, so that you will never hunger again spiritually. You believe in Jesus, who gives you the water of life, so that you will never thirst again.

Spend time in your secret place with your Father and you will be spiritually satisfied and fortified. You will be able to hear from your commander-in-chief. He will direct your paths. He will give you the strategy for your life and for your ministry. He will tell you how to be what you need to be for your family. He will show you how to provide for your family. He will tell you what it is that you are to do. Success is to be found as you spend time in the secret place with your Father – not in frenetic busyness and rushing around striving from morning until night. *"In returning and rest you shall be saved; in quietness and confidence shall be your strength"* (Isaiah 30:15b).

Prayer

My Father, thank You for Jesus, who is the bread of life and the living water. I sit at Your feet, my Lord; I drink and I eat. Thank You that nothing else can satisfy me. I am filled and satisfied by You alone. Lead me in Your ways and equip me to be a prayer warrior. Amen.

As God's warrior your focus is not consumed only by the temporal, because you realize that there is a bigger picture.

A strong, powerful warrior

Read Ephesians 6:10–18

Finally, my brethren, be strong in the Lord and in the power of His might. (Ephesians 6:10)

I n the book of Ephesians, Paul deals with some major themes, culminating with chapter six. In verse ten he says: *Finally, my brethren, be strong in the Lord and in the power of His might.* It's as if he is implying that you will not be able to do the other things he speaks of in the chapter if you are not strong in the Lord. Could this be the reason that so often we are weak and ineffectual in our Christian lives? Because we are not strong in the Lord and we do not have His mighty power coursing through us?

We expend a great deal of energy and time trying to achieve power in other areas of our lives. Some work to excel on the sports field. Whatever their chosen sport they train and work, often making huge sacrifices to become powerful sportsmen. Others work long hours to become successful in their business or career. They make more and more money believing that financial gain alone will bring them peace and security. True power is not to be found in worldly success or riches. God can certainly use these to His glory, if we commit them to Him. However, it's only in the secret place that we receive the input of lasting power into our lives. No one can take this power away from you.

Finishing strong is such an important thing. How many men have slipped and allowed themselves to be distracted away from the path God has ordained for them? How do we remain strong? Again it comes down to time in the secret place. John shares this with us: *I have written to you, fathers, because you have known Him who is from the beginning. I have written to you, young men, because you are strong, and the word of God abides in you, and you have overcome the wicked one* (1 John 2:14). You will be strong if God's Word abides in you. Spend time with God in His Word and you will become a strong, powerful prayer warrior.

Prayer

My Father, as I come before You I ask You to fill me with Your Spirit. Give me Your power and strength. As I spend time in Your Word strengthen me in my inner man so that I will be able to stand strong. Amen.

Spend time with God in His Word and you will become a strong, powerful prayer warrior.

Put on the whole armour

Read Ephesians 6:10–18

Put on the whole armor of God, that you may be able to stand against the wiles of the devil. For we do not wrestle against flesh and blood, but against principalities, against powers, against the rulers of the darkness of this age, against spiritual hosts of wickedness in the heavenly places. (Ephesians 6:11–12)

The armour that we are talking about is a spiritual armour, not a physical one. The devil you can see is so much easier to deal with than the devil you cannot see. So often he approaches us in subtle, sly ways that can catch us off guard. This is why we need to spend time in the secret place: we need to be in God's Word. When we put on the whole armour of God we will be able to stand against the wiles of the devil. You will recognize him no matter how clever he tries to be. Your God is mighty to save.

The devil knows that his time is short, so he will do whatever he can to deceive and destroy. This is why Paul warns us so strongly in verses twelve to thirteen of our reading. Don't be fooled, my friend. He is a deadly foe. The joyful news is that God has given you everything you need to fight him. You are a warrior for Jesus. You do not fight the devil with weapons such as guns and knives. You fight him with spiritual weapons. You have not been left defenceless. No matter what is going on in your life right now, stop and take count. If you are being beaten by the enemy, go to the secret place.

Your commander-in-chief will be there and He will walk through the valley with you. You will not be left alone; He will give you what you need to withstand the evil day. Then when you have done everything and the battle is over, you will still be standing victorious in Jesus. It is Jesus who won the battle for us on Calvary – He conquered death and the enemy. Philippians 4:13 assures us: *I can do all things through Christ who strengthens me.* Don't allow yourself to be pushed around by the enemy – Ephesians 6:13 says: *Therefore take up the whole armor of God, that you may be able to withstand in the evil day, and having done all, to stand.*

Prayer

My Father, I come before You battered and broken. I realize that I have taken my eyes off You. I have become sidetracked by the wiles of the enemy. I turn to You today. I come into the secret place and I lift my eyes to You. I put on the armour and I stand firm in Your power. Amen.

Your commander-in-chief will give you what you need to withstand the evil day.

Our weaponry

Read Ephesians 6:10–18

Stand therefore, having girded your waist with truth, having put on the breastplate of righteousness, and having shod your feet with the preparation of the gospel of peace; above all, taking the shield of faith with which you will be able to quench all the fiery darts of the wicked one. And take the helmet of salvation, and the sword of the Spirit, which is the word of God. (Ephesians 6:14–17)

Too many Christians are being mown down by the devil, because they don't know how to use the weapons that the Lord has given them. Many don't even know what their weapons are, or what they are to be used for. You have truth to gird your waist; a breastplate of righteousness; gospel of peace shoes; a shield of faith; a helmet of salvation and a sword of the Spirit. These are awesome weapons, my friend. Now is the time for you to be a prayer warrior. You need no weapons other than these to wage and win the war against the prince of this world. These weapons are mighty to wage battle. Once you have received your mission from your commander-in-chief then gird up your loins. Put on your armour piece by piece and go forth into battle.

Put on the belt of truth; always speak the truth – it will set you free. Jesus said in John 17:17: *"Sanctify them by Your truth. Your word is truth."* How often has the devil tried to hold you back by pointing out the sins from your past to you? This is why you need the breastplate of righteousness. We are not righteous in our own right – absolutely not – but we have the righteousness of God. Romans 3:22 says it like this: *even the righteousness of God, through faith in Jesus Christ, to all and on all who believe.* If you believe in Jesus and He is your saviour then the breastplate of righteousness is yours. Use it to deflect the darts of condemnation that the enemy fires at you.

The Lord says, blessed are the peacemakers, not blessed are the peace lovers. When you wear the shoes of the gospel of peace it sometimes means you have to say the hard things, folks. We're called to steadfastly speak the Word of truth. When people repent of their sin and accept Christ, then the peace comes. We are warriors for Christ bringing His peace to a lost world. Our feet are shod with the shoes of peace.

Prayer

My Father, I thank You that You have given me everything that I need to stand firm for You. As I sit at Your feet instruct me in the art of warfare. Help me to put on each piece of armour so that as I go out into the world I might be a mighty warrior for You. Amen.

Too many Christians are being mown down by the devil, because they don't know how to use the weapons that the Lord has given them.

The belt of truth

Read Ephesians 6:10–18

Stand therefore, having girded your waist with truth, having put on the breastplate of righteousness, and having shod your feet with the preparation of the gospel of peace; above all, taking the shield of faith with which you will be able to quench all the fiery darts of the wicked one. And take the helmet of salvation, and the sword of the Spirit, which is the word of God. (Ephesians 6:14–17)

The *New International Version* speaks about having *the belt of truth buckled round your waist*. When you dress in the morning, you thread your belt through the loops in your trousers and buckle it up. Your belt serves a very practical purpose – it stops your trousers from falling down. How embarrassing would it be if you were walking down the road and your trousers slid down around your ankles, because you forgot to put on and buckle up your belt? To avoid spiritual embarrassment buckle up the belt of truth around your waist.

How often has the devil tried to hold you back by pointing out the sins and failures from your past to you? *And the Word became flesh and dwelt among us, and we beheld His glory, the glory as of the only begotten of the Father, full of grace and truth* (John 1:14). Jesus is your truth, my friend. In Him you have received salvation. In Him you are righteous – all your sins are under His blood. Therefore, you stand in His grace and you are washed clean. Don't ever allow the enemy to make you doubt this. His aim is to rob you of the assurance of your salvation through his lies, then he knows he will have a foothold into your life.

Jesus had this to say about the devil: *You are of your father the devil… He was a murderer from the beginning, and does not stand in the truth, because there is no truth in him. When he speaks a lie, he speaks from his own resources, for he is a liar and the father of it* (John 8:44). Always speak the truth. It will set you free. In John 17:17 we read: *Sanctify them by Your truth. Your word is truth.* Paul had this to say: *Therefore, putting away lying, "Let each one of you speak truth with his neighbor," for we are members of one another"* (Ephesians 4:25). Defeat your enemy by putting on the belt of truth – walking in truth, living in truth and speaking the truth.

Prayer

My Father, thank You for Jesus, who is my truth. Help me to daily put on the belt of truth. By Your Spirit I want to walk, live and speak Your truth in every situation and circumstance of my life. I want to honour You by the way that I live. Amen.

Defeat your enemy by putting on the belt of truth – walking in truth, living in truth and speaking the truth.

The breastplate of righteousness

Read Ephesians 6:10–18

Stand therefore, having girded your waist with truth, having put on the breastplate of righteousness, and having shod your feet with the preparation of the gospel of peace; above all, taking the shield of faith with which you will be able to quench all the fiery darts of the wicked one. And take the helmet of salvation, and the sword of the Spirit, which is the word of God. (Ephesians 6:14–17)

A soldier puts on a breastplate in order to protect vital organs such as his heart, lungs and kidneys. Without it the soldier would face sure death. The enemy would be able to plunge his sword into the heart of the soldier, rendering a fatal wound. We live in a sinful world and we face danger on every side, each day. We are in a spiritual battle. You cannot fight in your own strength or on your own merits. Isaiah 64:6 tells us: *But we are all like an unclean thing, and all our righteousnesses are like filthy rags.* Paul confirms this: *"There is none righteous, no, not one"* (Romans 3:10). If you are depending upon your own righteousness you will be defeated.

You need the righteousness of God: *But now the righteousness of God apart from the law is revealed, being witnessed by the Law and the Prophets, even the righteousness of God, through faith in Jesus Christ, to all and on all who believe. For there is no difference; for all have sinned and fall short of the glory of God, being justified freely by His grace through the redemption that is in Christ Jesus, whom God set forth as a propitiation by His blood, through faith, to demonstrate His righteousness, because in His forbearance God had passed over the sins that were previously committed, to demonstrate at the present time His righteousness, that He might be just and the justifier of the one who has faith in Jesus* (Romans 3:21–26).

If you believe in Jesus and He is your saviour, then the breastplate of righteousness is yours. Use it to deflect the darts of condemnation that the enemy fires at you. You can live with confidence because you are protected by the breastplate of righteousness. When you get up in the morning be intentional about putting on your spiritual armour. Put on your belt of truth and your breastplate of righteousness. You have a suit of armour that will defeat your enemy. Go forth in the righteousness of God, your Father.

Prayer

My Father, I come before You realizing that I can never be righteous on my own merits. I stand before You today, so much in need of You. Thank You that I can claim Your righteousness, because I am Your child and I have been saved through the shed blood of Jesus. Amen.

If you believe in Jesus and He is your saviour, then the breastplate of righteousness is yours.

Spreading the gospel of peace

Read Ephesians 6:10–18

Stand therefore, having girded your waist with truth, having put on the breastplate of righteousness, and having shod your feet with the preparation of the gospel of peace; above all, taking the shield of faith with which you will be able to quench all the fiery darts of the wicked one. And take the helmet of salvation, and the sword of the Spirit, which is the word of God. (Ephesians 6:14–17)

Again the New International Version puts it well – *your feet fitted with the readiness that comes from the gospel of peace.* The Lord says: *Blessed are the peacemakers...* (Matthew 5:9), not blessed are the peace lovers. Folks, wearing the shoes of the gospel of peace sometimes means saying the hard things. We need to steadfastly speak the Word of truth to people. Jesus said about Himself: *"Do not think that I came to bring peace on earth. I did not come to bring peace but a sword"* (Matthew 10:34). What Jesus means is that when confronted with Him people are forced to make a choice. They have to choose to either follow Him or reject Him. As His followers we have to be uncompromising in speaking His truth.

There are people who will do anything to "keep the peace". Paul says our feet must be fitted with the readiness. Are you ready, eager and willing to share the good news of the gospel of Jesus Christ with those around you? This does not mean that we go around being judgmental or Bible-bashing. It simply means that we share the gospel with the people we come into contact with. It means that your actions must line up with your talk. We are meant to bring peace wherever we go. When someone repents of their sin and accepts Christ, then they meet the Prince of Peace and peace comes into their lives.

None of the pieces of the armour are meant to be used in isolation from each other. They work together to accomplish God's purposes. We speak the Word of truth (Jesus) to people – sharing His love and compassion with them. We reach out, bringing His peace into the lives of those who are troubled and lost. There is only one way to achieve peace: *Therefore, having been justified by faith, we have peace with God through our Lord Jesus Christ* (Romans 5:1). We are Christ's warriors bringing His peace to a lost world. Our feet are shod with the shoes of peace.

Prayer

My Father, I thank You again today for my salvation. You have given me the peace of Jesus in my heart and life. I live each day aware that my life is in Your hands. Help me to fearlessly share the good news of the gospel with people I come into contact with. I want to share the peace that I have with others. Amen.

"How beautiful are the feet of those who preach the gospel of peace, who bring glad tidings of good things!" (Romans 10:15b).

Taking up the shield of faith

Read Ephesians 6:10–18
Stand therefore, having girded your waist with truth, having put on the breastplate of righteousness, and having shod your feet with the preparation of the gospel of peace; above all, taking the shield of faith with which you will be able to quench all the fiery darts of the wicked one. And take the helmet of salvation, and the sword of the Spirit, which is the word of God. (Ephesians 6:14–17)

T*aking the shield of faith with which you will be able to quench all the fiery darts of the wicked one.* Folks, you know faith is something that I love to speak about – I could talk about it all day long. *Now faith is the substance of things hoped for, the evidence of things not seen* (Hebrews 11:1). Are you walking by faith or are you walking by sight? If you are walking by sight the devil is going to take you out, because we are living in his domain. There is nothing, nothing, absolutely nothing certain here on earth. Only one thing is certain and that is change. Things are changing all the time and in order to remain steadfast we have to walk by faith.

We have to stand on the promises of God and believe; this is the only way we can deflect the darts of the evil one. When the devil shoots his fiery darts at you, counter them by holding up your shield of faith. You will only be able to do this if you know God and His Word. The Word of God is your ammunition. Jesus used the Word to counteract the devil when he tried to tempt Him in the wilderness. Jesus said to the devil, *"It is written… "* (Matthew 4:4). There is nothing that puts fear into the enemy like the Word of God does. *For the word of God is living and powerful, and sharper than any two-edged sword, piercing even to the division of soul and spirit, and of joints and marrow, and is a discerner of the thoughts and intents of the heart* (Hebrews 4:12).

The Word of God is no less powerful today – you have your ammunition – so use it. Stand on the Word of God by faith and you will withstand the fiery darts of the evil one. It is sad to watch so many Christians live lives of defeat because they do not use the weapons that are at their disposal. Take up your shield of faith today.

Prayer

My Father, I give You thanks and praise today for Your Word. I take up the shield of faith. I stand upon Your Word and I will fight the enemy with all the weapons that are at my disposal. Amen.

The Word of God is just as powerful today – you have your ammunition – so use it.

Wearing the helmet of salvation

Read Ephesians 6:10–18

Stand therefore, having girded your waist with truth, having put on the breastplate of righteousness, and having shod your feet with the preparation of the gospel of peace; above all, taking the shield of faith with which you will be able to quench all the fiery darts of the wicked one. And take the helmet of salvation, and the sword of the Spirit, which is the word of God. (Ephesians 6:14–17)

The battle is in the mind – have you heard people say this? It is so true; you can ask any sportsperson. The game is won in the head. You can be as fit as you can be – you can train twenty-four hours a day – but if your mind is not right you are a goner. Another phrase that people use is "getting your head in the game". In a sense this is what we are talking about in our reading. If you do not have the right attitude you will be in trouble. Putting on the helmet of salvation means keeping your mind straight.

What do you fill your mind with, my friend? This is where the problem starts: junk in, junk out. You have been saved by the blood of the lamb. Therefore, it does not matter, my friend, what people say about you, because Jesus says in Romans 10:8b–9: "… *The word is near you, in your mouth and in your heart*" (that is, the word of faith which we preach): that if you confess with your mouth the Lord Jesus and believe in your heart that God has raised Him from the dead, you will be saved.

This is why your mind doesn't have to be a battlefield. Wear your helmet of salvation; then when the accuser comes reminding you of your past mistakes, you can tap your helmet and tell him to get behind you. With your helmet firmly in place the devil will not be able to gain a foothold in your mind. Sin begins in the mind, my friend. A thought pops into your mind and will take root if you do not apply God's Word to your situation. You must cut the thought off – using the Word of God (just like Jesus did when He was tempted). Jesus says to you: "*Peace I leave with you, My peace I give to you; not as the world gives do I give to you. Let not your heart be troubled, neither let it be afraid*" (John 14:27). Remember to put on your helmet.

Prayer

My Father, thank You for Your Word. Thank You for my salvation. Help me to focus upon You and Your Word. Give me the ability to be able to memorize Scripture so that when the enemy attacks me I can use Your Word to block his efforts in my life. Amen.

Fill your mind with the things of God and the Word of God, then there will be no room for anything else.

Wielding the sword of the Spirit

Read Ephesians 6:10–18

Stand therefore, having girded your waist with truth, having put on the breastplate of righteousness, and having shod your feet with the preparation of the gospel of peace; above all, taking the shield of faith with which you will be able to quench all the fiery darts of the wicked one. And take the helmet of salvation, and the sword of the Spirit, which is the word of God. (Ephesians 6:14–17)

The sword of the Spirit is my "spiritual rifle" – it's my protection. The sword of the Spirit is the weapon that keeps my mind sane – it is the Word of God spoken with the power of the Holy Spirit. *For as many as are led by the Spirit of God, these are sons of God. For you did not receive the spirit of bondage again to fear, but you received the Spirit of adoption by whom we cry out, "Abba, Father." The Spirit Himself bears witness with our spirit that we are children of God* (Romans 8:14–16).

Jesus promised us the Spirit before He left this earth. *"But the Helper, the Holy Spirit, whom the Father will send in My name, He will teach you all things, and bring to your remembrance all things that I said to you"* (John 14:26). The Holy Spirit helps us to remember the Word of God so that we can brandish our sword in the face of the enemy. The Spirit also helps us to pray when we don't have the words to express our feelings. Romans 8:26 says: *Likewise the Spirit also helps in our weaknesses. For we do not know what we should pray for as we ought, but the Spirit Himself makes intercession for us with groanings which cannot be uttered.*

Our warfare is not against flesh and blood: *For though we walk in the flesh, we do not war according to the flesh. For the weapons of our warfare are not carnal but mighty in God for pulling down strongholds, casting down arguments and every high thing that exalts itself against the knowledge of God, bringing every thought into captivity to the obedience of Christ* (2 Corinthians 10:3–5). You have nothing to fear because you have the sword of the Spirit in your hand. The sword can be used as an offensive as well as a defensive weapon. As you wear God's armour you have nothing to fear from anyone or anything. The armour of God is enemy-proof so go forth in the joy of the Lord.

Prayer

My Father, I stand tall today wearing each piece of Your armour. Finally I take up the sword of the Spirit. Thank You that You have given me everything that I need to grow and thrive in my Christian walk. Lord, I love You and I am so grateful to You. Amen.

You have nothing to fear, because you have the sword of the Spirit in your hand.

Lord, teach us to pray

Read Luke 11:1–4

Now it came to pass, as He was praying in a certain place, when He ceased, that one of His disciples said to Him, "Lord, teach us to pray, as John also taught his disciples." (Luke 11:1)

Jesus' disciples had watched His prayer life closely. They were used to Jesus disappearing to His secret place. They knew that when Jesus came back from spending time with His Father things happened. They observed the power with which Jesus ministered. They saw His focus and how He was able to zoom right in to the heart of a matter. The disciples were just regular guys, but they were savvy enough to understand the importance of prayer. They wanted to learn how to pray – so they asked Jesus to teach them: He said to them (Luke 11:1–4), *"When you pray, say:*

> *Our Father in heaven, Hallowed be Your name. Your kingdom come.*
> *Your will be done on earth as it is in heaven.*
> *Give us day by day our daily bread.*
> *And forgive us our sins, for we also forgive everyone who is indebted to us.*
> *And do not lead us into temptation, but deliver us from the evil one."*

Prayer is talking to the Lord like you would talk to a dearly loved friend. You may say, "Angus, it is one-way traffic; I don't hear God speaking to me." Of course He speaks to you! You have to give Him time, you have to listen and you have to wait. Waiting means learning to be quiet in your spirit. People ask me if God speaks audibly to me. No, He has never spoken to me audibly; I don't think He has spoken to too many people audibly and they have lived to tell the tale. After all He is Almighty God. There are many ways that He speaks to you though. He speaks to you in your spirit man through His Word and through nature as well as other Christians. God uses Christian television programmes and books. In fact there is no end to the ways that He speaks to you. Once God has spoken He will confirm His word to you. Not once, but as many times as you need Him to. Become a prayer warrior today. Gird up your loins, put on your armour and get ready to do battle.

Prayer

My Father, I know that I allow so many other things to take priority over spending time with You. Over this past month You have been challenging me through Your Spirit to change the way that I live. I need You and I know that the way to reach You is to spend time with You. Amen.

Prayer is talking to the Lord like you would talk to a dearly loved friend.

Praying to your Father

Read Luke 11:1–4

Our Father in heaven, hallowed be Your name. Your kingdom come. Your will be done on earth as it is in heaven. (Luke 11:2b)

O*ur Father in heaven…* I want to ask you, "Can you say, 'Our Father'?" Let's make it even more personal: "Can you say, 'My Father'?" You will find it difficult to do this if you have not had a relationship with your earthly father. I want to challenge you right now: If you have a problem with your earthly father, settle it so that you can communicate with your heavenly Father. *Hallowed be Your name…* Hallowed means holy or sacred. God's name is sacred, my friend. He is a holy God; He is the only one who is worthy to be praised, worshipped, adored and magnified. When you come before God you need to come recognizing and acknowledging who He is. Isn't it wonderful that He is also your heavenly Father? Spend some time before Him today telling Him how much you love Him.

Your kingdom come… Lord, please bring heaven to earth. The Bible tells us this world we are living in is going to burn. God is preparing mansions for us in heaven. However, we don't have to wait until we get to heaven to experience the kingdom of God. If you are a child of God the kingdom of heaven is in your heart. So why don't you pray this morning: "Thy kingdom come. Lord, renew me. Take the bitterness, ugliness, hatred, unforgiveness and fear out of my heart today. Replace these with Your love, joy and peace."

Your will be done on earth as it is in heaven. Jesus said: *For whoever does the will of God is My brother and My sister and mother"* (Mark 3:35). As God's children our lives are to be about doing the will of our Father. Our prayers are to be in line with the will of God. *Now this is the confidence that we have in Him, that if we ask anything according to His will, He hears us. And if we know that He hears us, whatever we ask, we know that we have the petitions that we have asked of Him* (1 John 5:14–15).

Prayer

My Father, today I come before You and pray. My Father in heaven, hallowed and holy is Your name. I pray that Your kingdom will come on earth in the same way that it is in heaven. Thank You that Your kingdom is in my heart. Your will be done in my life – I surrender to You. Amen.

If you are a child of God the kingdom of heaven is in your heart.

Give us this day, our daily bread

Read Luke 11:1–4

"Give us day by day our daily bread. And forgive us our sins, for we also forgive everyone who is indebted to us. And do not lead us into temptation, but deliver us from the evil one." (Luke 11:3–4)

Give us day by day our daily bread. Do you see the three little words: *day by day?* Isn't this where so many problems emanate from? We want to be able to see way into the future. God says day by day. We spend so much of our time worrying about tomorrow that we don't enjoy today. Philippians 4:6 says: *Be anxious for nothing, but in everything by prayer and supplication, with thanksgiving, let your requests be made known to God.* When you have a chance read Luke 12:22–34 again. God says do not be anxious; trust Him to provide for you; He is your Jehovah Jireh. Our problem is that we want the extra car, the holiday house and the new toys to play with. God has not promised you these: He has promised you daily bread – day by day.

And forgive us our sins, for we also forgive everyone who is indebted to us. Someone once wisely said that we should keep short accounts of our sins before God. In other words when you sin go to God, repent and ask His forgiveness. What about forgiving other people? Next month we are going to talk about forgiveness. Jesus said *"For if you forgive men their trespasses, your heavenly Father will also forgive you. But if you do not forgive men their trespasses, neither will your Father forgive your trespasses"* (Matthew 6:14–15).

And do not lead us into temptation, but deliver us from the evil one. My friend, you need to know today that God will never tempt you. He will test you, yes (we see this in the story of Job). God is your loving heavenly Father. He will only allow something into your life that has the potential to make you stronger. Temptation comes from the devil. He is the one who would lead us into temptation, but our God is greater than him. So pray to your Father today and ask Him to protect you; ask Him to deliver you from evil. Put on your helmet, tie on your breastplate and take hold of your sword.

Prayer

My Father, *for Yours is the kingdom and the power and the glory forever* (Matthew 6:13b). Amen.

He is your Jehovah Jireh. He has promised you daily bread – day by day.

A persistent prayer warrior

Read Luke 11:5–13

"For everyone who asks receives, and he who seeks finds, and to him who knocks it will be opened." (Luke 11:10)

At the beginning of Luke chapter eleven the disciples came to Jesus asking Him to teach them to pray. It is important to note that directly after He gave them the Lord's Prayer He went on to talk about the need for persistence in prayer. How often do we give up when we don't receive an answer to our prayers immediately? We are the victims of the instant society in which we live. These verses that we have read in God's Word this morning direct us back to the fact that prayer requires persistence. Are you trusting God for something specific? How long have you been praying about it? How long have you been waiting? Maybe you are at the place where you are ready to give up. Well I am here to say to you: don't give up.

Read the Word of God again. He is telling us to persevere. Check that you are praying according to God's will – God cannot go against His own will. If you are sure that what you are praying for is within God's will, then continue trusting Him. This month we have been speaking together about being a prayer warrior. Have you begun to establish your secret place? I hope that you are experiencing the joy of meeting with your Father in your secret place. The closer we get to the end of this age the more important it is going to be for us to be strong in the Lord.

You will only be able to stand firm and true if you know your God. You cannot know someone you do not spend time with. You cannot know God by osmosis. You need to spend time in His presence, sitting at His feet. This is how you will become a strong prayer warrior. Spend time in His Word; learn to know His will for your life and the lives of your family. Then you will be able to pray according to His will, and when you do this you will begin to see results. Be strong in the Lord, my friend.

Prayer

My Father, I worship You today; I praise You; I lift my hands in surrender to You. I sit at Your feet and I wait upon You. Meet me in my secret place, I pray. Show me Your will through Your Word. Teach me Your ways that I might glorify You through my life. Amen.

Spend time in His presence and sit at His feet. This is how you will become a strong prayer warrior.

OCTOBER

How much do you love Him?

Forgiven much

Nothing is too costly for Him

Mary Magdalene or Simon, the Pharisee?

Do you know who Jesus is?

Do you know that you are forgiven?

Do not give offence

Do not offend your brother

Do not pick up an offence

Walk in love

Walk in the light

Walk in wisdom

Love and respect

Jesus offends the leaders

Forgive us, as we forgive others

Your sins are forgiven

Binding and loosing

Seventy times seven

Forgiveness before worship

Who will throw the first stone?

Forgiving – no more than our duty

Father, forgive them…

Jesus restores Peter

God meant it for good

David forgives Saul

Stephen forgives his murderers

Paul's sins are forgiven

Love your enemy

Vengeance is Mine

Do not take vengeance

Forgive and forgiven!

How much do you love Him?

Read Luke 7:36–50

Now when the Pharisee who had invited Him saw this, he spoke to himself, saying, "This Man, if He were a prophet, would know who and what manner of woman this is who is touching Him, for she is a sinner." (Luke 7:39)

This month our topic is forgiveness. We are going to examine together what it means to leave retribution and judgment to God. Now is the time … "Vengeance is Mine," says the Lord. However, before we can look at forgiving other people, or for that matter allowing God to be the one who metes out judgment, we need to understand how much we have been forgiven. It is so easy to focus on other people and what they have done wrong. On the other hand we don't like to look too closely at our own shortcomings.

Simon, the Pharisee, had invited Jesus into his home to eat with him. He was not happy when the woman came in and interrupted their meal, and he was only too eager to point out her shortcomings. He sat there judging her in his heart. He was scandalized that she had the audacity to enter his home. Do you think that he might have been worried that her presence would reflect badly upon him? Jesus knew everything that was going on in his mind. Jesus said to him: *"There was a certain creditor who had two debtors. One owed five hundred denarii, and the other fifty. And when they had nothing with which to repay, he freely forgave them both. Tell Me, therefore, which of them will love him more?"* Isn't it just like Jesus to go to the heart of the matter? You can sense Simon's reluctance to admit, *"I suppose the one whom he forgave more"* (Luke 7:41–42, 43). My friend, where do you find yourself today? Are you like the woman or are you like Simon, the Pharisee?

So often we are self-righteous and judgmental. We forget that we would not even be able to stand in God's presence if it weren't for the fact that we have been redeemed by the blood of Jesus. We have been washed clean and our sins have been forgiven. You know what Romans 3:10 says, *"There is none righteous, no, not one."* Take some time to tell your Father how much you love Him.

Prayer

My Father, I come before You today and I bow at Your feet. I thank You that the only reason I can do this is because I am a sinner who has been saved by grace. Thank You, Jesus, for Your death on the cross. I am so grateful to You, my Lord. I love You and I worship You. Amen.

Take some time to tell your Father how much you love Him.

Forgiven much

Read Luke 7:36–50

"Therefore I say to you, her sins, which are many, are forgiven, for she loved much. But to whom little is forgiven, the same loves little." (Luke 7:47)

This is the story of Mary: she came and washed Jesus' feet with her tears and then she dried Jesus' feet with her hair. After that she took an alabaster jar of fragrant oil and anointed His feet. What an amazing encounter this was. Jesus said that because Mary had been forgiven so much, she loved Him so much. Whereas everyone at the table was ready to ridicule her, Jesus commended her. Jesus has forgiven me for a lot, folks; this is why I love Him so much. I know for a fact if it were not for Jesus Christ I would not be writing this. He took my ragged life and He restored it; He renewed me and He made me brand new. The day I gave my life to Him, He forgave me all my past sin.

Some people accuse me of being "over the top". I don't believe I am. I am an ordinary, normal Christian, who has been saved by grace, and I serve a mighty God. Romans 3:23 tells us, *for all have sinned and fall short of the glory of God.* So, if anyone reading this is like Simon, the Pharisee, and they think there is no sin in their life, they are in trouble, because that is the biggest sin of all. Isaiah 64:6a says: *But we are all like an unclean thing, and all our righteousnesses are like filthy rags.* There is no way to get to heaven other than through Jesus Christ. You have to acknowledge your sin, come to Him and ask Him for forgiveness. This is why Jesus died on the Cross, my friend: to save us.

Mary understood what it was to have her sins forgiven. She loved Jesus and she was grateful to Him for all He had done for her. She did not mind that she was ridiculed and humiliated – all that mattered to her was that Jesus should know how much she loved Him. Does your life reflect the fact that you are a sinner who has been forgiven much?

Prayer

My Father, I thank You that You have saved me. I am a sinner who has been saved by grace. I lift my hands in praise and adoration of Your holy name today. I thank You, I thank You, I thank You. I will never grow tired of saying it. I love You, my Lord and saviour. Amen.

Does your life reflect the fact that you are a sinner who has been forgiven much?

Nothing is too costly for Him

Read Luke 7:36–50

…and stood at His feet behind Him weeping; and she began to wash His feet with her tears, and wiped them with the hair of her head; and she kissed His feet and anointed them with the fragrant oil. (Luke 7:38)

M ary used a very expensive oil to anoint Jesus' feet. She was not a rich woman and it cost her everything – not only materially, but also emotionally and physically – … *and [she] stood at His feet behind Him weeping; and she began to wash His feet with her tears, and wiped them with the hair of her head; and she kissed His feet and anointed them with the fragrant oil.* Simon, the Pharisee, was a very religious man. He regularly went to the temple. He was a "church guy". Yet all he could see was his own social embarrassment at having a prostitute in his home. He totally missed the poignancy and the beauty of the moment because of his self-righteousness.

My friend, I go to church and so do you. We need to learn a lesson from the reaction of Simon, the Pharisee. We must be careful that we don't point fingers. Sometimes, those of us who go to church are blinder than the people in the world. Of course Jesus knew she was a prostitute. But, you see, Jesus came to save sinners; He is a friend of sinners.

"Do you see this woman? I entered your house; you gave Me no water for My feet, but she has washed My feet with her tears and wiped them with the hair of her head. You gave Me no kiss, but this woman has not ceased to kiss My feet since the time I came in. You did not anoint My head with oil, but this woman has anointed My feet with fragrant oil. Therefore I say to you, her sins, which are many, are forgiven, for she loved much. But to whom little is forgiven, the same loves little." Then Jesus turned to Mary and He said to her: … *"Your sins are forgiven … Your faith has saved you. Go in peace"* (Luke 7:44b–47, 48, 50). If you are self-righteous you will not be able to love Jesus with abandon. When you love Him in the same way that Mary did nothing will be too costly for Him.

Prayer

My Father, I realize that so often I hold back. I want to love You with the same abandon that Mary did. I give myself anew to You today. Help me by Your Spirit to share Your love with others as well. Amen.

When you love Him in the same way that Mary did nothing will be too costly for Jesus.

Mary Magdalene or Simon, the Pharisee?

Read Luke 7:36–8:3

…and certain women who had been healed of evil spirits and infirmities – Mary called Magdalene, out of whom had come seven demons. (Luke 8:2)

"**A**ngus, are you honestly telling me that a prostitute went to heaven?" I want to go further: If you get to heaven before me, look for her – she will be seated right near the master's feet. That is where you will find Mary Magdalene. Wherever Jesus was there you would find Mary Magdalene. *And many women who followed Jesus from Galilee, ministering to Him, were there looking on from afar, among whom were Mary Magdalene…* (Matthew 27:55–56a). *Now there stood by the cross of Jesus His mother, and His mother's sister, Mary the wife of Clopas, and Mary Magdalene* (John 19:25). *And Mary Magdalene and Mary the mother of Joses observed where He was laid* (Mark 15:47).

Now when the Sabbath was past, Mary Magdalene, Mary the mother of James, and Salome bought spices, that they might come and anoint Him. Very early in the morning, on the first day of the week, they came to the tomb when the sun had risen (Mark 16:1–2). *Now when He rose early on the first day of the week, He appeared first to Mary Magdalene, out of whom He had cast seven demons* (Mark 16:9).

Mary stuck close to Jesus because she was so in love with her master. She could not show enough appreciation for her new life. Are you in love with your master? Do you show Him appreciation? Jesus is more to me than anyone or anything in my life. Mary Magdalene, Mary the mother of Jesus and a couple of other women were the only ones who never ran away from the Lord. Mary was totally committed to Jesus. She had been forgiven so much; that's why she loved Him so much. There is no place for the lukewarm Christian in God's economy – it is all or nothing. The end of the age is approaching and it is only those who are sold out for Jesus who are going to be able stand to the end. Take stock today of where you stand with the Lord. Are you a Mary Magdalene or a Simon, the Pharisee?

Prayer

My Father, I bow in Your presence today. I come before You in the name of Jesus, my precious saviour. Lord, I want to be found at the feet of Jesus. Like Mary Magdalene I want to express my gratitude and love to You for all that You have done for me. Amen.

Where do you stand with the Lord? Are you a Mary Magdalene or a Simon, the Pharisee?

Do you know who Jesus is?

Read Luke 7:36–50

Now when the Pharisee who had invited Him saw this, he spoke to himself, saying, "This Man, if He were a prophet, would know who and what manner of woman this is who is touching Him, for she is a sinner." (Luke 7:39)

Imagine how embarrassed Simon was when he realized that Jesus had read his thoughts. Jesus knows everything even as you are reading this devotional; He can read your mind. He knows what is in your heart because He is God. … *Jesus answered and said to him, "Simon, I have something to say to you."* Then Jesus proceeded to share a mini-parable with Simon. *"There was a certain creditor who had two debtors. One owed five hundred denarii, and the other fifty. And when they had nothing with which to repay, he freely forgave them both. Tell Me, therefore, which of them will love him more?"* (Luke 7:40a, 41–42).

Simon had the head knowledge – he knew the answer. The pity was that it never reached his heart. He did not love Jesus the way Mary Magdalene did. Jesus turned to Mary and then back to Simon: *And He said to him, "You have rightly judged."* Then He *turned to the woman and said to Simon, "Do you see this woman? I entered your house; you gave Me no water for My feet, but she has washed My feet with her tears and wiped them with the hair of her head. You gave Me no kiss, but this woman has not ceased to kiss My feet since the time I came in. You did not anoint My head with oil, but this woman has anointed My feet with fragrant oil. Therefore I say to you, her sins, which are many, are forgiven, for she loved much. But to whom little is forgiven, the same loves little"* (Luke 7:43b–47).

We are saved by grace, my friend, not by works. Simon kept the law, he was a righteous man, he was a religious man – yet it didn't ensure a relationship with Jesus. Mary had broken the law, she was a sinner, she was not religious – yet she had a love relationship with Jesus. For all his knowledge Simon didn't know who Jesus was. But Mary did – she knew her Lord and saviour. Do you know Jesus, my friend? What is He to you?

Prayer

My Father, I come before You acknowledging my sin today. I realize that You know everything. As Your child this is comforting as opposed to being scary. I am thankful that at all times You know what I am thinking. Thank You that You know me so well. Lord, I in turn want to know You intimately. Amen.

Mary knew her Lord and saviour. Do you know Jesus, my friend? What is He to you?

Do you know that you are forgiven?

Read Psalm 51

For I acknowledge my transgressions, and my sin is always before me. Purge me with hyssop, and I shall be clean; wash me, and I shall be whiter than snow. (Psalm 51:3, 7)

The Psalmist, David, understood what it was to feel guilt. He had killed a man and he had blood on his hands. There are so many people who go through life feeling guilty. Guilt can kill you if you are not careful. It weighs you down and literally has a physically debilitating effect upon your body. It eats away at your psyche and keeps you in emotional turmoil. As you read Psalm 51 I am sure that you picked up on all of these aspects as David poured out his heart to God.

If you find yourself in the position today where you are walking around weighed down by a burden of guilt, follow David's lead. Bring your sin to Jesus; lay it down at the foot of the cross. 1 John 1:9 promises us: *If we confess our sins, He is faithful and just to forgive us our sins and to cleanse us from all unrighteousness.* Mary Magdalene understood what it was to have her sins forgiven. She learnt that she did not have to feel guilty about her past, because Jesus had forgiven her; her sordid past was history. Maybe people didn't want her to forget what she had done, but Jesus never reminded her of it. In fact Mary was one of Jesus' inner circle. All the time He walked on this earth Jesus mixed with sinners.

The Pharisees asked the question: *"How is it that He eats and drinks with tax collectors and sinners?"* Jesus answered them: *"Those who are well have no need of a physician, but those who are sick. I did not come to call the righteous, but sinners, to repentance"* (Mark 2:16b–17). The enemy wants us to feel guilty because that way he keeps us in his snare. Jesus came to set you free, my friend. Come to Him, repent and ask Him to forgive you. Then accept His forgiveness and walk in the victory of your forgiveness. As a child of God you do not bring glory to your Father when you walk around filled with guilt.

Prayer

My Father, I thank You for Your grace and mercy towards me, Your child. I pray that You will forgive me today. Cleanse me as I confess my sin before You. Fill me afresh with Your Holy Spirit. Help me to walk tall in the fullness of Your blessing and forgiveness. Amen.

As a child of God you do not bring glory to your Father when you walk around filled with guilt.

Do not give offence

Read Proverbs 18:1–24

A brother offended is harder to win than a strong city, and contentions are like the bars of a castle. (Proverbs 18:19)

There are many things that can offend people. For instance, in our story in Luke chapter seven, Simon, the Pharisee, was offended by Mary Magdalene. Throughout the Gospels there are many instances where the religious leaders of the day took offence at what Jesus had to say. With Jesus it wasn't because He was saying the wrong thing, but because they didn't like the truth He was speaking. Jesus came to speak God's truth here on earth – He didn't allow anything to prevent Him from doing this.

We, on the other hand, often offend because we say hurtful, uncaring things to people. It is one of the biggest problems in the church; people offend each other. The number one reason that you end up needing to forgive or to be forgiven is because of an offence – is that not so? For the next few days we are going to talk about this subject of taking or not taking offence. As you can see we are laying the groundwork for our topic "'Vengeance is Mine,' says the Lord." You need to know that you are forgiven. Like Mary you need to know that Jesus has washed away your past sins. You need to have confidence in what God has done for you through Jesus. Take a moment and examine your heart: Are you like Simon, the Pharisee? Do you go around judging and condemning other people? If you do then you need to repent of this and ask God to forgive you.

Once you have sorted this out then you are ready to approach the rest of the month and what God has in store for us. So getting back to taking and giving offence: Proverbs 18:6-7 says: *A fool's lips enter into contention, and his mouth calls for blows. A fool's mouth is his destruction, and his lips are the snare of his soul.* Our actions can give offence, but most times it is words that offend. There is great power in the tongue; in it lies the power to do both good and evil.

Prayer

My Father, I come before You and bow in Your presence. Thank You that I am forgiven. Help me to be gracious to other people. I know that I can so easily take offence and today You are talking to me about not giving or receiving offence. Amen.

There is great power in the tongue; in it lies the power to do both good and evil.

Do not offend your brother

Read Romans 14:1–23

It is good neither to eat meat nor drink wine nor do anything by which your brother stumbles or is offended or is made weak. (Romans 14:21)

P aul in writing to the Romans tells them: *For none of us lives to himself, and no one dies to himself* (Romans 14:7). We do not belong to ourselves; first and foremost we belong to God and then we belong to each other. When you accept Jesus Christ as your Lord and saviour you become a member of His body – the church. Once you are His you can no longer live as you like, doing what you like. Your life is meant to be lived glorifying God, your Father. It does not bring glory to Him if you live in a way that causes your brother or sister offence and results in them stumbling.

This means that I have to consider my lifestyle and how I live. In our reading Paul uses the examples of food and wine. *Do not destroy the work of God for the sake of food. All things indeed are pure, but it is evil for the man who eats with offense. It is good neither to eat meat nor drink wine nor do anything by which your brother stumbles or is offended or is made weak* (Romans 14:20–21). Freedom in Christ does not give you the liberty to disregard the effect your lifestyle has upon other people. Too often we have seen men of God stumble and fall, causing those who looked up to them to become offended and discouraged.

Paul further tells us that it is not our place to judge others. *So then each of us shall give account of himself to God. Therefore let us not judge one another anymore, but rather resolve this, not to put a stumbling block or a cause to fall in our brother's way* (Romans 14:12–13). You cannot hang out in the bar on a Friday night and be sitting in the church pew on a Sunday morning, my friend. Your walk and your talk need to line up with each other. We need to take our witness for Christ seriously; He calls us to live so that we do not offend our brothers or sisters.

Prayer

My Father, I ask You to help me examine my heart today. Show me through Your Spirit if there are things that I am doing that can cause an offence to a brother or sister resulting in them stumbling. Lord, forgive me, I pray. Help me to live a life that is pleasing to You, bringing glory to Your name. Amen.

Your walk and your talk need to line up with each other.

Do not pick up an offence

Read John 16:1–12

These things have I spoken unto you, that ye should not be offended. (John 16:1 King James Version)

W hat you say is what you get; so today we are going to rejoice in the Lord and not be offended. We choose not to pick up an offence. Jesus commands us: *Ye should not be offended.* They say that if you kick a dead dog it won't move: right? So, if you are dead to self, you should not be open to picking up any kind of an offence. If you kick a live dog, it will turn around and bite you, wont it? When we give our lives to Jesus, what happens to us? *Likewise you also, reckon yourselves to be dead indeed to sin, but alive to God in Christ Jesus our Lord* (Romans 6:11). We die to self and live for the Lord.

So if people offend you, you shouldn't respond. You should not pick up an offence. In our reading today Jesus warned His disciples: *They will put you out of the synagogues; yes, the time is coming that whoever kills you will think that he offers God service* (John 16:2). This is scary isn't it? There comes a time when people will persecute you, thinking that they are doing God a service. This was exactly what Paul, the apostle, did before he met Christ on the road to Damascus. He persecuted the Christians believing that he was doing it in the name of God.

When certain people offend you they actually believe that they are helping the Lord. One thing I have learnt in my Christian walk is not to point fingers. We are all sinners saved by grace. The only reason I have faith is because God gave it to me. *"The heart is deceitful above all things, and desperately wicked; who can know it?"* (Jeremiah 17:9). When I pick up an offence I have to repent of it and lay it down. God cannot use us if we are going to continually become offended. We are quick to criticize people for all sorts of superficial reasons. What concerns God is what is inside your heart. Ask the Holy Spirit to examine your heart today.

Prayer

My Father, help me not to become offended when other people do and say things that could be hurtful to me. Help me, I pray, to not be critical of other people. Above all help me not to cause offence because I believe I am doing You a favour. Amen.

What concerns God is what is inside your heart. Ask the Holy Spirit to examine your heart today.

Walk in love

Read Ephesians 5:1–7

And walk in love, as Christ also has loved us and given Himself for us, an offering and a sacrifice to God for a sweet-smelling aroma. (Ephesians 5:2)

Paul offers three antidotes to the possibility of giving offence – walk in love, walk in the light and walk in wisdom. The reason you and I can walk in love is because Christ died for us. He is love, He came to this earth and He was a living example of what it means to walk in love. God loved you and me so much that He was willing to send His Son to die on the cross of Calvary. Jesus was willing to hang on the cross to secure our salvation. His sacrifice on Calvary was a sweet-smelling aroma to the Father.

Our choosing to walk in love is a response to God the Father's and Jesus' love for us. This means that I do not live to please myself. The day I gave my heart to Jesus, in the little Methodist church in Greytown, was the day that Angus died. The old Angus, who cursed, drank, lived rough and pleased himself was no more. The new Angus became a new creation in Christ. From that day on the things that previously drew me and attracted me were no longer important to me. I fell in love with Jesus and He became the focal point of my life.

Walking in His love means that I view the world through His eyes. I am called to love those that He loves. This means that I cannot say and do what I want to. I have to take into account the effect that my words and actions will have on others. I do not want to be a stumbling block to anyone. If I love my wife then I am going to remain true to her. I am not going to provoke and discourage my children by being unnecessarily harsh towards them. I am not going to cheat my business partner because I belong to God and He has called me to walk in love. I will pay my taxes and my word will be my bond. When I walk in love I will not cause offence to people.

Prayer

My Father, thank You for Your great love for me. Jesus, thank You that You personified love when You died on Calvary for me. I choose to walk in love today. Fill me with Your Spirit of love, I pray. I want to bring glory to You, my Father. Amen.

Walking in love means that I do not live to please myself.

Walk in the light

Read Ephesians 5:8–14

For you were once darkness, but now you are light in the Lord. Walk as children of light. (Ephesians 5:8)

But you are *a chosen generation, a royal priesthood, a holy nation, His own special people, that you may proclaim the praises of Him who called you out of darkness into His marvelous light* (1 Peter 2:9). You have been chosen by God, my friend; you are special and you have a purpose in this life. Your purpose is to have fellowship with God and proclaim His praises. Before we came to Christ we were in darkness – spiritual darkness.

1 John 1:5 tells us: *This is the message which we have heard from Him and declare to you, that God is light and in Him is no darkness at all.* God cannot dwell where there is darkness. When His presence comes in the darkness has to flee. This is why we cannot walk with God and walk in sin at the same time. When His Spirit has control of our lives He leads us in the light. Walking in the light means that you will treat people in such a way that you will not cause them to stumble and fall. *But if we walk in the light as He is in the light, we have fellowship with one another, and the blood of Jesus Christ His Son cleanses us from all sin* (1 John 1:7).

Walking in the light means that every thought and every decision you make will be held up to the scrutiny of His light. In the beam of His light shining into your heart, mind and soul there will be no place for the darkness to lurk. The terrible things that people do to each other are the result of darkness lurking in our hearts. Don't allow the enemy to have a foothold in your life. He will do his best to cause you to take and give offence against your fellow brothers and sisters. When he manages to do this he knows that he has a foothold into your life. God cannot live in the darkness, but the enemy cannot live in the light. Therefore counteract his strategy by walking in the light.

Prayer

My Father, You are the Father of light. Jesus, You are the light of the world. Spirit, You illuminate the path before me. I choose today to walk in Your light, bringing honour and praise to Your name. Amen.

God cannot live in the darkness, but the enemy cannot live in the light. Walk in the light.

Walk in wisdom

Read Ephesians 5:15–21

See then that you walk circumspectly, not as fools but as wise, redeeming the time, because the days are evil. (Ephesians 5:15–16)

We are living in the end times and we are fast reaching the climax of the ages. You only have to look around you to see that man is not walking circumspectly; people are constantly doing foolish things. Wisdom is a scarce commodity in our world. Paul tells us that the reason for this is because the days are evil. In verse seventeen his counsel to us is: *Therefore do not be unwise, but understand what the will of the Lord is.* No matter what is going on in the world around us, you and I are called to walk in wisdom. We are called to understand what the will of the Lord is – and when we understand what His will is then we are to do it.

How will we know the will of God? By being *... filled with the Spirit* (Ephesians 5:18b). We are to be filled daily with the Spirit. The Spirit will lead us into all knowledge; the Spirit will reveal the things of God to us. As we spend time in God's Word He will reveal to us what His will is. God does not leave us hanging, my friend. He tells us clearly in His Word how we are to live. This month we are talking about forgiveness. We are talking about the things that would cause us to give and take offence. We are talking about allowing God to be the one who judges. The Word tells us that vengeance belongs to God alone. I cannot take revenge; you cannot take revenge. No matter what happens you have to trust God to do His will in your life and the lives of your loved ones.

What is the result of being filled with the Spirit? *Speaking to one another in psalms and hymns and spiritual songs, singing and making melody in your heart to the Lord, giving thanks always for all things to God the Father in the name of our Lord Jesus Christ, submitting to one another in the fear of God* (Ephesians 5:19–21). Can you see that if you live like this you will walk in wisdom?

Prayer

My Father, I thank You that You are wisdom. In You there is no confusion. You call me to live a life that is characterized by wisdom. I ask You to fill me with Your Spirit. Cause me to praise You and worship You in a new way today. Show me Your ways and lead me along the path of wisdom, for Your name's sake. Amen.

No matter what is going on in the world around us, you and I are called to walk in wisdom.

Love and respect

Read Ephesians 5:21–6:4

...submitting to one another in the fear of God. Nevertheless let each one of you in particular so love his own wife as himself, and let the wife see that she respects her husband. And you, fathers, do not provoke your children to wrath, but bring them up in the training and admonition of the Lord. (Ephesians 5:21, 33; 6:4)

We have said before that one of the trickiest and hardest places to consistently have a good witness for Christ is in our own homes. Yet, my friend, if we cannot be a witness at home anything we do outside kind of pales into insignificance. As the spiritual leader in your home God has called you to set the example. Our closest relationships can often be the ones that have the potential for causing us the most offence. They are also the ones where we can give the most offence. We need to stop for a moment and take stock of where we are.

What is it like in your home? Is it a safe haven for the members of your family or is it a battleground? If it is the latter then you have to put a stop to it. God has given you the privilege of being the head of your home. This doesn't mean that you get to lord it over your family. It means that you get to lead them by example. It is not an accident that Paul prefaced his comments on marriage and children with the injunction to live in love, to live in the light and to walk in wisdom. You are the one who has to show your family what it means to live in this way.

It all starts with verse twenty-one: *submitting to one another in the fear of God.* Do you fear God, my friend? If so you will live in a way that glorifies God. When you live life like this your family will follow your lead. It starts with you. It doesn't matter what the world thinks of you – it matters what your wife and children think of you. There are too many men who are one way when they are in the world and another entirely when they are at home behind closed doors. God is looking for men who will stand up and be counted. Now is the time, my friend, to be a mighty man of God – it starts at home.

Prayer

My Father, I am humbled as I bow in Your presence. I thank You for Your love and grace that You have extended toward me. Help me to be the spiritual leader in my home. Help me to be an example to my family. You know that I love them and I want the best for them. Amen.

As the spiritual leader in your home God has called you to set the example.

Jesus offends the leaders

Read Matthew 21:12–17

But when the chief priests and scribes saw the wonderful things that He did, and the children crying out in the temple and saying, "Hosanna to the Son of David!" they were indignant. (Matthew 21:15)

When you read the Gospels it would seem that Jesus spent a lot of time offending the religious leaders of His day. Just about everything He said or did caused them to become indignant and offended. Yet in Matthew 17:27 we read: *"Nevertheless, lest we offend them, go to the sea, cast in a hook, and take the fish that comes up first. And when you have opened its mouth, you will find a piece of money; take that and give it to them for Me and you."* Jesus didn't break the law. He was careful to do the right thing. The reason that the religious leaders of His day were offended by Him was because He spoke the truth and they didn't like this.

You will find that the same thing will happen to you when you speak God's truth. People will become offended. It is no different today, my friend: people don't like to hear the truth. We have spoken a lot about not causing offence. I hope that you can see the difference between living or speaking in a careless way and speaking the truth of God's Word. Jesus did not act in an uncaring way. He did not go around hurting people – no, not at all. Jesus loved sinners. He reached out to them. It was not the sinners that Jesus ran into trouble with; it was the religious people who became offended by what He said and did.

God calls us to be fearless when it comes to sharing the truth of the gospel of Jesus Christ. You can expect that there will be those who will not like what you are saying; however, if they take offence it must never be because you have been cruel or careless. Speak the truth in love – that is what God has commissioned you to do. When you do this you can leave the results up to the Holy Spirit – He is the one who convicts and draws people to Jesus. Your job is simply to obey, sharing God's love and mercy with people.

Prayer

My Father, You have called me to share Your truth with people. Help me to examine my heart so that I speak in love. Jesus, thank You for Your example. You always spoke with compassion and mercy. Help me to be fearless in sharing Your truth with others. Amen.

God has commissioned you to speak the truth in love. Leave the results up to the Holy Spirit.

Forgive us, as we forgive others

Read Matthew 6:5–15

"Our Father in heaven, hallowed be Your name. Your kingdom come. Your will be done, on earth as it is in heaven. Give us this day our daily bread. And forgive us our debts, as we forgive our debtors. And do not lead us into temptation, but deliver us from the evil one. For Yours is the kingdom and the power and the glory forever. Amen." (Matthew 6:9b–13)

J esus mentions several different things in the Lord's Prayer. In fact it is probably the most definitive prayer you can ever pray. Yet He chooses to highlight one aspect of it in Matthew 6:14–15. *"For if you forgive men their trespasses, your heavenly Father will also forgive you. But if you do not forgive men their trespasses, neither will your Father forgive your trespasses."* He couldn't be more explicit: If you don't forgive, then you will not be forgiven.

We live in a world where unforgiveness is rife. There is so much hatred and strife around. I live in a country that was for many years filled with unforgiveness. Sadly today people still harbour grudges and offences relating to things that were done to them in the past. There are no exclusionary clauses in the Bible when it comes to forgiveness. God doesn't say you need to forgive, but … He says if you want to be forgiven then you need to forgive. Terrible things have been done to people. There is nothing worse than man's inhumanity towards man. Without the love and grace of Jesus, where would we be?

The only hope for our world is for people to come to Jesus and experience His forgiveness for their sins; then they need to extend that same forgiveness to the people who have wronged them. When we realize how much God has forgiven us it will be impossible to withhold forgiveness from another person. Unforgiveness makes you physically, emotionally and mentally sick. It can eventually kill you. Families have been torn apart, marriages have been destroyed and lives have been ruined by unforgiveness. No one wins when there is unforgiveness – especially not the person who refuses to forgive. This is the reason that Jesus was so clear about forgiving. In fact He spoke a lot about the need to forgive. Over the next few days we are going to have a look at some lessons from Jesus' life regarding forgiveness. He is our ultimate teacher; He is the one we can emulate and model our lives upon.

Prayer

Take some time to carefully pray through the Lord's Prayer. Spend time examining your heart when you come to: *And forgive us our debts, as we forgive our debtors.* Ask the Holy Spirit to speak to your heart.

When we realize how much God has forgiven us then it will be impossible to withhold forgiveness from another person.

Your sins are forgiven

Read Matthew 9:1–8

But Jesus, knowing their thoughts, said, "Why do you think evil in your hearts? For which is easier, to say, 'Your sins are forgiven you,' or to say, 'Arise and walk'?" (Matthew 9:4–5)

Could anything be more liberating than hearing the words: *"Son, be of good cheer; your sins are forgiven you … Arise, take up your bed, and go to your house"* (Matthew 9:2c, 6c). Have you noticed how many times Jesus said the words "Your sins are forgiven" when He healed someone? Jesus knew that ultimately it was the forgiveness of sin that set people free. Knowing Jesus means knowing the truth. He said in John 8:32: *"And you shall know the truth, and the truth shall make you free."* Forgiveness is only to be found in Jesus.

Jesus didn't see people as compartmentalized; He ministered to the whole person – body, soul and spirit. This is why He instructed us in Mark 12:30: *"And you shall love the LORD your God with all your heart, with all your soul, with all your mind, and with all your strength."* God is interested in all of you – the whole package. Jesus didn't only come to this earth to redeem our souls – He came to redeem us, body, soul and spirit. You are a new creation in Him. His deliverance and renewal extends to every area of your life. I love to pray the prayer of faith for those who are sick. I believe that God wants us to trust Him for health and wholeness.

So many Christians settle for less than what Jesus gained for them on Calvary. My friend, I firmly believe that we can trust God to keep us and protect us until the day comes that our work here on earth is done. Until that day you can know His healing and wholeness in your life. This healing and wholeness extends to every area of your life. Don't allow yourself to be shortchanged. The religious leaders of Jesus' day took exception to Him saying to people: "Your sins are forgiven." They took exception to Him healing the sick. They took exception to Him setting people free from bondage. But it didn't stop Him – He went right on doing it. Are you living in your freedom today?

Prayer

My Father, I give You praise for my salvation today. Thank You that I have been forgiven. I have been redeemed, body, soul and spirit. I am a new creation in Jesus Christ. Thank You that I can live and walk in this freedom every day of my life. Amen.

Jesus didn't see people as compartmentalized; He ministered to the whole person – body, soul and spirit.

Binding and loosing

Read Matthew 18:15–20

"Assuredly, I say to you, whatever you bind on earth will be bound in heaven, and whatever you loose on earth will be loosed in heaven." (Matthew 18:18)

God has entrusted great power to us as His children. We should not take this power lightly. In Matthew 18:15 Jesus explained what to do when a brother sinned against another. He said: *"Moreover if your brother sins against you, go and tell him his fault between you and him alone. If he hears you, you have gained your brother."* What happens if he doesn't want to hear you? *"Take with you one or two more, that 'by the mouth of two or three witnesses every word may be established'"* (Matthew 18:16). We don't just give up on a brother; Jesus is saying we must walk the second mile to try and reconcile.

If that doesn't work then the final resort is to: *"… tell it to the church. But if he refuses even to hear the church, let him be to you like a heathen and a tax collector* (Matthew 18:17). It is never meant to be easy to turn your back on a brother in Christ. In 2 Corinthians Paul writes to the Corinthians regarding a brother who has offended in some way. We don't know what he did; but the important thing is the way Paul deals with the offending brother.

But if anyone has caused grief, he has not grieved me, but all of you to some extent – not to be too severe. This punishment which was inflicted by the majority is sufficient for such a man, so that, on the contrary, you ought rather to forgive and comfort him, lest perhaps such a one be swallowed up with too much sorrow. Therefore I urge you to reaffirm your love to him. For to this end I also wrote, that I might put you to the test, whether you are obedient in all things. Now whom you forgive anything, I also forgive. For if indeed I have forgiven anything, I have forgiven that one for your sakes in the presence of Christ, lest Satan should take advantage of us; for we are not ignorant of his devices (2 Corinthians 2:5–11).

Prayer

My Father, You are a great and merciful God. You love Your children and I thank You that You have given me Your Word so that I can know how I am to live. As Your child You give me power here on earth – help me to use this power wisely to the honour and glory of Your name alone. Amen.

God has entrusted great power to us as His children. We should not take this power lightly.

Seventy times seven

Read Matthew 18:21–35

Then Peter came to Him and said, "Lord, how often shall my brother sin against me, and I forgive him? Up to seven times?" Jesus said to him, "I do not say to you, up to seven times, but up to seventy times seven." (Matthew 18:21–22)

Have you ever noticed that Peter's question followed directly after Jesus spoke about how to deal with a brother who sins against you? Peter thought he was being generous when he suggested that seven times was an acceptable number of times to forgive someone. Jesus replied that no, he was to be prepared to forgive seventy times seven – in other words, as many times as was necessary. This was probably not what Peter or the disciples wanted to hear. It is not what we want to hear either, is it? We grow up and live in a world that loves conditionally. If we do what people want us to do they love us. Sadly, even parents can love their children conditionally.

So it stands to reason that we often offer our love conditionally to people. If they do what we want them to do then we love them. If they don't, then we withhold our love and forgiveness from them. To further illustrate His point Jesus shared a story with His disciples about two servants. One owed the king a lot of money, but he couldn't repay it. The king took pity on him and forgave him his debt. Then he went out and met a fellow servant who owed him a small amount of money by comparison to what he owed the king. Instead of extending the same mercy to his fellow servant that he had received from the king he threw his debtor into prison. Naturally, when the king heard about this he was angry and delivered him to the torturers until he could pay his debt.

If there is someone whom you are refusing to forgive today, Jesus is speaking to you when He says: *"You wicked servant! I forgave you all that debt because you begged me. Should you not also have had compassion on your fellow servant, just as I had pity on you?"* (Matthew 18:32–33). The inference is that the first servant could never repay his debt – and neither can you. Jesus says you will experience the same fate as the unforgiving servant if you do not forgive.

Prayer

My Father, I realize that I can never repay my debt to You. I stand in Your presence as a sinner saved by grace. Help me to extend the same love and forgiveness to others that I receive from You. Amen.

The inference is that the first servant could never repay his debt – and neither can you.

Forgiveness before worship

Read Matthew 5:21–26

"Therefore if you bring your gift to the altar, and there remember that your brother has something against you, leave your gift there before the altar, and go your way. First be reconciled to your brother, and then come and offer your gift." (Matthew 5:23–24)

Jeremiah said this about the heart: *"The heart is deceitful above all things, and desperately wicked; who can know it?"* (Jeremiah 17:9). Sin begins in the heart, then takes root in our minds and, if we entertain it, expresses itself in actions. It is hard to believe that Jesus was talking to people who were religious in Matthew chapter five: religious people who were ready and prepared to come to the altar to worship God, while knowing that there was a brother with whom they were out of fellowship. One of the verses that we frequently quote is from 1 Samuel 15:22: *So Samuel said: "Has the LORD as great delight in burnt offerings and sacrifices, as in obeying the voice of the LORD? Behold, to obey is better than sacrifice, And to heed than the fat of rams."*

Too often today we have the same situation in churches. There are people standing in the pews raising their hands in worship to God and they are not speaking to the brother standing across the aisle from them. If this is you, then God is speaking to you in our Scripture reading today. If you know that someone has something against you because of something you have done – go and make it right. Say you are sorry and ask for forgiveness. God is not interested in your sacrifice; He is interested in your obedience.

Maybe you are concerned about the reception you will receive. You might say to me, "Angus, you don't know what I did to this person. They will never forgive me for my sin against them." My friend, have you repented before God? Have you asked Him to forgive you? If you have then He is faithful and just to forgive you and to cleanse you from all unrighteousness. If your brother or sister refuses to forgive you, then that is between them and God. They have to answer to Him for their unforgiveness. Your responsibility is to sincerely say sorry and ask their forgiveness – you are not responsible for their decision to forgive or not to forgive.

Prayer

My Father, I thank You that You have forgiven me for my sin. I pray that when I ask my brother or sister for forgiveness You will soften their heart towards me. I know that You are more interested in my obedience than my sacrifices. I want to worship You with clean hands today. Amen.

Your responsibility is to sincerely say sorry and ask their forgiveness – you are not responsible for their decision to forgive or not to forgive.

Who will throw the first stone?

Read John 8:1–12

"He who is without sin among you, let him throw a stone at her first." Then those who heard it, being convicted by their conscience, went out one by one, beginning with the oldest even to the last. (John 8:7b, 9a)

Jesus has always been in the business of saving sinners. The religious people of Jesus' day were in the business of condemning sinners. I do not wish to generalize, please hear me; I am not pointing fingers at the church. I love the church. However, there are definitely people who consider themselves to be "good Christians", who too easily point fingers at those they consider to be sinners. Jesus is our example in everything: Jesus loved sinners, but hated sin. Too often we hate both the sinner and the sin.

In Mark 2:17 we read: *When Jesus heard it, He said to them, "Those who are well have no need of a physician, but those who are sick. I did not come to call the righteous, but sinners, to repentance."* We are often prone to disregarding this. As the body of Christ we are not called to live self-righteous lives. This was how the Pharisees in Jesus' day lived. They were so aware of the law, considering themselves custodians of the law. This was the reason they became so easily and often offended by Jesus. According to them He didn't uphold the law. They were too blind to see that He was the very embodiment of the law: the law of Love.

We should never confuse speaking the truth of God's Word in love with compromise. There is a big difference. If our motivation is love for God and love for people then we will get it right. We are also, like Jesus, called to help sinners repent and find healing for their sins. We must share the good news of the gospel that has the power to heal body, soul and spirit. If you allow unforgiveness, self-righteousness and prejudice to rule in your heart you will be of no use to God in furthering His kingdom here on earth. Don't be like the religious leaders in our reading in John chapter eight. If you are, Jesus says: *"He who is without sin among you, let him throw a stone at her first."*

Prayer

My Father, I thank You that Jesus came to save sinners – otherwise I wouldn't be able to come before You today. Help me to show Your love to everyone. Use me to share Your truth with people whom I meet. I want to be a witness for You sharing Your love and forgiveness with people. Amen.

Religious people are often too blind to see that Jesus was the very embodiment of the law: the law of Love.

Forgiving – no more than our duty

Read Luke 17:1–10

"So likewise you, when you have done all those things which you are commanded, say, 'We are unprofitable servants. We have done what was our duty to do.'" (Luke 17:10)

Jesus was walking along teaching and sharing with His disciples. By the way, have you ever tried to imagine what it must have been like to walk with Jesus when He was on this earth? I stood by the Sea of Galilee and imagined what it must have been like to be with Him. *Then He said to the disciples, "It is impossible that no offenses should come, but woe to him through whom they do come! It would be better for him if a millstone were hung around his neck, and he were thrown into the sea, than that he should offend one of these little ones. Take heed to yourselves. If your brother sins against you, rebuke him; and if he repents, forgive him. And if he sins against you seven times in a day, and seven times in a day returns to you, saying, 'I repent,' you shall forgive him"* (Luke 17:1–4).

On hearing this the disciples realized that it was beyond them to do it in their own strength. They said: *"Increase our faith"* (Luke 17:5b). Does it take faith to forgive? I believe it does. When I choose to forgive it means that I hand the result over to God. When someone wrongs me and I forgive them I no longer have control over what will happen next. This is one of the reasons that it is often so difficult to forgive. We feel that we are losing control when we do. As long as we hold onto the offence we feel we have some control of the person or situation. This is not true; all that happens is that the results of not forgiving begin to control us.

In Luke chapter seventeen Jesus goes on to tell a parable about a servant. He points out that a servant does not have the right to be served. It is the servant's duty to serve their master. Forgiving is no different – it is the command of our master that we should forgive. Therefore, Jesus is saying to us that forgiving is no more than our duty.

Prayer

My Father, I bow in Your presence as Your humble servant today. I recognize that I do not have any rights when it comes to forgiveness. Father, I gladly relinquish my will to Yours. Give me faith to trust You with my hurt and disappointment. I know that You love me and You will do what is best for me. Amen.

It is the servant's duty to serve their master. Forgiving is no different – it is the command of our master that we should forgive.

Father, forgive them …

Read Luke 23:26–49

Then Jesus said, "Father, forgive them, for they do not know what they do." (Luke 23:34a)

Have you ever stopped to think that Jesus doesn't ask you to do anything that He hasn't done or isn't prepared to do Himself? If you think that uttering the words, *"Father, forgive them, for they do not know what they do,"* was easy for Him, then I remind you of the Garden of Gethsemane. Take a few minutes and read the account in Luke 22:39–46 again. Verse forty-four tells us: *And being in agony, He prayed more earnestly. Then His sweat became like great drops of blood falling down to the ground.* It would not be possible for Jesus to stand in front of you today, telling you to forgive, if He did not understand what forgiveness costs.

If you have been betrayed by those you served and ministered to – He understands: the same thing happened to Him. If your closest confidants have abandoned you – He understands: it happened to Him. He had twelve disciples; only one of them was at the foot of the cross when He hung, suffered and died there. If you feel misunderstood and misquoted – He understands: He was misunderstood and misquoted every day of His life on earth. If you have been abused and mistreated – He understands: He regularly lived in fear of His life. Even if you are put to death for Your faith – He understands: He was put to death so that you can have faith.

Jesus went before us. He is our example. Proverbs 18:24b tells us: *But there is a friend who sticks closer than a brother.* You will never have to go through any trial or difficulty alone. Jesus will always be right beside you. Jesus knew that He could entrust His life to His Father in heaven. Even at that awful moment when the sin of the world pressed down upon Him and He was separated from His Father – He still trusted Him. You will never have to experience that separation because Jesus experienced it for you. You can forgive, no matter how painful, because you can entrust your heart to Jesus today.

Prayer

My Father, in the midst of my pain I look to Jesus. Thank You, my saviour, that You understand better than anyone else what forgiveness can cost. However, I am also aware that the cost of not forgiving is far greater. Therefore, I give my heart into Your hands today. Amen.

You can forgive, no matter how painful, because you can entrust your heart to Jesus today.

Jesus restores Peter

Read John 21:1–19

He said to him the third time, "Simon, son of Jonah, do you love Me?" Peter was grieved because He said to him the third time, "Do you love Me?" (John 21:17a)

P eter denied Jesus three times after His arrest, just as Jesus had predicted that he would. Peter was a broken man. Did Jesus hold this betrayal against Peter? No, He didn't because Jesus is in the business of restoration. In Mark chapter sixteen Jesus appears to Mary Magdalene and her friends after His resurrection. He tells her: *"But go, tell His disciples – and Peter – that He is going before you into Galilee; there you will see Him, as He said to you"* (Mark 16:7). Why do you think Jesus did this? Do you think He wanted to reassure Peter that He did not hold the denial against him?

Next we see the disciples fishing on the Sea of Tiberias and Jesus appears on the shore. They hadn't managed to catch any fish and Jesus told them to cast the net on the right side of the boat. When they did this the net was filled with fish. It was then that John realized it was Jesus. He told Peter and he immediately jumped over the side and began wading in to the shore. Jesus had a fire going and He cooked breakfast and ate together with His disciples. Then Jesus turned to Peter and asked him: *"Simon, son of Jonah, do you love Me more than these?" He said to Him, "Yes, Lord; You know that I love You." He said to him, "Feed My lambs"* (John 21:15). Three times Jesus asked Peter if he loved Him; and three times Peter replied that he did.

It says that the third time Jesus asked him *Peter was grieved* (John 21:17). Do you think maybe that Jesus asked him three times because Peter would deny Jesus three times? Each time he replied *"I love You"* it wiped out one of the claims of denial. Jesus totally restored Peter; he went on to become the one who delivered the sermon at Pentecost. Jesus is in the business of restoration, my friend. If you need restoring today, come to Him, kneel at His feet, repent, ask His forgiveness; then allow Him to restore you.

Prayer

My Father, I come into Your presence today. I bow at Your feet and ask Your forgiveness, Lord. In the name of Jesus, Your Son, forgive me, I pray. Cleanse me, restore me and use me once again to bring glory and honour to Your name. Amen.

If you need restoring today, come to Him, kneel at His feet, repent, ask His forgiveness; then allow Him to restore you.

God meant it for good

Read Genesis 50:15–22

Then his brothers also went and fell down before his face, and they said, "Behold, we are your servants." Joseph said to them, "Do not be afraid, for am I in the place of God? But as for you, you meant evil against me; but God meant it for good, in order to bring it about as it is this day, to save many people alive. Now therefore, do not be afraid; I will provide for you and your little ones." And he comforted them and spoke kindly to them. (Genesis 50:18–21)

Y ou know the story of Joseph, don't you? At a young age his brothers sold him off into slavery, then went home and told their father a wild animal had eaten him. Joseph landed in prison because of wicked Potiphar's wife. Joseph remained faithful to God and God blessed him. *The keeper of the prison did not look into anything that was under Joseph's authority, because the LORD was with him; and whatever he did, the LORD made it prosper* (Genesis 39:23). Joseph was betrayed by his friends whom he helped to be released from prison.

Still Joseph remained faithful. Many people would have become bitter and twisted, believing that God had deserted them. Two full years later Pharaoh had a dream. No one could interpret the dream, then the butler remembered Joseph. He interpreted the dream for the Pharaoh. As time went by Joseph became more and more indispensable to the Pharaoh. *And Pharaoh said to his servants, "Can we find such a one as this, a man in whom is the Spirit of God? You shall be over my house, and all my people shall be ruled according to your word; only in regard to the throne will I be greater than you"* (Genesis 41:38, 40). Joseph went from being in prison to being the second most important person in Egypt.

When the famine came Joseph's brothers journeyed to Egypt looking for food. It was Joseph's opportunity to get even with them. He didn't, though, because he realized that God was in control of his life. He knew that God had a plan and a purpose for his life. Neither adversity nor the betrayal of people could thwart that plan. Joseph kept the faith and God blessed his life as a result. Joseph knew His God and because of it he could forgive his brothers; and he could utter the beautiful words in our key text. Do you know your God like this? Do you trust Him enough to believe that no matter what happens in your life He can use it for good?

Prayer

My Father, I bow in Your presence. I am so encouraged and inspired by the story of Joseph. Thank You for using the story of Joseph to once again remind me that there is nothing that can touch my life that You cannot use to Your glory and honour, if I am willing to submit to You. Amen.

Do you trust God enough to believe that no matter what happens in your life He can use it for good?

David forgives Saul

Read 1 Samuel 24:1–22

Then he said to David: "You are more righteous than I; for you have rewarded me with good, whereas I have rewarded you with evil. And you have shown this day how you have dealt well with me; for when the LORD delivered me into your hand, you did not kill me."
(1 Samuel 24:17–18)

After killing Goliath, David went to live in the palace with Saul. David faithfully served Saul, but as God began to bless David more and more, Saul became jealous of David. The final straw was when David returned from war and the people praised David more than Saul. 1 Samuel 18:8–9 says: *Then Saul was very angry, and the saying displeased him; and he said, "They have ascribed to David ten thousands, and to me they have ascribed only thousands. Now what more can he have but the kingdom?" So Saul eyed David from that day forward.*

Saul tried many times to kill David, but David never retaliated in kind. In our reading today Saul is once again in pursuit of David. He goes into a cave to rest and while he is asleep David and his men enter the cave. David refuses to kill Saul; instead he cuts off a corner of his robe. David says to Saul: *"Moreover, my father, see! Yes, see the corner of your robe in my hand! For in that I cut off the corner of your robe, and did not kill you, know and see that there is neither evil nor rebellion in my hand, and I have not sinned against you. Yet you hunt my life to take it. Let the LORD judge between you and me, and let the LORD avenge me on you. But my hand shall not be against you"* (1 Samuel 24:11–12).

Saul responded: *"You are more righteous than I; for you have rewarded me with good, whereas I have rewarded you with evil"* (1 Samuel 24:17). The story of David and Saul is another example of how God undertakes for those who trust Him. God looked after David and helped him proper. Saul was not able to harm him because God's hand was upon David. He went through heartache and difficult times, yes; but never did God forsake him. Despite what Saul did to him David steadfastly did the right thing towards Saul. Are you steadfastly doing the right thing in the situation in which you find yourself?

Prayer

My Father, in the midst of chaos and uncertainty You are my rock and my anchor. I know that as I steadfastly cling to You, choosing to do the right thing, despite the provocation to retaliate, You will bless me as You did David. You are my deliverer; You are the lifter of my head. Amen.

Are you steadfastly doing the right thing in the situation in which you find yourself?

Stephen forgives his murderers

Read Acts 6:8–15; 7:54–60

Then he knelt down and cried out with a loud voice, "Lord, do not charge them with this sin." And when he had said this, he fell asleep. (Acts 7:60)

S tephen loved Jesus: *And Stephen, full of faith and power, did great wonders and signs among the people* (Acts 6:8). The religious leaders could not find anything against him so they had to resort to lies. They brought him before the Council; *And all who sat in the council, looking steadfastly at him, saw his face as the face of an angel* (Acts 6:15). Stephen then proceeded to preach the sermon of his life. The people could not handle the truth that Stephen spoke and they were incensed by his words.

They took hold of him and began stoning him. There was a young man, Paul, standing in the crowd watching and listening. He held the coats of the men who stoned Stephen. He believed that he was upholding God's law and helping God by doing this. Stephen was not afraid because he knew his God; he had committed his life to Jesus. As he knelt in the dust he looked up to heaven. *But he, being full of the Holy Spirit, gazed into heaven and saw the glory of God, and Jesus standing at the right hand of God, and said, "Look! I see the heavens opened and the Son of Man standing at the right hand of God!"* (Acts 7:55–56).

Stephen was not alone as he was stoned. The Holy Spirit filled him and Jesus was also right there with him. Hebrews 8:1b tells us: *We have such a High Priest, who is seated at the right hand of the throne of the Majesty in the heavens.* Yet Stephen says: *"Look! I see the heavens opened and the Son of Man standing at the right hand of God!"* Jesus didn't sit idly by; He stood up so that Stephen could see Him and know that He was right there with him as he died. Stephen was able to forgive the men who stoned him, because he knew what it was to have his sins forgiven. No matter what you go through, even death, you can know that Jesus is right there beside you. Like Stephen, He will never leave you.

Prayer

My Father, I come to You today, so grateful for Your love and Your forgiveness. I know that I need fear nothing that people can do to me. I have You by my side. You are in control of my life. Help me to be faithful to You to the very end, I pray. Like Stephen, help me to finish strong. Amen.

Stephen was able to forgive the men who stoned him, because he knew what it was to have his sins forgiven.

Paul's sins are forgiven

Read Acts 9:1–31

And Ananias went his way and entered the house; and laying his hands on him he said, "Brother Saul, the Lord Jesus, who appeared to you on the road as you came, has sent me that you may receive your sight and be filled with the Holy Spirit." (Acts 9:17)

Paul was spiritually blind long before he was physically blinded on the road to Damascus. When Ananias prayed for him, Paul gained spiritual sight as well as regaining his physical sight. The spiritual sight was far more important. It enabled him to accept Jesus as his Lord and saviour. That day on the road to Damascus, Saul's life was changed irrevocably. His name was changed to Paul. Paul suffered much for the gospel. When his spiritual eyes were opened Paul became as fanatical for Jesus as he had been against Him. Paul was willing to and eventually did die for Jesus.

The religious leaders of the day were constantly trying to imprison him, beat him, kill him and generally harass him. He suffered physically, mentally and often emotionally for the gospel. Paul never wavered, though; he never gave in or gave up. His motivation was his love for Jesus. Like Mary Magdalene, Paul had been forgiven much and therefore he loved much. Paul was so incredibly grateful to God for forgiving his sins. Can you imagine what it must have been like for Paul when he realized that his persecution of the Christians had been a sin against God Himself, and that Jesus was the Son of God? If anyone needed the assurance of their salvation and forgiveness it was Paul.

God also gave Paul a special love for the church. Paul's life was spent serving Jesus and His body. Paul learnt to trust God despite his thorn in the flesh. He learnt that God's grace was sufficient for him. My friend, where do you stand in your commitment to Jesus today? Like Paul, do you know what it means to be forgiven? If you do, what are you doing with your new life in Christ? Can you say with Paul: *But by the grace of God I am what I am, and His grace toward me was not in vain; but I labored more abundantly than they all, yet not I, but the grace of God which was with me* (1 Corinthians 15:10)?

Prayer

My Father, I thank You that I can say with Paul, I am what I am, and Your grace toward me is not in vain. I surrender my life afresh to You today. Use me, I pray, in Your service and for Your glory. Amen.

But by the grace of God I am what I am, and His grace toward me was not in vain.

Love your enemy

Read Matthew 5:38–48

"You have heard that it was said, 'You shall love your neighbor and hate your enemy.' But I say to you, love your enemies, bless those who curse you, do good to those who hate you, and pray for those who spitefully use you and persecute you." (Matthew 5:43–44)

I s it any wonder that the religious leaders of Jesus' day didn't understand Him? He turned popular wisdom on its head. Do not resist an evil person; if someone slaps you on the cheek, turn the other one; if someone sues you and takes your tunic, give him your cloak also – whatever was Jesus on about? He went still further: *love your enemies, bless those who curse you, do good to those who hate you, and pray for those who spitefully use you and persecute you.* He asks us the question: *For if you love those who love you, what reward have you?* (Matthew 5:46a)

Is God asking us to do the impossible? Philippians 4:13 tells me: *I can do all things through Christ who strengthens me.* Isn't that beautiful? God will never ask you to do anything that He cannot give you the strength to actually do. We are saved in order to live differently to the world around us. If there is no difference between the way Christians live and the way the world lives, then what will ever attract people to Jesus? People have to see that you are different. It is the peace and joy that comes from being forgiven that will make people want what you have.

Matthew 5:45b says, *for He makes His sun rise on the evil and on the good, and sends rain on the just and on the unjust.* This can be a difficult pill to swallow, can it not? So often we are in the forefront when it comes to taking revenge. This is not what Jesus saved us for. What kind of a world would we live in if every Christian lived out the principles that Jesus set out in our reading today? The world won't begin living like this until we do. No matter what happens we have to live according to the principles that Jesus has laid out for us in His Word. Choose today to walk and live in love.

Prayer

My Father, I choose today to walk and live in love. I realize that I cannot do this in my own strength. Thank You that You promise me in Your Word that I can do anything You ask me to because of the strength and power You give me in Jesus Christ, Your Son. Amen.

Choose today to walk and live in love. The world won't begin living like this until we do.

Vengeance is Mine

Read Romans 12:9-21

Beloved, do not avenge yourselves, but rather give place to wrath; for it is written, "Vengeance is Mine, I will repay," says the Lord. (Romans 12:19)

I don't know what feelings the readings this month have evoked in you. I am aware that I live in a country where countless people have experienced despicable things being done to them. My country is a violent one. Crimes of a violent nature are perpetrated against people every day. If you or a loved one have been the victim of a crime, you might feel that you want to take revenge against those who harmed you or your loved one. My friend, if you are a child of God, this is not an option for you. God is clear in His Word: *"Vengeance is Mine, I will repay."*

Unforgiveness is a terrible thing; it eats away at you, slowly but surely destroying you. This is the reason that Jesus was so definite and insistent that we have to forgive. Your very salvation is tied up with you forgiving. God is the one who judges; and He will mete out justice. Don't allow unforgiveness to rob you of your witness for Jesus. It could be that you have been betrayed by a loved one. Maybe your child has disappointed you – maybe they are on drugs or they drink. You have tried and tried; now you are about ready to give up. You might have been defrauded in business: your partner took all your money and your business is bankrupt. It could be that your wife has betrayed you with another man. My friend, whatever the situation that has brought you to a place of bitterness and unforgiveness – you have to let it go.

All through this month we have looked at many different aspects of forgiveness. We have read countless Scriptures that all say the same thing: forgiveness is not an option. If you want God to forgive you, then you have to forgive others. If you want God to hear your prayers, you have to forgive. It is only God, through His Holy Spirit, who can touch your heart and change it. I pray sincerely that you've been open to hearing Your Father as He's spoken to you.

Prayer

My Father, thank You for Your Holy Spirit who speaks to my heart. I come before You, grateful for Your Word that You have opened to me this month. I know that You are telling me to forgive and today I choose to do so. Father, I forgive … in Jesus' name. Amen.

I pray sincerely that you've been open to hearing Your Father as He's spoken to you.

Do not take vengeance

Read Romans 12:9–21

Let love be without hypocrisy. Bless those who persecute you. Repay no one evil for evil. Therefore "If your enemy is hungry, feed him; if he is thirsty, give him a drink; for in so doing you will heap coals of fire on his head." Do not be overcome by evil, but overcome evil with good. (Romans 12:9a, 14a, 17a, 20–21)

The Old Testament also has quite a lot to say about not taking vengeance. *You shall not take vengeance, nor bear any grudge against the children of your people, but you shall love your neighbor as yourself: I am the LORD* (Leviticus 19:18). Isaiah 35:4 says: *Say to those who are fearful-hearted, "Be strong, do not fear! Behold, your God will come with vengeance, with the recompense of God; He will come and save you."*

Obeying God's command not to take vengeance also means that we cannot wish vengeance upon those who have harmed us. In other words you have to be prepared for the fact that if the person finds Jesus, then God is going to forgive them for what they did to you. In the same way that your sins are washed away by the blood of Jesus, so will theirs be. 2 Peter 3:9 reminds us: *The Lord is not slack concerning His promise, as some count slackness, but is longsuffering toward us, not willing that any should perish but that all should come to repentance.* Our reading in Matthew 5:44 a few days ago told us; *pray for those who spitefully use you and persecute you.* My friend, are you praying for the people who have hurt you?

If you have forgiven them then you will be able to pray for them. God will give you the grace to be able to do this. God will never ask you to do what He is unable to give you the grace to do. If you are struggling with this you need to cling to this truth. There is enormous power in forgiveness; Jesus has entrusted us with this power. *"And I will give you the keys of the kingdom of heaven, and whatever you bind on earth will be bound in heaven, and whatever you loose on earth will be loosed in heaven"* (Matthew 16:19). My friend, the keys of the kingdom are in your hands – will you use them to forgive and set those who have hurt you free?

Prayer

My Father, I bow before You and I surrender to You today. I choose to forgive; I choose to obey You. I pray that You will continue to give me grace and love. Help me to love with Your love. I am so grateful that You have forgiven me, I realize that I can never withhold the peace and joy I have experienced from anyone else. Amen.

For we know Him who said, "Vengeance is Mine, I will repay" (**Hebrews 10:30a**).

Forgive and forgiven!

Read Psalm 86

For You, Lord, are good, and ready to forgive, and abundant in mercy to all those who call upon You. (Psalm 86:5)

> Bow down Your ear, O LORD, hear me; for I am poor and needy.
> Preserve my life, for I am holy;
> You are my God; Save Your servant who trusts in You!
> Be merciful to me, O Lord, for I cry to You all day long.
> Rejoice the soul of Your servant, for to You, O Lord, I lift up my soul.
> For You, Lord, are good, and ready to forgive,
> And abundant in mercy to all those who call upon You.

> Give ear, O LORD, to my prayer; and attend to the voice of my supplications.
> In the day of my trouble I will call upon You, for You will answer me.

> Among the gods there is none like You, O Lord;
> Nor are there any works like Your works.
> All nations whom You have made shall come and worship before You, O Lord,
> And shall glorify Your name.
> For You are great, and do wondrous things; You alone are God.

> Teach me Your way, O LORD; I will walk in Your truth;
> Unite my heart to fear Your name.
> I will praise You, O Lord my God, with all my heart,
> And I will glorify Your name forevermore.
> For great is Your mercy toward me,
> And You have delivered my soul from the depths of Sheol.

> O God, the proud have risen against me, and a mob of violent men have sought my life,
> And have not set You before them. But You, O Lord, are a God full of compassion,
> and gracious, longsuffering and abundant in mercy and truth.

> Oh, turn to me, and have mercy on me!
> Give Your strength to Your servant, and save the son of Your maidservant.
> Show me a sign for good, that those who hate me may see it and be ashamed.

> Because You, LORD, have helped me and comforted me.

Prayer

My Father, thank You that I can pray this prayer to You today. Even though it was written so long ago it is as relevant today as it was then. Amen.

But You, O Lord, are a God full of compassion, and gracious, longsuffering and abundant in mercy and truth.

NOVEMBER

Now is the time ... to glorify God through suffering

Glorify God through suffering

Perseverance under pressure

Jesus suffered for us

You will not be overwhelmed

Abba, Father is with you

Faith in the midst of difficulties

The school of sorrows

School will soon be out

Unmerited favour

A thorn in the flesh

My grace is sufficient

Submission to the will of God

Parable of the poplar and the thorn tree

The Lord is a fortress in adversity

Wrestling with God

Adversity breeds patience

The Lord of hosts is with you

Behold, I stand at the door

Hope does not disappoint

Laying it down on the altar

Strength in the inner man

Finishing strong

A different spirit

Strength of character

Results of premature blessing

God supplies all our needs

Sorrow is better than laughter

God uses the broken

Glory revealed to us

Glorying in His grace

Glorify God through suffering

Read 1 Peter 5:1–11

But may the God of all grace, who called us to His eternal glory by Christ Jesus, after you have suffered a while, perfect, establish, strengthen, and settle you. To Him be the glory and the dominion forever and ever. Amen. (1 Peter 5:10–11)

Now is the time to glorify God through suffering. We don't like to talk about suffering; it is not a popular subject. We are averse to pain and if we are honest we will go to great lengths to avoid it. This month we are going to explore and talk about suffering for Jesus. Are you going through a hardship at the moment? We have to be real with one another; there is nowhere in the Bible where it says, "Come to Jesus and all your problems will be over." I have said this to you many times. In fact it is quite the contrary.

Before I met Jesus Christ as my Lord and saviour I was on a downward spiral – I was close to the bottom. I cried out to the Lord and He saved me. Since that day He has been walking with me. He hasn't taken me out of the fire; no, He walks through the fire with me. I am growing through these experiences and I am maturing as a Christian as I walk through His refining fire.

I want to make something clear so that you don't get the wrong impression. I am not saying that the Lord brings disease and hardship on you because He wants to teach you something. I don't believe that the Lord will use a drunk driver to kill a little child running across the road to get his ball in order to teach you a lesson. God doesn't work like that. What I am saying is we live in an imperfect world and this is not our home. The devil goes around like a roaring lion, the Bible tells us: *Be sober, be vigilant; because your adversary the devil walks about like a roaring lion, seeking whom he may devour* (1 Peter 5:8). We are not exempt from the hardships of this world because we are Christians. Things like recession and sickness affect us also. The difference is the Lord takes us through them. The Lord heals the sick, turns businesses around and sets the captors free.

Prayer

My Father, You are with me through the good times and the bad times. This is the reason that I can get up every day and face life. I thank You for Your unwavering faithfulness no matter what happens. I am grateful for Your love and gracious presence in my life. Amen.

Since that day He has been walking with me. He doesn't take me out of the fire; no, He walks through the fire with me.

Perseverance under pressure

Read Philippians 1:19–30

For to you it has been granted on behalf of Christ, not only to believe in Him, but also to suffer for His sake. (Philippians 1:29)

I want to tell you something: since I became a believer I have experienced more fiery trials than I ever did before. The good news is that He gives me the grace, strength and courage to push through to the other side. There is a Scripture I found in Philippians 1:29: *For to you it has been granted on behalf of Christ, not only to believe in Him, but also to suffer for His sake.* What does this Scripture mean? Believe me, it is very hard for an unbeliever, a person in the world, to identify with a Christian who has never, ever had a problem. No one can relate to someone for whom everything always goes well; who has money pouring in; is 100 per cent healthy; is unfailingly positive; has a marriage made in heaven and all their children serving God. No one can identify with that – it is like trying to identify with Superman.

Now I am not talking contrary to the Word of God. You know me; I am a faith man – I believe in faith. Faith has kept us on this farm. I believe and I consider myself to be a son of Abraham. *"Abraham believed God, and it was accounted to him for righteousness." And he was called the friend of God* (James 2:23b). This didn't stop Abraham from going through hardships: He left his farm and travelled to an unknown destination. Pharaoh nearly killed him and in his weakness he passed his wife off as his sister to save his life. Later God told him to sacrifice his only son, Isaac.

What about the apostle Paul, known as Saul of Tarsus, who wrote two-thirds of the New Testament? You cannot tell me he didn't suffer. My friend, I don't know of another man, other than Jesus, who suffered more than Paul. Despite his suffering Paul could say; *... as always, so now also Christ will be magnified in my body, whether by life or by death. For to me, to live is Christ, and to die is gain* (Philippians 1:20b–21).

Prayer

My Father, You have been with Your children from the beginning of time as they have walked with You. You have never disappointed or deserted those who have placed their faith in You. Father, help me today to always look to You, no matter what I go through. Amen.

No matter what I go through He gives me the grace, strength and courage to push through to the other side.

324   NOW IS THE TIME

Jesus suffered for us

Read Matthew 26:36–46

… He went away and prayed, saying, "O My Father, if this cup cannot pass away from Me unless I drink it, Your will be done." "… Behold, the hour is at hand, and the Son of Man is being betrayed into the hands of sinners. Rise, let us be going. See, My betrayer is at hand." (Matthew 26:42, 45–46)

J esus' mandate when He came to this earth was to suffer and die for our sins. That was His mission; it started in a stable in Bethlehem and ended on a cross on Golgotha. Jesus never once shirked His calling. He may have sweated great drops of blood and He wrestled with it, but He never wavered from the course His Father had set for Him. Jesus is our example in suffering as He is in every aspect of life.

Jesus didn't ever have a home. *And Jesus said to him, "Foxes have holes and birds of the air have nests, but the Son of Man has nowhere to lay His head"* (Matthew 8:20). He was no sooner born than Herod tried to kill Him. Joseph and Mary had to flee to Egypt to keep Jesus safe. (Read about it in Matthew 2:13–18.) He was scorned time and again, including in His home town of Nazareth. *Then He said, "Assuredly, I say to you, no prophet is accepted in his own country. So all those in the synagogue, when they heard these things, were filled with wrath, and rose up and thrust Him out of the city; and they led Him to the brow of the hill on which their city was built, that they might throw Him down over the cliff* (Luke 4:24, 28–29).

He suffered, He was misunderstood and He was misrepresented. Why? Because He stood for righteousness. His greatest battle was in the Garden of Gethsemane as He prayed to His Father: *"O My Father, if this cup cannot pass away from Me unless I drink it, Your will be done"* (Matthew 26:42b). There was no relief for Jesus; He had to go to Calvary otherwise you and I would not be able to enjoy our salvation today. Jesus paid the price so that we can know the reality of His saying to us: *"I will never leave you nor forsake you"* (Hebrews 13:5b). You can know that no matter what you are going through today, Jesus is right there beside you.

Prayer

My Father, I come to You today in the precious name of Jesus, my saviour. Thank You, Jesus, that You were willing to suffer and die for me. Father, it is because of Jesus' sacrifice that I can bow before You today. Thank You, Father, for my salvation. Amen.

You can know that no matter what you are going through today, Jesus is right there beside you.

You will not be overwhelmed

Read Isaiah 43:1–15

"When you pass through the waters, I will be with you; and through the rivers, they shall not overflow you. When you walk through the fire, you shall not be burned, nor shall the flame scorch you. For I am the LORD your God, the Holy One of Israel, your Savior." (Isaiah 43:2–3a)

We are in a battle against evil, but in Christ we have the victory. You might be suffering even though you are doing everything you know to do. You say, "Angus, I am tithing, I am praying, I go to church; with God's help I am raising my children right." The Lord your God says: *"Fear not, for I have redeemed you; I have called you by your name; You are Mine."* Your business is failing despite your best efforts. Your crops have come to nothing. You have lost your job. God says to you: *"When you walk through the fire, you shall not be burned, nor shall the flame scorch you. For I am the LORD your God, the Holy One of Israel, your Savior"* (Isaiah 43:1b, 2b–3a).

When you go through the fiery trials the Lord is right beside you, to strengthen you. He is not punishing you, my friend, you need to know and understand this. He might be chastening you though. *You should know in your heart that as a man chastens his son,* so *the LORD your God chastens you* (Deuteronomy 8:5). *"For whom the LORD loves He chastens, and scourges every son whom He receives"* (Hebrews 12:6). What does chastening mean? Well, the blacksmith takes hold of the piece of iron with his tongs and holds it in the fire, until it is white hot. Then he places the piece of iron on the anvil. He then takes a hammer and he beats the iron. The process is repeated a number of times, to make the steel resilient. When he is finished it is strong and it can perform the task that it is designed for.

The Bible says in Romans 8:1: There is *therefore now no condemnation to those who are in Christ Jesus, who do not walk according to the flesh, but according to the Spirit.* So if you have given your life to Christ, you can know that any hardship you experience can only serve to make you better able to serve God, your Father and His purposes for your life.

Prayer

My Father, I submit myself to Your will for my life today. I acknowledge that I am in a battle against the evil one. How grateful I am to have Your assurance that no matter what I go through You have promised me that You have redeemed me and that I am Yours. Amen.

When you go through the fiery trials the Lord is right beside you, to strengthen you.

Abba, Father is with you

Read Romans 8:1–17

For you did not receive the spirit of bondage again to fear, but you received the Spirit of adoption by whom we cry out, "Abba, Father." The Spirit Himself bears witness with our spirit that we are children of God. (Romans 8:15–16)

*T*here is therefore now no condemnation to those who are in Christ Jesus… (Romans 8:1). The Holy Spirit convicts you, but He does not condemn you. It is the devil who condemns you; he is the one who wants to put you down. Jesus on the other hand only ever wants to raise you up. So, my dear friend, if you are going through a hardship today, do not automatically assume that there is sin in your life. Where does it say that in the Bible, my friend? Listen to me: if you are going through a hardship by all means sit down and say, "Lord, if there is anything in my life that is not pleasing You, please reveal it to me so that I can repent of it. Show me, so that I can move on with You."

When you go through a hardship it is often the time when you can be the greatest witness to the unbeliever: your work colleague; your next door neighbour. When things are going well for you, they can say you serve the Lord because everything in your life is perfect. However, if you faithfully serve Him even in the bad times it will send a message to them.

This is exactly what happened to Job, remember. He was tested and he came through pure. The devil said to God it is easy for Job to worship Him because he is a rich farmer and he has a beautiful family. Take that all away from him and see what happens. What happened? Job stood firm. He said: *"Though He slay me, yet will I trust Him"* (Job 13:15a). The Lord was with Job; and his end was greater than his beginning. Job prospered and everything that was taken away from him God gave back to him double. Whatever you are going through today, my friend, don't allow the enemy to shift your focus off of the Lord, your God. He loves you and He wants only what is best for you. You are His child and you can cry out to Him: "Abba, Father".

Prayer

My Father, I come before You today and I kneel at Your feet. Lord, I am tired, I am worn out and I need to feel Your special touch upon me. Abba, Father, put Your arms around me. Show me in a new way that You love me. Help me to remain strong; fill me with Your strength and courage. Amen.

He loves you and He wants only what is best for you. You are His child and you can cry out to Him: "Abba, Father".

Faith in the midst of difficulties

Hebrews 11:1–16

Now faith is the substance of things hoped for, the evidence of things not seen. For by it the elders obtained a good testimony. By faith we understand that the worlds were framed by the word of God, so that the things which are seen were not made of things which are visible. (Hebrews 11:1–3)

God runs a costly school and many of the lessons He teaches are learnt through tears – tears of sorrow. If you want more faith I will introduce you to the school of sorrow. It is there in the school of sorrow that faith is learnt. You don't learn faith when everything is going well. You cannot learn it then because you don't need faith when everything in your life is going well. It is usually only when the wheels begin coming off that we say, "Please, Lord, help me" – and He steps in. This happened to Peter, when he was walking on the water he was fine. It was only when he started sinking that he cried out, "Jesus, help me", and the Lord immediately lifted him up out of the water.

A man asked me the other day if I had ever thought about the fact that Jesus must have walked with Peter back to the boat. When talking about this story we always stop at the point where the Lord lifts Peter up out of the water. Have you ever thought about what happened after that? Well the Lord walked with him back to the boat, I am sure, or back to the shore and onto dry land. Whichever way it happened Jesus rescued Peter. He didn't leave him to drown. That day Peter's faith grew a little more.

This year we have been looking together at the theme: *Now is the time of God's favour; now is the day of salvation.* All of the subjects we have explored are geared to help you as you seize the day. They are meant to help you to live out your faith, so that you will be ready and well prepared as we move towards the end of this age. Faith in the midst of suffering and difficulties is one of the most important characteristics that a Christian needs to have. Faith gives us hope; you cannot have hope without faith. *Now faith is the substance of things hoped for, the evidence of things not seen.*

Prayer

My Father, thank You that You do not leave me when I am floundering. You are there when I call out to You just like You were for Peter. Increase my faith, I pray. Strengthen me by Your Spirit to live a life characterized by faith and hope. Amen.

If you want more faith I will introduce you to the school of sorrow. It is there in the school of sorrow that faith is learnt.

The school of sorrow

Read Philippians 1:19–30

For to you it has been granted on behalf of Christ, not only to believe in Him, but also to suffer for His sake. (Philippians 1:29)

I want to take you back to the portion of Scripture in Philippians that we read on the second of November. I also want to share a statement that I read in a daily devotional recently. Even this morning as I was praying to the Lord about what to share with you, He led me to this. I trust it will encourage and challenge you as it did me. The writer talks about the school of tears through which lessons are learnt. This reminded me of our Scripture verse: *For to you it has been granted on behalf of Christ, not only to believe in Him, but also to suffer for His sake.*

The writer went on to speak about Richard Baxter, the 17th-century puritan preacher. Baxter endured much persecution and difficulty throughout his life and he said: "O God, I thank You for the discipline I've endured in this body for fifty-eight years." Isn't this amazing? Of course he certainly isn't the only person who has turned trouble into triumph. Are you like this? Do you turn trouble into triumph? This is what a man of God is required to do: take a troubled situation and turn it into a triumphant situation. Success is simply turning failure inside out. That is the difference between failure and success, my friend. I have never met a person who is amounting to anything, who hasn't been through the school of trials and tribulations.

So, if you are going through difficulties and sorrows now, rejoice. Why? Paul tells us why in Romans 5:1–5: *Therefore, having been justified by faith, we have peace with God through our Lord Jesus Christ, through whom also we have access by faith into this grace in which we stand, and rejoice in hope of the glory of God. And not only that, but we also glory in tribulations, knowing that tribulation produces perseverance; and perseverance, character; and character, hope. Now hope does not disappoint, because the love of God has been poured out in our hearts by the Holy Spirit who was given to us.*

Prayer

My Father, I worship at Your feet and I give You praise and honour today. I thank You that when I go through trials and difficulties You are right beside me. Thank You that tribulation produces perseverance; perseverance, character; character, hope; and – praise You – hope does not disappoint. Amen.

I have never met a person who is amounting to anything, who hasn't been through the school of trials and tribulations.

School will soon be out

Read Jeremiah 33:1–11

"Call to Me, and I will answer you, and show you great and mighty things, which you do not know." (Jeremiah 33:3)

I f you want God to use you then you must be prepared to go through the school of hard knocks. Soon our heavenly Father's school will close, for the end of the school term draws closer every day. We do not have the option to run from a difficult lesson or flinch from the rod of discipline. One day soon we will go to heaven and it will be sweeter because we cheerfully endured until the end. Then the day will come when we graduate to glory.

My dear friend, this is good news, isn't it? We will not be in school forever. Our term is drawing to a close and then we are going to heaven to be with Jesus Christ forever. In the meantime we must continue to turn disaster into success, to turn tragedy into triumph, through patience, character-building and suffering for the Lord. There is a beautiful illustration about fiery trials that I want to share with you. The world's finest china goes through the firing process at least three times. Dresden china is always fired up three times. Why is it forced to endure such intense heat? Shouldn't once or twice be enough? No, it is necessary to fire the china three times so that the colours that are being used become brighter, more beautiful and permanently attached. We are fashioned after the same principle. The human trials of life are burned into us numerous times; and through God's grace beautiful colours are formed in us and made to shine forever.

Friends, don't run away or be afraid of the challenges and the fiery trials; just keep bringing them back to God and laying them at the cross of Calvary. Don't get disheartened. The race is not over yet; keep running with perseverance. The day is coming when our voice will join in the voices of joy and the voices of gladness that make up the bride of Christ as we sing together: *"Praise the LORD of hosts, for the LORD is good, for His mercy endures forever"* (Jeremiah 33:11b).

Prayer

My Father, I submit to Your work in my life. I know that whatever comes my way can only serve to further prepare me for the day when school is out and I come home to be with You forever. Keep me strong; keep me faithful. Thank You that I can call out to You and You answer me. Amen.

One day soon we will go to heaven and it will be sweeter because we cheerfully endured until the end.

Unmerited favour

Read 2 Corinthians 12:1–10

And He said to me, "My grace is sufficient for you, for My strength is made perfect in weakness." Therefore most gladly I will rather boast in my infirmities, that the power of Christ may rest upon me. (2 Corinthians 12:9)

The definition of grace is unmerited favour – undeserved loving kindness. Paul continued in verse ten, saying: *Therefore I take pleasure in infirmities, in reproaches, in needs, in persecutions, in distresses, for Christ's sake. For when I am weak, then I am strong.* Paul had learnt that when he was weak, then he was strong.

When a young man is strong and at the peak of his prowess it is often hard for him to understand the concept of strength in weakness. This can be particularly difficult for sportsmen, who can feel invincible when they are at the top of their game. Physical weakness seems very far removed from their reality; and yet it can strike at any moment. We are not only talking of physical strength and weakness but also spiritual strength and weakness. It is possible to be physically weak and spiritually strong; the converse is also true. As Christians we are to guard against spiritual weakness. Even when we go through hardships we can remain spiritually strong.

We all, including Paul, have to endure times of testing. In 2 Corinthians chapter eleven Paul lists the various trials he endured for the sake of the gospel: *... in labors more abundant, in stripes above measure, in prisons more frequently, in deaths often. From the Jews five times I received forty stripes minus one. Three times I was beaten with rods; once I was stoned; three times I was shipwrecked; a night and a day I have been in the deep; in journeys often, in perils of waters, in perils of robbers, in perils of my own countrymen, in perils of the Gentiles, in perils in the city, in perils in the wilderness, in perils in the sea, in perils among false brethren; in weariness and toil, in sleeplessness often, in hunger and thirst, in fastings often, in cold and nakedness – besides the other things, what comes upon me daily: my deep concern for all the churches. Who is weak, and I am not weak? Who is made to stumble, and I do not burn with indignation?* (2 Corinthians 11:23b–29).

Prayer

My Father, I am always amazed at the change You wrought in Paul's life. Change me too, I pray. I know that I shirk the process that change requires. I realize that what made Paul able to endure was that he fell irrevocably in love with Jesus. Help me to have this same love. Amen.

The definition of grace is unmerited favour – undeserved loving kindness.

A thorn in the flesh

Read 2 Corinthians 12:1–10

And lest I should be exalted above measure by the abundance of the revelations, a thorn in the flesh was given to me, a messenger of Satan to buffet me, lest I be exalted above measure. Concerning this thing I pleaded with the Lord three times that it might depart from me. (2 Corinthians 12:7–8)

We are going to spend some time with Paul over the next couple of days. Besides the other difficulties and afflictions Paul suffered, verse seven tells us he was given a thorn in the flesh. There are many opinions regarding what Paul's thorn was; humbly I believe that it was his eyes. On the road to Damascus he was blinded. God gave him his sight back, but you will find in some of his letters he writes, "I sign this letter in my own handwriting." I choose to think that maybe his sight was impaired, which would have slowed him down.

Paul was a rather aggressive type of guy (and I tend to be the same). He was certainly fanatical; he was also impulsive and very self-assured. He was a well-educated man (which I am not, by the way). He was a member of the Sanhedrin – the inner circle in Jerusalem. They were the intellectuals, the elders in the temple. He didn't apologize to too many people and you will pick up from the tone of some of his letters that he didn't suffer fools gladly. Yet, this same man was willing to die, not only for Jesus whom he loved more than life itself, but also for the church, the body of Christ.

What could bring about such a change in a man? Only an encounter with the living God and His Son, Jesus Christ; only a life that was filled with Holy Spirit power. All the fanaticism that Paul employed to persecute the Christians, he used to bring the good news of the gospel of Jesus Christ, to the lost and the church after his conversion. Paul was an all-or-nothing man – I really identify with him. He endured all the things we read about yesterday and he was willing to endure the thorn in his flesh – all for the sake of the gospel of Jesus Christ. What are you prepared to endure, my friend? If you are serious about your walk with the Lord, then the answer will be – everything.

Prayer

My Father, I am so humbled, as I bow in Your presence today. I realize that my commitment is so often lukewarm. Forgive me, I pray. Give me a fresh revelation of Yourself, Jesus. Fill me with Your Holy Spirit power today, so that my life can bring glory to You. Amen.

What are you prepared to endure, my friend? If you are serious about your walk with the Lord, then the answer will be – everything.

My grace is sufficient

Read 2 Corinthians 12:1–10

And He said to me, "My grace is sufficient for you, for My strength is made perfect in weakness." Therefore most gladly I will rather boast in my infirmities, that the power of Christ may rest upon me. (2 Corinthians 12:9)

Maybe you have been reading the devotionals this month and you would like to say to me: "I love God, I am a Christian, I serve Him, I have never departed from the truth since the day I came to Jesus and yet I am suffering." You know, my dear friend, Paul suffered, as we read a day or two ago, and he certainly didn't turn from the path of following Jesus after his Damascus experience. When things get difficult some people want to go back to their old life. Don't even think about it! There is nothing good about your old life. The Israelites constantly wanted to return to Egypt. They chose to forget about the slavery, the cruelty and how badly they were treated. We all have what is referred to as selective memory. Going back is never an option. There is only one way and that is forward towards our promised land – heaven.

Yes, there are hard times, but Jesus says to us: *"My grace is sufficient for you, for My strength is made perfect in weakness."* I have spoken to men who have been through fire; they are normally men who speak little, but listen a lot. You know the saying, "God gave us two ears and one mouth"? We are supposed to listen twice as much as we talk. You see, the men I am speaking of have learnt wisdom as they have gone through their times of trial and tempering.

If you are a younger person you can learn from someone like this. Seek out these men and listen to their experiences. Allow them to encourage you as you face your times of difficulty. This is what Paul did for the Christians in the early church. He visited them, teaching, encouraging and sometimes scolding them when they were tempted to stray from the truth. He wrote letters reminding them of what they had in Christ and how they should be living as a result. God's grace is sufficient for you no matter what you are going through today.

Prayer

My Father, I realize that I am tempted to give up sometimes when things become too difficult. I know that going back is not an option. Thank You for this wonderful promise – that Your grace is sufficient. I cling to this. I want to finish strong. Amen.

There is only one way and that is forward towards our promised land – heaven.

Submission to the will of God

Read 2 Corinthians 12:1–10

And lest I should be exalted above measure by the abundance of the revelations, a thorn in the flesh was given to me, a messenger of Satan to buffet me, lest I be exalted above measure. Concerning this thing I pleaded with the Lord three times that it might depart from me. (2 Corinthians 12:7–8)

P aul writes: *And lest I should be exalted above measure by the abundance of the revelations…* You see, Paul had revelations from God we could only dream of. The Lord used that man incredibly. Two-thirds of the New Testament was written by him. Paul continues, *a thorn in the flesh was given to me, a messenger of Satan to buffet me* (buffet means to beat) *lest I be exalted above measure.* Above measure means getting too big for your boots. He goes on: *Concerning this thing I pleaded with the Lord three times that it might depart from me.*

Three times Paul asked God to remove the thorn in his flesh. Some say it was a spiritual thing; I shared with you the other day that I don't believe that. Maybe God only restored his sight partially so that Paul would remain faithful to Him. We do not need to split hairs about what it was. The fact is he received the thorn. Three times he implored the Lord to remove it from him. Do you see the similarity here? Three times in the Garden of Gethsemane, Jesus asked His Father to remove the cup from Him. Each time He said: "Thy will be done." Jesus submitted to the will of His Father. His Father's grace was sufficient to take Him through the ordeal of the cross.

Three times Paul asks God for relief. God says to Paul: *"My grace is sufficient for you, for My strength is made perfect in weakness."* What is Paul's response to God's refusal to take away his thorn in the flesh? *Therefore most gladly I will rather boast in my infirmities, that the power of Christ may rest upon me. Therefore I take pleasure in infirmities, in reproaches, in needs, in persecutions, in distresses, for Christ's sake. For when I am weak, then I am strong* (2 Corinthians 12:9–10). There you have it, my friend. If you are looking for the answer as to how you can bear your trial, look to Jesus; look to Paul. The answer is – submission to the will of your Father.

Prayer

My Father, I come before You today and all I can do is quietly wait in Your presence. Lord, if Your answer to me is: *"My grace is sufficient for you"*, then, Lord, I accept Your will for my life. Help me and give me the courage and the strength that I need to live strong for You in the midst of hardship. Amen.

If you are looking for the answer as to how you can bear your trial, look to Jesus; look to Paul. The answer is – submission to the will of your Father.

Parable of the poplar and the thorn tree

Read Hebrews 11:1–22

Now faith is the substance of things hoped for, the evidence of things not seen. For by it the elders obtained a good testimony. (Hebrews 11:1–2)

I want to share a modern day parable with you. It is about the poplar and the thorn tree. Our next-door neighbours are the Lion Match Company. They grow poplars in huge areas of wetlands. When the poplar trees are cut down and dried out, they are very light. Poplars grow very, very quickly because they are comprised of about 90 per cent water. They are almost like balsam wood that we use to make model aeroplanes out of. Poplars have no stress because they have plenty of water as a result of the marshland.

Now thorn trees grow down in the Low Veld, about two hours' drive from where I live. It is a hot area and there is little or no rain. The trees are stunted and take at least fifty years to grow by comparison to the poplars' nine years. However, when they reach the same diameter and you cut them open the poplar has no weight, it catches fire easily and in no time is burnt up.

A thorn tree, on the other hand – you can ask any guy who enjoys making a braai – burns for days. It is dense, it is heavy and it is solid. The difference between the thorn tree and the poplar tree is that the poplar has no aggravation at all, no hardship. It has as much water and sun as it wants and it grows like a weed. The thorn tree, however, has to push its roots deep down to find water. It is buffeted by the weather, by the lack of rain, by hardship. As a result of this when it grows it is solid, it is strong and it is dependable. This is what Paul was writing about in 2 Corinthians chapter twelve. You do not grow strong in your faith when everything is going well for you. Hebrews chapter eleven tells us that it was through faith that *the elders obtained a good testimony*. They grew strong through their hardships. It is by faith that we too will endure, grow strong and end victorious.

Prayer

My Father, I thank You that You speak to me in so many different ways. Lord, I want to endure. I want to grow strong and I want to end victorious. I know that this will not happen by my taking the easy way. I am so grateful that through the trials and storms You are with me every step of the way. Amen.

It is by faith that we too will endure, grow strong and end victorious.

The Lord is a fortress in adversity

Read Psalm 31:1–15

But as for me, I trust in You, O LORD; I say, "You are my God." My times are in Your hand; deliver me from the hand of my enemies, and from those who persecute me. (Psalm 31:14–15)

The darkest moments that I have experienced in my Christian walk are the times when Jesus has been the closest to me. I say this reservedly, but I wouldn't change those times for anything. You see, my friend, it was through the hard times in my life that I have come to really know the King of kings and the Lord of lords. I wouldn't choose to go through those experiences again, but I realize that if I hadn't gone through them, I wouldn't have learned the lessons I did. Like our parable yesterday, you will learn nothing growing in the marsh with all the water and sunshine that you could want. You will, however, grow true and strong as you battle the elements in the harsh Low Veld climate.

So it is with the Christian. Most Christians that I have met who are worth their salt, when you listen to their story, all have an incredible testimony. Maybe they have been through hardship, or turmoil; possibly they have come from a background where they had very little, if anything. Each of them knows what it is to know the Lord as a fortress in adversity. They have called out to God in the midst of their turmoil like the Psalmist: *Have mercy on me, O LORD, for I am in trouble; My eye wastes away with grief, yes, my soul and my body! For my life is spent with grief, and my years with sighing; my strength fails because of my iniquity, and my bones waste away* (Psalm 31:9–10).

I look at one of the greatest evangelists who ever lived, D.L. Moody. He came from a large family and his dad died when he was a young boy. He had to go out to work as a shoe salesman and send money home to keep his family going. He knew about hardship. God used Moody's hardships to mould him into a man He was able to use greatly. What effect are your trials and difficulties having on your growth as a man of God?

Prayer

Pray with the Psalmist today: *In You, O LORD, I put my trust; let me never be ashamed; deliver me in Your righteousness. Bow down Your ear to me, deliver me speedily; be my rock of refuge, a fortress of defense to save me. For You are my rock and my fortress; therefore, for Your Name's sake, lead me and guide me* (Psalm 31:1–3). Amen.

What effect are your trials and difficulties having on your growth as a man of God?

Wrestling with God

Read Genesis 32:1–32

Then Jacob was left alone; and a Man wrestled with him until the breaking of day. Now when He saw that He did not prevail against him, He touched the socket of his hip; and the socket of Jacob's hip was out of joint as He wrestled with him. And He said, "Let Me go, for the day breaks." But he said, "I will not let You go unless You bless me!" (Genesis 32:24–26)

God also touched Jacob in the Old Testament. Jacob wrestled all night with God. *And He said, "Let Me go, for the day breaks." But he said, "I will not let You go unless You bless me!"* Have you noticed how often in the Bible when someone has an encounter with God He gives them a new name? Abram became Abraham; Saul became Paul. Here we see God doing the same for Jacob. *So He said to him, "What is your name?" He said, "Jacob." And He said, "Your name shall no longer be called Jacob, but Israel; for you have struggled with God and with men, and have prevailed"* (Genesis 32:27–28). His name was changed from Jacob, which meant "deceiver", to Israel – the name of God's people to this day. You cannot meet the living God and remain the same, my friend.

A change of name was not the only change that Jacob was left with. Verse twenty-five tells us: *Now when He saw that He did not prevail against him, He touched the socket of his hip; and the socket of Jacob's hip was out of joint as He wrestled with him.* God touched Jacob's hip; He actually dislocated it. For the rest of his life, he walked with a limp. I think it was a reminder to him of who God was – it slowed him down some.

Maybe as you are reading this today, sir, you are saying, "Yes; God has touched me. He has slowed me down some." You know Jesus says, *"If your hand or foot causes you to sin, cut it off and cast it from you. And if your eye causes you to sin, pluck it out and cast it from you. It is better for you to enter into life with one eye, rather than having two eyes, to be cast into hell fire"* (Matthew 18:8a, 9). Again, I don't say He causes it – I don't believe that. But He does allow us to go through hardships in order to temper us, to slow us down a little…

Prayer

My Father, I know that so often I run ahead of You so full of my own plans and purposes. I am tempted by the world around me to stray from the path You have set before me. You have to bring me up short and sometimes allow me to be tempered in order for me to keep on the straight and narrow. Amen.

I don't say He causes it – I don't believe that. But He does allow us to go through hardships, in order to temper us.

Adversity breeds patience

Read 2 Corinthians 12:1–10

Therefore most gladly I will rather boast in my infirmities, that the power of Christ may rest upon me. Therefore I take pleasure in infirmities, in reproaches, in needs, in persecutions, in distresses, for Christ's sake. For when I am weak, then I am strong. (2 Corinthians 12:9b–10)

Some time ago a twenty-five-year-old Australian man, who now lives in the United States, came to visit us at Shalom. He was born without arms or legs and he travels around the world as an evangelist. As we visited together he spoke more into my life than I could ever have spoken into his life.

Before he left this young man wanted a photograph taken with me. In order to take the photo they had to place him on the table, so that we could be the same height. I have very rarely in my life been as touched by the love of another human being as I was by that young man. He couldn't shake my hand so he said, "Angus, give me a hug." Of course he couldn't hug me back; he could only use his head when I rested my head on his shoulder. As he was leaving he gave me a DVD. He asked, "Can I sign it for you?" One of his friends gave him a pen, he held it between his teeth and he wrote a message on the front of the DVD. He had a better handwriting than I have, and I have two hands and two feet. My friend, I saw something in that young man that I have not seen in many young men his age.

Young men can sometimes be impatient; lacking in sensitivity and grace. I was a young man once and I remember the way I was. You see, without the rigours of life, without going through pain and suffering, you can become impatient with people. The young man who visited me had endured great hardship from the day he was born. Yet, he didn't sit around feeling sorry for himself. He made the decision to allow God to use his adversity to reach people. As I said, I experienced such incredible love from this young man. My friend, are you sitting around feeling sorry for yourself or are you allowing God to use your adversity to His glory?

Prayer

My Father, I realize that so often I sit around feeling sorry for myself. Forgive me, I pray. Help me to look to You and only You. In You I will find everything I need to not only be able to bear my burdens, but to rejoice in them. Give me the gift of faith, I pray. Amen.

Are you sitting around feeling sorry for yourself or are you allowing God to use your adversity to His glory?

The Lord of hosts is with you

Read Psalm 46

Be still, and know that I am God; I will be exalted among the nations, I will be exalted in the earth! The LORD of hosts is with us; The God of Jacob is our refuge. (Psalm 46:10–11)

I want you to understand something very clearly; I do not wish tribulation or a thorn in the flesh on anyone. I don't pray that over anyone. However, by the same token, you can be sure that when it comes growth will occur in your life. It will strengthen and mature you. In retrospect, not while you are going through it, you will look back and say, "It was the best days of my life." Maybe you are going through tribulation right now and you find it hard to believe that you will ever feel like that. I want to reassure you that you will. Those were the days during which I learned to trust God. During that time, if it weren't for my family, I wouldn't have made it. My business was fast sliding towards bankruptcy, but the Lord Jesus Christ saw us through.

It is during times of tribulation that we learn to trust God. We learn not to do everything our way, but to come to the place where we say: "Your will be done, Lord." It is said that the star players on rugby or soccer teams make the worst trainers. The reason is because they say: "This is the way you do it." Then they just go ahead and do it. If the rest of the team don't get it right the first time they think they are stupid. Sometimes the best trainer is a man who hasn't ever played the game himself, because he has the patience and understanding.

Remember the poplar tree? No hardship, no stress and no persecution – equalled soft, lightweight, weak and unreliable wood. The thorn tree which grew in drought, hardship and persecution equalled strong, heavy, dense and reliable wood. We use thorn trees as the corner posts when we erect fences on our farms. Why? Because even the ants and the termites cannot eat through them; they are too hard. If you are going through tribulation at the moment take a few minutes to be still in God's presence. He is the Lord of hosts and He is with you.

Prayer

My Father God, You are my refuge and my strength. You are a very present help in times of trouble. I trust my life into Your hands. I know that You know what You are doing with my life. Your grace is sufficient for me and I will not be afraid. Amen.

It is during times of tribulation that we learn to trust God and to say, "Your will be done, Lord."

Behold, I stand at the door

Read Revelation 3:14–22

"As many as I love, I rebuke and chasten. Therefore be zealous and repent." (Revelation 3:19)

Jesus says, *"My grace is sufficient for you"* (2 Corinthians 12:9). The grace of God is all you need. You might reply, "Angus, my wife has run off and left me. I am finished." No you are not, because Jesus says: *"My strength is made perfect in weakness"* (2 Corinthians 12:9). When you are weak that is when you are strongest. You see, when you say, "I want to do it my way", then God backs off. When you come to the place that you cannot go on any more and you say, "Jesus, help me," He replies, "Here I am." In many ways we are exactly like little children. They always want to do it their own way so they push your hands away. As soon as they get into trouble though, what do they do? They shout for their parents and then you can help them.

Have you ever watched a lifeguard save someone who is drowning? When a bather gets into trouble and calls for help, the lifeguard jumps right in and swims out to save them. It is said that a drowning person can be very dangerous because they are desperate and they often panic. Unintentionally they can drown the person trying to save them. Sometimes the lifeguards have to knock the person out in order to bring them back to shore. It is only when the drowning person has no strength left to fight that they can be saved.

We are like this sometimes; we think we are so strong. Suddenly we become desperate, then we thrash around and the Lord cannot do anything for us; He simply stands back. If this describes you then hear what He is saying to you: *"Behold, I stand at the door and knock. If anyone hears My voice and opens the door, I will come in to him and dine with him, and he with Me"* (Revelation 3:20). He doesn't only save you, He also promises you: *"To him who overcomes I will grant to sit with Me on My throne, as I also overcame and sat down with My Father on His throne"* (Revelation 3:21).

Prayer

My Father, this is me exactly. I think I am so strong, believing I can cope on my own. I realize that I make life difficult for myself. Lord, I surrender. Thank You that You graciously stand at the door to my life – I open it and I invite You in. I trust You, Lord, to take over – I submit to Your will. Amen.

When you come to the place that you cannot go on any more and you say, "Jesus, help me," He replies, "Here I am."

Hope does not disappoint

Read Romans 5:1–11

And not only that, but we also glory in tribulations, knowing that tribulation produces perseverance; and perseverance, character; and character, hope. Now hope does not disappoint, because the love of God has been poured out in our hearts by the Holy Spirit who was given to us. (Romans 5:3–5)

D id the devotional yesterday speak to your heart? Did it describe where you are in your life? Maybe you have been trying to do things in your own strength. I hope that as you have looked into your heart you have made a decision to look to Jesus. He is ...*the author and finisher of* our *faith*... (Hebrews 12:2). Paul exhorts us: ... *let us run with endurance the race that is set before us*... The reason you can endure, the reason you can run the race is because you are *looking unto Jesus, the author and finisher of* our *faith*... You are not left alone to run this race – no, *you are surrounded by so great a cloud of witnesses*... (Hebrews 12:1, 2, 1). All the men and women of faith who have gone before you are cheering you on; and most importantly Jesus is right in the front leading them.

We are running the race of our lives and we need the Lord Jesus Christ to help us like never before. The young man that I told you about a few days ago is totally helpless. He cannot perform the simplest physical functions for himself. He cannot eat, go to the bathroom or climb out of bed in the morning. He has to rely on help all day, every day; talk about grace. He understands patience and perseverance, my dear friend.

In our reading today Paul says: ... *but we also glory in tribulations, knowing that tribulation produces perseverance; and perseverance, character; and character, hope.* When this young man spoke, he spoke with hope, wisdom, grace, gentleness, love and perseverance. He understands what it means to rejoice in his tribulation. The wonderful thing is that it doesn't stop with tribulation. This hope we have is not a "maybe" hope nor is it a "fickle" hope; no, verse five says *Now hope does not disappoint, because the love of God has been poured out in our hearts by the Holy Spirit who was given to us.* It is true, it is strong, it is enduring and it is sure.

Prayer

My Father, thank You for Your faithfulness and love towards me. Thank You for Your grace and that You have not left me without hope. On the contrary I am overflowing with hope. I stand in this hope today. I cling to it; I rejoice in it. Amen.

This hope we have is not a "maybe" hope nor is it a "fickle" hope: It is true, it is strong, it is enduring and it is sure.

Laying it down on the altar

Read Matthew 19:16–22

Jesus said to him, "If you want to be perfect, go, sell what you have and give to the poor, and you will have treasure in heaven; and come, follow Me." But when the young man heard that saying, he went away sorrowful, for he had great possessions. (Matthew 19:21–22)

This walk was never ever meant to be a bed of roses. The Lord Jesus says there is no servant that is greater than his master. If Jesus Christ suffered and died for us, how can we expect anything better? You see, it is in giving that we receive. There seems to be a misconception about Christian prosperity. The things in life worth having cannot be bought. Things such as love, peace of mind, contentment, health, faith, hope and salvation. No amount of money can buy any of these; they are all gifts from God.

My God, whom I love so much, is a giving God. *"For God so loved the world that He gave His only begotten Son, that whoever believes in Him should not perish but have everlasting life"* (John 3:16). What He wants in return is for you to give Him your life. Why? So that He can give it back to you. This is what the rich young ruler didn't understand. He thought Jesus wanted to take away his money. No, Jesus didn't need his money. The Father owns the cattle on a thousand hills: Jesus has all the money in the world. Jesus wanted to know that nothing was more important to the young ruler than serving Him.

You can never out-give God. If you are like the rich young ruler and you are holding out on God – don't. Maybe for you it isn't money. It can be anything – anything that you are not willing to place on the altar of sacrifice. God is committed to completing the good work He has started in your life. Don't make God take the thing you are holding onto away from you, my friend: rather, voluntarily place it on the altar yourself. Maybe He will give it back, maybe He won't, but whatever happens He will do what is best for you because He loves you. As you stand at the altar He says to you: *"My grace is sufficient for you"* (2 Corinthians 12:9). What do you say to Him?

Prayer

My Father, I surrender to You today. I lay the thing that I have been withholding from You on the altar. Thank You for speaking to me so clearly through Your Word. Lord, I realize that I can trust You no matter what happens. You are in control of my life. Amen.

As you stand at the altar He says to you: *"My grace is sufficient for you."* What do you say to Him?

Strength in the inner man

Read Ephesians 3:14–21

For this reason I bow my knees to the Father of our Lord Jesus Christ, from whom the whole family in heaven and earth is named, that He would grant you, according to the riches of His glory, to be strengthened with might through His Spirit in the inner man.
(Ephesians 3:14–16)

This month we have been discussing the fact that suffering is part of the Christian journey. At some point in all our lives we will go through trials and tribulations. It seems as if some people suffer more than others. What we have learnt together is that no matter how much we suffer or what we go through we can trust God when He tells us: *"My grace is sufficient for you."* I want us to spend some time now looking at inner strength. What part does inner strength play in our ability to be able to endure suffering and tribulations in our lives?

Paul prays for the Ephesians: *... that He would grant you, according to the riches of His glory, to be strengthened with might through His Spirit in the inner man* (3:16). It is this strength that comes from knowing the sufficiency of God's grace that makes it possible for us to endure all things. It is the knowledge that Christ dwells in our hearts that gives us faith; we are not in this battle alone. I want to ask you a question, my friend: Do you know that God loves you? Your answer to this question will determine how you handle suffering in your Christian life. Listen to what Paul prayed for the Ephesian Christians – he prays the same for us:

... that you, being rooted and grounded in love, may be able to comprehend with all the saints what is the width and length and depth and height – to know the love of Christ which passes knowledge; that you may be filled with all the fullness of God (Ephesians 3:17b–19). The key to knowing God loves you is found in the first part of verse seventeen – *that Christ may dwell in your hearts through faith. Paul completes his prayer: Now to Him who is able to do exceedingly abundantly above all that we ask or think, according to the power that works in us, to Him be glory in the church by Christ Jesus to all generations, forever and ever. Amen* (Ephesians 3:20–21).

Prayer

My Father, thank You for the wonderful encouragement I have received today from this prayer of Paul's. You are the one who gives me inner strength. As I rest in the fact that Your grace is sufficient for me, I believe in my heart that Christ dwells inside of me and I know that You love me. Amen.

The key to knowing God loves you is found in the first part of verse seventeen –
that Christ may dwell in your hearts through faith.

Finishing strong

Read 2 Timothy 4:1–18

I have fought the good fight, I have finished the race, I have kept the faith. Finally, there is laid up for me the crown of righteousness, which the Lord, the righteous Judge, will give to me on that Day, and not to me only but also to all who have loved His appearing. (2 Timothy 4:7–8)

I read something very interesting about another aspect of inner strength in a book entitled, *On the Highroad of Surrender*, written by Frances J. Roberts. She writes: "That we must have inner strength in order to cope with the outer blessing." In other words, we pray, "Lord, please help me to be one of the greatest preachers that has ever lived." God gives you your heart's desire; but then because you haven't spent time with God, you do not have inner strength and you don't cope. The most terrible thing to imagine would be nearly finishing the race and then running out of petrol. To be close to the finish line only to run out of steam and then to be unable to complete the course.

Paul understood about this and he was able to say: *I have fought the good fight, I have finished the race, I have kept the faith. Finally, there is laid up for me the crown of righteousness, which the Lord, the righteous Judge, will give to me on that Day, and not to me only but also to all who have loved His appearing.* After having invested his life in serving God and spreading the good news about Jesus, Paul was able to rest in God's grace. Paul understood the balance between weakness and strength. You are never stronger than when you realize your own weakness and dependence upon God. His strength is made perfect in your weakness.

Do you think that maybe our problem is that we tend to depend upon our own strength? This results in our inherent weaknesses surfacing when we are under pressure. It means that we do not have the inner strength to cope with the outer blessing in our lives. Could this be why so many of God's servants crash and burn? Paul encourages us with these words in Hebrews 12:1 today: *Therefore we also, since we are surrounded by so great a cloud of witnesses, let us lay aside every weight, and the sin which so easily ensnares us, and let us run with endurance the race that is set before us.*

Prayer

My Father, I acknowledge my dependence upon You today. I know that I can do nothing on my own that will have lasting worth. Father, keep me at Your feet. Like Paul and the many who have gone before I want to finish strong. I can only do this as I rest in Your grace that is more than sufficient for me. Amen.

You are never stronger than when you realize your own weakness and dependence upon God.

A different spirit

Read Numbers 14:1–25

"But My servant Caleb, because he has a different spirit in him and has followed Me fully, I will bring into the land where he went, and his descendants shall inherit it." (Numbers 14:24)

aleb had *a different spirit* – a spirit of faith, my friend. He called those things that weren't, as if they were. He looked at the mountain and it became a molehill in his sight. Why? Because everything he did, he dedicated to God. As I think of this I am reminded of David who looked at Goliath and didn't see a giant, but rather an opportunity for God to be magnified and glorified. When you face a mountain or a giant what do you see? Your answer will give you an insight into the kind of spirit you have. Paul told Timothy in 2 Timothy 1:7 the following: *For God has not given us a spirit of fear, but of power and of love and of a sound mind.*

In order for you to access this power and love and the resultant sound mind you will need to submit yourself to God. We are talking about an all-out commitment – one that acknowledges God as everything in your life. This is the kind of person that Caleb was. The other scouts responded, saying: ... *"We went to the land where you sent us. It truly flows with milk and honey, and this is its fruit. Nevertheless the people who dwell in the land are strong; the cities are fortified and very large..."* (Numbers 13:27–28). The people responded as usual that they wanted to return to Egypt. Caleb however had this to say: ... *"Let us go up at once and take possession, for we are well able to overcome it"* (Numbers 13:30b).

Do you see the difference between the two reports? The one was all about the difficulties; the other was all about the possibilities. Was Caleb's response one that was based upon positive thinking? Not at all. *"If the LORD delights in us, then He will bring us into this land and give it to us ... their protection has departed from them, and the LORD is with us. Do not fear them"* (Numbers 14:8a, 9b). Caleb knew his God; it was this knowledge that resulted in him having a different spirit.

Prayer

My Father, I bow in Your presence. I thank You that I do not have faith that is based upon positive thinking. Like Caleb's, my faith is based upon knowledge of You. You have never let me down and I stand strong in Your love and faithfulness today. Amen.

Caleb looked at the mountain and it became a molehill in his sight. Why? Because everything he did, he dedicated to God.

Strength of character

Read Luke 16:1–13

"He who is faithful in what is least is faithful also in much." (Luke 16:10a)

The Israelites had been waiting for forty years to enter the Promised Land. When the time came their strength deserted them and they were overcome with fear, pessimism and doubt. Caleb had a different spirit though; he trusted God and he knew that his God would supply everything that they needed to take down the giants. As we said a few days ago, we need to have inner strength to be able to deal with outward blessing. Maybe your dream is to have your own farm one day. If you haven't been to agricultural college to learn about farming you will be in trouble. You need to learn the theory of farming as well as the practical aspects if you want to be a successful farmer; otherwise you won't last a season when God gives you the farm.

Whatever your dream, whatever you have asked God for, you need to prepare in order to cope with the blessing once God gives it. Spend the time while you are waiting preparing your inner man. You must ensure that you are growing stronger in the Lord, so that you are prepared for the big test when it comes. You prepare for the big test by passing the smaller ones. You make the most of each day so that you are ready for the big day. When it comes will you be like the ten scouts or will you be like Caleb?

Our reading today tells another story about passing the test in the smaller things in order to cope with the big things. It is the story of the unrighteous steward. This man did not have inner strength; because, my friend, along with inner strength comes strength of character. There is nothing like trials, tribulations and suffering to build strength of character. This steward did not have strength of character. Jesus' pronouncement on the way that he behaved was: *"He who is faithful in what is least is faithful also in much; and he who is unjust in what is least is unjust also in much"* (Luke 16:10).

Prayer

My Father, I want to be faithful in the little things so that You will be able to trust me with the big things. I realize that this takes strength of character and this comes from persevering and enduring. I love You, Lord, and I want to be faithful to You in all things. Amen.

There is nothing like trials, tribulations and suffering to build strength of character.

Results of premature blessing

Read Matthew 25:14–30

"His lord said to him, 'Well done, good and faithful servant; you have been faithful over a few things, I will make you ruler over many things. Enter into the joy of your lord.'"
(Matthew 25:23)

A s we said yesterday inner strength and strength of character are both results of perseverance, faithfulness and integrity. You need all of these to cope with God's blessing upon your life. Often God will test us to see how we will react when put under pressure. This testing can take many forms; what is important is our reaction to it. So many people moan and complain because of their lot in life. Paul has this advice for us in 1 Thessalonians 5:16–19, 21–22. *Rejoice always, pray without ceasing, in everything give thanks; for this is the will of God in Christ Jesus for you. Do not quench the Spirit. Test all things; hold fast what is good. Abstain from every form of evil.*

Our story today speaks to the three servants and their reaction to the test that their master set for them. They each reacted differently. The one talent that the unfaithful servant had was taken away and given to the faithful servant. The lesson that Jesus wanted His disciples to learn from this story is: *"For to everyone who has, more will be given, and he will have abundance; but from him who does not have, even what he has will be taken away"* (Matthew 25:29).

The faithful servant like Caleb had a different spirit. They served God with abandon, not holding anything back. Through the good and the bad times they were faithful. The result was that they were entrusted with great blessing. This is the key that we so often don't get. Job had to endure much suffering and hardship before God restored to him double what he had lost. We want everything and we want it now. We become angry and disgruntled like the Israelites when we don't get our own way. We want to return to our "Egypt", believing that life will be easier there. We are not prepared to pay the price for blessing. When we receive the blessing prematurely we are in danger of crashing and burning. Are you like the faithful or the unfaithful servant?

Prayer

My Father, I come before You in humility and thankfulness today. You are showing me that perseverance and faithfulness are characteristics that You value highly. I want to be the kind of person to whom You can entrust blessing. Help me to be faithful in the smaller things first. Amen.

When we receive the blessing prematurely we are in danger of crashing and burning.

God supplies all our needs

Read Philippians 4:8–20

And my God shall supply all your need according to His riches in glory by Christ Jesus. (Philippians 4:19)

Joshua and Caleb were not concerned about the giants in the land of Canaan. The other scouts, however, were petrified of them. Those scouts clean forgot about all the miracles God had performed for the children of Israel during the forty years since they left Egypt. God parted the Red Sea so that they could walk across it on dry ground. He caused water to flow out of a rock so that they had drinking water. He sent manna from heaven to feed them; provided shade by day and light by night. They experienced all of those miracles, and yet in that moment when they were faced with the giants they allowed fear to take hold of them. Their faith in God totally deserted them.

Hebrews 11:6 says: *But without faith it is impossible to please Him, for he who comes to God must believe that He is, and that He is a rewarder of those who diligently seek Him.* God puts a high premium on faith. Every miracle in the Bible happened because someone had faith. The parting of the Red Sea – that was by faith. *By faith they passed through the Red Sea as by dry land, whereas the Egyptians, attempting to do so, were drowned* (Hebrews 11:29). God does not operate outside of faith, my friend.

Caleb had a spirit of faith. What spirit do you have today? If you are going through difficulties how are you handling them? You need to trust God to give you the victory in His own way. It might be one step at a time, then one day He reaches down, bringing His salvation into your situation. Or it could be like Paul's thorn in the flesh; God might never lift the suffering you are enduring until you go home to heaven. You have to trust that He knows what is best for you. Whatever happens you continue to trust Him when He says: *"My grace is sufficient for you."* Trust Him to provide for each and every one of your needs as He promised He would.

Prayer

My Father, I realize anew that You do nothing outside of faith. As I think of all the mighty men of God down through the ages – it was because of faith that they overcame. Today, I commit myself once again to You and Your ways. I trust You, my God, to supply all my needs according to Your riches in Jesus. Amen.

Trust Him to provide for each and every one of your needs just like He promised He would.

Sorrow is better than laughter

Read 2 Timothy 2:1–13

You therefore, my son, be strong in the grace that is in Christ Jesus. You therefore must endure hardship as a good soldier of Jesus Christ. No one engaged in warfare entangles himself with the affairs of this life, that he may please him who enlisted him as a soldier. And also if anyone competes in athletics, he is not crowned unless he competes according to the rules. (2 Timothy 2:1, 3–5)

Sorrow is very much part of our lives. Paul tells Timothy that he *must endure hardship as a good soldier of Jesus Christ.* Ecclesiastes 7:3 says: *Sorrow is better than laughter, for by a sad countenance the heart is made better.* Is the writer saying we must be miserable? No, of course not. Paul says in 1 Thessalonians 5:16, 18a: *Rejoice always… in everything give thanks.* In Philippians 4:4: *Rejoice in the Lord always. Again I will say, rejoice!* What he is saying is that we must become serious about serving God and the things of God.

When you are sorrowful you think less about the world and more about home. The early Christians were persecuted; they were martyred for their faith. They were sorrowful people. They spoke about heaven more than they did about earth. Again Paul told Timothy: *Yes, and all who desire to live godly in Christ Jesus will suffer persecution* (2 Timothy 3:12). It saddens me that we hear more from the pulpit about the here and now than we do about eternity. We have read several times this year from Hebrews about the fathers of the faith: *These all died in faith, not having received the promises, but having seen them afar off were assured of them, embraced them and confessed that they were strangers and pilgrims on the earth* (Hebrews 11:13).

Their focus was not on this world with its sorrows and tribulations; no, it was on the promise of eternity. Hebrews further says that the reason Jesus could endure the Cross was because His focus was on what came after: *looking unto Jesus, the author and finisher of our faith, who for the joy that was set before Him endured the cross, despising the shame, and has sat down at the right hand of the throne of God* (Hebrews 12:2). Once you have a correct understanding of eternity you will be in a better position to minister to people who are suffering. It will also help you to have a different perspective on your own suffering. Suffering is passing; eternity is forever – *sorrow is better than laughter.*

Prayer

My Father, I thank You that You speak to me so clearly through Your Word. I realize that so much of my focus is on the here and now. This is why everything that happens takes on such gigantic proportions. When I look at all of this as transient then I begin to get a more balanced perspective. Amen.

Once you have a correct understanding of eternity you will be in a better position to minister to people who are suffering.

God uses the broken

Read 1 Peter 5:1–11

Resist him, steadfast in the faith, knowing that the same sufferings are experienced by your brotherhood in the world. But may the God of all grace, who called us to His eternal glory by Christ Jesus, after you have suffered a while, perfect, establish, strengthen, and settle you.
(1 Peter 5:9–10)

Peter reassured his readers that the suffering they were experiencing was also being *experienced by your brotherhood in the world*. When people haven't experienced suffering and hardship they can be very judgmental and harsh. God never uses anyone to any great degree until that person has been broken. As you move through the Bible starting with Adam and Eve you will see that people suffered. Sometimes it was because of their own failure and sin. Other times it was as a result of the tethering work of God in their lives.

Many of these men (and women) are mentioned by name in the book of Hebrews; others are referred to collectively as *so great a cloud of witnesses* (Hebrews 12:1). These witnesses are not only biblical characters but people down through the ages who have been faithful to God through thick and thin. We have mentioned the names and stories of several of them over the months as we have shared together. What they all have in common, no matter the century they lived in, is their deep, abiding commitment to Jesus Christ, irrespective of what they endured here on earth.

As you reflect back over this past year and you think of what is going on in your life at the moment, ask yourself: "How am I shaping up?" If you are moaning and complaining about your lot and what is happening in your life then you are not standing steadfast in the faith. We need to humble ourselves before God and accept His will for our lives. Peter says: *Therefore humble yourselves under the mighty hand of God, that He may exalt you in due time, casting all your care upon Him, for He cares for you* (1 Peter 5:6–7). Due time means His time. In the meantime you can stand in faith. You can also share the good news of God's love with those who are suffering. Allow God to use you to bring encouragement to others. Even if you are suffering yourself, you can still be a witness of God's goodness to other people.

Prayer

My Father, I want to stand tall. I want to stand firm. I do not want to be someone who moans and groans, giving the enemy a foothold in my life. Help me to rejoice always. Lift my focus from my own pain and help me to be a blessing and an encouragement to someone else. Amen.

God never uses anyone to any great degree until that person has been broken.

Glory revealed to us

Read Romans 8:18–30

For I consider that the sufferings of this present time are not worthy to be compared with the glory which shall be revealed in us. (Romans 8:18)

My friend, if your life is all about now then you are not going to understand what Paul is speaking about in Romans chapter eight. If our lives were all about now then we wouldn't need salvation. It would not have been necessary for Jesus to come to this world to die for us. This is what faith is about: *Now faith is the substance of things hoped for, the evidence of things not seen* (Hebrews 11:1). Certainly while we are on this earth we are to enjoy the blessings God gives us. Our lives are to be lived establishing His kingdom here on earth, doing His will and glorifying Him through our lives. However, we are always to be aware that we are pilgrims passing through.

Why do you think Jesus cautioned us not to store up treasure here on earth? *For where your treasure is, there your heart will be also* (Matthew 6:21). This doesn't mean that God doesn't give us prosperity here on earth. It is what we do with the prosperity that counts – it is to be used to further His kingdom. When we can reach the place that we begin to live like this then Matthew 6:33 will become true for us: *But seek first the kingdom of God and His righteousness, and all these things shall be added to you.* It takes sorrow to expand and deepen the soul. I don't wish sorrow on anybody but that's what it does.

The deepest and most sorrowful times in my life have been the times when I have been the closest to Jesus. I can remember them with fondness. That's when He held me. Sometimes I didn't want to climb out of bed in the morning. I didn't want to face another day; yet Jesus gave me strength every day to get up and walk a little farther. He can do it for you too. Every nation and every person must endure lessons in God's school of adversity. This is how we grow and it is how we mature.

Prayer

My Father, I realize that my life is not only about the here and now. Thank You for lifting my focus. I know that the sufferings I am enduring now are nothing compared to the glory I will enjoy with You in heaven one day. Amen.

Our lives are to be lived establishing His kingdom here on earth, doing His will and glorifying Him through our lives.

Glorying in His grace

Read 2 Corinthians 12:1–10

And He said to me, "My grace is sufficient for you, for My strength is made perfect in weakness." Therefore most gladly I will rather boast in my infirmities, that the power of Christ may rest upon me. (2 Corinthians 12:9)

What about you today? Jesus says: *"My grace is sufficient for you."* A lot of us make mistakes, including me. I am honestly sharing from my heart, as I always do. We have to stop crying over spilt milk though. Do you know what that means? It means that we have to put the past behind us and we have to press on. Paul exhorts us to do exactly this in Philippians 3:13–14: *Brethren, I do not count myself to have apprehended; but one thing I do, forgetting those things which are behind and reaching forward to those things which are ahead, I press toward the goal for the prize of the upward call of God in Christ Jesus.*

If there was anyone who had to make a decision not to cry over spilt milk it was Paul. The enemy would have loved him to be so filled with guilt over his persecution of the Christians that he was never of any use to God. This is why he said in 1 Corinthians 15:10: *But by the grace of God I am what I am, and His grace toward me was not in vain; but I labored more abundantly than they all, yet not I, but the grace of God which was with me.* Through his commitment to Jesus what could have been debilitating was turned around to be a blessing and useful to God. Paul learnt to live in God's grace. Are you living in God's grace today, my friend?

Don't let His grace towards you be in vain. As a result of everything you have learnt from God this month I pray that your faith has been strengthened. I pray that you have been built up in your inner man. I trust that you have received insight and perspective on your suffering through what God's Word has said to you. Don't allow either the past or your present circumstances to hold you back. Whatever your challenges, disappointments and sufferings, today Jesus says to you: *"My grace is sufficient for you, for My strength is made perfect in weakness."*

Prayer

My Father, thank You for this past month. I am so grateful to You for Your faithfulness to me, Your child. Thank You that I too can say today; *by the grace of God I am what I am, and* [Your] *grace toward me was not in vain.* Your grace is everything to me. Amen.

Don't let His grace towards you be in vain. I pray that you have been built up in your inner man.

DECEMBER

Now is the time ... to fulfil your purpose

Now is the time of God's favour

Now is the accepted time

Justified by faith

Stumbling between two covenants

Obedience – key to fulfilment

A man of purpose asks for help

Your purpose – a man of promise

Your purpose – a living sacrifice

Your purpose – abiding in the Word

Your purpose – fulfilling the Great Commission

Your purpose – overcoming the world

Your purpose – living in humility

Your purpose – being a watchman

Your purpose – to live a godly life

Deal purposefully with sin

When you sin

Dealing with guilt

Putting the past behind you

Keep your heart with all diligence

The heart of a servant

Are you afraid?

Do not worry

Open your eyes

Jesus makes it possible to persevere

A Son is given

Every spiritual blessing

Bold access through faith

Fullness of joy

Now is the accepted time

A man fulfilling his purpose

Looking unto Jesus

Now is the time of God's favour

Read Malachi 1:6–14

"But now entreat God's favor, that He may be gracious to us. While this is being done by your hands, will He accept you favorably?" Says the LORD of hosts. (Malachi 1:9)

Our theme this year has been "Now is the time of God's favour – now is the time of salvation." We have looked at various sub-themes all with the purpose of helping us to be men who live our lives with purpose and vitality. We are not on this earth for our own gratification or pleasure. We are here to fulfil the purposes of God in our generation. We are ambassadors of Jesus Christ and as such we need to live bringing honour to His name. We have the privilege of living in an exciting time. Never before has there been such opportunity to serve God. Are you making the most of the time you have on this earth?

In our reading today God is not happy with His people. Why? Because they are not giving their best to Him. Have we not said several times during this year that God is not interested in our sacrifices: *"Has the LORD as great delight in burnt offerings and sacrifices, as in obeying the voice of the LORD? Behold, to obey is better than sacrifice, And to heed than the fat of rams"* (1 Samuel 15:22). God is berating His people in Malachi chapter one because they were not obeying Him. God places a very high premium on obedience – it is everything to Him.

If you want to enjoy God's favour upon your life then obedience is your starting point. You will never experience blessing if you are not obedient to God. You cannot reach your full potential in God if you are not prepared to submit to Him in all things. My friend, "all things" means exactly that: all things. Your own life, your marriage, your family, your ministry, your business and your interaction with people. So often we want to withhold areas of our lives from God. We bargain with Him: "Lord, I'll give You this, but You cannot have that." This is not how it works. There is no exclusionary clause when it comes to living as an ambassador of Jesus Christ, representing the kingdom of God on earth.

Prayer

My Father, You have called me to be a man of purpose, a man who serves at Your pleasure, my heavenly Father. You require a total, complete and absolute surrender of my life to You. Lord, thank You for Your love and faithfulness to me. I surrender to You. Amen.

There is no exclusionary clause when it comes to living as an ambassador of Jesus Christ, representing the kingdom of God on earth.

Now is the accepted time

Read 2 Corinthians 6:1–10

We then, as workers together with Him also plead with you not to receive the grace of God in vain. For He says: "In an acceptable time I have heard you, and in the day of salvation I have helped you." Behold, now is the accepted time; behold, now is the day of salvation.
(2 Corinthians 6:1–2)

*N*ow is the accepted time... what a privilege to live in these days. Now as never before men of God have to live in the awareness of their calling. Paul never forgot for a moment who he was in Christ and what he had been called to do. It consumed his whole life. My friend, I have committed my life unreservedly to serving Jesus; there is nothing more important to me than loving Jesus. How about you? Where does Jesus fit into your priorities? Paul had this to say in our reading today about what it means to follow Jesus:

We give no offense in anything, that our ministry may not be blamed. But in all things we commend ourselves as ministers of God: in much patience, in tribulations, in needs, in distresses, in stripes, in imprisonments, in tumults, in labors, in sleeplessness, in fastings; by purity, by knowledge, by longsuffering, by kindness, by the Holy Spirit, by sincere love, by the word of truth, by the power of God, by the armor of righteousness on the right hand and on the left, by honor and dishonor, by evil report and good report; as deceivers, and yet true; as unknown, and yet well known; as dying, and behold we live; as chastened, and yet not killed; as sorrowful, yet always rejoicing; as poor, yet making many rich; as having nothing, and yet possessing all things (2 Corinthians 6:3–10).

I have included these verses because I want you to take the time today to read through them again. As you do, ask the Holy Spirit to speak to you about how your life lines up with the level of commitment Paul is writing about here. My friend, the time for messing about is over. We are living in changing times and we do not know what the future holds. What we do know is Whom we serve. *Now is the accepted time...* Are you going to seize the day for God? Are you going to stand up for Jesus and walk in the power of the Holy Spirit?

Prayer

My Father, Your call upon my life is clear. I surrender to it. Lord, I want to seize the day for You. *Now is the accepted time...* I want to be Your man for this hour. Thank You for the privilege of being Your child. Amen.

Now is the accepted time... Are you going to seize the day for God? Are you going to stand up for Jesus and walk in the power of the Holy Spirit?

Justified by faith

Read Galatians 3:1–14

Therefore He who supplies the Spirit to you and works miracles among you, does He do it by the works of the law, or by the hearing of faith? – Just as Abraham "believed God, and it was accounted to him for righteousness." (Galatians 3:5–6)

n Galatians chapter four we read about two babies being born. I want to compare these two babies. The one baby, Ishmael, was born to Hagar – a slave of Sarah, Abraham's wife. The other child was born of the promise to Sarah and his name was Isaac. Baby Ishmael came from Mount Sinai where the law, the Ten Commandments were given. Baby Isaac came from the New Jerusalem, the place of promise, where you and I are going.

This is the difference: Ishmael was born because Sarah doubted God. She told her husband to sleep with her maid so that she might have a child and not be shamed in the district. Abraham listened to her, slept with Hagar and the result was Ishmael, who was born of the flesh. On the other hand Isaac, the child of promise, was born of the Spirit. I want to ask you a question: Are you walking by faith, or are you making a plan? The "plan" that Sarah made, and that Abraham agreed to, is the very challenge that the Jewish people are struggling with to this day. A thorn in the flesh, that's right; because remember Ishmael is the half-brother of Isaac, making the Muslims and the Jews half-brothers.

If only Abraham and Sarah had trusted God; if only they had truly believed that the Lord would honour their desire for a child and His promise to give them one. However, they became impatient. Can you identify with them? Some of you have done this; I know I have. The truth is you cannot trust God and make your own plan; it never works out. If God has given you a promise, trust Him to fulfil it in His perfect time. *Therefore He who supplies the Spirit to you and works miracles among you, does He do it by the works of the law, or by the hearing of faith?* (Galatians 3:5). You are justified by faith, my friend. This means you have to walk and live by faith. You cannot move between the law and the promise.

Prayer

My Father, I bow before You today and I ask You to forgive me. I am so forcefully reminded that I all too often make my own plans. Help me today to walk in the confidence of the promise I have in You. I choose to trust You to fulfil Your promise to me in Your own perfect time. Amen.

You are justified by faith, my friend. This means you have to walk and live by faith.

Stumbling between two covenants

Read Galatians 3:10–29

For as many as are of the works of the law are under the curse; for it is written, "Cursed is everyone who does not continue in all things which are written in the book of the law, to do them." But that no one is justified by the law in the sight of God is evident, for "the just shall live by faith." Yet the law is not of faith, but "the man who does them shall live by them." (Galatians 3:10–12)

This Scripture tells us that if we want to follow the law then we have to make sure that we fulfil and keep every single aspect of it. This is not possible and it is why the Word tells us we are under the curse. *"Cursed is everyone who does not continue in all things which are written in the book of the law, to do them."* The law is there to lead us to Christ to make us aware of our need. Under the law there is only condemnation, failure and disappointment. Why then do we spend so much time moving back to it? This is why Paul admonished the Galatians: *Stand fast therefore in the liberty by which Christ has made us free, and do not be entangled again with a yoke of bondage* (Galatians 5:1).

The enemy likes nothing better than keeping us under the yoke of bondage. He knows that there is no power there. If you are going to live out your purpose, if you are to live as a child of the promise, it can only be done under the new covenant. You can only fulfil your potential if you walk by faith. Abraham learnt that lesson when he collaborated with Sarah to try and make their own plan to fulfil God's promise to them – it was a dismal failure.

Our plans take many shapes and forms. For each of us it will be something different that tempts us to make our own plan instead of believing God. I know that by now you can quote Hebrews 11:1 and 6: *Now faith is the substance of things hoped for, the evidence of things not seen. But without faith it is impossible to please Him, for he who comes to God must believe that He is, and that He is a rewarder of those who diligently seek Him.* If you have tried to make your own plan then come to God today and ask His forgiveness, confess your sin and allow Him to forgive you. Then make sure that you don't do it again.

Prayer

My Father, You are the mighty God and I am Your child. Lord, forgive me for not trusting You to fulfil Your Word to me. I am so sorry that I stumble between the old and the new covenant. Lord, I don't want to live a life that is cursed. I want a life that is blessed. Amen.

You can only fulfil your potential if you walk by faith.

Obedience – key to fulfilment

Read Mark 12:28–34

"'And you shall love the LORD your God with all your heart, with all your soul, with all your mind, and with all your strength.' This is the first commandment. And the second, like it, is this: 'You shall love your neighbor as yourself.' There is no other commandment greater than these." (Mark 12:30–31)

T he thing above all others that God requires from us is obedience. The degree to which we are prepared to obey God is the degree to which we trust Him. You cannot blindly do what someone tells you to do if you do not believe that they have your best interests at heart. If you have an obedience problem, then you also have a trust problem. As we read the other day even father Abraham – renowned for his faith, known as a friend of God – had his moments when he mistrusted God. It never worked out well for him when he didn't. It won't work out well for you either.

Have you ever taken the time to consider the link between obedience and trust? Maybe now is the time to do it. In February we spent an entire month discussing obedience. One of the key Scriptures coming out of our study together was Mark chapter twelve: *"'And you shall love the LORD your God with all your heart, with all your soul, with all your mind, and with all your strength.' This is the first commandment. And the second, like it, is this: 'You shall love your neighbor as yourself.' There is no other commandment greater than these."* The logical progression of thought is that you cannot love someone that you do not know. So as men of God we need to be growing in our knowledge of God.

I am talking about experiential knowledge, not academic or intellectual knowledge. The better you know God, the closer you will grow to Him. The closer you grow to Him, the more you will love Him. The more you love Him, the more you will trust Him. The more you trust Him, the easier it will be for you to obey Him. It is when you have this quality of relationship with God that you will be in a position where He can begin to use you. Then He will be able to entrust His blessing to you, because He will know that He in turn can trust you.

Prayer

My Father, I worship You today. I realize that You are not interested in sacrifices and outward expressions of worship as much as You are the condition of my heart. Father, I long to be a man who obeys You unconditionally. Thank You for Your patience with me. Amen.

The more you trust God, the easier it will be for you to obey Him. Then He will be able to entrust His blessing to you, because He will know that He in turn can trust you.

A man of purpose asks for help

Read Matthew 14:22–33

But when he saw that the wind was boisterous, he was afraid; and beginning to sink he cried out, saying, "Lord, save me!" And immediately Jesus stretched out His hand and caught him, and said to him, "O you of little faith, why did you doubt?" And when they got into the boat, the wind ceased. (Matthew 14:30–32)

We men don't easily ask for help do we? We seem to be wired to go it alone. There is that well-known joke about men never wanting to ask for directions. Most men would rather drive around in circles than admit that they are lost and don't know where they are going. In many ways we feel the responsibility to be "the man"; to take responsibility. On the one hand this is admirable, as we are meant to be responsible and dependable. We believe that one of our God-given responsibilities is to look after our families and be the leader of those God has entrusted to us. You cannot do this on your own though; you need to commit your responsibilities to God and allow Him to lead you, then you in turn can lead others.

Peter was a man's man. He had a spirit of adventure and daring. He was out of the boat in a shot to walk towards Jesus on the water. You can imagine that he must have been feeling quite good for a few minutes as he walked on the water – I mean how many people have done that? Then reality set in and he began to sink. He faced a choice at that moment. He could have tried to make the most of it. As a fisherman surely he would have known how to swim. His other choice was to admit he was in trouble and ask for help.

Peter chose to ask for help and the moment that he did Jesus was there to rescue him. Notice the words that Peter used: *"Lord, save me!"* He didn't try and tough it out – he admitted that he was in trouble and he needed saving. If you are in trouble today, don't try to tough it out – ask for help. Say the words: *"Lord, save me!"* The Bible says: *And immediately Jesus stretched out His hand and caught him.* Jesus won't make you beg for help – the moment you call out He will be there. A man of purpose asks for help.

Prayer

My Father, I come to You and I ask You to help me. I know that I have tried for too long to tough it out on my own. Forgive me for my misguided sense of responsibility. I need Your help, Lord. As You did for Peter, please reach out and save me. Amen.

Jesus won't make you beg for help – the moment you call out He will be there.

Your purpose – a man of promise

Read Galatians 4:1–6, 21–31

Now we, brethren, as Isaac was, are children of promise. (Galatians 4:28)

Some of you reading this are blessed to have descended from a godly heritage. You can look back over your family history and thank God for those who have gone before you. You have godly family members who have prayed for you, instructed you and kept you on the straight and narrow. As you know my parents did not come to know Jesus until late in their lives, but they were always an example to me and I thank God for them.

There are others who are reading this and you look back over your family history with shame and possibly bitterness. Your father (or your mother) may have been an abusive alcoholic. You grew up knowing only emotional and maybe even physical deprivation and punishment. You look around and you envy those who come from the kind of godly background that I described in the previous paragraph. Your lack of "credentials" have made you feel like a second-class citizen in the kingdom of God, no matter how much you know in your mind that all men are equal before God.

It is time that you let this head knowledge sink down to your heart. There is only about a ruler's length between our head and our heart but sometimes it might as well be the distance between the earth and the moon. Our reading tells us that if we are a child of God then we are children of promise. You are a son of the free woman; you are no longer in bondage. Jesus did this for you on Calvary. The choice you have to make is: Are you going to live as a man of promise or are you going to forever remain a child of the slave-woman? You have been adopted out of your earthly family and into a heavenly family: *But when the fullness of the time had come, God sent forth His Son, born of a woman, born under the law, to redeem those who were under the law, that we might receive the adoption as sons* (Galatians 4:4–5).

Prayer

My Father, because I am Your son, You sent forth the Spirit of Your Son into my heart, crying out, "Abba, Father!" Therefore I am no longer a slave but a son, and if a son, then an heir of God through Christ. Thank You for this, my Father. In the name of Jesus, Your Son. Amen.

The choice you have to make today is: Are you going to live as a man of promise or are you going to forever remain a child of the slave-woman?

Your purpose – a living sacrifice

Read Romans 12:1–21

I beseech you therefore, brethren, by the mercies of God, that you present your bodies a living sacrifice, holy, acceptable to God, which is your reasonable service. And do not be conformed to this world, but be transformed by the renewing of your mind, that you may prove what is that good and acceptable and perfect will of God. (Romans 12:1–2)

I t saddens me to meet up with people who are disillusioned in their walk with the Lord. I sometimes have them come up to me at places where I am preaching. Other times I receive letters or emails. Sometimes when I listen to their stories they tell me of how they wanted to do great things for God. They started a ministry, went off as a missionary or did whatever it was that they believed God was telling them to do. After a time things didn't work out so they ended up burnt out and disillusioned. My friends, I have to tell you if God has told you to do something then He will bring it about. It might take a while, you might go through great trials and difficulties in the process, but in the end He will do what He has said He will do.

So where does the problem come in, then? It could be that in our haste to serve God and do something for Him we rush ahead of Him. God is never in a hurry, my friend – remember that. We have said many times that God is more interested in you having a relationship with Him than in what you can do for Him. Our Scripture speaks of this; *present your bodies a living sacrifice, holy, acceptable to God, which is your reasonable service.* Place not only your body, but your ambition upon the altar.

When we place ourselves on the altar God renews our minds so *that you may prove what is that good and acceptable and perfect will of God.* Once you know the mind of God then you can move ahead in confidence. It all hinges upon knowing God. You can be sure that God has a purpose for your life; He has a task uniquely designed for you to accomplish. First, though, you have to place yourself upon the altar of sacrifice. You can only fulfil the purpose God has for you from a position of submission to Him.

Prayer

My Father, I thank You for Your Word to me. I know that in my eagerness I have run before You in the past. Forgive me for this and help me to slow down. I realize that it is only in sacrifice that I will be able to be used by You. I lay down my own plans and I place myself upon the altar of sacrifice. Amen.

You can only fulfil the purpose God has for you from a position of submission to Him.

Your purpose – abiding in the Word

Read John 8:31–36

Then Jesus said to those Jews who believed Him, "If you abide in My word, you are My disciples indeed. And you shall know the truth, and the truth shall make you free." (John 8:31–32)

Romans 10:17 tells us: *So then faith comes by hearing, and hearing by the word of God.* A man of purpose abides in God's Word. I am always saying – on my television programme and when I preach – that God's Word is your manual. If you are in business it is your business manual; in farming it is your agricultural manual; if a lecturer or a teacher, it is your teaching manual. If you are a parent, then it is your parenting manual; everything you need to know about rearing your children is to be found in the Bible.

2 Timothy 3:16 instructs us: *All Scripture is given by inspiration of God, and is profitable for doctrine, for reproof, for correction, for instruction in righteousness.* Our problem is that we consult every other form of opinion on God's Word. We read books and place the opinions of people above the wisdom of the Word. It is our last port of call instead of being our first one. Jesus says: *"If you abide in My word, you are My disciples indeed."* If you want to be a disciple of Jesus you need to abide in His Word. The word "abide" implies more than a cursory glance now and again. It means exactly what it says: You need to "live" in God's Word. The Psalmist has this to say about God's Word: *How sweet are Your words to my taste, Sweeter than honey to my mouth!* (Psalm 119:103)

Are you in a place today where you are feeling that everything around you is dark and you don't know which way to turn? Listen to what the Psalmist said: *Your word is a lamp to my feet and a light to my path* (Psalm 119:105). Go to God's Word, my friend, abide in His Word and wait on Him. As a man of God you need the wisdom of God's Word if you are going to fulfil your purpose. You will only know satisfaction and freedom if you are a man who abides in God's Word.

Prayer

My Father, thank You for Your Word. I am so grateful that You have not left me without a lamp and a light for my path. I ask You to forgive me that so often I turn to other avenues for counsel – not any more. I want to be a man of the Word. Amen.

As a man of God you need the wisdom of God's Word if you are going to fulfil your purpose.

Your purpose - fulfilling the Great Commission

Read Mark 16:1–20

And He said to them, "Go into all the world and preach the gospel to every creature."
(Mark 16:15)

One of our main purposes as men of God is to fulfil the Great Commission. Before Jesus returned to heaven He spoke to His disciples and commissioned them to spread His gospel. Each and every one of them gave their lives to the work of the gospel. Throughout the Acts of the Apostles we see the disciples working tirelessly to establish the church of Jesus Christ. We as Jesus' modern day disciples are commissioned in the same way that the original disciples were. How are you faring in your fulfilment of the Great Commission?

Sharing the gospel should be the most natural thing in the world for us. All you have to do is to share your story of what Jesus has done for you and tell people how much you love Him. Whatever a person's personal belief or persuasion they cannot argue with your experience. I have rarely found anyone who is not prepared to listen to a story. Once you have shared with them it is up to the Holy Spirit to convince them – conviction is not your job or responsibility. You can trust the Holy Spirit to do His work. The important thing is that the people you live with and work with must be able to see the difference that Jesus has made in your life. This does not mean that you are perfect; none of us are. However, when you make a mistake be sure to respond in humility and ask for forgiveness.

Your walk matching your talk is your greatest witness, my friend. Be careful how you live. Do not allow the enemy to gain a foothold in your life and ruin your testimony. You are a man of God and you have a divine purpose, which is to bring glory to God. Do not allow anyone or anything to deflect you from that purpose. No temporary gain in this life, no matter how beguiling, is worth losing your testimony over. God's Word to you today is: *"Go into all the world and preach the gospel to every creature."*

Prayer

My Father, I thank You that I am Your man for this hour. Help me, I pray, to courageously and sensitively share the story of what You have done for me. I realize that I have a responsibility to line my walk up with my talk. Fill me with the power of Your Holy Spirit to enable me to be a faithful witness for You. Amen.

No temporary gain in this life, no matter how beguiling, is worth losing your testimony over.

Your purpose – overcoming the world

Read 1 John 5:1–13

For whatever is born of God overcomes the world. And this is the victory that has overcome the world – our faith. (1 John 5:4)

I don't know what kind of a year you have had. I certainly pray that our daily times together in God's Word have helped to build you and strengthen you in your inner man. I am only too aware, though, that life can press in upon us. When these times come our way it is important that our reaction and response is to run to God and not away from Him. Jesus has gained the victory over any and every situation that you could possibly experience. Our Scripture says: *For whatever is born of God overcomes the world.* If you have accepted Jesus as your Lord and saviour, if you are a child of God, then you have everything you need to live as an overcomer.

There is another step to the implementation of this victory though, isn't there? Our Scripture gives it to us: *And this is the victory that has overcome the world – our faith.* What is it that helps us to appropriate our victory? It is our faith. It is by faith that we walk in victory. It is by faith that we can implement the full extent of our salvation and what Jesus did for us on Calvary. So if you are experiencing difficulties and failures in your life right now you have a faith problem. Hear me: I am not saying that as a child of God you will never know tribulation and suffering; we spent the whole of last month sharing together about this very subject. However, even in the midst of suffering we are not defeated.

No matter how difficult the circumstances in your life you can still live in victory. We make a big mistake when we think that victory means a life that is without any challenges. We have spent a lot of time this year looking at the lives of men of God, who even in the midst of great tribulations lived victorious lives for Him. You are a man with a purpose: your purpose is to live in victory – irrespective of your circumstances – to the glory of God.

Prayer

My Father, I thank You for the victory that Jesus gained for me on Calvary. Help me to walk in that victory no matter what is happening in my life. I am so grateful that I am not at the mercy of what is going on in and around my life. My faith is in You, Lord, and You are my victory. Amen.

You are a man with a purpose: your purpose is to live in victory – irrespective of your circumstances – to the glory of God.

Your purpose – living in humility

Read James 4:1–10

Humble yourselves in the sight of the Lord, and He will lift you up. (James 4:10)

E very mighty man of God, down through the ages from Bible times onwards, has been a man of humility. God cannot use someone who is filled with pride. He will not share His glory with anyone, my friend. Satan learnt this to his detriment when he was thrown out of heaven for thinking he was equal to God. Proverbs 16:18 tells us: *Pride goes before destruction, and a haughty spirit before a fall.* How many men have started out with great gusto only to crash and burn along the way?

Many times this is due to pride. You can be sure that if you entertain pride in your heart the devil will use it to gain a foothold in your life. From there it is a short journey for him to find a way to trip you up. Proverbs has a lot to say about pride. Listen to this sage advice: *When pride comes, then comes shame; but with the humble is wisdom* (Proverbs 11:2). Humility and wisdom go together. *Who is wise and understanding among you? Let him show by good conduct that his works are done in the meekness of wisdom* (James 3:13). Your purpose is to glorify God through your life. So any ministry or any prominence you may have is not for your benefit, but for the benefit of the gospel. We said the other day that one of our purposes is to fulfil the Great Commission; you will only be the witness you need to be if you walk in humility.

As His man this is what God expects from you: *He has shown you, O man, what is good; and what does the LORD require of you but to do justly, to love mercy, and to walk humbly with your God?* (Micah 6:8). It is always sad and frankly embarrassing to see someone who claims to be a servant of God lording it over other people. A final word from Proverbs 29:23 on this: *A man's pride will bring him low, but the humble in spirit will retain honor.*

Prayer

My Father, forgive me for the times that I allow pride to surface in my heart. I realize that You have called me to walk in humility. I want to glorify You and live as Your man fulfilling the purposes You have for my life. Lord, I submit to You in all things. Amen.

A man's pride will bring him low, but the humble in spirit will retain honor (Proverbs 29:23).

Your purpose – being a watchman

Read Ezekiel 33:1–11

Again the word of the LORD came to me, saying, "Son of man, speak to the children of your people, and say to them: 'When I bring the sword upon a land, and the people of the land take a man from their territory and make him their watchman.'" (Ezekiel 33:1–2)

P art of the purpose God has for you to fulfil is to be a watchman. In May we spent the month sharing around what it means to be a watchman to the house of Israel. *"Say to them: 'As I live,' says the Lord GOD, 'I have no pleasure in the death of the wicked, but that the wicked turn from his way and live. Turn, turn from your evil ways! For why should you die, O house of Israel?'"* (Ezekiel 33:11). The house of Israel is your brothers and sisters in Christ, the fellowship of believers. God has called you to sound the warning trumpet, to speak the word of truth. You are a guardian of God's truth and one of your purposes is to share the truth. Compromise is not an option for a watchman. So often we are tempted to remain silent – to keep the peace. This is not a valid option or excuse.

While we are looking the other way the enemy is moving in upon God's people. *"But if the watchman sees the sword coming and does not blow the trumpet, and the people are not warned, and the sword comes and takes any person from among them, he is taken away in his iniquity; but his blood I will require at the watchman's hand'* (Ezekiel 33:6). This is a sober warning, my friend. Time is running out and the enemy is hard at work amongst the body of Christ. If you don't bring God's truth, who is going to do it?

It is a good time to evaluate how you have fared this year as a watchman on the walls. Your family need you to be there as a protection for them. Have you been fulfilling your purpose as watchman over your family? At your place of work, do you bring God's truth into situations there? What about your brothers and sisters? Can they depend upon you as a watchman who guards the walls keeping watch for the enemy? God has given you this important task – how are you doing as His watchman?

Prayer

My Father, I praise You and worship You. I am Your servant to be used by You as You desire. I will continue to be a watchman on the walls guarding my family, my brothers and sisters in Christ and everyone You bring into my life. Give me wisdom as I speak Your truth. Amen.

You are a guardian of God's truth and one of your purposes is to share the truth.

Your purpose – to live a godly life

Read 2 Peter 1:1–11

...as His divine power has given to us all things that pertain to life and godliness, through the knowledge of Him who called us by glory and virtue. (2 Peter 1:3)

We live in a world where integrity is not a high priority. So much of what we see, read and hear is geared to endorse a lifestyle that is not godly. If you look around, how many leaders are there who can be held up as examples of virtue? Sadly, even in the church we find all too often that leaders are falling because their walk is not lining up with their talk. Yet God has not left us without a moral compass and a reminder of how He expects us to live. One such reminder is found in our reading today.

Peter is speaking to Christians here; he is reminding them of the fact that they have everything they need to live a godly life. He says the way they do this is by putting controls in place. These controls are: *But also for this very reason, giving all diligence, add to your faith virtue, to virtue knowledge, to knowledge self-control, to self-control perseverance, to perseverance godliness, to godliness brotherly kindness, and to brotherly kindness love. For if these things are yours and abound, you will be neither barren nor unfruitful in the knowledge of our Lord Jesus Christ* (2 Peter 1:5–8). If these characteristics are part of who you are then you will live a godly life. The very heart of it all is *knowledge of our Lord Jesus Christ.*

This is the question, my friend: Do you know Jesus? We have spoken about this knowledge many times during the past year. It is an experiential knowledge where Jesus is everything to you; not an intellectual knowledge that has no power. Peter continues saying: *For he who lacks these things is shortsighted, even to blindness, and has forgotten that he was cleansed from his old sins* (2 Peter 1:9). Do you think this is what our problem is sometimes, that we forget what we have been saved from? It is a good thing to look back occasionally and remember your life before you met Jesus. Then look forward and live the godly life He saved you to live.

Prayer

My Father, thank You that You saved me through Your Son, Jesus Christ. I am saved not only to go to heaven one day when I die, but also to live a godly life here on earth. My salvation covers every area of my life. Lord, I pray that You will fill me with Your Spirit so that I will be empowered to live as Your man. Amen.

Therefore, brethren, be even more diligent to make your call and election sure, for if you do these things you will never stumble (2 Peter 1:10).

Deal purposefully with sin

Read Psalm 51

O Lord, open my lips, and my mouth shall show forth Your praise. For You do not desire sacrifice, or else I would give it; you do not delight in burnt offering. The sacrifices of God are a broken spirit, a broken and a contrite heart – These, O God, You will not despise.
(Psalm 51:15–17)

Man of God deals purposefully and ruthlessly with sin. David was known as a man after God's own heart. God had this to say about him: *"I have found David the son of Jesse, a man after My own heart, who will do all My will"* (Acts 13:22b). When God chose David to be king He said to Samuel, His prophet; *"Do not look at his appearance or at his physical stature, because I have refused him. For the LORD does not see as man sees; for man looks at the outward appearance, but the LORD looks at the heart"* (1 Samuel 16:7).

Despite David being a man after God's own heart he stumbled and fell. He committed adultery and then compounded his sin by having his mistress's husband, Uriah, murdered. In 2 Samuel chapter twelve God sends the Prophet Nathan to confront David with his sin. David chooses to respond in humility to the revelation and he comes before God to ask forgiveness. Psalm 51 is David's prayer of repentance. It is a poignant and beautiful outpouring of his heart. David realizes that he has sinned first and foremost against God, whom he loves so much. David's heart is broken by his sin. God forgave David's sin, but there were consequences for him and his family.

If you have failed God what is your response to your sin? One response is choosing to harden your heart. On the other hand you might have been walking around for years under a cloud of guilt. Neither of these responses are going to make you fit for purpose – to serve God and fulfil His plan for your life. If you have sinned against God come to Him and repent; ask Him to forgive you and restore you. Then walk in the light of His mercy and grace. *If we confess our sins, He is faithful and just to forgive us our sins and to cleanse us from all unrighteousness* (1 John 1:9). David went on to be mightily used of God; He can do the same for you.

Prayer

My Father, I come to You in the name of Jesus Christ, my Lord and saviour. Father, I ask You to forgive me for the sin I have committed. I pray that in Your love and mercy You would cleanse me from the guilt and shame of what I have done. Restore me and fill me with Your Holy Spirit. Amen.

If you have sinned against God come to Him and repent; ask Him to forgive you and restore you. Then walk in the light of His mercy and grace.

When you sin

Read 1 John 1:1–10

If we confess our sins, He is faithful and just to forgive us our sins and to cleanse us from all unrighteousness. (1 John 1:9)

We are saved and redeemed to live godly lives. We all know that life happens and we fall. Our sins can haunt us and fill us with guilt, making it impossible for God to use us. If you are someone who is not able to live an abundant Christian life because you are mired in guilt please re-read our key text. *If we confess our sins, He is faithful and just to forgive us our sins and to cleanse us from all unrighteousness.* The sins that haunt us fall into three categories: the sins we committed before coming to salvation; those we committed after coming to know Jesus, which – although we have repented and asked for forgiveness – still haunt us; and then the sins that we are currently committing.

Now we cannot categorize sin. In God's eyes sin is sin. However, there are the sins that we all commit on a daily basis such as snapping at our family, or becoming angry because someone stole our parking space (you know what I am talking about – the list is endless). We should keep short accounts of these sins. Generally they are not the ones that keep us mired in guilt. I want to address the sins that have had a life-changing effect upon our lives or the lives of someone else. These are the ones that eat at us. They keep us awake at night and they prevent us from being useful to God.

Hear me today, my friend. If it happened before you came to Jesus *it is under the blood.* God has forgotten about it – so who are you to keep remembering it? If it happened after you came to salvation and you have repented and asked forgiveness – then move on and don't do it again. If you are still involved in the sin – **stop**! Right now – immediately. It is not worth losing your testimony over. God's grace is there for you, but you have to stop what you are doing. Come to God, repent and ask His forgiveness and then don't do it again.

Prayer

My Father, I come to You so grateful for Your grace and forgiveness. Please forgive me for the things that I have done that separate me from You. I acknowledge them today. I lay them at the foot of the cross. Cleanse me and fill me, I pray. Then help me to live as Your man serving You. Amen.

Come to God, repent and ask His forgiveness and then don't do it again.

Dealing with guilt

Read 1 Corinthians 15:1–11

But by the grace of God I am what I am, and His grace toward me was not in vain; but I labored more abundantly than they all, yet not I, but the grace of God which was with me. (1 Corinthians 15:10)

The apostle Paul knew all about the sins of the past haunting a man. Several times this past year we have mentioned Paul's past, how he persecuted the Christians. He stood holding the coats of the men who stoned Stephen to death. His name was both feared and reviled by the early church. When he came to salvation in Jesus he had to deal with this guilt. God had a special task for him to perform and the debilitating effects of guilt could not be part of it. Paul had to make a choice: either he was going to stand in the grace and forgiveness of God, or he was going to allow guilt to ruin him.

Paul chose to glory in the grace of God. It was as a result of this choice that he was able to write the words: *But by the grace of God I am what I am, and His grace toward me was not in vain; but I labored more abundantly than they all, yet not I, but the grace of God which was with me.* The best way for Paul to counteract the lies that the enemy wanted him to believe was for him to focus upon the grace of God and serving Him with all his heart. The same is true for you, my friend: if you find that guilt is holding you back, go to God and talk to Him about it. In His presence you will find not only forgiveness but restoration as well.

I have a word for anyone who is holding someone's past over them – not allowing them to forget their mistakes or the effects of what they did. If you are such a person, then you need to repent before God today. You are not God and you do not have the right to withhold forgiveness from another person. You do not have the right to punish someone. God is the one who deals with each individual. You have to trust Him. If He has forgiven the person you have to accept it and move on.

Prayer

My Father, I am so in awe of who You are. Thank You for Your boundless love, mercy and forgiveness. As I sit in Your presence today I ask You to restore me. Fill me with the assurance of my salvation and the comfort of Your acceptance. I want You to be able to use me in Your service. Amen.

If you find that guilt is holding you back talk to God about it. In His presence you will find forgiveness and restoration.

Putting the past behind you

Read Philippians 3:1–16

...but one thing I do, forgetting those things which are behind and reaching forward to those things which are ahead, I press toward the goal for the prize of the upward call of God in Christ Jesus. (Philippians 3:13b–14)

Whatever the negative things are that have happened in your past and are holding you back – let them go. The most debilitating thing is guilt. There are those of you reading this who are walking around with a weight of guilt upon your shoulders that is almost humanly impossible to bear. Yesterday I mentioned how the apostle Paul had to deal with his guilt over persecuting and killing the Christians. If he hadn't overcome that guilt he would have been useless to God. It was God's grace that made it possible for Paul to do this. Paul used his past to fuel his future. It was his incredible love for Jesus that motivated him to be able to achieve what he did in his ministry.

So, my friend, whatever you have done or whatever has been done to you – the question is: What are you going to do about it? Are you going to sit in a corner and allow the devil to stomp all over you? Or are you going to allow God to use your past for His glory in the future? If you have confessed your sin to God, asked Him to forgive you and turned from it, then it is covered by the blood of Jesus. God is no longer interested in it. What He is interested in is: What are you going to do with the forgiveness and grace He has given to you through His Son, Jesus Christ?

You are a man with a destiny; God has a plan and a purpose for your life. Do not let your past stand in the way of you fulfilling that purpose. The truth is that none of us would be able to be used by God if it was down to our own worthiness. We are all sinners saved by grace – these are your credentials, my friend. These were Paul's credentials, Peter's and those of every man of God from the beginning of time. Put the past behind you and press forward toward the prize in Christ Jesus.

Prayer

My Father, I ask You to forgive me for holding on to my guilt for such a long time. I realize that in many ways I have used it as an excuse not to move forward. Today, I choose to look to Jesus, my Lord and saviour. I want to be used by You, my Lord, I want to fulfil my purpose. Amen.

If you have confessed your sin to God, asked Him to forgive you and turned from it, then it is covered by the blood of Jesus.

Keep your heart with all diligence

Read Proverbs 4:20–27

Keep your heart with all diligence, for out of it spring the issues of life. (Proverbs 4:23)

God has a plan and a purpose for your life. He has a vision that only you can fulfil. As a man with a purpose you need to guard and *keep your heart with all diligence.* Our key verse says *out of it spring the issues of life.* Jeremiah 17:9 has this to say about the unredeemed human heart: *"The heart is deceitful above all things, and desperately wicked; who can know it?"* You cannot control your heart in your own strength. It is in the heart that both good and evil originate. This is why we need to be constantly filled with God's Spirit.

Paul had this to say in Romans 7:18–19: *For I know that in me (that is, in my flesh) nothing good dwells; for to will is present with me, but how to perform what is good I do not find. For the good that I will to do, I do not do; but the evil I will not to do, that I practice.* Paul knew that the only chance he had was to walk in the Spirit. It was in the Spirit that he was able to overcome the desires and evils of the flesh. We are no different, my friend; we have to walk in the Spirit of God every day of our lives. Matthew 12:35 says: *"A good man out of the good treasure of his heart brings forth good things, and an evil man out of the evil treasure brings forth evil things."*

God is looking for good men who will be a witness for Jesus Christ; men of purpose who live out what they believe; men who live out the things they talk about. Don't allow the enemy to short-change you out of your destiny. Your heart is at the centre of all you think, say and do – it is precious because out of it spring the issues of life. Protect it, guard it and place the protection of God's Spirit around it. Take care of it so that it serves you and your master well.

Prayer

My Father, I bring my heart before You today. Shine the light of Your Spirit into my heart. Father, I want my heart to be a wellspring of all that is good and pure. Place Your Spirit as a guard around it. Amen.

Your heart is at the centre of all you think, say and do – protect it, guard it and place the protection of God's Spirit around it.

The heart of a servant

Read Matthew 20:20–28

"And whoever desires to be first among you, let him be your slave – just as the Son of Man did not come to be served, but to serve, and to give His life a ransom for many."
(Matthew 20:27–28)

The greatest service that has ever been performed was by Jesus when He came to this earth to suffer and die for our sins. He did not withhold anything of Himself – He poured His life out to ransom you and to ransom me. Jesus is our greatest example of servanthood. He was truly a servant leader in every sense. His leadership style was radically opposed to so much of what we see around us. Many people believe that a position of leadership entitles them to dominate and lord it over other people. We see leaders extorting their followers; we witness leaders perpetrating the most awful crimes, seemingly believing that they have immunity against any kind of retribution.

This is not what spiritual leadership is about. The sad thing is that all too often we see Christian leaders behaving in the same way that worldly leaders do. This breaks Jesus' heart because He came to model what true leadership should look and act like. My friend, whatever the leadership role is that you fill please stop and examine your heart, your motives and your actions today. We said yesterday that it is out of the heart that both good and evil originate. It stands to reason, then, that the state of your heart will determine the quality of your leadership.

A servant leader is one who serves those God has entrusted to him. It doesn't matter if it is your family or a multimillion-rand company with thousands of employees. God calls you to be faithful in every sphere of your life. He is not interested in the size and scope of your leadership; no, He is only interested in the quality of your leadership. God is interested in whether you are a servant leader or not, whether you have a servant heart beating in your chest. Remember, *whoever desires to be first among you, let him be your slave*. This is His mandate to you today. As you come to the end of this year how would you evaluate the quality of your leadership?

Prayer

My Father, I bow in Your presence. Thank You, Jesus, for the wonderful example You are to me of servant leadership. You are so wonderful. I long to be like You. Help me to be the same kind of leader that You are. Amen.

It stands to reason that the state of your heart will determine the quality of your leadership.

Are you afraid?

Read Luke 21:25–28

"...men's hearts failing them from fear and the expectation of those things which are coming on the earth, for the powers of the heavens will be shaken." (Luke 21:26)

We live in uncertain times, don't we? Today as never before people are fearful about what the future holds for them. Some people are leaving the country in search of a safer environment in which to raise their children. Others are looking to take advantage of economic opportunities in other countries. Every day we read stories in the newspapers or watch reports on television of violent crimes being perpetrated against innocent people. Many of you reading this will either yourselves have been the victims of crime or you will know someone who has. All around us men's hearts are literally failing them from fear.

As a Christian what is your response to these very real challenges meant to be? God has entrusted you with the task of leading your family – what are you meant to do to keep your family safe? As men we have a God-given need to protect those we love. Over and above the challenges we face in our country, the world at large is on a slippery slope going downhill fast. *"And there will be signs in the sun, in the moon, and in the stars; and on the earth distress of nations, with perplexity, the sea and the waves roaring"* (Luke 21:25). It would be easy to become overwhelmed if we didn't know that our confidence is not in human beings or circumstances. Our confidence is in Jesus. He is the one to whom we look in all things. He is the one whom we look to for protection.

I have said many times that I do not fear any man because I know that nothing can touch me until my work here on earth is done. When that day comes the next thing for me will be heaven and being with Jesus. Our problem is that we are so tied to this world that we forget that we are only passing through. Jesus is coming back to fetch us – we have nothing to fear. *"Now when these things begin to happen, look up and lift up your heads, because your redemption draws near."* (Luke 21:28)

Prayer

My Father, I know that I am living in the end times. I look to the day when Jesus will return, bringing an end to all sin and suffering. Lord, thank You that You are my protector: You care for me and those I love. I know that when this life is over the next thing for me will be heaven and being with You. Amen.

You have nothing to fear – because your redemption draws near.

Do not worry

Read Luke 12:22–34

"For all these things the nations of the world seek after, and your Father knows that you need these things. But seek the kingdom of God, and all these things shall be added to you. Do not fear, little flock, for it is your Father's good pleasure to give you the kingdom."
(Luke 12:30–32)

There are always two sides to a coin, aren't there? On the one side: *But if anyone does not provide for his own, and especially for those of his household, he has denied the faith and is worse than an unbeliever* (1 Timothy 5:8). On the other: *Then He said to His disciples, "Therefore I say to you, do not worry about your life, what you will eat; nor about the body, what you will put on. Life is more than food, and the body is more than clothing"* (Luke 12:22–23). God's Word does not contradict itself so these two seemingly opposing commands must balance each other out.

The crux of the matter, my friend, is that in all things God is your provider – He is the one who gives you the ability to climb out of bed in the morning and do a good day's work. He is the one who gives you success. Yes, we are meant to work hard – no man ever accomplished anything sitting around doing nothing. The Word has a lot to say about lazy people. What Jesus is talking about in Luke chapter twelve is an attitude of the heart. He is talking about faith – Jesus is challenging His listeners to consider in whom they have faith. Is it their jobs, is it in the economy or is it in their own ability? If your faith is in any of these things you are in trouble.

It means that you are going to worry from morning until night. There are so many things that can go wrong – trying to keep control of all the various aspects of your life is going to drive you crazy. This is not faith. Read the key texts at the top of the page again. Jesus says this, *"Sell what you have and give alms; provide yourselves money bags which do not grow old, a treasure in the heavens that does not fail, where no thief approaches nor moth destroys. For where your treasure is, there your heart will be also"* (Luke 12:33–34). Where is your heart?

Prayer

My Father, help me to get my head sorted out about my responsibility versus Your responsibility. I realize that I take everything upon myself and this is why I end up worried and anxious. Give me a kingdom perspective, I pray. Increase my faith and help me to walk this road trusting You. Amen.

"For where your treasure is, there your heart will be also" (Luke 12:34).

Open your eyes

Read 2 Kings 6:8–23

So he answered, "Do not fear, for those who are with us are more than those who are with them." (2 Kings 6:16)

A s we approach the end of the year, poised at the beginning of a new one, it is always good to spend some time in reflection. Looking back over this past year I hope that you have managed regular times of fellowship with the Lord. My prayer is that you will have grown in your faith and in your relationship with the Lord. I trust that you have taken the time to be in God's Word and that the subjects we've discussed together have spoken into your life. As you have spent time before God I know that the Holy Spirit will have worked in your heart and life leading you closer to the Father every day.

You know that I am a faith man – I would not have been able to do any of the things that I have done were it not for trust in God. Each day, every day I trust God to undertake, lead, guide and reveal His will to me. I know without a shadow of a doubt that I can do nothing without Him. On the other hand I also know without a shadow of a doubt that with Him there is nothing that I cannot do. In our Bible reading today we have the story about Elisha and his servant. The servant saw in the natural – and what he saw was trouble and disaster.

Elisha prayed to God asking Him to open the eyes of his servant. ... *"LORD, I pray, open his eyes that he may see." Then the LORD opened the eyes of the young man, and he saw. And behold, the mountain was full of horses and chariots of fire all around Elisha* (2 Kings 6:17). My friend, whatever the situation you find yourself in today, stop and ask God to open your eyes. Ask Him to give you the eyesight of faith so that you can see His provision and abundance all around you. Don't allow yourself to be overwhelmed by the circumstances of your life – God is greater than anything you are facing right now.

Prayer

My Father, I bow in Your presence. I exalt Your holy name. Lord, give me the eyesight of faith today so that I can see Your provision for my life. I know that with You all things are possible. I no longer want to walk in the natural. I want to walk in the Spirit trusting You in all things. Amen.

Ask God to give you the eyesight of faith so that you can see His provision and abundance all around you.

Jesus makes it possible to persevere

Read Revelation 3:1–12

"Because you have kept My command to persevere, I also will keep you from the hour of trial which shall come upon the whole world, to test those who dwell on the earth. Behold, I am coming quickly! Hold fast what you have, that no one may take your crown."
(Revelation 3:10–11)

Today we stand on the eve of the birth of Jesus Christ, our saviour. We know that this was not the date of His real birth, but it doesn't change the fact that He was born. Therefore this is a good time for us to reflect upon what His birth means to us. One of the things we have received as a result of Jesus' birth is the assurance of spending eternity with Him and the Father in heaven. I don't know what you are going through in your life right now. Whatever it is I want to take another opportunity as we come to the close of this year to encourage you to persevere. Don't give up, my friend; don't give in.

The enemy would love you to throw in the towel, but remember today that because Jesus was born in a stable in Bethlehem you have eternal life. Your eternity is not about what is going on right now – your eternity is in heaven with Jesus. This is what John encourages us with in our reading today. *"Behold, I am coming quickly! Hold fast what you have, that no one may take your crown."* Maybe as you look back over the past year you are disappointed because the thing you have been trusting God for still hasn't come to be. If you are feeling like giving up then read Revelation chapter three again. God's timing is perfect and He is never too early nor too late. This is where faith comes in, my friend: To your faith add perseverance.

Ultimately it is not about whether you receive the thing you have been praying for – it is about remaining faithful and knowing that in the end God will work all things out for good. We cannot see the big picture – only God can. *"He who overcomes, I will make him a pillar in the temple of My God ... And I will write on him My new name"* (Revelation 3:12). Don't give up, my friend, determine today that you will continue to persevere and trust God.

Prayer

My Father, I come before You and I kneel in Your presence. Lord, You know that I am tired and I am discouraged. I have been waiting so long. Thank You for Your Word to me today reminding me about perseverance. I trust You and I believe You will do what is best for me. Amen.

Ultimately it is not about whether you receive the thing you have been praying for – it is about remaining faithful.

A Son is given

Isaiah 9:1–7

For unto us a Child is born, unto us a Son is given; and the government will be upon His shoulder. And His name will be called Wonderful, Counselor, Mighty God, Everlasting Father, Prince of Peace. (Isaiah 9:6)

"*F*or *God so loved the world that He gave His only begotten Son, that whoever believes in Him should not perish but have everlasting life*" (John 3:16). Is your heart filled with gratitude today, my friend? Have you taken a moment to stop and thank God for sending His Son to this world to die for you? If He hadn't done this you would not be able to call yourself a son of God. Jesus' birth meant that the process was put in motion that would lead to Calvary, an empty tomb, the ascension, Jesus seated at the right hand of the Father on high and eventually His second coming.

Christmas is not about gifts wrapped in pretty paper – it's about the greatest gift this world has ever known. It is not about festive food – it's about Jesus, the bread of life. It is not about drinking and being merry – it's about Jesus, from whom flows rivers of living water. Colossians 1:13–14 tells us that because Jesus, God's Son was born: *He has delivered us from the power of darkness and conveyed us into the kingdom of the Son of His love, in whom we have redemption through His blood, the forgiveness of sins.* You no longer live in darkness, but instead you live in the kingdom of God's Son.

If you don't know Jesus as your personal saviour then don't delay another minute. Don't let another year go by without making a commitment to Jesus. If you are reading this then God's Spirit has been moving in you. Today is your day of salvation – take hold of it. John 3:17 tells us: *"For God did not send His Son into the world to condemn the world, but that the world through Him might be saved."* Read John 3:1–21 then rejoice that *unto us a Child is born, unto us a Son is given.* Kneel at the feet of your saviour today, thank Him for His precious, wonderful gift to you, then respond by recommitting your heart and your life to Him.

Prayer

My Father, I worship You. Thank You for sending Jesus Christ, Your Son, to save me. Jesus, I worship You today – *Wonderful, Counselor, Mighty God, Everlasting Father, Prince of Peace* (Isaiah 9:6). Amen.

Kneel at the feet of your saviour today, thank Him for His precious, wonderful gift to you, then respond by recommitting your heart and your life to Him.

Every spiritual blessing

Read Ephesians 1:1–23

Blessed be the God and Father of our Lord Jesus Christ, who has blessed us with every spiritual blessing in the heavenly places in Christ. (Ephesians 1:3)

*T*herefore I … do not cease to give thanks for you, making mention of you in my prayers: that the God of our Lord Jesus Christ, the Father of glory, may give to you the spirit of wisdom and revelation in the knowledge of Him, the eyes of your understanding being enlightened; that you may know what is the hope of His calling, what are the riches of the glory of His inheritance in the saints, and what is the exceeding greatness of His power toward us who believe, according to the working of His mighty power which He worked in Christ when He raised Him from the dead and seated Him at His right hand in the heavenly places, far above all principality and power and might and dominion, and every name that is named, not only in this age but also in that which is to come. And He put all things under His feet, and gave Him to be head over all things to the church, which is His body, the fullness of Him who fills all in all* (Ephesians 1:15–23).

My friend, this is God's gift to you: His child. Take some time today to sit in His presence and thank Him for Jesus and all that He means to you. So often Christians can allow themselves to feel under siege from the world around them. This could not be further from the truth. Paul says: *that you may know what is the hope of His calling, what are the riches of the glory of His inheritance in the saints.* Do you understand what your inheritance is? Are you living in the fullness of it?

As you contemplate the end of this year and the beginning of a new year, I hope that your spirit is quickened and that you are excited about your walk with Jesus. In Jesus you have everything you need to live a life of blessing and abundance. It doesn't matter what comes your way; as long as you are walking with Jesus you are more than a conqueror.

Prayer

My Father, thank You for everything that I have in Jesus, Your Son. I realize that I have blessings that I haven't even begun to fathom or understand yet. I know that so often I allow myself to walk a second-class walk with You. Forgive me for this. Today I choose to walk in victory with Jesus. Amen.

It doesn't matter what comes your way; as long as you are walking with Jesus you are more than a conqueror.

Bold access through faith

Read Ephesians 3:1–21

…that now the manifold wisdom of God might be made known … according to the eternal purpose which He accomplished in Christ Jesus our Lord, in whom we have boldness and access with confidence through faith in Him. (Ephesians 3:10–12)

F or this reason I bow my knees to the Father of our Lord Jesus Christ, from whom the whole family in heaven and earth is named, that He would grant you, according to the riches of His glory, to be strengthened with might through His Spirit in the inner man, that Christ may dwell in your hearts through faith; that you, being rooted and grounded in love, may be able to comprehend with all the saints what is the width and length and depth and height – to know the love of Christ which passes knowledge; that you may be filled with all the fullness of God. Now to Him who is able to do exceedingly abundantly above all that we ask or think, according to the power that works in us, to Him be glory in the church by Christ Jesus to all generations, forever and ever. Amen (Ephesians 3:14–21).

As you come into God's presence make this prayer of Paul's your own today. Ask God to strengthen you in your inner man. Tell Jesus that you want Him and Him alone to dwell in your heart through faith. It is through faith that you have access into God's presence, my friend. It is by faith that you can boldly come before His throne of grace. Faith is what makes it possible for you to bring your requests before God, your Father.

I pray that as you read these words God will speak to you from His Word and you will be overwhelmed by His love for you. If you experience God's love in the way that Paul is describing in Ephesians chapter three you will never falter or fall. You will be so encapsulated in His love that you will be completely safe and secure. It is God's love that has seen you through all your yesterdays, it is His love that is present with you today and it is His love that will carry you through all your tomorrows until Jesus comes or calls for you. This is your confidence as you face the new year.

Prayer

Now to Him who is able to do exceedingly abundantly above all that [I] ask or think, according to the power that works in [me], to Him be glory in the church by Christ Jesus to all generations, forever and ever. Amen (Ephesians 3:20–21).

It is God's love that has seen you through all your yesterdays; it is His love that is present with you today and it is His love that will carry you through all your tomorrows.

Fullness of joy

Read Psalm 16

You will show me the path of life; in Your presence is fullness of joy; at Your right hand are pleasures forevermore. (Psalm 16:11)

*P*reserve me, O God, for in You I put my trust. O my soul, you have said to the LORD, "You are my Lord, my goodness is nothing apart from You." ... O LORD, You are the portion of my inheritance and my cup; you maintain my lot. The lines have fallen to me in pleasant places; yes, I have a good inheritance. I will bless the LORD who has given me counsel; My heart also instructs me in the night seasons. I have set the LORD always before me; because He is at my right hand I shall not be moved. Therefore my heart is glad, and my glory rejoices; my flesh also will rest in hope. You will show me the path of life; in Your presence is fullness of joy; at Your right hand are pleasures forevermore (Psalm 16: 1–2, 5–9, 11).

This is a wonderful prayer to pray as you come to the end of the year. Look back and remember all the times that God has directed and led you through the past year. Remember and thank Him for the many blessings He has given to you and your family. Don't generalize – thank Him for each one as they come to mind. Acknowledge that outside of Him you are not capable of any goodness. Have you been enjoying your inheritance in Jesus this past year? You know you do not need to wait to get to heaven to enjoy the kingdom of God. We are meant to be enjoying it right here and right now – arriving in heaven is simply a continuation of kingdom living.

I hope that as you end this year your heart is filled with joy, gratitude, praise and adoration for all that God has done for you. I pray that you are excited about the coming year and all that you will experience with God as He continues to lead, guide and use you for His kingdom's purposes. You can move forward in hope because the Lord is always at your right hand. In His presence is fullness of joy.

Prayer

My Father, I lift my hands in praise and worship to You. I open my heart and sing of Your goodness and mercy to me. I thank You today that You have been with me every step of the way this past year; through the good and the bad. Lord, thank You for giving me fullness of joy in Your presence. Amen.

You can move forward in hope because the Lord is always at your right hand. In His presence is fullness of joy.

Now is the accepted time

Read 2 Corinthians 6:1–10

For He says: "In an acceptable time I have heard you, and in the day of salvation I have helped you." Behold, now is the accepted time; behold, now is the day of salvation. (2 Corinthians 6:2)

*B*ut in all things we commend ourselves as ministers of God: in much patience, in tribulations, in needs, in distresses, in stripes, in imprisonments, in tumults, in labors, in sleeplessness, in fastings; by purity, by knowledge, by longsuffering, by kindness, by the Holy Spirit, by sincere love, by the word of truth, by the power of God, by the armor of righteousness on the right hand and on the left, by honor and dishonor, by evil report and good report; as deceivers, and yet true; as unknown, and yet well known; as dying, and behold we live; as chastened, and yet not killed; as sorrowful, yet always rejoicing; as poor, yet making many rich; as having nothing, and yet possessing all things* (2 Corinthians 6:4–10).

In the verses above Paul reminds the Corinthian Christians of the example he has set them; and by extension he is saying to them this is the way they too are to live. If Paul was standing in front of you and me today he would say the same thing to us – "this is the way you are to live." Paul lived his life aware of the urgency of the moment. His primary, burning desire was to do as much as possible to spread the good news of Jesus to those who had not heard it. His second desire was to establish those who come to Christ in their faith.

Our salvation does not stop at the moment we accept Jesus. He says to the Philippians: *Therefore, my beloved … work out your own salvation with fear and trembling* (Philippians 2:12). We continue working out our salvation until the day we go home to be with Jesus. Working out your salvation is about growing in Jesus; it is about holy living, about maturing in Jesus. Daily we are to be growing in our faith – becoming more like Jesus. Our greatest witness to the world around us is when people see Jesus in us. Your primary ambition should be to have people look at you and say: "I want what you have. Please tell me how I can have it."

Prayer

My Father, thank You for my salvation. Thank You that I have the assurance that I will spend eternity with You and Jesus, my saviour. Lord, fill me with the power of Your Holy Spirit so that I will live a life of holiness and integrity, one that will draw people to You. Now is the accepted day; now is the time for me to work out my salvation. Amen.

Working out your salvation is about growing in Jesus; it is about holy living, about maturing in Jesus.